CHRISTIANS IN THE MARKETPLACE SERIES
Biblical Principles and Public Policy: The Practice

Richard C. Chewning, Ph.D., Series Editor

W FARWELL

NAVPRESS (*)®
A MINISTRY OF THE NAVIGATORS
P.O. BOX 6000, COLORADO SPRINGS, COLORADO 80934

The Navigators is an international Christian
organization. Jesus Christ gave His followers
the Great Commission to go and make disciples
(Matthew 28:19). The aim of The Navigators is to
help fulfill that commission by multiplying laborers for Christ in every nation.

NavPress is the publishing ministry of The Navigators. NavPress publications are tools to help
Christians grow. Although publications alone cannot make disciples or change lives, they can help
believers learn biblical discipleship, and apply
what they learn to their lives and ministries.

The Scripture quotations in this publication are
from several translations: the *Good News Bible:
Today's English Version* (TEV), copyright © Ameri-
can Bible Society 1966, 1971, 1976; the *King
James Version* (KJV); the *New American Standard
Bible* (NASB), © The Lockman Foundation, 1960,
1962, 1963, 1968, 1971, 1972, 1973, 1975, 1977;
the *Holy Bible: New International Version* (NIV).
Copyright © 1973, 1978, 1984, International Bible
Society. Used by permission of Zondervan Bible
Publishers; the *New King James Version* (NKJV),
copyright © 1979, 1980, 1982, Thomas Nelson,
Inc., Publishers; the *Revised Standard Version
Bible* (RSV), copyright 1946, 1952, 1971, by the
Division of Christian Education of the National
Council of the Churches of Christ in the U.S.A.,
and used by permission with all rights reserved.

The individual authors of this book have used
the following translations unless otherwise noted:
Chewning—NASB; Henry—none; Kosters—KJV;
Wilkinson—KJV; Mason—NIV; Vickers—KJV;
Anderson—NIV; Wood—NIV; Hill—NIV; Wilson—
none; Skillen—none; Henderson—NASB; Grinols—
NKJV; Malloch—KJV.

Printed in the United States of America

CONTENTS

SERIES EDITOR

Dr. Richard C. Chewning is the Chavanne Professor of Christian Ethics in Business at the Hankamer School of Business of Baylor University in Waco, Texas. He received baccalaureate, master's, and Ph.D. degrees, all in business, from Virginia Polytechnic Institute, the University of Virginia, and the University of Washington, respectively. He began formal academic training in business ethics and corporate social responsibility as a doctoral student and pursued postdoctoral study in comparative ethics at St. Mary's College, the seminary arm of the University of St. Andrews in Scotland.

Dr. Chewning began teaching at the University of Richmond in 1958 where he taught finance, served for some years as a department chairman, and also as an academic dean. In 1979 he was invited by the business faculty to develop and teach courses in the field of business ethics. He moved to Baylor University in 1985. He has published over forty-five essays and articles integrating Scripture with business and economics, and he has authored and coauthored books in the field of ethics and business from a biblical perspective, including *Business Ethics in a Changing Culture* and *Business Through the Eyes of Faith*.

For years Dr. Chewning has been a consultant to government bodies, trade associations, and corporations in matters of both finance and ethics, while maintaining a busy schedule of public lectures and seminar participation. He is the editor of the CHRISTIANS IN THE MARKETPLACE Series. Volume 1 is *Biblical Principles and Business: The Foundations* and Volume 2 is *Biblical Principles and Economics: The Foundations*. Volume 3 is *Biblical Principles and Business: The Practice*.

PREFACE

Amos, Ezekiel, Isaiah, and other prophets spoke of God's judgment of the nations (Ammonites, Moabites, Edomites, etc.) because they had transgressed God's requirements for righteousness and justice in their lands. God will judge all people and nations according to the light of the truth evident in the minds and hearts of all—unbelievers and believers alike (see Rom. 1:18-21; 2:12-16). But prior to the Final Judgment, and while we are functioning on earth, God has given us external guides to assist us in fulfilling our obligations for doing what is fair and just.

To the Church—the scattered body of heavenly citizens—God has given the Bible, the Holy Spirit, and spiritual gifts to renovate and restore us to the image of Christ so we will, through knowing Him, become like Him in character and conduct (see Eph. 4:24; Col. 3:10). But citizens of Heaven, so long as we live on earth, have a dual citizenship. We are also citizens of a nation-state with citizenship obligations in this realm as well.

The nation-state, however, is composed primarily of people who have rejected their opportunity for heavenly citizenship and have chosen their inheritance in this life, not in the life eternal (see Ps. 16:5-6; 17:14). Although these people may, by God's common grace, subscribe to many prudent precepts of Scripture, their allegiance is to themselves or other fake gods. But they do accept and obey, in the normal course of things, the authority of those who govern them. And Christians, better than other people, know that those who govern us have been established by God to be His ministers for the good of the community. Despite the world's rejection of God's sovereign rule, He has not left the world without leaders who are responsible for maintaining economic, political, legal, and social justice through rules and regulations (see 1 Sam. 8:1-22). We have been told that laws are for the ungodly who refuse to exercise self-restraint (see 1 Tim. 1:9-11).

7

Christians are therefore confronted with the triple duty of walking in God's paths, obeying the requirements of the world's governing authorities, and seeking to positively influence the course of public justice. We are particularly concerned with this latter duty in this volume. But the task of determining how to seek public justice in a pluralistic society is not easy. God's Word was given to the Church to light its way. It was not directed specifically to those who govern the world's affairs and are ultimately responsible to God for the oversight of public justice among the unregenerate.

Christians must try to discern in God's Word those principles that have application where public justice is to be maintained. We must also find the most responsible way to influence the political process so it will incorporate those principles effectively.

The foundational chapters of this volume are conservative but not exhaustive efforts to open the doors of a significant number of public policy arenas to the light of Scripture. These chapters elicit further study and discussion. They are cautious in character and not dogmatic and doctrinaire. But they are substantive and provocative in that they identify biblical principles and apply them to the problems of the public arena. The chapters do take positions.

Economists, though, are trained to recognize the complexity of the world. Furthermore, the variables in the natural order are so numerous that all perceptive economists realize from the outset that their proposals may bring about consequences as troublesome as the original problems they set out to solve. Human nature is such that predictive economic models must always be understood as reasoned "guesstimates" only one psychological step away from being substantially wrong; for the human mind is difficult to predict.

When we consider public policies, we confront the decisions of government. Governments make public policies. In the United States, governmental laws are made in the context of certain constitutional stipulations and a federal system where the responsibilities of legislatures, executives, and the courts are distributed at three different levels.

Reflection on public policy takes for granted various assumptions about the nature and responsibility of the state—of the political community of citizens under a constitutional government. It is not enough, therefore, to look only at the outcomes one might wish to achieve through a policy decision—better education, better health, a cleaner environment, or a stronger economy. Outcomes may depend more or less on public policy decisions, and if justice is to be done, they may require more or less responsibility on the part of nongovernmental institutions and individuals. Government's actions should not be viewed as simply the means to whatever end a particular interest group wants to achieve. Rather, government should be recognized as having a responsibility in its own right to do justice to the political community (or state) it governs.

Since Christians understand that God has ordained government to establish justice, they should not simply aim to keep government away from society. Government should not be reduced to a playground for mere interest-group competition, nor should governmental policies attempt to do everything and thus assume totalitarian control of society. In the United States today Christians have the task of seeking biblical wisdom for understanding the proper nature, limits, and responsibilities of government.

Though we do not try to develop a Christian political philosophy in this book, or even focus attention on the nature of the state and the limits of public policy, we must keep in mind that the public policy considerations outlined in the following chapters rest on a set of basic assumptions made by the authors about the nature and task of government. Not all of them make the same assumptions, though they share many of the same ones about the government's responsibility to do justice within constitutional limits that should also respect the integrity and responsibility of nongovernmental institutions and activities.

The reader should notice, in particular, that the chapters deal with two different kinds of public policy issues. The first kind involves issues that the government itself controls directly—regulating the money supply and organizing the military and the police, for example. The second kind concerns the relation of government to nongovernmental institutions and organizations whose responsibilities do not originate with government, but the government seeks to encourage, discourage, regulate, or protect them, depending on the circumstances. Family life, health care, and economic productivity, for example, are not the direct responsibility of government. But government's tax rules, insurance policies, and criminal statutes will affect the activities of parents in their homes, workers on the job, and students in schools.

What follows is a responsible demonstration of the integration of Scripture with twelve areas of public policy. The chapters do not illuminate every dimension of the issues with the light of Scripture, but they do expose several aspects of each policy area to discernible biblical principles. The efforts here are specifically directed at overcoming an historic barrier that has constrained Christians from making such a broad attempt to integrate Scripture with public policy matters in modern society. That barrier has been one of economists complaining that theologians know too little economics to correctly address such an array of economic matters on an in-depth basis, and of the economists feeling inadequate to wade off into sophisticated theological debates.

We assembled twelve evangelical Christian economists with thoroughgoing interests and expertise in specific public policy areas. They were to search for several biblical principles—aggregated biblical propositions all speaking to the same concern—that address the basics of their specific public policy area and to integrate those principles into their work. They were asked not to plumb the depths of their field or theology but to lead the way through the door of understanding concerning a sound approach for integrating Scripture with public policy. This, I believe, they have accomplished. It is hoped that other Christian economists will take what has been done in this volume as an invitation to join the efforts of these men and pick up the pace in going farther with the work.

The work contained in this volume is not technical economics at its mind-jarring best (or worst). However, it is economics as reflected in the marketplace of ideas—the press, Congress, public debaters, and the classroom. All of us will benefit by engaging it.

Richard C. Chewning
Chavanne Professor of Christian
Ethics in Business
Hankamer School of Business
Baylor University
Waco, Texas

ACKNOWLEDGMENTS

Any literary project as large as this four-volume series must, of necessity, involve the dedicated work of many people. The fifty scholars who contributed chapters to the series have been recognized, to a degree, through the brief biographical sketches appearing at the beginning of their chapters. There are, though, six other people who have contributed immeasurably to the successful completion of this undertaking and without their efforts and support the venture would have been either impossible or of a lesser quality.

Dr. Richard C. Scott, Dean of the Hankamer School of Business at Baylor University, from the moment the project was presented to him became its advocate in the deepest sense. Without his backing and deep commitment, this series could never have begun or been completed.

Authors must work closely with their editors (this is not always easy, as any experienced author can testify). I have never been so encouraged and uplifted by an editor as I was by Jon Stine, who shepherded this project through to completion. Writers can be their own worst critics, but Jon has the ability to offer genuine encouragement while calling for further refinements. He has been a true Barnabas—a son of encouragement.

Dr. Phil Van Auken, a friend and colleague at Baylor, read every word before it was submitted to the publisher. His editorial help and comments often boosted my confidence when it was sagging.

The toughest task of all—trying to "even out" the work and style of fifty scholars, giving their combined effort a pleasing flow and rhythm—became the lot of Dimples Kellogg, a freelance editor employed by NavPress. She is truly a master craftsman, and my admiration of her work knows no bounds.

Then there is always the person who types the manuscripts (I do all my writing in longhand) and the person who is given the responsibility to over-see the details of travel arrangements, housing, and meals that accompany the running of a Colloquium. (Four such week-long meetings were held.) These responsibilities fell on Virginia Gero, and she handled them with great professional skill and tact.

My wife, Shirley, undertook the task of proofreading all the manuscripts. She spend hundreds of hours burning the midnight oil in her tireless efforts to support me and do what I do poorly. As in so many areas of my life, she blesses me.

Proclamation
example

PART I

GOD: THE JUDGE
OF THE NATIONS

Most evangelicals hold the view that since New Testament times the regenerate Church has been universally and intentionally scattered under diverse forms of government in order to witness to the lordship of Jesus Christ as final judge of the nations. By proclamation and by example they are to promote universally the justice God seeks and the justification He offers penitent believers in Christ. Although evangelicals do not equate democratic or republican political structures with the Kingdom of God, most nonetheless consider democratic government preferable in present fallen history because of its promotion of political self-determination and the safeguards it offers against secular totalitarianism.

This quote, from Dr. Carl F. H. Henry's chapter "Linking the Bible to Public Policy," is most appropriate to open this concluding volume in the CHRISTIANS IN THE MARKETPLACE Series. I wish to highlight four significant presuppositions in the paragraph that ought to undergird our thinking as we link the Bible to public policy. It is important to examine our own assumptions about Christians' relationships to world governments before we read into Dr. Henry's chapter, which strikes a marvelous biblical balance between the countervailing tensions of our individuality, on the one hand, and our obligations as members of a community, on the other hand.

First is the assumption that the "Church has been universally and intentionally scattered under diverse forms of government in order to witness to the lordship of Jesus Christ." This is more than a biblical assumption; this is a biblical reality. We need to believe and act responsibly on this fact. Figuring out what it means to act responsibly as witnesses to the lordship of Christ brings us full circle to the opening discussions in the first book of this series where

Kenneth Kantzer's chapter ("God Intends His Precepts to Transform Society") and Philip Wogaman's chapter ("Christian Faith and Personal Holiness") both acknowledged that God gives no evidence in Scripture of a conflict between the creation mandates, which include working and ruling over the created order, and the Great Commission. Christ made it plain that His Kingdom is not an earthly kingdom, in the traditional sense, but is first and foremost a Kingdom in the hearts of His disciples (see John 18:36-37). But His Kingdom is to be in the world as Christ lives in us and as we live for Him, having made Him Lord of every aspect of our lives.

The second assumption Dr. Henry sets before us is that Jesus Christ is to be the "final judge of the nations." Over 450 times the Scripture speaks about nation(s), many of them being the nations around Israel or the nations into which the Church was dispersed. Scripture also makes it abundantly clear that God establishes all governing authorities and that He raises up and puts down worldly kingdoms as He wills (see Dan. 2:21; 4:17, 25, 32; Rom. 13:1; 1 Pet. 2:13-14). Presidents, governors, senators, kings, dictators, and princes shall all stand before God and give an accounting of the just and unjust activities they shared in or were responsible for during their tenure in public office.

The third point Dr. Henry makes is that Christians "are to promote universally the justice God seeks" among the nations "by proclamation and by example." (He, of course, also added the responsibility of Christians to proclaim the justification God offers penitent believers in Christ.) We cannot afford to miss the clear implications of Dr. Henry's point. Christians are sprinkled among the nations to be the salt of the earth. We are dispersed abroad to be the light of the world (see Matt. 5:13-16). We are not to be "secret disciples" of Jesus as were Joseph of Arimathea and Nicodemus (see John 19:38-39). We are to openly promote justice through our conversations (oral and written), our decisions, and our actions. We are not to hide our light in some monastic closet.

Dr. Henry closes his paragraph with the fourth point that most evangelicals, while not equating a free and democratic or republican political structure with God's Kingdom, nonetheless prefer this type of government in a fallen world. He gives two reasons: (1) it promotes political self-determinism, and (2) it offers safeguards against secular totalitarianism. I would simply add that enjoying such freedoms also presents us with special responsibilities (because we have special opportunities) to foster justice. Those who live under a totalitarian regime may legitimately be discharged from being held primarily accountable for public justice in their nation, but those residing in freer societies must seek public justice in the town square and the marketplace.

Readers who have been following the thoughts of Carl Henry over the years will immediately recognize that he is comfortable with the subject before him—the appropriateness of relating the Bible to the formulation and administration of public policy. Dr. Henry, as much as any other leader in the evangelical wing of Christendom, has labored for the past half century to define and call us to a world view thoroughly shaped by the Scripture and reflected in every facet of our lives.

evangelism   redemption

creation   mandate   stewardship

Proclamation

example
  · conversations (ORAL + WRITTEN
  · DECISIONS
  , ACTIONS

economics — marketplace

politics —   town square

CHAPTER 1

LINKING THE BIBLE TO PUBLIC POLICY

Carl F. H. Henry

Dr. Carl F. H. Henry is an evangelical theologian and author of more than thirty books in the areas of religion and ethics. He was founding editor of Christianity Today *magazine. He holds the Th.D. degree from Northern Baptist Theological Seminary and Ph.D. degree from Boston University and has pursued postgraduate research at Cambridge University, England, and New College, Edinburgh. He has also been awarded these honorary degrees: D.D. by Gordon-Conwell Theological Seminary and Northwestern College; L.H.D. by Houghton College; Litt.D. by Seattle Pacific University and Wheaton College; and LL.D. by Hillsdale College. His six-volume work* God, Revelation and Authority *is available in Korean and Mandarin.*

Many devout American economists take quite for granted that public policy and social action ideally involve some clear linkage to biblical values.

Even radical academicians enamored of recent theologies of revolution and/or of liberation present Marxist theory, justifiably or not, in the context of the Hebrew Exodus from Egyptian oppression and of Jesus' promise of final deliverance from injustice.

During the forepart of our century, ecumenical churchmen addicted to the so-called Social Gospel politicized their expectation of the coming Kingdom of God and professed to derive from Jesus of Nazareth and from the Old Testament prophets their confidence that history moves inescapably toward a socialist utopia. They displaced the evangelical insistence on humanity's need of personal spiritual regeneration by speculative evolutionary notions that mankind is essentially good and that earthly history edges inexorably toward a flawless future.

At the same time most fundamentalist Protestants withdrew from cultural involvement and abandoned public affairs to theological modernists. They did so for several reasons. Dispensational premillennialists viewed religious liberalism's disavowal of basic New Testament beliefs as telling evidence that history had declined into end-time apostasy. Since modernism had defaulted from the Christian Church's redemptive task, fundamentalists made personal evangelism and foreign missions their primary burden. Modernist effort to reform culture and society while neglecting the salvific role of Jesus Christ, religious conservatives complained, was a betrayal of the mission of the Church.

By mid-century a rectification of fundamentalist/evangelical withdrawal from social concerns was already getting under way. An awakened interest in public involvement was encouraged in part by my lamentation *The Uneasy Conscience of Modern Fundamentalism* (1948) and by a social action commission subsequently sponsored by the National Association of Evangelicals (NAE). NAE did not, however, go much beyond adopting resolutions at annual conventions and sporadically conferring with sympathetic public officials.

Gradually, however, evangelical colleges enlarged course offerings in political science and economics. Graduates pursued doctorates in law and related fields, and some evangelicals ventured political campaigns for public office. The emergence of the Moral Majority—in response to federal intrusion into the arena of religious values such as prayer in public schools and public funding of abortions—activated large masses of fundamentalists and other religious conservatives. They engaged in public demonstrations and wrote officeholders expressing their views on specific legislative proposals.

In contrast to modernism's Social Gospel program, the religious right concentrated on an agenda of specifics more than on a comprehensive social vision. To be sure, modernist churchmen had their own agenda of specifics. But local church constituencies more and more repudiated ecumenical hierarchies that professed to speak for them. The religious right demonstrated massive numerical strength, even when allowance was made for promotional exaggeration. The religious right did not, to be sure, speak for all evangelicals, any more than Pat Robertson's presidential candidacy was a "panevangelical" effort. Many evangelical college students were turned off by the confrontational tactics of Jerry Falwell's followers, and some were less "radically right." Evangelical college professors, especially sociologists, moreover, tended to be less conservative than their students.

What was clear, however, was that evangelicals had ended their public silence and civic nonparticipation. Insofar as they specified public objectives and opposed social evils, they recovered continuity with the eighteenth- and nineteenth-century Evangelical Awakening in England and with American abolitionist evangelicalism of the post-Civil War era.

Emphasis on the regenerate Church as a new society over which Christ rules by the Holy Spirit through the inspired Scriptures was correlated afresh with two convictions.

capitalist utopia
socialist utopia

First, the Church as light to the world is called to model in society at large what happens when God's people live by the precepts and power of the risen Lord. Creative pilot projects could mirror the community of faith's endeavor to live by both neighbor love and social justice. The Church need not survive only as a subsociety of Amish believers or of Hasidic Jews withdrawn from the world and confined to their own institutions. The separatist option had made evangelism difficult and had deprived the Christian community of some values of modernity. But, no less important, it deprived the Church of its divinely intended role of public light, salt, and leaven. The Creator's moral creation mandate no less than Christ's evangelistic mandate presupposes universally valid ethical imperatives and divinely established social institutions like the monogamous family and governmental authority.

Second, the Church is to proclaim to the world the criteria or standards by which Christ, at His end-time return in power and glory, will finally judge all humanity and the nations, and by which He is anticipatively judging them even now. As redeemed sinners once identified with the world's rebellion, but now by divine grace on privileged speaking terms with the coming King, the people of God are to share with secular society the best of all good news: God offers forgiveness of sins and new spiritual life to all who trust in Christ's saving work.

Yet this return to social involvement lacked a dimension that evangelical scholars are now beginning to address more earnestly, the arena of public policy. Reasons for their recent neglect of this area are not difficult to identify. To speak compellingly about public philosophy and about policy concerns requires both cognitive competence and vocational expertise. Forfeiture of social concern by an earlier generation had left evangelicals with few qualified spokesmen in many areas of government and economics. Few things served the evangelical movement more poorly than mere aphorisms and verbal blips on the thin surface of worthy debate. A secular press readily probed evangelists and televangelists rather than evangelical educators and editors for a clue to the direction of Christian social thought.

But a still deeper reason accounts for evangelical timidity and confusion in public policy matters. Religiously conservative scholars have not developed a comprehensive Christian social ethics that connects the universal divine creation mandate with the Decalogue as a divine covenant-republication of creation ethics. To neglect God's creation ethics mandated before the Edenic Fall and its relationship to the Decalogue tends to leave nebulously in midair the significance of the Mosaic law and the ethics of the Old Testament prophets for contemporary Christian social engagement.

Some of this confusion is evident when, for example, extreme dispensationalists wholly dismiss Mosaic legislation as belonging to a now superseded dispensation (and then divert the Sermon on the Mount away from the Church

Age to a future Kingdom Age or millennium). Theonomists, on the other hand, insist on the universal and permanent validity of the entire corpus of Mosaic legislation for civil government in all times and places.

The confusion that here concerns us exists among avowed evangelicals, not simply among nonevangelical interpreters who deny the propositional validity of biblical morality, and who substitute for objectively revealed principles and precepts an internal disposition identified as a vague sentiment of love.

The failure of evangelical ethicists to engage in public policy formulation has had costly consequences. For it cast evangelicals in a pluralistic society in a role of concern only for their own special interests, and not for justice and equity as a public cause that embraces an evangelical agenda along with that of all other citizens.

Evangelicals in earlier centuries shared a concern for the public good. At our country's founding, Americans embraced a sense of the nation's universal mission and manifest destiny. Some regarded the United States as "the new Israel" standing in a covenant relationship to God and divinely assigned a mission of Christianizing the world. They particularized a universal conviction that divine providence underlies the origin of all nations and stressed that America's destiny as an intentionally pluralistic republic was nonetheless contingent upon faithfulness to the Judeo-Christian heritage.

Only public policy involvement that transcends a partisan agenda and envisions social justice as a universal due—reflecting God's universal demand for righteousness—can invalidate the complaint that evangelical orthodoxy is concerned for justice only when and as its own interests are violated.

Although humanity's fall into sin precipitated a catastrophic culture shock, the tragedy of Eden did not strip rebellious humans of all moral illumination. God holds humans responsible for their rebellion in Adam and also on their own account.

The Old Testament leaves no doubt that the Gentiles, although unenlightened by special revelation and nonparticipants in covenant ethics, nonetheless have light they deliberately spurn. Cain is held accountable for his murder of Abel; Israel's pagan neighbor-nations—Syria, Edom, Ammon, Moab, and others—are condemned for crimes of treaty breaking, enslavement of captives, violence, and savage conduct.

Any society that does not deal ethically with sex and marriage, with labor and economics, and with divinely willed structures of authority will accommodate the sinful warping of social components that need to be reclaimed for their divinely created intention. So, too, attention is required to civil government as a divinely intended context for human preservation and order in a fallen society.

If one neglects God's creation ethic, which the redemptive scriptural ethic restates and aims to reinforce, the risk multiplies of propounding only partisan policy preferences, and of doing so on extrabiblical grounds. When evangelicals seek to distill a program of contemporary moral policy and action solely from Israel's specially revealed covenant ethics, they are prone to compensate for their neglect of the significance of general or universal revelation by speculative theories of natural law, or to rely on unacknowledged ecclesiastical tradition to strengthen their positions. Or they are prone to imply a revelatory basis for their own social judgments.

What is espoused as "Christian public policy" inferred from biblical principles is readily promoted as normative Christian commitment and regarded as a necessary expression of a well-formed faith. But the authenticity of such inferences depends on their biblical legitimacy and the logical rigor of an intellectual process. Whenever God's will is precariously identified with acceptance of certain political or social preferences, what begins as a worthy effort to preserve the relevance of biblical revelation to the pressing social problems of modernity may through misjudgment or overstatement unwittingly invite doubts over what is declared to be biblical. When relativities are changed into absolutes, absolutes are more easily perceived as relativities. In view of this absolutizing of the relative in the name of God, other professedly Christian sociologists and political scientists, moving from sociology to theology with unclear theological priorities, may in turn even question whether divine revelation actually takes the form of rational propositions and objective principles.

For all that, biblical principles are indeed a verbal particularization of God's will. Beyond their significance for personal obedience in the world lies their equally important significance for public life and policy. Scripture is interested in comprehensive righteousness—personal and social. The self-revealing Creator and Governor of the universe commands universal justice. Scripture concerns itself with human thought and action in government and in business and economics no less than in education and culture and in marriage and the family.

Does that concern embrace the nature and purpose of economic systems and legislation touching the marketplace? Do scriptural references to labor and economics hold priority—in part or whole—over the sphere of civil government, or does the state have the final say? Does "doing the truth"—a basic Christian requirement—involve a definitive view of the state's role in the foundation and practice of business? Ancient Hebrew society operated within certain divinely stipulated structures. Is their significance limited wholly to the ancient faith community? Are those structures relevant to secular society today?

The Bible is not, of course, a guidebook on policy; however, to ignore it in public policy formulation is to neglect the brightest moral and spiritual illumination available. Yet it is an easy—and also a risky—leap from the conviction that the Bible is a divinely inspired book whose moral imperatives illumine every sphere of human behavior to the emphasis that it offers ready-made solutions—if only we trouble ourselves to find them—for any and every social dilemma. True as it is that Scripture constitutes a transcendent ethic that surpasses even "the wisdom of the ages," it is nonetheless the case that the Bible gives no direct answers to numerous contemporary problems. We are left to make inferences from revealed principles. To have revealed social and political principles is, to be sure, an immense asset. But our inferences from such foundation truths are not necessarily infallible. Attention to logic and hermeneutics will no doubt go a long way toward keeping us on the proper track. If we fall into error, the fault is not with guiding principles but with unsound exegesis.

The need for caution is illustrated by proposals for political action that some well-intentioned religious spokesmen promote. In the area of foreign policy, both the right and the left have claimed Christian legitimacy for very diverse positions on such matters as nuclear defense, troop reductions, the Panama Canal treaty, and much else. Nobody need be surprised, therefore, that what some interpreters view as "an evangelical recovery of political responsibility" is regarded by others as "a politicizing of evangelical piety."

Some political scientists warn that both the religious left and the religious right have promoted public policy positions and taken specific legislative positions presumably on Christian grounds, when their positions in fact arise less (if at all) from an expressly scriptural basis than from a subjectively preferred political stance. Whether one thinks the minimum wage in the United States should presently be raised, and if so by how much, may well turn more upon one's political outlook than upon direct biblical sanction. Some radical Christians have even revered Marxian economic analysis as an extension of general divine revelation. If religious conservatives often were unwitting apologists for the status quo, religious liberals have tended to view themselves as successors of the biblical prophets.

Fervent appeals have been ventured—on supposedly biblical grounds—in behalf of the so-called Social Gospel (usually a form of socialism), liberation theology, theology of revolution, and dispensational fundamentalism's withdrawal from politics and the world at large. In such cases not only have wrong inferences been drawn from biblical principles, but philosophical prejudices extraneous to the Bible were antecedently imposed upon it.

The governing hermeneutical approach to biblical ethics, all too much ignored in the effort to shape Christian policy decisions, is therefore critically important. Confusion is unavoidable if one begins by merely transferring to present-day secular society those ethical elements from the Old or New Testament that seem to have burning moral relevance while skipping over those that have fallen by the cultural wayside. On what basis does one avoid transferring to our times all—and not only part—of the biblical ethic? Are we to resort to natural law? Or should one function like a closet theonomist? Or do a divine creation mandate and general revelation contribute factors that we dare not ignore? Does it make a vital difference that the Old Testament prophetic vision of a universal era of justice and peace is correlated with the return of Messiah?

Some interpreters hold that the Sermon on the Mount provides all the revealed principles and divine guidance we need for any and every role in public affairs today. But the Sermon deals essentially with interpersonal relationships, not with official and international relationships. The Sermon is intended basically, moreover, for the new community of Christ's followers; it is not to be coercively imposed on unbelievers. To transfer the Sermon to official public life would disadvantage public agencies as well as misunderstand its intention.

Most contributors to this volume support the sanctity and perpetuity of the Old Testament moral law but find no reason to perpetuate the institutional forms of theonomic rule in which it was first expressed. In legal affairs we are not now legislating for a future millennium or for a contemporary theocracy.

Biblical principles nonetheless have a decisive importance for public policy matters in our fallen society in which God mandates the state to restrain injustice and to preserve order. God in His providence restrains human inordinacy and faces His people with the continuing task of reaffirmation and reformation in legislative and policy specifics. Since human unregeneracy will not automatically lead to justice and the public good, will not legislative regulation have some necessary role in a fallen world? Or are the principles of a market economy laws of nature? Are the checks and balances of a free market system adequate to contain entrepreneurial greed and inordinate self-interest?

So-called Christian Reconstructionists would superimpose upon all the nation-states Old Testament law, which was the basis of ancient Israel's theocratic rule. That law remains permanently valid, theonomists insist, not simply as an expression of God's moral will for humanity but as a legal corpus that civil government should universally enforce even in the present era.

But are the 613 divine laws in the Torah to be received and promoted as obligations of all modern states? Are Christians, as a test of their submission to the lordship of Christ, to champion an "all or nothing" restoration of theonomic rule?

Most evangelicals hold the view that since New Testament times the regenerate Church has been universally and intentionally scattered under diverse forms of government in order to witness to the lordship of Jesus Christ as final judge of the nations. By proclamation and by example they are to promote universally the justice God seeks and the justification He offers penitent believers in Christ. Although evangelicals do not equate democratic or republican political structures with the Kingdom of God, most nonetheless consider democratic government preferable in present fallen history because of its promotion of political self-determination and the safeguards it offers against secular totalitarianism.

Much Mosaic teaching is doubtless ongoingly significant for politics and economics, not least of all its support for private property, free enterprise, and concern for human welfare. Yet the modern state of Israel, although Jewish to the core, has not revived Jewish religious law but deliberately pursues a secular economic program.

Meir Taman, chief economist of the Bank of Israel, holds that the ideal would be an entrepreneurial religious Jewish state. It would preclude Jews from charging other Jews interest on loans, he declares, avoid inflation, balance employment levels with preservation of the work ethic with social morality, rely on a tax to provide survival funds until the unemployed find work, and shut down failing companies rather than bail them out.

These proposals face us with specific interpretations that some exegetes of the Torah may well question and disavow as reading into the Torah some social proposals not self-evidently inherent. No less important is the question of selectivity. Is all Mosaic legislation to be carried forward as an obligation of a modern Jewish religious state? Orthodox Jews seek literally to follow the Torah's more than six hundred commandments. Should the Israeli state then revive death by stoning for all crimes so designated by the ancient theocracy, in which capital punishment was stipulated for adultery, homosexuality, and juvenile delinquency, among other offenses?

Christian Reconstructionists would extend theocratic legislation to all modern nation-states on the ground that all the Mosaic teaching has permanent and universal validity for civil government. Some dissension is occasioned within the movement's ranks by Reconstructionists who would make certain exceptions—for example, retention of the menstrual laws—whereas others insist that every "jot and tittle" of the Mosaic teaching remains applicable.

The alternative view shared by most evangelicals was reflected by British Prime Minister Margaret Thatcher's address to the General Assembly of the Church of Scotland in May 1988. Mrs. Thatcher granted that democracy as a form of government is "not in itself especially Christian, for nowhere in the Bible is the word democracy mentioned. Ideally, when Christians meet, as Christians do, to take counsel together, their purpose is not (or should not be) to ascertain what is the mind of the majority but what is the mind of the Holy Spirit—something which may be quite different. Nevertheless," Mrs. Thatcher continued, "I am an enthusiast for democracy. And I take that position not because I believe majority opinion is inevitably right or true—indeed, no majority can take away God-given human rights. But because I believe it most effectively safeguards the value of the individual, and, more than any other system, restrains the abuse of power by the few. And that is a Christian concept."

We should go on to echo Prime Minister Thatcher's further comment, since few Christian leaders have served as effectively as Mrs. Thatcher in leading a powerful modern nation in public policy affairs. She added, "There is little hope for democracy if the hearts of men and women in democratic societies cannot be touched by a call to something greater than themselves. Political structures, state institutions, and collective ideals are not enough. We parliamentarians can legislate for the rule of law. You, the church, can teach the life of faith." Then she recited from a cherished hymn about "another country" whose King cannot be seen and whose armies cannot be counted, yet "soul by soul and silently her shining bounds increase."

The difficulties attending the formulation of "evangelical public policy" are helpfully indicated in *Evangelicals and Foreign Policy: Four Perspectives*, which is concerned with international more than economic policy.[1] After assessing conflicting attempts to derive an evangelical public philosophy based on biblical revelation, the political scientist Dean Curry concludes that "no distinctively biblical approach to foreign policy" seems possible. Alberto Coll, professor of international law, thinks we are locked up to prudential decision making that presupposes broad Christian principles. Richard John Neuhaus more fully emphasizes the democratic process in which evangelicals along with others seek to shape a public philosophy. The sociologist James Davison Hunter cautions that lack of consensus may deprive evangelicals of the public policy influence they might otherwise have.

In a doctoral dissertation completed in the late 1980s at Boston University under sociologist Peter Berger and titled "Recent Evangelical Appraisals of Capitalism and American Class Culture," Craig M. Gay notes that the evangelical debate over social and economic policy has arisen within a specifiable social context that pulls the "right" and the "left" quite predictably in contrary directions, and that the debate itself, moreover, has become one of the more important frameworks through which contemporary culture is unsuspectedly "modernizing" or secularizing Protestant orthodoxy. He gives an overview of the divergent evangelical appraisals of capitalism, from those on the right who, like Carl McIntyre, defend capitalism as a natural outgrowth of biblical Christianity, to those on the left who, like Jim Wallis, have declared capitalism to be an unjust system and have blamed it for many of the world's ills.

Gay then charts less extreme and more centrist views. He protests that many views succumb to ideological abuse of Scripture and to the de facto confession of the ultimacy of economic life and of material existence. The resulting confusion, he thinks, was reflected even by the 1974 International Congress on World Evangelization in Lausanne, where leading evangelical activists put social engagement on a par with evangelism in direct contradiction of Billy Graham's keynote emphases.

More recently, Christian Reconstructionism has essentially equated capitalism with the emerging Kingdom of God, he protests, while evangelical radicals like Ronald Sider and a growing circle of Christian Reformed spokesmen champion government interventionism, and World Evangelical Fellowship increasingly provides a sounding board for related emphases. The left identifies capitalism as an economic system essentially incompatible with Christian theology and ethics and promotes "an evangelical theology of liberation," taking its lead from radical secular analysis charging that a capitalist political-economic elite manipulates society for its own advantage.

Meanwhile the defenders of capitalism, Gay suggests, fall into several groups. Some anchor capitalism in the laws of nature; others hold that only Christian values make it work; still others ground it in Mosaic legislation assumed to be perpetually and universally valid. Gay notes the influence of socialist sources even on the evangelical center, through its interaction with the intellectual "new class" as a knowledge elite, an influence that not even neofundamentalists wholly escape. Gay does not express final judgment on the conflicting views, but emphasizes the urgency of further evangelical discussion of the relation of evangelical theology to rival contemporary social, economic, and political approaches. Significantly, he comments that not "'separatism' but . . . socio-political activism" comprises the most pressing temptation facing evangelical intellectuals.

Amid the ideological conflicts of our times, the first temptation may be to identify capitalism as Christian or biblical, all the more so now that socialism almost everywhere is emptying into disillusionment. To escape economic despair and to share in the capitalist creation of wealth, erstwhile socialist leaders are returning in stages to the market system they have long despised. But do the striking loss of confidence in socialism and the equally striking resurgence of the free market system justify us in dignifying capitalism as Christian economics? Socialism seems to have been an artificially contrived collectivist theory, whereas free enterprise is compatible with the deepest human instincts. Yet to claim that capitalism is essentially Christian is to assimilate to Christianity an economic system capable of ethical indifference and injury.

Is it more factual, then, simply to hold that free market economics was superimposed on a religious outlook stressing voluntarism, hard work, and prudent management, and that the providential result was an unprecedented expansion in material production and wealth and in a remarkable improvement in the living standards of much of the citizenry? Shall we regard free enterprise as an ethically neutral system, or is it not rather the case that Christianity requires us to forgo the notion of value-free mechanisms? Given humanity's present fallen condition, capitalism is readily placed in the service of human inordinacy. While it is true that competition and the law restrict such inordinacy, does not mass media advertising create for shysters an unprecedented opportunity to disadvantage the consumer?

In a speech at the American Enterprise Institute's annual policy conference, Paul Johnson remarked that capitalism needs to address the exclusion of perhaps a fifth of society from a life of modest decency.[2] Capitalism offers hope

evangelism

Social engagement

that "this minority problem of failure . . . the biggest single task our societies [face] today . . . can and will be overcome." The socialist systems cannot produce wealth; capitalist society knows that "a solution can be found" for permanent mass poverty, "and we have an inescapable moral obligation to find it." Yet Johnson granted the compatibility of the capitalist market system with Christianity, and he exhorted all who are rooted within the Judeo-Christian system of ethics "who value freedom, who strive for the just society, and who recognize the enormous productive potential of market capitalism" to engage in the entrepreneurial tasks of linking the free market system to the principles and practices that will promote regenerate moral ends. "It is a mistake," Johnson affirmed, to consider capitalism inherently moral rather than to recognize it as an incomparable system for producing wealth. But, he held, "it is possible to run it in tandem with public policies which make use of its energies while steering it in a moral direction." This task, Johnson averred, calls for a considerable agenda: absolute equality before the law; equality of opportunity, in which he included giving the poor access to education and to capitalism itself (as by stock ownership and small businesses); free trade; and by instructing the poorer nations in the skills of market capitalism. Capitalism is not the economics of the Kingdom of God, but neither is it a grotesque ideology; it has openly exhibited its efficiency as a wealth-producing system, and biblical principles can prod it toward the ethical purposes that protect it from inordinate misuse.

Evangelical economists are unanimous that the current distribution of wealth is not morally ideal. This is evident from the biblical exhortation that we respond to the poor and to cases of hardship. Yet they are equally unanimous in declaring that complete equality of income distribution is not a biblical standard. Indeed, as Marvin Kosters comments, such redistribution would offend other principles of fairness in relation to rewards and needs.

We are often told nowadays that the ideal state will be marked by justice and by compassion or love. This emphasis gets a ready hearing in the once-Christian West, in which all the humanitarian movements arose in the past from the theology of the Cross and evangelical affirmation of the *imago Dei* in all humanity. But love, or compassion, is a relationship between persons, not between institutions or between institutions and persons. No improvement can be made on an entirely just government; in community relationships, justice is the course that neighbor love takes. The continual modification of government policy in the name of compassion contributes to a misunderstanding of both compassion and justice. Love is always preferential; it gives itself voluntarily, not because the giving is legally due another. These confusions, which have important bearing on Christian social ethics, lead also to a speculatively compromised view of God. For they tend to elevate compassion as the essence of divinity and subordinate to it all other divine perfections, including righteousness or justice. One consequence is that God is depicted as not seriously offended by sin and iniquity; another is that the concept of justice itself is weakened, while that of compassion is distorted. The unhappy end product of compassionate government is the hoax of the welfare state.

The contributors to this present volume discuss the bearing of the biblical tenets of creation, fall, and redemption on the legal aspects of economic structures and on the regulation and control of business. Their concern not to ignore the public political route is great gain unless one confuses such involvement with "bringing in the Kingdom of God." The relationship of particular political and economic proposals to theological orthodoxy is quite tenuous. If one thinks that a particular position on a nuclear weapons freeze is more sure and more important than the doctrine of a final resurrection of the dead to divine judgment, one seriously confuses his priorities. How then, we may and must ask, are public policy commitments to be legitimated as Christian or biblical? Or is any and every such claim made on their behalf misleading?

In respect to the governing biblical sources, Christian economists differ over the nature and meaning of the supposedly relevant scriptural data, and differ also over precisely what illuminating inferences to public policy we are to derive from Scripture. Are these differences more a matter of semantics than of substance?

When writers speak of "broad implications of a biblically based vision," of Bible-engendered "nuances" and "insights" and "perspectives," and of Scripture as a major "source of ethical discernment," we are far removed from objective principles from which valid inferences can assuredly be drawn. The greater the gulf between express biblical doctrine and an agenda of precise legislative specifics, the harder it becomes to invoke express biblical authority for policy.

To be sure, each Testament is primarily addressed to a single faith community. In what way does the biblical ethic "apply to" and "illumine" public policy problems in a secular society?

Need a policy that is "compatible with" biblical principles rule out the possibility that another policy might also be compatible? "The spirit" of biblical teaching is sometimes invoked—in distinction from the teaching itself—in a manner that implies a devout mysticism. Some writers rely so much on parables for the content of social ethics that one wonders whether they are inclined to channel all biblical principles into subjective relational concerns. When economists speak quite generally only of knowing "God's desires" or of nurturing human desires that are truly scriptural, our task becomes more demanding. How does one compare desires if the validity of propositional revelation is unsure?

The Bible deals with human nature and with personal relationships more than with specific problems. But much of its teaching nonetheless expressly bears on public policy concerns. All humans are finite creatures, yet all are made in God's image. We are fallen sinners, yet we are responsible for our choices and stewardship of possessions. We must not confuse the abundant life with materialism, and we must be compassionate toward the poor. The biblical work ethic implies that in a fallen world labor is not to be shunned because it is sometimes an exasperating experience.

Even if Scripture includes general governing principles, say about the dignity of and the need to work, can we confidently infer that government is obliged to enforce one's right to work as an absolute right or merely insist that society must create a climate disposed to provide more jobs? Can one get assuredly from scriptural principles to cooperatives and to profit sharing?

The confusion over the Bible and public policy is in some respects due to the questions we address to Scriptures. The Bible does not contain an answer to all twentieth-century public policy concerns; in respect to some other issues it says very little. If we ask specifically whether the development of nuclear energy is the best option to cope with the fuel shortage in the future, the biblical writers are silent. Devout Christians know no more than do secular humanists about some of these concerns; indeed, all our calculations may be upset if cold fusion turns out to be more than a hoax.

So intricate are public policy issues, moreover, that an economist may well distinguish positions that rest obviously on governing principles from those that depend on fallible inferences and from still other positions that seem simply to be prudent.

Biblical principles can provide direction for rational priorities and inherent goals. Economics can define a decision-framework and specific approaches, but Scripture must remain the norm if we are to avoid reducing Christian concern to mere world concern. As responsible carriers of light and leaven, Christians are to be identified with the world, speaking to the soul of the nation, pointing to a higher way, and modeling and exhorting the masses to obey the coming King.

A scholar is to be commended rather than criticized if caution requires him to avoid claiming direct biblical authority for a view that seems compatible with Scripture and yet is not expressly demanded by it. To claim biblical justification for certain aspects of public policy is both unnecessary and ill-advised, when all that is clear is consistency within a concern for justice. Sincere Christians may differ over particular guidelines for national policy, but they should not blame the Bible for differences that arise from contrasting political platforms. Policy decisions are a response to God's call to justice, but we should be cautious about unqualifiedly calling them "God's will." Yet in a pluralistic society Christians must strive as individuals and as a new community to approximate as fully as possible the Creator-Redeemer's moral imperatives. But the difficulties of transforming scriptural general principles into specific policy prescriptions must not discourage us. In a fallen world, utopia must wait for the Lord's return.

EDITOR'S PERSPECTIVE

Arise, O God, judge the earth!
For it is Thou who dost possess all the nations. (Ps. 82:8)

God will judge the nations! God has revealed His universal demand for right-eousness. God has established the state and mandated that it restrain injustice, promote justice, and preserve order. God did not give the Church an imbalanced and limited gospel, neither a Social Gospel nor a gospel solely interested in evangelism. God gave the Church a gospel that is to leaven every aspect of life—private and public, individual and community. As Carl Henry stated, "The Church is to proclaim to the world the criteria or standards by which Christ, at His end-time return in power and glory, will finally judge all humanity and the nations, and by which He is anticipatively judging them even now."

Dr. Henry expounded on each of these ideas, and he rightly argued that evangelical orthodoxy must vigorously pursue social justice as a universal due that transcends any partisan or self-serving agendas. Until the world knows we are willing to have our own economic ox gored for the sake of justice, the world will continue to think ill of any pronouncements that seem to serve the status quo or personal interests. He also distinguished appropriate from fallacious ways of identifying and using biblical principles as shaping elements for public policy. This aspect of his chapter is, of course, central and critical to this entire series. We must at all costs avoid reducing the Scripture to a set of principles or baptizing our business and economic activities and policies with Scripture in an effort that results in our boasting about particular structures, policies, methods or, worse yet, our own insights. Jeremiah reported,

Thus says the LORD, "Let not a wise man boast of his wisdom . . . but let him who boasts boast of this, that he understands and knows Me,

29

that I am the LORD who exercises lovingkindness, justice, and righteousness on earth; for I delight in these things." (Jer. 9:23-24)

Certainly, though, one of Dr. Henry's more profound insights appears in
the following paragraph near the end of his chapter:

We are often told nowadays that the ideal state will be marked by justice
and by compassion or love. This emphasis gets a ready hearing in the
once-Christian West, in which all the humanitarian movements arose in
the past from the theology of the Cross and evangelical affirmation of
the *imago Dei* in all humanity. But love, or compassion, is a relationship
between persons, not between institutions or between institutions and
persons. No improvement can be made on an entirely just government; in
community relationships, justice is the course that neighbor love takes. The
continual modification of government policy in the name of compassion
contributes to a misunderstanding of both compassion and justice. Love
is always preferential; it gives itself voluntarily, not because the giving is
legally due another. These confusions, which have important bearing on
Christian social ethics, lead also to a speculatively compromised view of
God. For they tend to elevate compassion as the essence of divinity and
subordinate to it all other divine perfections, including righteousness or
justice. One consequence is that God is depicted as not seriously offended
by sin and iniquity; another is that the concept of justice itself is weakened, while that of compassion is distorted. The unhappy end product of
compassionate government is the hoax of the welfare state.

The paragraph is really self-explanatory, but the point that "justice is
the course that neighbor love takes" when governments, businesses, and other
institutions seek to fulfill their obligations in the community is a profound truth
to contemplate and take to heart. As Dr. Henry noted, this fact ought to have an
important bearing on Christian social ethics.

Dr. Henry also observed that our governing hermeneutical approach to
biblical ethics is significant as Christians work to shape public policy decisions.
He is quite right. Dr. Walter Kaiser, Jr., in fact, stated in his chapter ("A Single
Biblical Ethic in Business," volume 1, pages 77, 79) that determining how the
Old Testament and the New Testament relate to each other—a hermeneutical
issue—is the biggest problem Christians face in applying Scripture to our
lives. Hermeneutics (how we interpret Scripture) is therefore worthy of further
consideration.[1]

Tomes have been written about hermeneutics. Denominations are formed
around hermeneutical perspectives. Seminaries are known for their hermeneutical positions. People are labeled Augustinian or Thomists, or Calvinists and

Arminians. All of this must be passingly humorous and extremely disappoint-
ing to our gracious and merciful Savior. As Abraham Lincoln is reported to
have said, "Everybody in this conflict [Civil War] claims that God is on their
side, but I really wonder who is on God's side." I often wonder who is in what
hermeneutical camp because of upbringing, the camp a "spiritual mentor" is in,
the fit of the hermeneutic with logical orientation, psychological needs being
shored up by the truths of Scripture, personal experiences prior to this regeneration, and other similar view-shaping phenomena.

Several things seem self-evident to me. Our personal experience and logic
are not the solutions to untying the hermeneutic knot. The Holy Spirit, the only
true teacher we all have in Christ, is never double-minded, so He is not to be
credited with the difficulty. The Scripture the Spirit has brought forth, and
kept intact for our nurturing through the centuries, is completely sufficient in
the hands of the Holy Spirit to produce (1) an accurate understanding of God,
(2) the truth about mankind, and (3) light that is adequate to show us the way
God would have us travel. Then what is the problem?

I believe our hermeneutical difficulties arise from three major problems:
(1) our inherent propensity to seek resolution, psychological comfort, and security (needs emanating from the Fall) rather than remain open to hermeneutical
tensions; (2) our self-perpetuated ignorance of the Scripture; and (3) our substitution of a knowledge about God for a relationship with Christ.

The first problem tempts me greatly to carry on at length about our disinclina-
tion to simultaneously embrace knowledge and mystery, certainty and uncertainty,
and conditions that are resolvable and unresolvable. But this is neither the time nor
the place to wade off into such deep waters. I will simply observe that God's love
for us is so genuine and far reaching that it is not constrained by or dependent
on our psychological willingness (openness) to embrace many more profound
realities about His nature and our finitude. For example, how many Christians
have ever taken the time or gone through the mental pain to reconcile the wrath
of God with the love of God? Both are clearly taught in Scripture. Who dares
to discover the equal joy and mental security that come from the grandeur of
knowing an inscrutable, incomprehensible God who is still self-revealing? All
too frequently we are guilty of wanting a small God who will leave us comfortable
with our logic and our imagination and cater to our psychological needs.

Biblical ignorance, on the other hand, is harder to justify. At least in the
first case we can halfheartedly blame our fallen nature. I need to explain,
though, what I do *not* mean by biblical ignorance. I do not mean that we are
unfamiliar with Bible verses. I do not mean that we do not know who Jesus
Christ is and that He died for our sins and was raised from the dead on the third
day. I am not thinking about an ignorance of Bible stories, parables, miracles,
and other such matters.

We speak of the God of the Scripture. We testify to the fact that the Holy

Spirit writes God's Word on our hearts. But how much time do we spend reading the Scripture, believing God will speak to us personally through it? Do we pore over it as carefully as we did the love letters from our sweethearts when our hearts were on fire for them? Or have we really left our First Love? Are our minds being fed more by television than by the Living Word?

At the Scholars' Colloquium accompanying the writing of the first volume of this series, Walt Kaiser told of his dad's profound biblical knowledge, despite no formal theological training. Evening after evening his dad read the Bible, moving back and forth through its pages, searching out what God might have to say on each and every matter the Scripture brought to his attention. A single account in one place would find him looking up the same idea in other places in the Bible. I am afraid that today our culture offers too many distractions for most people to view what Walt Kaiser's dad did as an appealing alternative to their current practices in the evening. But this is precisely the reason we are a biblically ignorant people today. We devote little time to studying the contents of the Bible.

> How blessed is the man . . . [when] his delight is in the law of the LORD,
> And in His law he meditates day and night. (Ps. 1:1-2)

> "Behold, days are coming," declares the Lord GOD,
> "When I will send a famine on the land,
> Not a famine for bread or a thirst for water,
> But rather for hearing the words of the LORD.
> And people will stagger from sea to sea, . . .
> They will . . . seek the word of the LORD,
> But they will not find it." (Amos 8:11-12)

However, biblical knowledge must never become a substitute for a personal walk with the Lord Jesus Christ, which is the third reason we have so many hermeneutical difficulties. Claiming to have a personal relationship with Christ without testing every thought and examining every intention and action against the Word of God is being disobedient to the Word (see 2 Cor. 10:5; 1 John 4:1). On the other hand, some people are "always learning and never able to come to the knowledge of the truth" (2 Tim. 3:7), or they have not heard Christ say, "You search the Scriptures, because you think that in them you have eternal life; and it is these that bear witness of Me; and you are unwilling to come to Me, that you may have life" (John 5:39-40). Our life in Christ is guided by, but not simply made up of, biblical doctrines or spiritual experiences. A true relationship with Christ is harmonized and balanced with sound biblical teaching, an obedient response to what we know, and a genuine fellowship with our Lord through the work of the indwelling Spirit who has been given to us as a seal signifying the certainty of eternal life.

PART II

INCOME DISTRIBUTION IN A JUST SOCIETY

When a mother has ten peach halves to distribute among three children, she faces an equity question. What is the just way to distribute the peaches? Do the two oldest (or biggest) children each receive four halves and the youngest (or smallest) child two halves? Or should they be divided four, three, three? Or does it matter since we are not dealing with people who are poor or starving? Are there rules or principles to guide us as we seek justice, fairness, and equity in a system of distribution?

The world has presented us with many models for distributing wealth over the centuries. In some societies, the greatest hunters or warriors received the greatest rewards, according to their contribution to the care of the larger group. In other cultures, the patriarch ruled and the eldest son was automatically the heir apparent—a system of tradition honoring the firstborn male. Still other economies were ruled by command structures, and those in charge got all they wanted and the others got what was left. There have been efforts also to construct utopian societies where everything was shared equally or according to need.

Every system of distribution that has ever been employed has created some very unjust side effects. Both fallen human nature and natural human differences (mental, physical, and life experiences) guarantee that inequities will exist. Persons responsible for justice in the marketplace have to work at minimizing the consequences of unjust inequities while not subverting or stifling the enormous benefits flowing to the entire society from human inequalities that are neither unfair nor inherently unjust. The mixture of sin with natural human inequalities creates the opportunity for serious economic injustices. Every economic/political/social system has experienced difficulties trying to figure a way to harmonize and balance the consequence of these fixed realities—sin and inherent human inequalities.

Dr. Marvin Kosters sets before us an analysis of the distribution of income in our country, and he clearly identifies several groups who constitute the "poor" in our society—single-parent households, those with little education, and those with nontraditional working patterns. Identifying these groups allows us to sharpen our questions about the type of national policy we should follow. Dr. Kosters observes that our national policy to date has relied extensively on free market forces, family help (care of children and aged), involvement of federal and state governments, and voluntary acts of charity instituted by the private sector. (Readers who desire more analysis of what gives rise to poverty can review Section E, pages 207-246, of volume 2 of this series, and especially T. M. Moore's chapter, "The Private Sector and the Poor," pages 211-225.)

Kosters also indicates that people may seek to redress inequities in the distribution of wealth either by taking steps to redistribute the currently available wealth or by seeking ways to increase the average income levels so that all groups are economically elevated. Our society has, at different times, acted to do both. Has God revealed His desires on this matter? While not trying to be dogmatic or absolutely definitive, Marvin Kosters notes some biblical themes (principles) and rightly reminds us that we need to glean from them the eternal verities God has given us to assist us in acting responsibly before Him. Kosters points us in a direction (the correct one, I believe) and takes a clear position on our need to discern and implement practices that will help people grow in their ability to care for themselves—a truly godly ingredient in any effort to address the larger issues associated with questions of income distribution.

CHAPTER 2

BIBLICAL PRINCIPLES APPLIED TO A NATIONAL POLICY ON INCOME DISTRIBUTION

Marvin H. Kosters

Marvin H. Kosters is Director of Economic Policy Studies at the American Enterprise Institute, a Washington-based nonprofit public policy research organization. His research and publications have mainly addressed national policy issues concerned with labor markets, income maintenance, and government regulation. He previously served as a Senior Economist at the Council of Economic Advisers, Director for policy at the U.S. Cost of Living Council, which administered wage and price controls from 1971 to 1974, and as a Senior Economist at the White House. A graduate of Calvin College, he received a degree in Economics from the University of Chicago.

I n our daily working lives we encounter two broad subject areas of economics: how goods and services are produced, and how they are apportioned among us. We are both producers and consumers. The distribution of income involves the second area. Its subject matter extends beyond our working lives, of course, in two directions—to children and to retired people.

The distribution of income has always been one of the most controversial areas of economics. One reason is that perspectives from outside economics need to be brought to bear for a full discussion of the issues. In particular, whether the needs of the poor are being met adequately—especially for people with handicapping or disabling conditions, those with health problems, and those who can neither work nor turn to others for support—is a question that cannot be addressed exclusively or even primarily in economic terms. Economic analysis is certainly relevant for examining this issue, but it does not supply the moral imperative for addressing the question.

Just as judgments about whether a particular pattern of income distribution is fair or provides economic justice require criteria from outside economics, it should also be recognized that the purely economic concept of access to

35

material resources described by the income distribution comprises only one dimension of what is relevant and important in our lives. A moment of thoughtful introspection about what would be high on a list of blessings for which gratitude should be expressed on Thanksgiving Day, for example, is perhaps sufficient to confirm this point. Although economic well-being is obviously significant, the limited range of human experience it describes must be kept in mind. Moreover, the available measures of the income distribution are incomplete and often crude approximations to represent how well people and families are faring in economic terms.

After sketching the main elements in our current national policy on income distribution, my discussion will draw heavily on empirical information on how income is distributed. This discussion is intended primarily to shed light on the issues that need to be addressed and on the dilemmas posed by policies designed to change the distribution of income. The discussion is also intended to provide an empirical basis for exploring how biblical principles should be applied in our current economic and policy context.

Two broad themes can be drawn from biblical teachings that I believe are most relevant for examining income distribution issues. The first stresses fairness and equity (not equality), especially as these aspects of economic justice can be applied to relations between contributions and rewards, between work and pay, and between good stewardship and economic well-being. The second involves exercise of charity, compassion, and personal assistance to people in need. This second theme includes the responsibilities of society and its members toward the poor, a persistent biblical topic. The first theme, emphasizing choices and their consequences, is particularly applicable to the commercial relationships involved in economic exchange. The second recognizes that individual circumstances are often not attributable to behavioral choices, and that indifference is not a moral response to economic adversity irrespective of whether it arises from misfortune or limited endowments, or whether instead it can be traced to improvident choices. The biblical text that best summarizes these themes is the well-known injunction in Micah 6:8 "to do justly, and to love mercy, and to walk humbly with thy God." The third theme in the text seems particularly appropriate in an effort to apply the first two to an analysis of income distribution policies.

These two broad themes—justice and love—have an all-encompassing quality. Lewis Smedes states,

> Justice and love are the two absolute commandments. They cover every
> conceivable human situation. . . . Everything we do must be fair; if it
> is not fair, it is not right. And everything we do must be helpful, or at
> least not hurtful; if we mean it to hurt and not help people it is not right.
> Justice and love form a kind of moral counterpoint in life.[1]

The quotation also hints that there is often tension between these two principles. We should accordingly expect to encounter dilemmas in efforts to apply them to income distribution policies.[2]

U.S. INCOME DISTRIBUTION POLICY

It seems useful to consider at the outset our national policies as they affect the income distribution. The central element in U.S. national policy toward the income distribution is certainly extensive reliance on the marketplace. The marketplace is the institution that directly and indirectly influences what is produced and how income is in turn apportioned to individuals and family units. It influences directly what people are paid for their work, and workers' earnings account for some three-fourths of total income.[3] Its indirect influence includes how savings and investments are guided by incentives generated in the marketplace, and how prices and availability of material goods are set—and thus the consumption opportunities into which earnings and income can be translated.

Government is another institution that plays an essential role. The federal government's largest and most visible task is administering income transfer payments, especially social security retirement payments and a set of income support programs collectively referred to as welfare. Some of these programs involve providing money, but many others supply services directly (Medicaid, for example) or subsidies for particular kinds of consumption (food stamps and housing). Still other income transfer programs are conditioned on unemployment, disability, or veteran status.

Among other institutions, the family undoubtedly is most fundamental. Its role ranges from providing for children and young people through often intermittent assistance during adult life to offering various forms of personal and financial support for the elderly. Economic support through families is only one element in their role, and perhaps not the most important one, but its significance for the income distribution should not be overlooked.

Finally, the distribution of access to material goods is also influenced by voluntary and charitable organizations (including churches) and by local government and affiliated organizations, such as schools, that provide assistance in cash and in kind.

The two prominent features of our national policy on income distribution are its heavy reliance on money income earned in the marketplace, principally from labor earnings, and the varied and diverse roles of other institutions. The federal government also influences the distribution in substantial ways, particularly through the tax revenues it collects and the major programs such as social security it administers. Other institutions, however, provide both money and access to services.

MEASURES OF INCOME DISTRIBUTION

An examination of measures of how money income is actually distributed sets the stage for a discussion of the extent of inequality and the factors that should be taken into account in assessing the efficacy of the policies influencing it. The most commonly cited measures describe shares of income received by equal numbers of units when ranked according to their income levels. Measurements are usually made separately for families (people living with relatives) and unrelated individuals (people living alone or with nonrelatives). Summary measures are presented in table 2.1 for ten-year intervals for the past forty years.

The data for families show, for example, that a little more than 50 percent of total income is received by the middle three quintiles (which account for 60 percent of all families). In the broad middle section of the distribution, in other words, the share of income received compares reasonably with the share of families involved. The income share is somewhat lower for unrelated individuals, but it has risen close to 50 percent. The big differences, of course, are near the ends of the distribution.

Table 2.1

TRENDS IN INCOME INEQUALITY: 1947-87

	SHARE OF TOTAL INCOME RECEIVED BY:			
	Lowest Quintile	Middle Three Quintiles	Top 5 Percent	Index of Income Concentration
Families				
1947	5.0	51.8	17.5	.392
1957	5.1	53.3	15.6	.364
1967	5.5	54.2	15.2	.348
1977	5.2	54.6	15.7	.351
1987	4.6	52.0	16.9	.376
Unrelated Individuals				
1947	2.0	41.4	29.3	.552
1957	2.6	46.4	19.7	.489
1967	3.0	45.5	21.1	.490
1977	4.1	47.7	19.6	.443
1987	3.6	48.0	19.3	.451

Source: *Money Income of Households, Families, and Persons in the United States: 1987,* Current Population Reports, Series P-60, No. 162, U.S. Department of Commerce, Bureau of the Census, Table 12, pages 42-43.

At the low end of the distribution, the bottom 20 percent of families receive some 5 percent of total income, with the share noticeably lower in 1987 than earlier. One way of describing this pattern is by observing that families in the lowest quintile on average receive only about one-fourth the income they would receive if income were distributed equally among all families. When their share is compared with the top 5 percent of the distribution, it shows that these families, on average, receive three times the income that they in turn would receive if income were equally distributed. For unrelated individuals, income is distributed even more unequally, partly perhaps because the circumstances of those who make up this group are even more diverse.

The distribution can also be described by various indexes that measure degree of inequality across the entire distribution. Such a measure is also reported in table 2.1 for both groups. Although an index of this type has no simple intuitive explanation, it is worth noting that it would approach zero as incomes approach complete equality.[4]

The absence of any inequality provides a convenient benchmark for interpreting the various income distribution measures, but departures from complete equality should not by themselves be considered as bases for assessing the degree to which a distribution accords with moral or ethical principles. Moreover, equality of distribution is certainly not a general biblical theme.

These simple measures of annual money income are only crude measures of economic well-being. For one thing, measures of money income leave out the contributions to economic well-being represented by housing, automobiles, and other durable goods already paid for by owners, and income or subsidies in kind such as food stamps, medical services, rent, and so on. Another characteristic of these measures is that they cover only a single year, and income often varies considerably over time. Farmers are sometimes affected by drought, businesspeople and independent contractors have good and bad years, urban working people sometimes suffer bouts of unemployment, and income may be temporarily high for people who realized large capital gains from the sale of a farm or business even though their income throughout their working life was near the average. For people in these circumstances, what they actually spend during each year is likely to be far more stable than their incomes. Still another factor is that the family units whose incomes are being compared are very diverse in terms of both their incomes and their needs.

In table 2.2, data are presented that show both the diversity of family types and the changes in their composition over time. Each of these seven family types (which include two groups of unrelated individuals) is much more homogeneous than the two groups discussed earlier, but a great deal of diversity still remains in each group. The two most prominent trends in composition by family type are the rising share of unrelated individuals who are not elderly and the declining share of married-couple families with children. Among families with children, changing composition is particularly noteworthy, with a decline in the proportion of married couples and a large increase in single mothers with children.[5] These compositional changes influence measures of income distribution for broader groups because the needs and the incomes of these family types are quite different.

Table 2.2
DISTRIBUTION OF FAMILIES BY FAMILY TYPE: 1970 and 1986

Type of Family Unit	1970	1986
All families	100%	100%
Nonelderly units with no children		
Childless families	22	21
Unrelated individuals	14	23
Elderly units with no children		
Childless families	10	10
Unrelated individuals	9	10
Families with children		
Married-couple families	36	25
Single-mother families	5	7
Other units with children	3	3
(Percent Breakdown of Families with Children)		
Families with children	100%	100%
Married-couple families	81	71
Single-mother families	11	20
Other units with children	7	9

Source: *Trends in Family Income: 1970-1986*, Congressional Budget Office, February 1988, Table A-1, page 66. (Note that percentages do not always add to 100 because of rounding.)

As a further step toward making comparisons among individual family units and groups, incomes can be adjusted to take into account the fact that while two cannot live as cheaply as one, the total cost of two people living together is less than twice the cost of each living separately. Moreover, the needs of additional children can generally be provided at lower cost than for a single child. In table 2.3, data on adjusted family incomes are reported, with the adjustments based on standard measures of equivalency at the poverty level. In addition, median adjusted family income is expressed in percentage multiples of the poverty level to permit comparisons among groups.[6]

Measured in these terms, the level of economic well-being that could be achieved with the money income they received during 1986 was highest for childless families who were not elderly. Median income for them was almost five times the poverty line (491 percent). Those who fared worst were single mothers with children, nearly half of whom had money incomes below the poverty line. Median family income for all units taken together was about triple the poverty level.

Based on these measures cited here, it seems clear that single-mother families with children deserve special concern. In terms of their economic status, they are the contemporary counterparts of the widows so frequently named for consideration in the Bible. One indication of the relatively recent emergence of single-mother families as a behavioral phenomenon is provided by data on the family characteristics of children receiving assistance under welfare programs. In 1937-38, the father was deceased for 48.4 percent of the children, and the father was not married to the mother for 2.8 percent. By 1982, those relationships had reversed to less than 1 percent where the father was deceased and 46.5 percent where the father was not married to the mother.[7]

Table 2.3
MEDIAN INCOME AND POVERTY RATES BY FAMILY TYPE: 1986

Type of Family Unit	Median Adjusted Family Income as Percent of Poverty Line	Percent Below Poverty Line
All families	313	13
Nonelderly units with no children		
Childless families	491	4
Unrelated individuals	289	18
Elderly units with no children		
Childless families	323	4
Unrelated individuals	161	20
Families with children		
Married-couple families	336	7
Single-mother families	114	46

Source: *Trends in Family Income: 1970-1986*, Congressional Budget Office, February 1988, Figure 7, page 17, and Table C-2, page 110.

Significant fractions of unrelated individuals also had incomes below the poverty level, but many of them may receive support from others—from parents in the case of college students, for example, and from children in the case of the elderly. Although there is a great deal of diversity within these groups, money income is likely to be temporarily low for many of them; persistent poverty is less likely for most of them than for many single-mother families.

The adjusted income and poverty data reported in table 2.3 reflect both money income generated in the marketplace and payments received from various transfer programs. Information on income sources in the middle and at the bottom of the distributions is presented in table 2.4.

Table 2.4
INCOME TRANSFERS BY FAMILY TYPE AND INCOME RANGE: 1986

(Percent of Income from Transfers)

Type of Family Unit	Middle Three Quintiles	Bottom Quintile
All families	8	41
Nonelderly units with no children		
Childless families	2	15
Unrelated individuals	2	27
Elderly units with no children		
Childless families	41	80
Unrelated individuals	66	93
Families with children		
Married-couple families	1	9
Single-mother families	22	69

Source: *Trends in Family Income: 1970-1986*, Congressional Budget Office, February 1988, Tables A-7 and A-8, pages 74-77.

According to these data, nonelderly units without children and married-couple families rely to only a very small extent on income transfers throughout the middle range of the income distribution, and to only a modest extent at the low end. The elderly, however, rely extensively on transfers—mainly social security retirement payments—and transfers account for most of their income in the bottom quintile. Most single-mother families rely to only a limited extent on transfers, but for those at the bottom, transfers account for a very large share because transfers are mainly conditional on their income.

All of these data include only cash income, and for many of the poorest families, income and services in kind are of some importance. For single-mother families, for example, an average income of about $9,000 was needed in 1986 to achieve a level of spending at the poverty level. For single-mother families below the poverty level, average income was only about $1,500 before any transfers. Transfers in cash raised their average income level to about $4,100, and food and housing benefits raised it further to about $5,500. In addition, many of these families could receive medical services and other services provided by local government units. As these figures indicate, reliance on public assistance by these poorest among family units is very extensive, but their income levels still remain very low.

These data on how income is distributed reflect considerable inequality. Examination of differences in the composition of family units and simple comparisons of differences in their needs, however, show that departures from complete equality do not provide either an unambiguous or a reasonable basis for judging the extent to which income is distributed in ways consistent with biblical principles. Moreover, the money income measures used are only a partial measure of the distribution of economic well-being.

The measures that show families in poverty and in the lower part of the income distribution also indicate, however, that many families—and in particular many families with children—have very limited incomes. Despite programs that provide a large fraction of the income of many of these families, their material well-being is still far below that of the average family. The measures also show that the contemporary poor are heavily concentrated among single-mother families. Improving their well-being is one of the most difficult policy challenges.

INCOME, WORK, AND FAMILY TYPE

Differences in working patterns influence money income, and both the composition of families and the working patterns systematically vary between races. The well-known disparity between incomes of white and black families is illustrated for several family types in table 2.5. Much of the gap is attributable to individual workers' earnings levels. A significant portion, however, is a result of differences in family types and work patterns.

In 1987 the median income for all black families was only 56 percent of that of all white families. The gap is somewhat smaller for more homogeneous family types, but differences in working patterns within types of families also account for much of that. For example, among married-couple families in which the head works year-round and full-time and the spouse also works, median income for blacks is 90 percent of that for whites.

Table 2.5
MEDIAN INCOME BY FAMILY TYPE, RACE,
AND WORK EXPERIENCE: 1987

Family Type and Work Experience	All Races	White	Black
All families	$30,853	$32,274	$18,098
Married-couple families	34,700	35,295	27,182
Head worked year-round and full-time	41,951	42,214	36,677
Spouse employed	44,909	45,160	40,772
Spouse not in labor force	36,201	36,586	25,019
Single-mother families	14,620	17,018	9,701
Unrelated individuals	12,559	13,337	8,093

Source: *Money Income of Households, Families, and Persons in the United States: 1987*, Current Population Reports, Series P-60, No. 162, U.S. Department of Commerce, Bureau of the Census, Tables 17 and 18, pages 61-77.

A clearer picture of the significance of variations in working patterns can be obtained by considering only family units headed by people of working age. In table 2.6, poverty rates are presented for family types according to working patterns. The strong relationship between the likelihood of poverty and the amount of work during the year stands out in these data. Diversity among family types remains, of course, partly because of important differences in working patterns. In married-couple families, for example, more than one adult may be working, but this is less likely for single-mother families with children.

Table 2.6
POVERTY STATUS OF FAMILIES WITH HEADS 22 TO 64 YEARS OLD, BY FAMILY TYPE AND WORK EXPERIENCE: 1986

Family Type and Work Experience of Head	Percent Below Poverty Line
Married-couple families with children	7.9
No work during the year	40.1
Worked during the year	6.4
Year-round, full-time work	3.7
Single mother families with children	44.5
No work during the year	84.8
Worked during the year	26.8
Year-round, full-time work	7.9
Unrelated individuals	17.7
No work during the year	60.8
Worked during the year	11.0
Year-round, full-time work	4.3

Source: *Poverty in the United States: 1986*, Current Population Reports, Series P-60, No. 160, U.S. Department of Commerce, Bureau of the Census, Tables 21 and 22, pages 94-98.

The income comparisons among family types with different working patterns highlight a noteworthy point: Income levels attained and the incidence of poverty are strongly influenced by behavioral choices. Living arrangements constitute one area of choice. The economic circumstances of single-mother families show very dramatically how dissolution of marriage and childbearing outside marriage result in increased inequality and poverty and in serious economic disadvantage for the children involved. The second area of behavioral choice illustrated by these data is the linkage between work and income. The lesson for policy is that the importance of behavioral choices should not be overlooked. The dilemma for policy is how to encourage stable marriages, family relationships, and working patterns and at the same time alleviate economic hardship, particularly among children.

A report produced by a group led by Michael Novak points out that people are extremely unlikely to remain in poverty if, as adults, they "get married and stay married (even if not on the first try)" and "stay employed, even if at a wage and under conditions below their ultimate aims."[8] Both behavioral patterns can be urged on the basis of biblical principles. Assumption of responsibilities for support of family members—even for what we would call extended families—and willingness to work on the part of those who are able—even tolerance of some degree of hardship for those who are not—are, I believe, biblical themes that should continue to shape our attitudes and policies toward income distribution.

REWARDS FROM WORK

The wages and earnings of people who work also vary widely, even for those whose work effort is similar. It is therefore appropriate to explore briefly some sources of these differences and to reflect on how they should be regarded. A major portion of these differences in earnings arises from diverse abilities or special skills—pay levels received by people with outstanding ability in sports, music, or management often provide memorable examples. In contemporary economies, however, education and work experience acquired on the job contribute systematically to pay patterns. The systematic contribution of work experience and schooling levels to pay differences is illustrated in table 2.7 and figure 2.1. The figures charted there show that wages rise gradually during early working years and subsequently taper off and decline.

Table 2.7
MEDIAN HOURLY WAGES OF MALE FULL-TIME WAGE AND SALARY WORKERS, 1988

AGE CATEGORY	YEARS OF SCHOOLING				
	<12 Years	12 Years	13-15 Years	16 Years	>16 Years
16-19	$4.00	$ 5.00	$ 5.00	—	—
20-24	5.75	6.45	6.00	$ 8.33	$ 9.54
25-29	6.03	8.00	9.00	11.11	12.49
30-34	7.50	9.50	11.00	13.52	14.28
35-39	7.50	10.13	12.31	14.17	16.33
40-44	8.37	11.00	12.50	15.00	16.52
45-49	9.50	11.53	14.23	17.14	17.94
50-54	8.75	11.70	13.39	17.50	18.05
55-59	9.44	12.00	12.50	17.32	16.65
60-64	8.04	10.38	12.51	16.65	16.88

Source: Current Population Survey Microdata Files, April-June 1988.

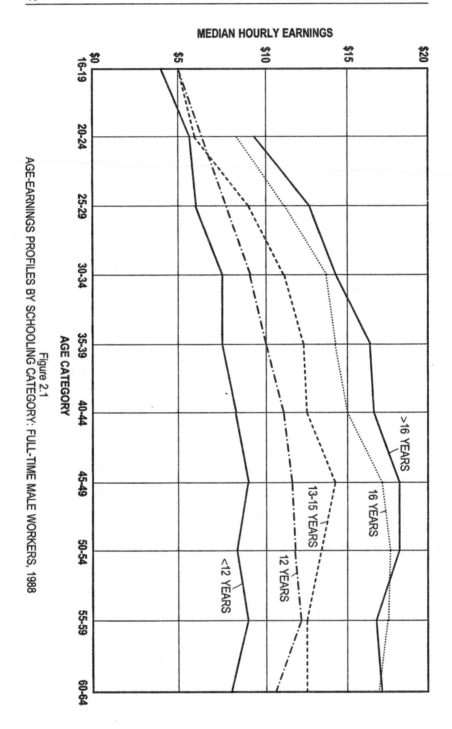

Figure 2.1
AGE-EARNINGS PROFILES BY SCHOOLING CATEGORY: FULL-TIME MALE WORKERS, 1988

Table 2.7 and figure 2.1 also show that significantly higher pay is received at higher schooling levels. In economic terms, both schooling and learning on the job can be considered investments made by individual workers that improve their earning capability. Also, again in economic terms, fairness suggests that making worthwhile investments should be rewarded. Estimates suggest that differences in schooling and work experience account for more than half of earnings inequality.[9]

The agricultural and pastoral economy that dominates the setting of the biblical teachings provides little experience that can be applied directly to assessing individuals' earnings. Diligence probably receives more biblical attention than technical skills, but it may also have been particularly important in tending flocks and fields. Careful stewardship in tending flocks, vine-dressing, and tilling fields is generally commended, however, and rewards from prudent investments are favorably regarded.

REDISTRIBUTION ISSUES

The total income available for apportionment among members of a society is produced by a combination of labor earnings generated by work and income from capital that has been accumulated by saving and investment on the part of workers, their parents, and earlier generations. A very large percentage of income is apportioned informally to individuals through sharing arrangements within families, by working-age people supporting their children. For this reason, measures of income distribution commonly take families as the relevant units for comparisons.

Another substantial component of income is apportioned to the elderly, most of whom are no longer working for pay. They receive much of their income through intergenerational transfers, transfers through taxes paid by working-age people to retired persons. Some of their income also comes from their own savings in the form of their housing and private pensions. Much of the diversity in income distribution arises from differences in circumstances over the life cycle, and corresponding differences in the units for which distributional shares are measured.

Among working-age people, their choices—about family formation, stability of marriage, and living arrangements—affect distributional measures. Their most noteworthy effects are their implications for children. Other aspects of the development and nurture of children, however, are perhaps even more important than their economic well-being. A second area of choice involves whether and how much to work. Variations in working patterns often reflect factors other than choice, of course, but behavioral choices have an impact on those patterns. A third area concerns preparation for making a valuable contribution through work. Good schooling, skill training, and development of constructive work habits are the main ingredients in investments rewarded by higher pay.[10]

The marketplace strongly conditions choices about work and preparation for it in the U.S. economy. The market has frequently been criticized as an impersonal institution preoccupied with material values. A serious limitation of markets and their role is their interest only in things on which a monetary value can be placed when they are offered for exchange. Things that are readily traded in markets are part of life, but a pervasive biblical theme is the reminder that economic matters and material well-being should not dominate our thoughts.

Opportunities for making economic choices in the marketplace allow people to develop their individual potential, which is a constructive feature of the market compared with most other institutions. Extensive reliance on personal choices, however, leads to wide differences in outcomes, such as those reflected in money income measures. One source of such differences is each person's unique capacity for making economic contributions. Other factors in addition to choice can have an impact. Whether to assume responsibility for work and self-support, for example, is primarily a matter of choice, but it is conditioned by opportunity, self-motivation to acquire knowledge and skills, and attitudes shaped by the home and community. Illness, disability, and misfortune (personal and economic) also affect incomes. The distinctions that should be made in response to such differences in circumstances, and how such differences should be taken into account, are issues that need to be considered in designing ameliorative policies.

The character of policy prescriptions often reflects, at least implicitly, perceptions about the process of income and wealth creation. One representation of this process is frequently described in terms of the earth's riches and bounty in which all should share. The biblical metaphor for this view would be manna falling daily from Heaven that each can pick up freely to meet his needs. According to a very different view, income is generated by persistent daily work efforts, careful management and maintenance of accumulated investments, and new additions to our production capabilities if we are to experience income growth. The biblical metaphor for this view is the condition after the Fall and expulsion from Eden that is described in terms of "thorns" and "thistles" in the fields and bread eaten "in the sweat of thy face."[11] Each viewpoint has an element of validity; the earth provides the resource base for our work, but the living standard that we buy with the money income at our disposal is predominantly the product of steady, continuing work efforts.

Recognizing that our level of living standard depends on how effectively we can organize and carry out ongoing production processes does not answer the question about the priority to be placed on efforts to redistribute income compared with policies to maintain or increase average income levels. Redistribution policies have very significantly raised the lower part of the income distribution for the elderly.[12] But for families as a whole, rising average incomes—shifting upward the entire distribution of income—have contributed much more to reducing poverty than changes in the shape of the distribution.

Efforts to substantially redistribute income among people of working age confront a serious dilemma. Unless income support policies are advanced well into the middle of the distribution, work effort becomes less worthwhile to the extent that such income support is available and is conditioned on total income of an individual or a family unit. Total income generated in an economy diminishes and adverse incentives result: a reduced sense of achievement and a lack of motivation for assuming family support responsibilities for fully developing skills and earnings capabilities. To limit such effects, income support policies have employed administratively complex and impersonal eligibility criteria that are only partially successful in maintaining constructive participation in the economy and society.[13] The influence of incentives does not absolve well-off persons from responsibilities for alleviating poverty and hardship, or even for providing decent conditions regarding the essentials of life, but it does mean that simply reshuffling money income toward greater equality can play only a limited role.

A proper recognition of the complex role of economic incentives makes it clear that the challenges for dealing with poverty are more complicated and demanding than simply providing money income to meet particular levels of need. As one fundamental element in responding to this challenge, ways need to be found to involve the poor in meeting their own needs—not mainly to lighten the burden on those who are better off, but instead to encourage the poor to make contributions, to develop their capabilities, and to help them become more fully integrated into the larger society. The Old Testament requirement to provide opportunities for gleaning emphasizes by example the mutual responsibilities of those who are poor and those who are not. It demonstrates how enabling the poor to make a contribution can play a role in policies to assist them.[14] Those who are well-off, in other words, cannot fully meet their responsibilities to the poor by providing money income transfers through an impersonal bureaucracy and then averting their eyes from serious problems of motivation, self-esteem, and lifestyles among the poor.

Although economic incentives exert powerful force on behavior, it is not necessary or appropriate to rely exclusively on incentives. Persuasion and encouragement can also play a role, and in some circumstances sanctions may be necessary. Efforts to build constructive cultural attitudes, perhaps as part of provision of schooling, could be valuable. Finally, opening up opportunity and heightening awareness of possibilities for achievement and contribution are most beneficial for children and youth. Policies that would facilitate broader exercise of parental responsibility, such as providing more scope for choice among schools, may be particularly important for enlarging opportunities for children in poor families, both because this would stimulate closer parental involvement and because their choices are otherwise very limited.

CONCLUSIONS

The general rise in living standards in advanced industrial countries has improved the economic well-being of those who are well-off and the poor. Economic growth has virtually removed the threat of famine in these countries, for example. Development of our capacity for feeding the poor and meeting their other most basic needs, however, has transformed our concerns about the poor to examining the responsibilities we share to alleviate their relative poverty and considering the ways this should be accomplished.

Economic growth and development have greatly enhanced our capacity for helping those most in need, but they also challenge us to reinterpret biblical principles and apply them in the context of our higher incomes and more complex economy. I will summarize my understanding of how broad biblical themes should be applied to income distribution policy by brief comments on the legitimacy of extensive reliance on the market, the standards they set for income inequality, the acceptability of current distributional patterns, and the way in which national policies should evolve.

In judging the legitimacy of the market (and its processes) we must avoid the extremes of rejecting it because it is concerned only with material values and driven by profit motives or embracing the specific results it produces as embodying special moral content.[15] The market should instead be viewed as a framework for structuring economic aspects of our lives, and as an institution for carrying out economic processes that is itself shaped by legal structures and personal and social ethics. Extensive reliance on relatively simple markets is not discouraged in biblical teaching. It may be more accurate to suggest that market processes are taken for granted as part of the context in which ethical and moral judgments need to be exercised. Lessons from experience are also relevant, and market institutions are increasingly being recognized for contributing to the very economic growth that has shifted our concerns about the needy to their relative material well-being.

No matter how it is measured, inequality in the distribution of income is quite pronounced. There is no support in biblical teachings, however, for the idea that complete equality should be the standard with which the distribution should be compared. In practice, complete equality under any particular measure of income distribution would offend other principles of fairness with respect to contributions in relation to rewards and material resources in relation to needs.

Nevertheless, the acceptability of substantial departures from equality should not suggest that the current distribution should meet with approval on moral grounds. Instead the Christian conception of the human condition provides a strong basis for the view that the Christian conscience can never be entirely comfortable in the presence of the poverty and hardship accompanying significant inequality of incomes. Certainly, concern about the condition of the poor is a pervasive biblical theme directly applicable to income distribution policies. Our responsibilities toward the poor mean that we have a continuing obligation to examine and adapt our policies in light of these responsibilities and constantly changing circumstances.

In response to the biblical mandate to consider the needs of the poor, Christians may legitimately differ in their views about the shortcomings of policy and the character of changes that may be constructive. In my view, more resources should be made available to low-income people, particularly to improve the economic well-being of children. This shift in the balance of our tax and transfer policies should come at the expense of people in the middle- and upper-income ranges and of those who are best-off among the older, retired generation. Expansion of current money income transfer programs should not be the main thrust of policy change, although some increases may be recommended.[16]

New directions for income support policies should motivate parents to assume more responsibility for supporting their children, they should encourage work effort by those receiving assistance, and they should seek to broaden the scope for involvement of the poor in activities and decisions affecting their own well-being. These approaches are surely difficult to design and implement, and an element of compulsion may sometimes be necessary as a complement to incentives. In introducing approaches along these lines, we should be guided more by their effects on the poor—in terms of their morale and the long-term well-being of their families—than by implications for the incomes of those who are well-off. These are idealistic, but not utopian, goals. Both the call to pursuit of ambitious ideals and the recognition that the goals are destined to be only imperfectly achieved are perspectives with firm bases in biblical thought.

EDITOR'S PERSPECTIVE

Marvin Kosters wrote,

> The complex role of economic incentives makes it clear that the challenges for dealing with poverty are more complicated and demanding than simply providing money income to meet particular levels of need . . . [and] ways need to be found to involve the poor in meeting their own needs—not mainly to lighten the burden on those who are better off, but instead to encourage the poor to make contributions, to develop their capabilities, and to help them become more fully integrated into the larger society.

Any effort to redress perceived injustices in a system of income distribution that ignores or plays down the principle embodied in this opening statement is certain to produce new problems that are as great or greater than the ones being addressed. God created us to be engaged in constructive, contributory work. Our very identity in God, the Master Creator, is incomplete and diminished when we are not pursuing creative activities. Being denied the opportunity to work, or refusing to work, eliminates a major portion of the means God designed to build in us a sense of purpose and worth. Godly self-worth can be wholesomely realized only through the means God designed, and being creatures who "know" and "do" means we must have constructive ways to develop and use our capacities, or we will further deform our godly image.

The idea of having an *opportunity* to work recurs in Scripture. Nowhere does Scripture say, "Thou shall have an opportunity to work," or "Thou shall give others the opportunity to work." But laws regulated what a man was to do when his neighbor became so poor that he desired to sell himself into indentured servanthood, or the original purchaser who met his need in that way subsequently sold him as a slave (see Exod. 21:2-6; Lev. 25:39-43; Deut. 15:12-18). I have little interest at this point in the details of the law, although some of it (like the owner's responsibility to "not send him away empty-handed [in the seventh year, but] . . . furnish him liberally from your flock and from your threshing floor and from your wine vat" [Deut. 15:13-14]) contains other principles of liberality and concern for another's ability to care for himself in the future. The central point of our interest here is in the fact that God was willing to let people take rather extreme, but honorable and dignified steps to alleviate their poverty rather than to beg, steal, or become destitute.

Dr. Kosters mentioned the gleaning laws (see Lev. 19:9-10; 23:22; Deut. 24:19-22; Ruth 2:1-23). They were designed to offer opportunities for the poor, widows (such as Ruth and Naomi), and others deprived of their land through personal misfortune (or poor judgment) to provide for themselves with dignity through their own efforts. Once again, the core principles of *liberality, opportunity,* and *self-help* are revealed. These three ingredients need to be present if the poor are to have a hope of constructively addressing their own needs. When the private sector fails to generate the conditions and opportunities that allow those who would help themselves to do so, then it is just for the public sector to seek ways to stimulate the private sector to such ends and, if necessary, to act to deal with the problem.

God's institution of the Jubilee (see Lev. 25:8-17) manifests some of these same concerns but in a larger and longer-range context. The apportioning of the Promised Land by lot to the eleven tribes of Israel (two portions for Joseph's descendants, making twelve territories; the Levites, the twelfth tribe, were to be cared for through the tithes of the people) reveals the two realities of inequality and equality in the very division of the land. The lot did not provide the most land to the largest tribe and so forth. The lot was no respecter of the size of the tribe, but within each tribe there was to be proportioned equality according to the size of the family (see Num. 26:52-56; Josh. 13-21).

The Jubilee Year maintained a hope of a better day to come if a family had been forced either through circumstances of providence or through poor judgment to relinquish their portion of the Promised Land. The land represented spiritual promises and realities to come as well as temporal ones, but it enabled each family of each tribe to be self-sufficient through the combination of work and barter. No family was to be permanently cut off from the opportunity to possess private property and to be productive in the use of possessions.

I do not want to push these points too far, but when we couple the concepts of indentured servanthood, the gleaning laws, and the Year of Jubilee, we have substantial evidence of God's concern for His people's opportunity to care for themselves. An expressed concern was necessary because sinful people will take advantage of their natural, positive inequalities (larger wealth, better opportunities, greater strength, brighter mind, etc.) and ignore or even take advantage of those individuals who are less-endowed. Justice, therefore, is not an automatic or a natural outcome of human endeavors in a fallen world. *Justice must be actively sought and maintained.*

The economic problems and tensions flowing from the moral and physical realities that all people are inherently equal in their common imagery and God-assigned worth—while simultaneously being unequal in their intellectual, physical, and experiential dimensions of life—are horrendous in a fallen world. What understanding and solutions are Christians to offer the world in such a case?

First, we are called to exhibit an attitude of contentment with the providential provisions we enjoy in our lives. Paul carries this point to the limit by stating that we should be content if we merely have food and covering (see 1 Tim. 6:8). This is not an argument for the status quo, though. Nor does it mean that we should not take advantage of opportunities to better our condition in life (see 1 Cor. 7:21). It is a call to an attitude of contentment (see also Phil. 4:11-12; Heb. 13:5).

We are also called to be concerned for the plight of the poor, unfortunate, orphans, and widows (see Prov. 29:7; 31:8-9; Jer. 5:28). We are to speak out for them; we are to seek justice for them; we are to advance their rights; we are to love them. However, God does not spell out a formula for economic justice nor tell us how to divide the wealth available. For example, God instructed Moses to "divide the booty between the warriors who went out to battle and all the congregation" (Num. 31:27), but God did not say how to divide the spoils. Joshua gave the people the same command and also left the actual division up to them (see Josh. 22:8). David, on the other hand, was more prescriptive. He told the warriors who completed the battle to share equally with those who fell behind and those who stayed at home with the baggage (see 1 Sam. 30:24). And Christ refused to become the judge or arbiter in a family squabble over the division of an inheritance. He warned instead against all forms of greed (see Luke 12:13-15).

It is obvious that God has left us with the responsibility, obligation, and freedom to decide how to divide the wealth available, but He has provided some principles and a sense of direction. We are to respect personal choice. We are to respect private property. We are to respect human diversity and inequality. We are to seek justice for the disadvantaged and those whose plight in life cries out for help. We are to respect those who govern us. We should want those who govern us to foster justice and redress injustices. A system of distributive justice should encourage stewardship, productivity, and imaginative efforts in the practice of worldly dominion; it should award retribution and oversee justice when either our sin or our finitude creates negative consequences for our neighbors in a fallen, rebellious world where "self" is the resident god in the minds of most people.

PART III

UNEMPLOYMENT AMIDST PLENTY

The distribution of wealth across a population, as noted in the previous chapter, is clearly tied to the patterns of family structure, levels of education, and the working patterns experienced by specific segments of the population. The issue addressed in this section is unemployment, one ingredient of the "working pattern" component that affects the distribution of wealth. It is evident, therefore, that income distribution and unemployment are "kissing cousins"—related but not absolutely causative. For example, unemployment figures influence the reported statistics for the distribution of wealth, but unemployment did not cause the existing pattern of wealth distribution to emerge.

Unemployment, like all macroeconomic concerns, is extremely complex in its origin. People get fired for both just and unjust reasons. People get mad or bored and quit their jobs. Economic conditions turn down and businesses release workers. Domestic and foreign competition makes life difficult, and cost-cutting efforts lead to layoffs in the name of "tightening the belt." New technology makes old products and old skills less attractive. These are a few of the things that happen to those who have previously enjoyed employment.

Many things hinder or keep people from securing or retaining employment. Educational and training deficiencies make people unattractive to potential employers. Mental and physical handicaps cause prospective employers to be reluctant to risk taking additional measures to employ people with such conditions. People with chronic illnesses or addictions to drugs and/or alcohol often have problems keeping jobs. Lack of self-discipline—tardiness, temper, and so on—causes many people trouble in the job market. And some people are psychologically defeated before they start. Perhaps they have been rejected six or eight times and have developed a hopeless outlook that essentially paralyzes them. Just plain ignorance about how to locate employment or how to get to the other side of the city to look for a job hampers others. Pride, too, keeps a number of people from doing work they consider to be "beneath them."

Nobody can do anything for a neighbor who elects to enter the ranks of the unemployed, for whatever reason. The questions we face and need to address arise when people who desire to work find themselves unemployed. What are the responsibilities of the individual confronted with the trauma of unemployment? Do those of us who are employed and enjoy a surplus of wealth have any personal obligations to unemployed persons? Do businesses or other private institutions have any God-assigned responsibilities to actively deal with such problems? Do local, state, and federal authorities have any inherent responsibilities for the unemployed?

Our society had no defined national policy on unemployment until the enactment of the Employment Act of 1946. Congress was faced at that time with the memory of the Great Depression when unemployment had been at record levels and little had alleviated its worst consequences until the armed services absorbed the unemployed in World War II. But in 1945-46 millions of servicemen and women were being discharged, and it was then that Congress acted—as much as anything to provide a psychological lift to the country. (The Employment Act itself had few "teeth" at that time to accomplish much.) Prior to that, the nation had accepted various efforts to meet specific trying conditions, like the creation of the Civilian Conservation Corps (1933 to 1942), which employed thousands of men to build federal park roads, plant trees on public land, and work on hundreds of other public projects.

In this chapter Dr. Bruce Wilkinson looks at the feasibility of having a national employment policy and the unemployment issues that need to be examined in the light of Scripture. He identifies sixteen biblical principles that address the issues related to employment. These principles represent the most exhaustive biblical survey on this matter that I have ever encountered. I am certain readers will be as delighted with Dr. Wilkinson's work as I was.

CHAPTER 3

BIBLICAL PRINCIPLES AND UNEMPLOYMENT

Bruce W. Wilkinson

Dr. Bruce W. Wilkinson is Professor of Economics at the University of Alberta, Edmonton, Canada, where he has been since 1967. Born in Saskatchewan, Canada, he received a Bachelor of Commerce degree from the University of Saskatchewan, an M.A. from the University of Alberta, and a Ph.D. in Economics from the Massachusetts Institute of Technology. He has been a consultant for the Economic Council of Canada and was Chairman of the Department of Economics at the University of Alberta from 1972 to 1977. His publications include numerous books and many articles on a variety of topics including education policy, natural resource development, international trade and commercial policy, and most recently the Canada-U.S. free trade agreement. Over the years he has been a frequent speaker to government, business, professional, and family-life groups on economic issues from a Christian perspective.

U nemployment has undoubtedly been the economic issue of greatest continuing concern to individuals in our Western industrialized societies. Although, as we shall see, the Bible has in it many perspectives relating to unemployment, and Christians have discussed the issues in earlier decades,[1] the fact that Christians have an important contribution to make has achieved new prominence in the 1980s through the statements made in Canada and the United States by the Roman Catholic Bishops.[2]

Before we attempt to examine the relevance of the Bible regarding unemployment, it will be useful to review briefly what contemporary economic theory and empirical work have to say about employment-creating policies. Some economists doubt whether anything can or should be done to reduce unemployment. However, among a growing body of economists, and I number myself among them, there is a strong conviction that it is not appropriate to

57

resign ourselves to accept whatever level of unemployment market forces of one sort or another produce. I take the space to do this in this short chapter not because I think that we as Christians must wait for economists to tell us whether policy actions are deemed possible by the profession before we can apply the words of Scripture to our contemporary scene.[3] Rather, my purposes are to point out two things. First, we are not going against reason and economic analysis in wanting to draw upon the Bible for guidance on employment issues. Second, although man in his thinking may from time to time believe that he has found "truths" that seem to be at odds with the Bible, sooner or later he must recognize that the Bible stands the test of time.

After we have satisfied ourselves about this matter, we will consider which biblical precepts apply to policies on employment. Finally, we will investigate how several of these principles might be used in the real world.

One clarification is necessary before we continue. When I write about national employment policy, I am not implying that we must focus only on what the federal government might do or refrain from doing. Such a perspective would eliminate many of the questions that need to be raised about this subject. Rather, I interpret the concept of a national employment policy to refer to the host of issues that need to be raised on a national scale regarding attitudes to unemployment and the unemployed. These include the moral and ethical issues involved, and the actions that might be taken by the federal government, other levels of government, individuals, businesses, the Church, and other community organizations.

IS A NATIONAL EMPLOYMENT POLICY FEASIBLE?

After the Second World War, the federal government of countries like the United States and Canada openly assumed responsibility for achieving and maintaining full employment in their respective economies. At that time, *The General Theory of Employment, Interest, and Money* by John Maynard Keynes was fresh in economists' and policy makers' minds. And with the surge of government spending generated by the war effort having raised aggregate demand and produced very low unemployment rates (less than 3 percent on average), there was much optimism that the scourge of long periods of high unemployment, such as occurred in the 1930s, could henceforth be avoided. That optimism grew for some years, and economists for a time believed that fine-tuning of the economy, practically from quarter to quarter, was possible. Substantial inflation, although of periodic concern—as during the Korean War—was not seen to be a continuing problem.[4]

All that changed as the 1960s drew to a close. With the U.S. build-up in Vietnam, financed without major tax increases, inflation became an important concern. As the oil and food price shocks of the early 1970s also raised production costs and prices, much more attention had to be given to inflation—what caused it and what to do about it. A variety of institutional and other changes, plus some misunderstanding of the causes of the price increases, combined with overreaction by government authorities to them, contributed to rising unemployment rates as well. At this time, the term *stagflation*, a combination of high unemployment and significant inflation, was introduced to summarize the results. The Phillips curve, showing an historical, negative, stable relationship between unemployment and inflation, no longer appeared to be stable. Inflation was higher at each inflation rate than previously estimated Phillips curves suggested should be so. The long-neglected concept of aggregate supply began to assume new prominence, too.

New theories with strong neoclassical microeconomic foundations were developed. Because the emphasis of economic theory had long been on the neoclassical, market-oriented approach, many economists favored the new theories. Also, arising as they did—when an ideological shift to the right was taking place among the public and economists—meant that because they supported minimal government involvement in the economy, they received warm support from many economists. And given the sociology of the academic world where there are incentives to develop new methodologies and clever theories, regardless of whether they accurately represent the real world, the new theories gained much appeal over the "old" Keynesian analysis.[5]

The more important policy-oriented conclusions of these theories may be enumerated as follows:

1. Any unemployment that exists is essentially voluntary. People are unemployed only because they desire too high a wage, prefer leisure, or are delaying the taking of a new job until they find the one that suits them.
2. Wages will move quickly to clear labor markets and thus eliminate any unemployment except what is of a voluntary nature.
3. There is a long-run natural rate of unemployment to which the actual unemployment rate will move expeditiously. Market forces working through flexible wages and prices will bring this about.
4. There is no such thing as a valid short-run Phillips curve. It is a flawed concept, and we should not expect to find any stable relationship between unemployment rates and inflation rates in the short run.
5. Business cycles with the accompanying fluctuations in employment need not be of great concern and may even represent the optimal result of adjustment to changing technological conditions.
6. The above five positions taken together imply that there is little need to act to reduce unemployment in our societies, for natural

market adjustments will do this. In fact, attempting to lower unemployment may actually result in net social costs.

7. If we add to these views the additional perspectives that, on the one hand, anticipated changes in the money supply are not supposed to have any real effects on the economy and, on the other hand, people and businesses all behave on the basis of rational expectations, then governments cannot really do much to enhance employment. Any action they might take would have been correctly anticipated by the public and allowed for in their actions already taken. Only if government acts unpredictably may it have an effect on the economy for a time.

If I subscribed to these beliefs, my chapter would probably have to end here with the conclusion that since little can be done to lower unemployment rates, it is irrelevant to worry about whether the Bible contains any principles that might be useful in developing a national employment-creating policy. But I do not subscribe to them. In my judgment, the accumulated empirical evidence supports what can only be labeled a more Keynesian type of analysis.[6] To be sure, it is not the simple Keynesian analysis of the 1950s and 1960s that concentrated almost solely on pushing up or regulating aggregate demand.[7] The newer analysis allows for an upward-sloping short-run aggregate supply curve, with very little slope when unemployment rates are high, and a higher slope as unemployment rates are reduced. It recognizes that there may be a long-run vertical aggregate supply curve at some natural rate of unemployment—while recognizing that there are resurgent questions about the validity of this natural rate and that what it is at any point in time may very much depend on the policies that have been followed and the path the economy travels to get there. Different paths may result in different natural rates.[8] It is aware that we may not easily be able to get unemployment rates down as low as in the latter part of World War II because of a number of institutional changes since then[9] and that family units may not necessarily be worse off economically because of higher unemployment rates, because the participation rates of women have risen (although this may be a very mixed blessing if the wife working is not what the family wants but is an economic necessity to make ends meet). And it comprehends that the lags in recognizing, making, and carrying out policy decisions, and in responses to actions taken, mean that fine-tuning as envisaged thirty or more years ago is not practical.

Nevertheless, this Keynesian perspective also observes that several other nations have had more success at reducing unemployment on a consistent basis—even after allowing for part of the difference between their rates and U.S. and Canadian rates being due to definitional variations. Japan, with unemployment rates around 2.5 percent, and Sweden and Switzerland at 2 percent and 1 percent, respectively, come readily to mind.[10] It is also very much aware that international monetarist stabilization policies as were employed in some southern Latin American countries, with their emphasis on monetary policy for balance of payments policy and exchange rate policy for controlling inflation, with an accompanying neglect of fiscal policy, have had a disastrous effect on those economies, particularly on the poor and unskilled working class.[11] Thus, although no one thinks that the path will be easy, there are good economic grounds for believing that scope exists for improved economic policies to reduce considerably the unemployment in our nations. In other words, economics seems to be coming around once again to where, as we shall discuss in subsequent sections, the Word of God has been all along—with its recognition that man was not meant to be without work. Let us turn, then, to consider this issue and the many subsidiary issues related to it that need to be explored from a biblical perspective.

UNEMPLOYMENT ISSUES FROM A BIBLICAL PERSPECTIVE

A host of different issues about unemployment arise. Some obviously can be explored from a biblical viewpoint, while others do not easily lend themselves to such an examination. Some of them have been treated at length in other studies, while others have been ignored or handled only tangentially. In this section we can do little more than list the more important of these questions, indicate briefly why they are significant, and mention a few of the views that have been offered about them.

Is unemployment wrong? The fundamental question to be asked is whether unemployment is wrong—whether it is even something that should concern us. After all, unemployment means more leisure, and is not leisure to be desired? If the Western world, because of its technology, suffers from overcapacity, the argument could be made that there is no need for everyone to work. Perhaps, as one author has put it, "The necessity to work is a neurotic symptom . . . a crutch . . . an attempt to make oneself feel valuable even though there is no particular need for one's working."[12] Should man be taught to free himself from the compulsion to work?

We shall see in the fourth section that biblical principles answer these questions and clearly indicate the significance of work for mankind. It is sufficient to note here that the argument asserting that we should somehow get over the neurosis to work simply because there has been, and continues to be, a substantial amount of long-term unemployment is on the same level as the argument stating that because many people are sinning, or because sinning has increased, we should remove the concepts of sin and guilt from our vocabulary and thinking. Such an approach does not deal with the problems; it only masks them—with the result that new problems evolve that eventually have to be handled. The Roman Catholic Bishops have carefully documented the secular studies demonstrating the waste of human and societal resources that occurs from unemployment. Individual and family health and stability are damaged. Human dignity is lost as people are essentially informed by the economic system that they are of no use to it. Lawlessness increases and creative effort is thwarted.[13]

What are the sources of unemployment? At first glance, this second question may seem to be a technical, economic issue, not something about which the Bible has anything to say. We know that some unemployment is seasonal (for example, a number of agricultural and fishing industry jobs), or frictional (due to families having to move for one reason or another, or individuals changing jobs and the like—or perhaps because unemployment benefits are overly generous). Cyclical unemployment arises as the economy experiences downturns in activity, often because of inadequate aggregate demand. Structural and secular unemployment occurs for several reasons: changing job requirements differ from the education, training, and skill levels of workers available; industries face a loss of competitiveness because of technological change and the development of lower-cost production elsewhere, perhaps in other countries; capital-intensive technology is adopted; consumers' changing tastes reduce demand for products. More labor force participation by young people and women—who typically have higher rates of unemployment than do older males—may contribute to this problem, too.

Some economists will argue that these factors primarily produce unemployment because there is insufficient flexibility in wages and prices of all types, and that all we need to do is to encourage more flexibility—including, where necessary, the removal of minimum wage levels and/or unemployment benefits. We have suggested earlier that even from an economic perspective, this purely market-oriented approach is inadequate. The issues need to be addressed from a biblical perspective, too. On the one hand, the Bible has something to say about people who would live without working or who are poor workers. On the other hand, it also talks about greed, selfishness, and increasing concentrations of power that result in people being thrown out of their means of making a living and/or employees being mistreated.

That there is great concentration of economic wealth and influence, for example, is well known.[14] The current merger movement has been shown to result in reduced employment, and at the same time the newly formed corporate giants can charge their costs of takeover as expenses, consistently pay the lowest average rates of corporate tax, and not infrequently raise their prices to cover their merger costs.[15] They may thus contribute to both inflation and unemployment.

David Hollenbach argues that at a fundamental level, unemployment is "the consequence of human perversity on both the levels of the economic choices made by individuals and of the economic patterns which institutionalize the dominance of some groups over others."[16] He goes on to indicate the origins of this in the initial sin of men attempting "to become 'like God' (Gen. 3:5) and to avoid being their brother's keeper,"[17] resulting at "the individual level in Cain's murder of his brother Abel (Gen. 4:8ff.) and at society's level in men wishing to 'make a name' for themselves which in turn led to the confusion of languages and the breakdown of community (Gen. 11:1-9)."[18] He thus suggests, "We will not eliminate unemployment by the declaration of the existence or the right to a job, but by participation in the sustained struggle to overcome the distortions of human community and work introduced by human duplicity and selfishness."[19] As we shall see, the Bible has much to contribute as we engage in this struggle.

What sort of work should be provided? The third major set of questions involves the sort of work that might be furnished to people. Three categories might be distinguished here: (a) What should be the nature of the work itself? (b) Who should the work be provided for? and (c) How much income should be earned by those working?

What should be the nature of the work provided? Perhaps the most fundamental question—and yet one that sometimes seems to be ignored—is whether people should be provided with the wherewithal to be self-employed or whether they should simply be hired by someone else. This needs to be addressed from a biblical perspective for, as we shall see later, the Bible gives quite a different view from what we may be accustomed to. It emphasizes the ownership and working of one's own property rather than the increasing concentration of wealth and more wage or salary labor.

Other questions might be addressed from a biblical viewpoint. Should an attempt be made to provide unemployed individuals with relatively long-term, secure work in a particular industry and/or location, or should the goal be limited to short-term jobs of various types and in various places or industries? Should the work be provided where the worker wishes to live, or should he or she be obligated to move to where the work is located? Should it be of a type that allows him to develop new skills and have some chance of advancement, or is it enough just to give him a job that provides a paycheck? Should the worker be able to see the meaningfulness of his work? Should it have some social significance? Should the work give him skills and keep his mind alert so that he is keeping or increasing his flexibility and adaptability for the future? Should the work be of a type that no one else wants, possibly involving risks to health and/or life? Should the worker have to take whatever is offered him or be considered ineligible for unemployment benefits or welfare assistance?

Should housework and home repair and maintenance work be included?

It will take some effort to derive biblical direction pertaining to all of these questions. Yet, the Bible mentions the authority of leaders to make decisions about where people live—as in the allocation of land to tribes and individual families (see Num. 2; 32; Josh. 13ff.). The Bible also speaks about how workers are to be treated by employers. And men are admonished in the Bible to use their gifts, spiritual or otherwise (see Matt. 25:14-28; Luke 12:48; Rom. 12:4-8; Eph. 4:11-13). These few comments indicate what the Bible has to offer us along these lines so that time devoted to gaining scriptural guidance for these issues would seem to be well spent.

Who should work be provided for? This second category of questions also deserves detailed study. Should *everyone* who wants to work outside the home be provided it? In other words, how low should we attempt to push the unemployment rate? Should priorities be set in the provision of jobs to men, women, youth, the disabled or handicapped, blacks, native people, immigrants, men or women with children versus those without children, families with one income earner already versus those with no income earners, those over sixty-five, and so on? In some instances today, the argument could be made that the secular world has turned some time-honored principles on end so that instead of eliminating discrimination, we may have simply replaced one form of it with another form. We need to search out biblical principles that can help us answer these questions.[20] What do the concepts of justice and equity mean in the present context? Should "hardship" or "need" be the basis for assistance as was suggested years ago in the United States with regard to the definition of unemployment?[21]

What income should be provided? This subject involves the following questions. Should the wage or the salary be sufficient to meet all the earner's basic needs? If not, should income be augmented by the employer or supplemented by the state? The Bible discusses exploiting others while living in luxury ourselves, a topic to which we will return in the next section.

Who should provide the employment, and how should it be provided? This question ties in closely with the fundamental issue of whether there should be more opportunity provided for self-employment as opposed to hired employment. But it goes beyond this issue to ask where responsibility falls for the creation of the work. Should families—not just the nuclear family of father, mother, and children, but the extended family so common in other cultures—be primarily responsible for their members? At what point should corporations—large, medium, and small—be responsible? Should they provide lifetime employment—as has been the custom for large Japanese corporations? What should be the role of each of the three levels of government in this regard? What part should Christian churches and the Christian community generally be responsible for? The Roman Catholic Bishops highlight the "principle of subsidiarity," which advocates that the association at the lowest level should be permitted to handle those social functions they are capable of handling rather than having such functions assumed by some "greater and higher association."[22] Further study of the Bible should enable Christians individually and collectively—in churches, businesses, and government—to see more clearly their responsibilities and possible roles.

A host of other questions deal with how additional employment should be provided. Many of them get into matters addressed in greater detail in other chapters in this volume. The financing of employment-creating expenditures by other than charity or business funding involves questions of whether taxation, debt, or money creation should be used; whether some sharing of public and private funds should be employed; the appropriate level of taxation by each level of government; what types of taxation should be used; whether interest rates for particular types of loans (e.g., home mortgages, new small businesses) should be established by government fiat or allowed to fluctuate freely in the market; and so on. Some writers believe they have already derived precise directives from the Bible on many of these matters.[23] But their views could hardly be deemed representative of the Christian community at large. Additional work in these matters is obviously required.

A major issue, probably the key one with regard to federal government involvement in employment creating policies, concerns how unemployment might be reduced without generating additional (possibly accelerating) inflation. Economists may be inclined to think that this is purely an economic issue about which little can or should be said by Christians. Yet I would argue that the Bible can yield much fruit on this matter because, other than the ideology that unregulated market will solve all our economic problems, one factor in Western society's reluctance to accept or operate within the framework of wage and price controls, or some variant thereof such as a tax-based incomes policy, or wages that vary with profits, is surely acquisitiveness or greed. And the Bible speaks eloquently and extensively about that.

In other words, the task before us goes beyond determining whether the Bible teaches that unemployment is wrong and whether it gives any guidance on structures and mechanisms that might alleviate unemployment. It goes beyond asking whether policies affecting aggregate demand, aggregate supply, or both aggregate demand and supply are consistent with biblical principles. It is necessary to examine biblical statements about our individual and collective responsibilities to our fellow human beings and to God, and about a wide range of ethical and moral questions relevant in this context. With these thoughts in mind, let us consider some biblical principles that can be applied to the types of issues raised here.

BIBLICAL PRINCIPLES RELATING TO EMPLOYMENT

A variety of biblical principles are relevant to this discussion. Some we have touched upon in the preceding section. Many of them tend to overlap one another.

1. Work is to be man's normal routine. The Creation message is that God worked to create the world and all that is in it (see Gen. 2:1-3), that man was made in the image of God (see Gen. 1:27) and he was to be fruitful, subdue the earth, and have dominion over everything in it (see Gen. 1:28). After man's disobedience in his desire to "be like God" (Gen. 3:5), work was ordained to be more of a struggle (see Gen. 3:17-18), but it was still set forth as the normal fare for mankind. The Fourth Commandment made it clear not only that man was to have a day of rest, but that work should be done in the days prior to it (see Exod. 20:9).

Throughout the Bible, man is admonished to work and warned that a failure to do so would bring poverty (see Prov. 10:4; 28:19), hunger (see Prov. 19:15), and want (see Prov. 13:4). Work is also deemed to be a way of providing not just for oneself, but for one's family (see 1 Tim. 5:8) and for others in need of assistance (see Eph. 4:28). Through it, one can gain the respect of others and not depend on other people for one's daily needs (see 1 Thess. 4:12). Man is "to be ready for any honest work" (Titus 3:1), and if he is not willing to work, he should not eat (see 2 Thess. 3:10). Idleness was deemed wrong (see Eccles. 10:18; 2 Thess. 3:11; Heb. 6:12).

The biblical standard, then, is that man has an obligation to work. This also implies that there must be an opportunity for him to work and that he must have *something to work with*, either his own property or someone else's.

2. Man's normal work was to be done on and with his own property. The Bible clearly supports the concept of private ownership of property under God's sovereignty. The land of Canaan was allocated as equally as possible to the individual tribes of Israel and the various families within the tribes (see Num. 26; Josh. 13:23). The prophet Ezekiel foresaw the day when aliens would have their allotment, too (see Ezek. 47:21-23). And if through misfortune or bad management or some other reason families lost their land, it was to be restored to them at the Jubilee (see Lev. 25:8-17, 25-28; 27:17; Num. 36:4; Ezek. 46:17).

3. Even when individuals or families were dispossessed and/or poor, they were expected to work. That is, even the welfare system involved work. If people lost their land, they could offer themselves to work for another family until the Jubilee (at which time they were to be restored to the land of their inheritance [see Lev. 25:39-41], with a share of the flocks and grain from the family they had been with [see Deut. 15:12-15]). They, along with other poor, such as "the sojourner, the fatherless, and the widow," were to be allowed access to the harvest fields after the main reaping of grain, grapes, and olives had been done.

Owners were instructed to leave unharvested the edges of their grain fields, some grapes on the vines as well as those that fell to the ground, and olives that remained on the boughs after the first beating, so that the poor would be able to work and provide for themselves (see Lev. 19:9-10; Deut. 24:19-22; Ruth 2).

4. Wage earners working for others also have an obligation to show their superiors honor and respect, to be obedient and faithful, and to work hard, not just to look good when their supervisors are watching, but all the time, as though they were working directly for Jesus (see Eph. 6:5-8; Col. 3:22-25; 1 Tim. 6:1-2; Titus 2:9; 1 Pet. 2:18-20). They can be a blessing to their superiors in the process (see Prov. 25:13; 1 Tim. 6:2). If, on the other hand, they are slack in their work, they are as "a brother to him who destroys" (Prov. 18:9).

In most writings examining biblical principles with respect to the unemployed, the poor, and lower income groups generally, all too often little, if anything, is said regarding their responsibilities. The emphasis is almost solely on their rights.[24] But clearly they have a responsibility to do the best they can with their talents and opportunities, whether they pertain to work itself or to education and training. If they do so, they are less likely to need welfare (and there may be less incentive when they are employed for management to replace them with labor-saving equipment).

5. Those who have property should recognize that it ultimately belongs to God: "All that is in the heavens and in the earth is thine" (1 Chron. 29:11); "All things come from thee" (1 Chron. 29:14); "The earth is the LORD's and the fulness thereof, the world and those who dwell therein" (Ps. 24:1); "For every beast of the forest is mine, the cattle on a thousand hills" (Ps. 50:10); and "The silver is mine, and the gold is mine, says the LORD of hosts" (Hag. 2:8).

6. Man is in turn accountable to God, a steward for God, for the possessions entrusted to him. The Creation story itself highlights this principle as God places man in charge of His creation. The New Testament emphasizes that time and talents as well as material possessions are to be handled wisely (see Matt. 25:14-30; Luke 12:48; 19:11-27; Rom. 14:12; 1 Cor. 4:2; 1 Pet. 4:4, 10).

This principle holds true not just for owners but for managers, or stewards as the Bible refers to them. They are to do the best they can for the owners who have entrusted assets to their care. Jesus clarifies this point in several of His parables (see Matt. 25:14-18; Luke 16:1-12; 20:9-16). Although in these parables He primarily refers to the proper treatment of the spiritual heritage entrusted to man, His use of examples of material stewardship indicates that He believes the principles of good stewardship should apply in the material case. If He did not believe so, one would have to wonder at His choosing such examples.

However, this principle does not justify executives' taking the position that they are to do whatever is necessary to maximize the profits of their firm and to maximize the return to the shareholders as long as it can somehow be defended before the law of the land. That attitude shows a callous disregard for all other principles of integrity, righteousness, and justice set forth in the Scriptures and an abdication of personal moral responsibility before God—for which all men must answer on the Day of Judgment.

7. A fundamental aspect of man's stewardship is that the resources in his possession are to be shared with the poor and needy or to be lent (without interest in the case of fellow Hebrews in the Old Testament). All this is to be done ungrudgingly (see Lev. 25:35; Deut. 15:7-11; 23:19-20; Prov. 19:17; 25:21; Isa. 58:7) even for strangers in the land (see Exod. 23:9; Lev. 19:33-34; 25:35-38; Deut. 5:14-15; 10:17-19; 24:17-18, 21-22). The New Testament reaffirms the merit and significance of giving generously to those in need, even if they are not family members or fellow believers or persons one likes (see Matt. 5:4-48; Acts 20:35; Rom. 12:13; Gal. 6:10; 1 Tim. 6:18; Heb. 13:16). *That we are to love our neighbors as ourselves* is one of the great underlying principles of the Bible (see Lev. 19:18; Mark 12:31).

These ideas are at odds with the "me first" Western world of today where people are encouraged to do their own thing, actualize themselves, please "number one," and the like. Nowhere in the Bible is it even remotely suggested that we are to make the "pursuit of happiness" one of life's main objectives. It is not a virtue, a right, or a responsibility. The Bible leaves no doubt that pursuing our own pleasure will lead to anything but happiness, and concomitantly will result in God's disapproval (see Prov. 21:17; Eccles. 2; Isa. 22:12-14; 47:8-9; Amos 6; 1 Tim. 5:5-6; 2 Pet. 2:13). True joy or happiness always comes from worshiping and praising God, loving Him, hoping and trusting in Him, seeking His will for our lives, obeying Him to the best of our ability, serving others (see 2 Chron. 30:13-27; Ezra 6:22; Ps. 16:11; Isa. 35:10; Jer. 31:13; John 16:20), and remembering that our "names are written in heaven" (Luke 10:20).

8. Offerings or gifts to the Lord or assistance to others should be on the ability-to-pay principle (not according to the benefits-received principle, which is often endorsed as an alternative principle of taxation today; see Lev. 14:21; Deut. 16:17; Ezra 2:69; Acts 11:29; 2 Cor. 8:12). This goes beyond the scriptural tithe, which is a proportional tax.

9. Increasing concentration of wealth and power in the hands of the few is not in accord with God's plans. A small group of families were not to end up with most of the assets. This principle is clearly established in the concept of the Jubilee Year when those who had earlier lost possession of their lands were to have them returned to them (see Lev. 25:10, 13, 23; Num. 36:6-9; Deut. 19:14; Prov. 22:28; Ezek. 46:16-18). People's land was their means of livelihood, their avenue to participating effectively in the production and social network of their nation.

This principle of avoiding the concentration of power is perhaps best expressed in a way meaningful to us today by the prophets Isaiah and Micah:

> Woe to those who join house to house,
>> who add field to field,
> until there is no more room,
>> and you are made to dwell alone
>> in the midst of the land. (Isaiah 5:8)

> Woe to those who devise wickedness
>> and work evil upon their beds!
> When the morning dawns, they perform it,
>> because it is in the power of their hand.
> They covet fields, and seize them;
>> and houses, and take them away;
> they oppress a man and his house,
>> a man and his inheritance. (Mic. 2:1-2)

Today, on average, the large corporations do not create the jobs. In Canada, for example, between 1978 and 1984 nearly 94 percent of the 875,000 new jobs created were in firms employing fewer than 20 employees. Employment during that period in firms of over 100 persons actually declined.[25]

10. Nevertheless, wealth in itself is not wrong. Some of God's special people, such as Abraham, Isaac, and Jacob, had great riches (see Gen. 13:2, 6; 26:12-14; 30:43). It may represent a gift of God (see Deut. 8:18; 1 Chron. 29:12; Prov. 22:2; Eccles. 5:19; 6:2; Hos. 2:8) or the fruit of much honest labor (see Prov. 10:4; 12:11, 24, 27; 28:19). But if riches increase, man is not to set his heart upon them (see Ps. 62:10).

11. There are many things to be valued more than wealth, such as love and peace in the home (see Prov. 15:17; 17:1), righteousness (see Prov. 11:4, 28; 16:8; Matt. 6:33), integrity (see Prov. 19:1, 22; 28:6, 20), wisdom (see Job 28:16; Prov. 3:13-15; 8:11), and more generally, the Kingdom of Heaven itself and our relationship with God (see Matt. 6:33; 19:21).

12. Wealth also holds serious potential dangers, which in today's world are often not mentioned, even in the Christian community. The possession of it can result in man's becoming self-satisfied and disinterested in God (see Deut. 8:13-14; Prov. 30:8-9; Hos. 13:6; Luke 12:15-21), so that it becomes difficult for him to enter the Kingdom of Heaven (see Mark 10:23-25). And whether one has it to begin with, whether one is already rich or poor, the pursuit of it as a dominating focus of life is identified in the Bible as the sin of greed or avarice. (The wealthy may have a greater opportunity to commit this sin, although not necessarily.) It can thus lead people away from God, make them insensitive

to the things of God, and produce much anguish for them and their families (see 1 Tim. 6:9-10; Mark 4:18-19; James 5:3; Prov. 15:27; 28:20). Wealth may also result in a sense of great emptiness and meaninglessness once it has been attained and used for selfish pursuits (see Eccles. 2:1-11), and a forfeiture of eternal life with God (see Mark 8:16-37). Covetousness, a corollary of greed, is also condemned in the Bible—by the Tenth Commandment (see Exod. 20:17), on many occasions by the Old Testament prophets (see Jer. 6:13; Ezek. 33:31; Mic. 2:2; Hab. 2:9), by our Lord (see Luke 12:15), and by His followers (see Col. 3:5; Heb. 13:5; 1 John 2:15-16). Contentment with what we have is a virtue espoused by the Bible (see Luke 3:14; Phil. 4:11-13; 1 Tim. 6:6-8; Heb. 13:5).

Unfortunately, as Hirschman has so eloquently pointed out, the deadly sin of greed tended to be played down from the late sixteenth century onward.[26] By the time of Hume and then Adam Smith, emphasis was placed on man's pursuing his self-interest—a virtue rather than a sin. Yet, inordinate self-interest is still greed, and even Keynes, with all the personal degradation in other dimensions of his life, recognized it, even though he was willing to condone it if it led to greater employment for the masses.[27] In our own thinking we need to reexamine, and heed, what the Bible says on the subject.

13. God requires that justice be a prominent principle of man's relationship with his fellowman (see Ps. 82:3; Prov. 21:3; Isa. 56:1). The prophet Amos proclaimed, "But let justice roll down like waters, and righteousness like an ever-flowing stream" (5:24). The biblical reference to justice is to no mere vague theoretical construct. It has very specific dimensions, relevant to the current discussion.

First, workers are not to be exploited so that others might live in luxury (see Jer. 22:13-17; Ezek. 22:6-7, 13, 25, 27, 29; Hab. 1:6-17).

Second, workers, whether brothers in the Lord or strangers, are not to be oppressed (see Exod. 23:9; Deut. 24:14; Job 31:13-14; Ps. 62:10; Prov. 14:31; Eccles. 5:8; Eph. 6:9). This is true even if the oppressor is also poor (see Prov. 28:3). Wages are to be paid to them (see Gen. 31:7; Deut. 25:4; Jer. 22:13; 1 Tim. 5:18; James 5:4), and paid promptly (see Lev. 19:13; Deut. 24:14; James 5:4), and such wages are to be adequate for the workers' needs (see Lev. 19:13; Mal. 3:5; Matt. 10:9-10; 1 Cor. 9:4, 7-12; Col. 4:1).

One might like to debate what *adequate* means in today's world—whether it goes beyond food and clothing, as the Scriptures assert, to include proper housing, health care, and other services. Although the Bible does not list these details, the general principles of justice and sharing should give us a sufficient basis to develop appropriate policies. The Golden Rule of doing unto others as we would have them do unto us applies here. As Jesus said, "For this is the law and the prophets" (Matt. 7:12).

In this context one might also think about the relationships between wages and salaries and other economic magnitudes, such as whether the spread between the highest and lowest paid people in an organization should be narrowed, or how lower interest rates (such as prevail in nations like Japan and Switzerland) could mean that workers on modest salaries might better be able to afford home mortgages.

Third, although profits or business gains certainly are not shunned in the Bible (see Prov. 10:4; 22:29; Matt. 25:14-28; Luke 19:12-24), they are not to be obtained by unjust means. The example most frequently cited in the Bible is that of dishonest weights and measures (see Lev. 19:35-36; Deut. 25:15; Prov. 11:1; 16:11; 20:10; Mic. 6:11); taking advantage of a brother's misfortune by charging him interest on a loan is also condemned.[28] In the commerce of that day, weights and measures were undoubtedly one of the most common areas in which injustice could be practiced. But the principle can easily be extended in our day to include any practice involving misrepresentation of performance or quality, or the sale of unsafe products or products endangering human health.

Fourth, people are not to be favored or treated differently depending upon their poverty or wealth (see Exod. 23:3; Lev. 19:15; Job 13:10; Mal. 2:9; Acts 10:34; 1 Tim. 5:21; James 2:4), or their status as immigrants or aliens or Hebrews (see Exod. 12:49; Lev. 19:34; Num. 15:16), for God Himself is no respecter of persons (see Deut. 10:17; Rom. 2:11; Eph. 6:9; 1 Pet. 1:17).

In essence the message of justice in the Bible is that God wants His people to be free, not just spiritually, but economically, socially, and politically.[29] Injustice, oppression, or exploitation by those in positions of power, such as the economic ways we have been discussing, violates one or more of these freedoms. God instructs man "to do justice, and to love kindness, and to walk humbly with your God" (Mic. 6:8).

14. People need to have a vision based not on man's mind but on God's plans and God's Word. The scripture most commonly quoted in this context is from the *King James* translation: "Where there is no vision, the people perish" (Prov. 29:18). In more recent translations such as the *New International Version* that verse states, "Where there is no revelation, the people cast off restraint." Although this is the only scripture that is so specific, the principle is unquestionably one of the most clearly established in the Bible. Men need to be guided and encouraged by the vision that God has for His world and for the people He has created. This principle is seen in the lives of men like Noah, Abraham, Joseph, Moses, Samuel, David, and all the prophets of those days and thereafter. Similarly, Jesus and His followers in the New Testament—Stephen, Philip, Paul, Ananias, Cornelius, Peter, and so on—received and were sensitive to the visions God provided, so that God's plans were advanced accordingly.

The Bible also makes explicit that if men simply follow their own minds or others who profess to be true prophets of God but are caught up in the deceit of their own minds or of Satan, they will be led to ruin (see Gen. 3:6; 1 Kings 22; Jer. 14:14; 23:16-17).

We need, therefore, to study very carefully and prayerfully the Word of God to ensure that we correctly capture God's vision for mankind with regard to economic matters such as employment, and what can be done to improve the lot of the poor and the unemployed.

15. The role of the state requires consideration. Some students highlight the dangers of the untrammeled power of the state as cited in Samuel's response to the people when they wanted a king. He warns them of the heavy taxes to follow and the taking of their lands and people to serve the king's interests (see 1 Sam. 8:11-18). Others emphasize the New Testament passages indicating that we are to respect and be subject to the governmental authorities because God has appointed them or permits them to be in these positions (see John 19:11; Rom. 13; Titus 3:1; 1 Pet. 2:13-17) and allows them to do such things as to collect taxes (see Matt. 17:24-27; 22:17-22). Yet according to the record of both Old and New Testaments, where injustices are being perpetrated by those in power and the Word of God is not being followed, it is appropriate to speak out against these things (see 2 Sam. 12; 1 Kings 18; Isa. 1; Jer. 2; Ezek. 45:9; Matt. 23). The state has a primary role, but it, too, is subject to the principles of justice, avoidance of oppression, and concern for the poor and dispossessed.

16. Nevertheless, individuals, families, and the Church have the first responsibility for those in need of assistance, such as the unemployed and the other poor. In keeping with Old Testament declarations, the extended family had a responsibility for employing and helping those who had lost their land or were otherwise in need. But assistance was to be given to the stranger in the land, too. The same principles are clear in the New Testament in Jesus' parable of the good Samaritan (see Luke 10:29-37), His teaching in the Sermon on the Mount (see Matt. 5:43-48), and His story about the sheep and the goats (see Matt. 25:31-46), and in the concerns of the early Church for those in need (see Acts 4:34-37; Rom. 15:25-28; 2 Cor. 9:6-15). It would seem to be missing the point of the Scriptures to assume that today individuals, the Church, or even other community organizations should leave all responsibility for employment creation to the national government.

We have, then, an array of biblical principles relating to unemployment issues. Taken together they present a picture of the importance of work for man in God's eyes; the need for us to be good stewards of all that God has graciously given us of talents, material things, and His creation generally; the necessity of not letting greed for wealth and power become the driving force or rationale for our lives; the significance of sharing what we have, helping those less fortunate than ourselves, and treating all people with justice and respect; the value of catching the vision of God's ways and plans for His world; and finally the fundamental responsibility of the individual, family, and community to take initiatives to resolve unemployment problems rather than leave the entire task to a national government.

Some may wonder how these principles can be applied to unemployment issues today. There are no simple answers. But we can take one or two of them to see how they might be worked out in actual practice.

THE APPLICATION OF BIBLICAL PRINCIPLES

If we accept the precepts that it is good for man to work and that God desires man to work rather than be on welfare, we must evaluate the best way(s) to provide such work and, if necessary, the training that may be required. If we also accept the principle that individuals, families, or local community groups such as a Christian church or fellowship have a responsibility, we can ask how the local group may participate in helping our brothers without simply providing welfare.

An excellent example of what can be done has been provided by the Mennonite Central Committee (MCC) in the city of Edmonton where I live.[30] The committee initiated a program to hire welfare recipients and some persons getting unemployment insurance to renovate and refurbish completely a number of houses condemned and scheduled to be destroyed by the city. Concurrently, those in the program (native Indians, refugees from Vietnam and Central America, several women, and some with prison records) spent about one-half their time in classes learning both work and communication skills. The vision, planning, and overall administration and direction of the program were handled by MCC-appointed and -financed staff, with the cooperation and assistance of city-appointed supervisors. The city furnished materials and paid for the specialized tradesmen such as gasfitters and electricians to do some tasks. The rest of the financing came from the federal government. An overall assessment of the project indicated that even without allowing for multiplier effects, the benefits in taxes received, reduced welfare and unemployment insurance benefits, enhanced value of city property for rental or sale purposes, and the training given to workers exceeded the outlays. In addition, most of the people were able to get jobs elsewhere as they finished their commitments, and there were some remarkably positive personal and family benefits from work being again a reality for them. This program is continuing, and presently about thirty-five people are participating.

The same committee has a similar program to employ and train about thirty workers in landscape improvement, which is also producing comparable favorable effects. Another dimension of their work has involved specialized garbage collection and a recycling program (of bottles and cans); mentally handicapped persons are employed to sort recyclable materials. This program has a contract with the city. Its profits are used to share with employees, hire additional people, and increase recycling endeavors. Currently over forty people are employed in it.

Here we have, then, local initiatives based on scriptural principles, working with governments at different levels to utilize and train people otherwise not "useful" to society while concurrently performing valuable services for the community.

The results are, interestingly enough, also consistent with a study done by the Sub-Committee on Training and Employment of the Standing Senate Committee on Social Affairs, Science and Technology of the Senate of Canada in 1987.[31] That work, based on both widespread consultation with economists throughout the country and two large-model econometric exercises, concluded that it was cheaper and more beneficial for society to have specific job creation plus training programs than to leave people on welfare or unemployment—and that it could be done in a noninflationary fashion to a large degree.

A second application of biblical principles might involve a combination of measures to assist in discouraging inflationary pressures should they tend to arise as job creation and training programs are undertaken. Greater publicity could be given to the principles that we are responsible for the welfare of those less fortunate and that sharing, generosity, and absence of greed and selfishness are virtues that benefit others and bring greater meaning and blessings to us. If this possibility is too unrealistic for our fallen world, we might still resort to practical applications of some of these principles by encouraging firms to have more profit-sharing schemes such as employee stock ownership plans,[32] or by encouraging the establishment of producer cooperatives as have been so successful in the northern Spanish city of Mondragon,[33] or by experimenting with some form of tax-based incomes policy for the larger pace-setting corporations. Any of these suggestions warrants a paper or monograph unto itself; I mention them only as illustrations of the potential available to us as we attempt to apply biblical principles to the unemployment problem.

EDITOR'S PERSPECTIVE

It is fair to say that a consensus has emerged in the work of the ten scholars who have touched on the plight of the poor and unemployed in this four-volume series. (Udo Middelmann, Robert Wauzzinski, Ronald Nash, Harold O. J. Brown, Richard Mouw, Calvin Beisner, T. M. Moore, Joseph McKinney, Marvin Kosters, and Bruce Wilkinson have all discussed it.) They have established a ranked priority of those responsible for the economically disadvantaged. They all agree that a clear biblical principle asserts that the unemployed are first and foremost responsible for finding a solution for their unemployment, and that any person or organization seeking to assist them should first help the unemployed learn how to help themselves.

When individuals have exhausted their avenues of self-help, their extended family is the next responsible "community" called on. That help, though, must not foster an attitude of false dependence on the provider of help. The self-respect of unemployed persons must be promoted while they seek gainful employment. Family, friends, and neighbors can generally best accomplish providing assistance that lets the unemployed maintain their dignity by *lending* them goods and/or money rather than giving those things to them. The biblical prescription is that we give to people when they are hungry and naked, but we lend to people when the need is ongoing (see 1 John 3:17 for giving; Deut. 15:7-11 and Luke 6:34-35 for lending). Lending allows borrowers to assume an obligation for the personal care of those for whom they are accountable and provides them with the support they need. In such cases, the lending is to be without interest, and without regard for how long they may need to repay the loan. In fact, we are to be prepared to forgive the loan in the future if necessary—do not suggest forgiving it when it is being loaned, however, for that will rob the borrowers of the necessary sense of obligation allowing them to keep their self-respect.

The third party with an obligation to the unemployed is the Church—first to its members, then to other brothers and sisters, and finally to the world—and other nongovernmental organizations that specifically assist the poor and unemployed.

The fourth group on the ladder of responsibility to help the unemployed consists of owners and operators of businesses, who offer the best long-run hope. They are the most skilled in addressing the problem. They also face the greatest temptation to deal callously with the problem as they seek self-preservation in economic downturns. Businesses are not charities. They are economic associations whose existence depends on their ability to make a profit. But businesses, whether they employ five people or five thousand, generate job opportunities—Dr. Wilkinson reminded us that small businesses are currently creating more jobs in North America than large ones. They are first in providing opportunities but fourth on the scale of those responsible for the unemployed.

Businesses are not without their responsibilities in this area, however, for they are also primarily releasers of people who were formerly employed. Businesses can contribute significantly to the reduction in the trauma of unemployment through better training and retraining programs. It is fundamentally a myth that people over forty or forty-five are not good candidates for retraining. They are, and are more likely to remain loyal to the businesses they have been with for some years than are younger and newer employees. Businesses (and labor) also need to explore flexible wages and job tasks that may allow management to seek alternatives other than layoffs during down cycles in the economy. I am a long way from being convinced that business cycles, technology, and foreign competition need to create the vast problems they are accused of. Most of our macro-unemployment problems arise when we collectively feel the need to take almost immediate action to reduce costs, and labor is generally seen as the variable cost that can best be eliminated first. Business has expended little or no effort to discover alternatives that could keep work forces more intact during slow times. Unions have "strike funds"; governments have "unemployment funds"; businesses have no funds. We must ask why.

The public sector is the fifth and final entity responsible to act on matters of unemployment. Government's role is, however, different in character from that of the other four—individual, family, the Church and other nongovernmental organizations, and businesses. Governments are the only segment of our society with coercive powers. They have the authority to require what they want. They can speak in the name of the social order, levy taxes on the people to fund their will, and exact penalties on those who refuse to cooperate. Our generation has forgotten that the Sixteenth Amendment to the Constitution, allowing the federal government to levy income taxes on the people, was not passed until 1913. The amendment reads as follows:

The Congress shall have power to lay and collect taxes on incomes, from whatever source derived, without apportionment among the several States, and without regard to any census or enumeration.

We ran our nation from 1789, when the Constitution was adopted, until 1913 without granting those who govern us at the national level the authority to tax our incomes. This change of philosophy opened the door to many well-intended governmental actions, many of which proved helpful and many of which created side effects as troublesome as the problems being addressed. At this point we need to remind ourselves of what Dr. Henry said: "Love, or compassion, is a relationship between persons, not between institutions or between institutions and persons. [Therefore], no improvement can be made on an entirely just government; in community relationships, justice is the course that neighbor love takes." So we should ask, "What is the just thing for governments to do to address the problems associated with unemployment?" I believe they can do three things to further the cause of justice.

First, governments can foster responsible economic growth in the private sector. By responsible economic growth, I mean growth in economic activity that does not ignore future hidden costs so often associated with the unaccounted-for consequences of technology. Or putting it another way, the costs of technology must be accounted for and paid for, as much as they can be discerned, as we go along with true economic growth being the additions to the economy after all such costs are subtracted. (We have not yet paid many of the economic costs associated with acid rain, poor water conservation, hazardous waste controls, and other technologically related side effects.)

As a generalization, I also believe that the stewardship of resources tends to be better where both massive governmental bureaucracies and economic monopolies are avoided. This being the case, allowing the private sector to retain its economic wealth through the minimization of taxes is a more prudent long-term goal than the prevailing practice of calling on the government to solve more and more social problems. And those segments of the private sector that can gain monopoly positions in the marketplace through efficient, competitive operations should be allowed to do so and then be rewarded through an incentive to redivide themselves into smaller competing units. That way, creative, imaginative, progressive tendencies can be kept alive. I know of no good reason to allow monopolies to exist that are created by financial transactions rather than the microdecisions of the competitive marketplace where economic value can be freely determined.

The third thing governments can do to encourage justice that will reduce unemployment is to focus on a few specific needs that would benefit everybody if they were addressed—more retraining, increased use of persons with physical disabilities, the employment of eighteen- to twenty-three-year-old minorities, etc.—and provide economic incentives to the private sector that would reward those with the resources to redress the specific problems. This approach would be more efficient than taxing those same resources and trying to create another system of economic activity apart from the more efficient ones already in the private sector. It is my opinion that little has been done in this area because it means lower tax revenues, which are the life-stream of an ideology that has often confused "public compassion" with public justice.

Finally, when we fail to bring about justice for the unemployed by fostering a growing private sector, by eliminating inefficient and powerful bureaucracies and monopolies, and by creating constructive incentives for the private sector to act in helpful ways to do things they might not otherwise do, then and only then should the governments tax and take direct action to alleviate unemployment problems—remembering that direct government action is the fifth and last resort.

PART IV

IN SEARCH
OF THE RIGHTS
OF THE POOR

Income distribution, unemployment, and public welfare matters are obviously three closely related subjects. This section addresses the public welfare issue, the collective public response to the problems of the poor—those at the lower end of the income scale who are either unemployed or unable to secure sufficient income from their employment to adequately meet their genuine requirements for housing, food, medical care, and other basic necessities.

The plight of the poor should be a serious concern to all of us in the Christian community. We should be at the forefront of efforts to respond justly to the *rights* of the poor. Scripture has much to say about this topic. Those of us who are not part of the poor—about 85 percent of the population—are one day going to be examined by God regarding our attitudes and conduct toward the poor.

People like to talk about the poor, but in fact most people feel threatened when confronted with personal (not governmental) responsibility for them. Few will admit that they want to avoid the poor, but how many neighborhoods have welcomed public efforts to build welfare housing in their communities, whether it be in the form of concentrated housing or scattered-site housing? The attitude is generally one of fear—fear that their presence will cause the local property values to go down, crime to rise, and education to be watered down. The "nice" poor are not welcomed, either, for they are a constant reminder that pricks our hearts concerning our personal obligations to them and their rights. How many individuals show a genuine concern, on a sustained basis, for even one poor family? We generally avoid the psychological discomfort associated with the presence of the poor. Scripture acknowledges this fact very bluntly:

The poor is hated even by his neighbor,
But those who love the rich are many. (Prov. 14:20)

79

Wealth adds many friends,
But a poor man is separated from his friend. . . .
All the brothers of a poor man hate him;
How much more do his friends go far from him! (Prov. 19:4,7)

God tells us that the poor, downtrodden, and needy have rights and that the righteous care about those rights (see Prov. 29:7; Jer. 5:28). But Scripture goes on to say that worldly people do not understand such concerns. The plight of the poor is generally rationalized away so that they are perceived as reaping the fruit of their own inferiority. God's children (even if we pay only cursory attention to Scripture) must acknowledge, however, that we are admonished to open our hearts to the poor. We are called to remember God's mercy on us; He delivered us from moral bankruptcy, and He showered compassion on us in every regard. If God's acts have not opened our hearts to the needs of others, we ought to wonder if we have really received the benefits we profess to have received from Him.

The question before us here, however, is very different. It is not about the moral obligations individuals are admonished by Scripture to shoulder on behalf of the poor; it is a question of the appropriateness of the state's defining a set of legal rights of the poor that then become a public obligation. If such legal obligations are appropriate and are to be instituted, what form should they take, and how should they be administered?

In his chapter, Dr. John Mason does three things that clarify this whole issue of doing justice with regard to the poor. He first delineates the public welfare issues as they are debated in the U.S. public arena today. Next, he thoroughly reviews the scriptural principles that apply to the problems of poverty. As is generally the case, even though the principles point us in the right direction, they must be mixed with an enormous amount of godly wisdom when we set out to implement them constructively. Misused principles can generate as many problems as they are intended to solve. And finally, Mason illustrates how we might make wholesome application of the biblical principles in the public welfare arenas. His biblical exegesis is solid; his conclusions, therefore, are compelling.

CHAPTER 4

BIBLICAL PRINCIPLES APPLIED TO A PUBLIC WELFARE POLICY

John D. Mason

Dr. John D. Mason is Professor of Economics at Gordon College in Wenham, Massachusetts. The chapter was written while he was visiting Professor of Economics at Calvin College in Grand Rapids, Michigan, during the 1988-89 academic year. He is the Secretary-treasurer of the Association of Christian Economists. For fifteen years he has served on the governing board of the Emmanuel Gospel Center, an urban ministry in Boston, Massachusetts, an experience that helped refine the ideas of the chapter.

The twentieth century has been marked by the growth of "public" welfare (state-mediated assistance to poorer citizens) in economically developed, market-based societies. Prior to the industrialization and accompanying urbanization that helped lift these societies to general economic well-being, poorer and weaker citizens were cared for through networks of extended families and locally mediated assistance (churches and local public provision). With the spread of both industrialization and urbanization (and generally in the midst or wake of the Great Depression of the 1930s) these private and local responses were considered insufficient. Was it that the social and psychological adjustment of the citizens did not match the new economic realities, such that the old social remedies did not work as well? We know, for example, that the extended family often gave way to the nuclear family in more urban settings—and today even the nuclear family is under severe attack. Is it the case that in the midst of general economic improvement for the masses, industrialized and urbanized societies know a certain "fragility" in terms of occasional bouts of unemployment and poverty for some of their citizens? We continue to seek answers to such questions.

It *is* clear that these nations responded to the potential and reality of both unemployment and poverty by erecting various types of national public welfare programs. However, a half-century after the Great Depression and the advent of most welfare programs, these nations are struggling to achieve the proper balance between private and local responses and a national response. As the decades since the 1930s have come and gone, we have learned a great deal about how hard it is to assist the poor without at the same time erecting incentives that encourage behaviors harmful to the poor and wasteful of society's resources. A too-easy response has been that the state simply cannot handle public welfare. But is there any other alternative, given all that has happened since the Great Depression? The more appropriate question today is, How can the national state along with private and local public initiatives cooperate to provide programs that work better than what we have known to the present? Such is our agenda here.

The purpose of this chapter is to learn from the postdepression experiences, in particular, of the economically developed societies, and then to use biblical insights to help us determine the appropriate balance of private and public responses to the presence of poorer citizens in our midst. The working conviction of this volume is that the God of creation, through His special revelation to us in the Bible, offers useful insights on the appropriate balance between public and private responses, and that we have to this point not sufficiently mined this source of ethical insight. The structure of the chapter is as follows: a review of recent experiences surrounding public welfare to show where fresh insight is needed; a consideration of relevant biblical emphases applicable to public welfare today; and the development of several of these emphases in more detail as guides to contemporary policy. Though much of the discussion fits any economically developed society, expositionally it is more beneficial (and interesting) to set the treatment within a particular society. That society will be the United States.

REVIEW OF PUBLIC WELFARE ISSUES

Our topic, then, is *public* welfare. But how broadly is this to be construed? In the United States since the early 1960s, "welfare" generally has been associated with three specific programs: Aid to Families with Dependent Children (AFDC), Food Stamps, and Medicaid. These programs assist primarily nonelderly families. A relatively recent and less well-known federal tax provision should be added because of the role it may play in the future; the Earned Income Tax Credit (EITC) allows the working poor to shrink their taxes and thus keep more of their income. Where publicly subsidized housing is available, it, too, would be seen as welfare.[1]

Social security and Medicare have helped many elderly citizens stay free of poverty, but these programs are considered "insurance" and not welfare. They are directed to the general population (and not only to those who otherwise would be poor). Similarly unemployment "insurance," in the midst of assisting all those who experience unemployment and qualify, also assists some who otherwise might be poor. The Supplemental Security Income (SSI) program is set up for aged, disabled, and blind citizens who are poor, but it typically is seen as part of social security and not welfare.

One final and important qualification must be recognized. The most effective means for lifting people out of poverty over the generations has *not* been welfare. General economic growth and the education of the citizens of a nation (what economists call "human capital" accumulation) have been the major forces attacking poverty in the long run. Indeed public welfare, if not structured properly, could well be a deterrent to economic growth and perhaps even to human capital accumulation. The goal, then, is to make these joint processes mutually supporting and not at odds with each other. Other chapters in this book (particularly those on money and banking and education) should be consulted for insight on the objectives of achieving economic growth and a good educational system.

So we will confine ourselves to the three main "welfare" programs: Aid to Families with Dependent Children (AFDC), Food Stamps, and Medicaid. Enacted as part of the Social Security Act of 1935, AFDC is state-administered cash assistance to poor families with funding coming primarily from Washington (a "federal" system). AFDC was seen initially as short-term assistance to those few poor mothers with small children and no husband, but the decades following World War II witnessed an unexpected and substantial increase in the numbers of female-headed families (as well as chronically insufficient child support by a majority of absent fathers). Responding to this in the 1960s, Congress provided supplemental assistance in Food Stamps and Medicaid and modified AFDC. Modification of AFDC meant a general liberalization in administration of assistance (the extent of which depended on the particular state) and *incentives* to encourage welfare recipients to work—lowering the effective tax rate (benefit reduction rate) on earnings and providing funds for schooling and retraining.

As the sixties bled into the seventies and eighties, and in the midst of growing inflation and a number of years of recession (and a failure of incomes to grow in real terms for many families), the states and Congress acted to limit the availability and adequacy of welfare. In a significant reform in 1981, the Congress raised the effective tax rate on earnings for welfare recipients back to 100 percent (one's welfare benefit falls dollar-for-dollar with any reported earnings) and encouraged the states to experiment with work rules, thus ending the era of incentives (seeking to induce welfare recipients to work more).

By the mid-1980s, some problems with welfare were generally recognized. The system of support was somewhat arbitrary and spotty—with considerable state differences—and it possibly induced two-parent families to split up; the system had too few "expectations" for welfare recipients to work or for absent parents to make support payments; and poor and welfare-dependent families were increasingly concentrated and isolated in urban ghettos.

Basic reforms in 1988 were addressed to these problems, to take effect gradually over the 1989-93 period. Assistance was extended to poor two-parent families in *all* states (ideally lessening the incentives for families to split up in order to qualify for assistance), with one of the parents being expected to work. Poor single parents whose youngest child was three or over were expected to take jobs or to be involved in educational and/or retraining programs to ease the transition from welfare to work. The states were ordered to locate nonsupporting parents and to have employers deduct child support from the wages of absent parents who have court-awarded support payments. Unlike the reforms of the 1960s, which stressed incentives to encourage people to work, this legislation contained *requirements* to work as a condition of continued eligibility for welfare. "Workfare" replaced welfare, some would say.

Though public welfare in the United States was reformed during the 1980s in fundamental ways, a number of important and difficult issues remain. The concern that troubled the broader citizenry so much and that fueled the reforms of both 1981 and 1988 is the presumption that many welfare recipients could, with a bit of effort, work more than they do. Otherwise, welfare is subsidizing idleness. This reaction is not just a preoccupation with getting lower taxes. If poorer citizens are allowed to remain idle, they fail to develop competent job skills or gain a sound educational background, which then destines them to long-run welfare dependency (with likely harmful effects on their children as well).

The reforms of 1988 require work. But will state administrators of welfare mandate that welfare recipients take "just any job"? Conservative and liberal voices debate whether welfare recipients should be forced to take a job (*any* job) or whether they should be prepared for work and "encouraged" to take a job. A related issue is the point in time at which a single mother on welfare be compelled to take a job: when her youngest child becomes three, as the reforms of 1988 specify, or when the child is younger or older. How tough should the state be in requiring work?

If welfare recipients are compelled to work, are there sufficient jobs available? This is the inevitable companion issue to workfare. Since the mid-1960s in North America and Western Europe, this question has been focused on the seemingly high levels of unemployment generally, and has been the grist for much discussion by economists and others on what precisely is the "full employment level of unemployment" (3 percent, as left-of-center observers have argued, or something higher—even 6 percent)—and on whether the state is indeed pursuing policies to lower unemployment to the full employment level.

In the latter decades of the twentieth century in the United States a further issue has been raised: whether a "structural twist" in the overall labor market has developed. The twist refers to the demise of low-skilled but well-paying manufacturing jobs (making cars and steel), and their replacement by service sector jobs that either pay little (hamburger flipping) or pay well but require much higher levels of education than necessary for the jobs being eliminated (computer programing). The outcome (so it is argued) is that sustaining a family with but a high-school diploma is far more difficult today, and for someone who drops out of high school before graduation, short of engaging in illegal activities, earning a sufficient income is nearly impossible. In the context of "workfare" the question is whether the wider community (the state) has a greater obligation than it has carried to this point to assure that sufficient jobs of an appropriate kind exist for poorer citizens to take.

As general economic growth and the opportunities gained through the accumulation of human capital (education) have allowed the vast majority of citizens to rise above poverty over the past two centuries, the remaining poverty increasingly has become concentrated in small pockets, such as Indian reservations and especially urban ghettos. The percentage of the United States poor population residing in the central cities of metropolitan areas has taken a sharp upturn in most recent years, and this poverty is characterized by a much higher incidence of female-headed families and a far more troubled surrounding environment than is true for the poor in other regions of the country.

At the same time that poverty is becoming more of a ghetto reality, well-paying entry-level jobs are moving from urban centers to the surrounding suburbs (and ex-urbs): a movement dubbed the "spatial mismatch" phenomenon. What may well compound the problem of compelling welfare recipients to take jobs, given these emerging realities, is a well-documented resistance by suburban communities to allow the construction of low-income housing (whether scattered-site or concentrated). The end result too often is that the families most likely to experience long-term (even intergenerational) welfare dependency may, because of the nonavailability of housing, be kept from those areas where good jobs are most likely to be found.

As noted earlier, the process of industrialization and urbanization from the nineteenth century to the present has witnessed the slow demise of the extended family—and in the years since World War II the breaking up of the nuclear family in economically unhealthy proportions (a reality of much greater intensity in the Afro-American family). We have come to realize rather recently what should have been apparent all along, that the extended and nuclear families are marvelously efficient units for achieving and maintaining economic well-being. Prior to the 1988 reforms, AFDC generally had not been allowed where a nuclear family was intact and provided assistance to the broken nuclear family without imposing any obligation on an absent father; those policies probably led to more broken families (and consequently more families on welfare) than otherwise would have existed.

The reforms of 1988 were designed to reinforce the nuclear family. Negative incentives still stand, however. Under these reforms, if there are not court-awarded support payments, an absent father is not obligated to help support the family. In what sense, then, should the state modify its provision of public welfare so as to create even stronger incentives for nuclear families to form and stay together?

Medical insurance in the United States for most families and individuals has been built into the perquisite package at their place of employment. As the cost of this insurance has increased with the general cost of medical care, increasing numbers of employers are reducing the extent of their provision, and some low-paying employers offer no such coverage at all. In an attempt to reduce the perquisite costs of employment, more employers are using temporary workers (who may have no medical coverage). In other words, the traditional system of employer-provided medical insurance slowly is cracking: a reality that most likely will be antagonized if there is a "structural twist" in the labor market. All of this comes home to roost particularly with the working poor, who may have little or no medical insurance protection provided on the job (and individual provision is inordinately expensive).

Public welfare in the United States is, as noted, a federal system with considerable freedom left to individual states to administer programs in unique ways. This characteristic has been seen as both a genius of the system and a fundamental weakness. Prior to the reforms of 1988, states had the freedom to offer AFDC and Medicaid to two-parent poor families or not, and only about half did so. Under the reforms, all states were compelled to do this. The financial provisions for the poor still vary considerably among the states, and critics long have called for a "national" standard. At the same time this system allows for a number of experiments with ways of assisting the poor effectively, and ideally will produce better means than otherwise would be forthcoming. But how can the system permit local and state initiative without incurring local and state irresponsibility? That question is troublesome.

Other issues surrounding public welfare might be raised that need clarification, but the ones mentioned so far have been the most discussed lately. For example, a longstanding concern is the appropriate "standard" to use in assisting poorer citizens, very meager subsistence or something more adequate. An extension of this is the "form" of assistance, whether as cash or "in-kind" (the direct provision of the good or service rather than the cash to purchase it); the latter has been used in housing, food, medical care, and retraining. Another issue long discussed is the degree to which the nature of welfare provision does and should "stigmatize" the poor (call attention to them in demeaning ways). For example, food stamps inevitably mark the poor in a way that cash assistance would not. Public housing "projects" do this as well, whereas housing vouchers would not.

BIBLICAL EVIDENCE APPLICABLE TO PUBLIC WELFARE

The material in the previous section reviews areas where public welfare policy needs fresh insight. In some cases the needed insight is technical: Is the United States experiencing a "structural twist" in the overall labor market; Has public welfare tended to separate nuclear families or discourage them from forming; Is medical insurance less and less available from employers? With a number of issues, however, the questions raised are primarily ethical: Should welfare mothers be compelled to take "just any job"; Should suburbs be compelled to allow the construction of more scattered-site, low-income housing; Should we set even tougher support requirements for absent fathers? Our concern lies primarily with the ethical issues, and to explore them, we turn to a major source of ethical discernment that undergirds Western civilization, the Judeo-Christian tradition—and to the primary source of this tradition, the Bible.

The biblical principles (or ethical emphases) examined will be organized around three major themes: (1) the Bible commends a special concern to be shown to those who are poor through little fault of their own; (2) in assisting the poor there should be mutual responsibility expected from the poor and the nonpoor; and (3) the nature of assistance should know as much decentralized administration as possible. We will consider some specific obligations confronting early Israel as the basis for much of the guidance we seek.

Reference has been made for some time in the Christian community to a "preferential option for the poor." This theological/ethical emphasis—often associated with Latin American theologians in the twentieth century but very clearly with a much broader and longer heritage—requires Christians (and typically the state as well) to pay *special* attention to the socioeconomic circumstances affecting the poorer citizens, and to respond in compassionate ways to them. We affirm this ethical emphasis without at this point committing to any particular means for achieving it—which is, after all, what the remaining paragraphs of this chapter are all about.

The God of the Bible desires justice and righteousness, and He orders us to act in just and righteous ways in our dealings with one another.[2] That assisting poorer and weaker members of society constitutes a practical meaning of justice and righteousness is a theme running boldly throughout the Bible: from the Mosaic laws ("Do not deny justice to your poor people" [Exod. 23:6]; see Lev. 25; Deut. 10:18; 14:28–15:11; 16:9-15; 24:10-22; 27:19), through the wisdom literature (see Job 29:7; 11-17; 31:16-23; Ps. 72:1-4, 12-14; Prov. 28:27; 31:20), to the prophetic complaints (see Isa. 1:16-17; 10:1-4; Jer. 22:3, 16; Amos 2:6-7; 5:7-11), and reinforced in the New Testament (Matt. 25:31-46; Luke 1:46-55; 3:10-11; 4:16-21; 16:19-31; 2 Cor. 8:1-15; 1 John 3:17).[3]

The basic question is *how* this special concern for the poorer and weaker members of society should be expressed: whether selectively to members of the household of faith or to all who are poor and weak in society; whether through private charity (a moral admonition on the nonpoor) or through some state action (a legal obligation).

The Law was given initially to Israel but was commended to all nations ("a light to the nations" [Isa. 51:4-5]; see Gen. 18:18; 2 Chron. 6:32-33; Isa. 2:2-4; 42:1-4; 49:6; 60:1-3; Joel 3:12; Mic. 4:1ff.; Rev. 15:3). Similarly the gospel was given initially to Israel but was commended to all the people of the world (a light to the Gentiles; see Luke 2:32; Acts 14:27; 17:31). Though the people of the household of faith are to express a particular concern for one another (see John 13:35; Acts 4:34-35), compassion should extend to all who are poor and needy (note the standard inclusion of the sojourners in the Mosaic legislation; see Gal. 6:10).

Though a charitable response to the poor and needy fulfills the highest intentions of the Law and is to be commended (ideally state action never would be needed), Scripture speaks of the "rights" of the poor (see Exod. 23:6; Deut. 24:17; 27:19; Ps. 140:12; Prov. 29:7; 31:9; Isa. 10:2; Jer. 5:28), and these words have clear legal significance. The admonitions of Psalm 72:1-4, 12-14 call upon the king to act in his official capacity. One can argue on biblical grounds that a proper function of the state is to assist citizens who are poor and needy when private charity is insufficient.[4]

A special concern for the poor commends a "compassionate" response to them. God was compassionate in rescuing Israel from demeaning slavery in Egypt; God in Christ takes compassion on us, forgiving our sins and imparting the gift of the Holy Spirit. An implication of this ideal compassion would have the poor in no way being stigmatized by whatever assistance they receive—though this is honored in the breach in the honest reality recorded for us in Scripture (Boaz had to warn his harvesters not to bother Ruth as she gleaned in his field, for example [see Ruth 2:9]). The use of a compassionate loan for the poor brother and his family (see Deut. 15:1-11) rather than a handout affirms the dignity of the poorer brother. The Jubilee land return (see Lev. 25) supports the norm cited elsewhere in the Old Testament that each man should be able to "sit under his own vine and under his own fig tree" (Mic. 4:4); each family should be able to provide for itself and not depend on others—attesting to the regard for the dignity of each family.

A final implication of compassionate concern noted here specifies the "standard" of assistance—liberal sufficiency for need: whether the specific provision is a compassionate loan, access to fallow-year fields, or the right to glean. The specific provisions in the Mosaic laws dealing with assistance to the poor designate sufficiency for need (see Deut. 15:8). The general concern for compassionate treatment of the poor, along with occasional ethical expressions of equality (see Ezek. 47:14; 2 Cor. 8:13), serves to bias the interpretation to "liberal" sufficiency for need.

If families, churches, and the state are to assist the poor, what specific obligations lie upon the poor and the nonpoor in this interchange? The second major ethical theme we want to consider calls both parties to mutual responsibility. Unlike the surrounding nations of the time, early Israel obligated its citizens broadly in most all social, political, and economic affairs. There was no standing army of professionals, but when the call went out, virtually all Israelite men were to respond. Legal proceedings involved all community members interacting with the "elders at the gate" (the heads of families in the small Israelite communities who would gather to hear legal disputes), and if the person were found guilty of a capital offense, all members of the community were to carry out the stoning. This same concern for broadly diffused responsibility seems clearly reflected in Christ's teaching that responsible leadership is service (see Matt. 23:8-11) and Paul's teaching on the Church as a body (see 1 Cor. 12).

So it was, then, that when poverty afflicted some members of society, all members were to bear responsibility. The primary means for assisting the poor were a compassionate loan (most likely for families with able-bodied workers), gleanings (most likely for the more dependent members of society), and access to the fallow-year fields; each obligated the poor to work in some way.[5] The nonpoor members of society bore responsibility as well: to make the compassionate loan (zero interest, with the possibility that full repayment would not be forthcoming); to allow gleaners into their productive fields and the poor generally into fallow-year fields; and in a much longer-run sense, to make sure that each Israelite family had a secure productive base (the Jubilee provision of Lev. 25).[6] The elders (the main form of primitive state in early Israelite communities) ideally would assure that all those activities transpired (a likely implication of passages such as Job 29:11-16 and Amos 2:6-7), and when God allowed a king to rule over Israel, he was charged with the same responsibility (see Ps. 72:1-4).

The third ethical theme—dealing with decentralized administration in assistance to the poor—builds from the second. The main provisions for assisting the poor in early Israel as outlined reflect the general concern for decentralization, with reliance primarily on extended family and neighbor-to-neighbor assistance. More well-to-do Israelites were to share with poorer surrounding residents at feast times (see Deut. 16:9-15; also Luke 16:19-31) and would be the obvious ones to make compassionate loans and to open their fields for gleaning.

An aversion to hierarchy and centralization generally marks the biblical record. God acted in history to establish a people and a land characterized by radical democracy in many areas. Recent scholars have shown the distinctiveness of Israel in the midst of the nations of the time: no standing army, no central state or king. Indeed the aversion to hierarchy is so striking that some prominent scholars see in early Israel a practical anarchy and the absence of any state. But there *was* a state. A legal corpus existed—the Law of Yahweh as Moses had mediated it. There were those who would enforce that law/covenant/constitution. There were sanctions (see Num. 35:12; Josh. 20:6-9). In the small communities in which most Israelites lived, administrative oversight and justice would have been carried out by the elders of the extended families, using the Law of Yahweh as the primary basis.

Accordingly, as strong as the general case for decentralization is, it must not be overdrawn. At the request of the Israelites, God allowed a king (though that was not His ideal preference). When the people felt threatened (in that case by military incursion from without), God allowed more administrative centralization. A similar reality may explain the otherwise troubling concentration of economic power brought about by the patriarch Joseph in Egypt (see Gen. 47:13ff.): a concentration that could be used to oppress and *was* used to enslave the people of Israel. A saving aspect of the concentration, however, was the stockpiling of food that helped save both Egypt and Israel at a time of extreme emergency.

New Testament teaching affirms the general preference for decentralized administration. Christ instructs His disciples that they should not erect artificial (and hierarchic) titles, "for whoever exalts himself will be humbled, and whoever humbles himself will be exalted" (Matt. 23:8-12); sacrificial service is to mark the lives of Christian men and women. Paul's teaching on the Body of Christ and how each part is vital and to be honored appears designed to prevent the dangers of arbitrary assignments of importance (and power?). Yet when the people were threatened and local responsibility was inadequate, a practical centralization developed. The apostles appointed seven men to oversee the distribution of food to the needy in Jerusalem (see Acts 6:1-7). In his travels among the churches, Paul admonished the more well-to-do communities of believers to send provisions to the poorer communities (see 2 Cor. 8:1-15).

In terms of the biblical record, God's ideal preference was for problems such as poverty to be handled as locally as possible. But when that was inadequate, there was a willingness to allow more centralized structures: typically in response to some clear threat to the continued viability of society. Those in authority (the elders of the small communities; the king under the monarchy) would have been charged to oversee the ideal local administration and to effect a more centralized response when local responsibility was not possible or forthcoming.

It is interesting to speculate why God preferred such local assistance and the peculiar forms that He did. Anthropological research provides evidence of reciprocal gift giving as a popular means of assistance in primitive societies. Several of the surrounding nations at the time of early Israel used more centralized means. Yet Israel was instructed to use compassionate loans, gleaning, and access to fallow-year fields—and, in a much longer time period, the return of a family's patrimony (Jubilee). Is there greater protection of the poor's dignity through such means? Might these forms place a greater sense of responsibility on the ordinary citizen to tend to society's problems, which thereby would instill a more profound sense of "ownership" of society—and thus a more stable society than otherwise would be true if most such problems were assigned to some removed bureaucracy?

BIBLICAL PRINCIPLES APPLIED
TO CONTEMPORARY PROBLEMS

In this last section the ethical emphases of Scripture are applied to the problems of public welfare policy today. The warrant for doing so is the conviction that the God of all creation has revealed in the Bible, particularly through His dealings with early Israel, instructions to guide all nations. A number of points of entry are before us. The Bible commends a compassionate response to the poor, and we could investigate the adequacy of the typical financial standard that various states use in assisting the poor, or whether the poor are stigmatized in unhealthy ways. The Bible commends widespread responsibility among members of society, and thus we might investigate the nature of a work obligation for those poor citizens who reasonably can be expected to work as well as the mutual obligation of the broader society to make sure that sufficient work opportunities exist. Our treatment here will address primarily the last theme, however, the concern for decentralized administration.

The Great Depression of the 1930s posed a clear national threat to economically developed, market-based societies. In terms of the biblical teaching just reviewed, such a threat could justify some type of centralized response. But in the actual programs developed over the decades, have the lines between national and local, and between public and private, been drawn appropriately? Could the problem of poverty have been handled more effectively than it has been?

One chapter cannot consider all dimensions of poverty in the United States. The ethical impetus of a "preferential option for the poor" would counsel that the most desperate piece of the poverty puzzle be addressed. In the latter decades of the twentieth century that piece is ghetto poverty. In or near the center of most major cities lies a concentration of poor citizens, characterized by high percentages of female-headed families and welfare dependency, high rates of teen pregnancy and out-of-wedlock births, low levels of labor force participation (and high levels of unemployment), excessive rates of high-school dropouts, and an unhealthy incidence of crime and drug involvement. The expert chronicler of these realities, sociologist W. J. Wilson, observes a growing condition of "social isolation" as regularly employed citizens move out of these areas, leaving them without a stabilizing network of social organizations (two-parent families, churches, civic organizations) to maintain order within a community. Unlike poverty generally in the United States, these poor settings are filled largely by Afro-American and Hispanic citizens—a particularly sad reality given the long history of restrictions and discrimination facing these citizens.[7]

In ghetto settings most public schools are so overcome by the problems of the surrounding environment that little useful education is provided to a majority of students. In these settings the labor market seems least likely to offer the types of jobs that promise long-run release from poverty; the more promising jobs at relevant skill levels are increasingly available in the suburban rings rather than the urban centers. In these settings the problem of young men not marrying and supporting the girls they impregnate is more evident: due in part to the fact that more babies are brought to term; due as well to perceived poorer labor market opportunities, such that either the mother or the father is unwilling to commit to a marriage relationship. One wonders whether the availability of welfare provision or medical protection only to a single mother might be a factor as well?

In a setting with poor schools, poor employment opportunities, and a social environment that often discourages behavior promising long-run economic benefits, does it seem likely that the standard provision of welfare, including the welfare reforms of 1988, will prove adequate? One certainly hopes so, in order to beat back the pervasive hopelessness there, but a sober assessment is far from optimistic. Welfare is becoming workfare. But what types of jobs exist in these settings that give some glimmer of long-run improvement? Both a structural twist in the overall labor market and a spatial mismatch of jobs within greater metropolitan areas work against such hope. And the high number of high-school dropouts continues unabated!

Since the early post-World War II years, many large public housing "projects" have been built in most urban poverty areas. Although these seemed hopeful housing arrangements in those earlier years when most residents were intact nuclear families earning low incomes (and more jobs were in the cities), they have become generally seed-grounds for despair when the vast majority of families are female-headed and living largely off public welfare. Indeed the "projects" have become symbolic of the general concentration of our most desperately poor citizens in areas set apart from the broader society. The more recent afflictions of these areas with high incidences of AIDS (even among newborns), crack addiction (even among newborns), and murder only add to the general despair and hopelessness.

How might we rethink the mix of local/national and private/public when it comes to ghetto poverty? The first thing that must be done is to restore a strong nuclear (if not extended) family as the main social base. The family is the Bible's first line of defense, and it has remained that throughout history in virtually all societies—including the United States in the twentieth century. Restoring this base will involve a combination of public and private initiatives. Parents need to be held responsible for their children; this goal is healthy for both the children and the parents. The welfare reforms of 1988 mandate absent-parent support only where there is a court order, albeit the desire of the legislation goes beyond this. A growing chorus of experts on the right and the left have called for becoming even more aggressive, and for the state to help establish paternity and compel through the tax system financial support by any absent parent. Otherwise, an often-unhealthy burden is forced on the remaining parent to pursue a court order.

Where natural families do not exist, loose or tight surrogate families can be formed. Single mothers often require all sorts of very practical assistance: from having questions answered about child care, to needing occasional day care, to balancing checkbooks, to doing repairs around the apartment—the list goes on and on. The presence of concerned friends and acquaintances can offer help in ways that public welfare officials doing the best possible job never could. A number of observers have testified to the extremely important role that adult "mentors" play in explaining why certain children from the ghetto survive to responsible adulthood: whether the adult is an extended family member, a youth worker on the street, a teacher in the schools, or someone like Eugene Lang (the wealthy businessman who promised a group of East Harlem elementary school graduates he would pay for their college education if they finished high school, *and then* became personally involved in their lives to help them get through high school—and almost every child graduated). Being a friend to a poor family and serving as a mentor to a poor child are ready-made for private activity, though the state could act to fund mentors and friends—perhaps through a type of domestic peace corps.[8]

Practically, the mentoring and the befriending are not likely to happen when the poor are isolated in settings where *they* are fearful of going out (let alone those who might consider going to the settings). We must wonder about the wisdom of the "projects" and the general concentration of the poor away from the rest of society. The Bible calls for the well-to-do to assist the poor in direct, personal ways. Such responses would come more naturally and frequently were the poor scattered throughout a metropolitan area (including the surrounding suburbs) rather than concentrated in the urban ghettos. Scattered-site, low-income housing would bring the poor closer to more promising jobs (and information networks about job opportunities as well as conventional commuting patterns) and within improved educational settings. Such a resolution would place them closer to a number of churches (some of which were relocated away from urban centers in earlier years) and the ideal development of individual-to-individual assistance.

Has it been wise administrative oversight, in terms of biblical ethical instruction, to allow the communities surrounding urban ghettos to prevent the construction of scattered-site, low-income housing, as they have been doing? Put more forcefully, should the "elders" of contemporary society compel the surrounding communities to undertake construction of scattered-site, low-income housing—and *all* the communities rather than just a few, with truly scattered-site and not reconcentrated housing in more diverse settings? Our judgment is that herein lies a case of local irresponsibility on the one hand (the surrounding communities) and local inadequacy on the other hand (the urban ghettos), such that a crisis has developed and greater centralization and hierarchy are needed. But we must proceed cautiously and honor as much local and private initiative as possible in redressing this situation.

It was noted at the beginning of the first section that in a more complete program to attack poverty, great stress should be placed on both general economic growth and human capital accumulation (a good education). A final brief implication will be drawn in terms of education. Public education in the United States at the elementary and secondary levels has been provided primarily at the local level (with increasing amounts of state funding). This otherwise commendable concession to local control has left many public schools in the urban ghettos virtually nonfunctional in any meaningful sense. Serious rethinking is needed on the public/private and local/state roles to make "public" involvement with education in these settings at all meaningful. Does the crisis of the ghetto offer strong support to a policy of funding students rather than schools, allowing the student (and family) to assign the funding to a school that offers greater hope for a socially beneficial education to take place? We believe so.

In his excellent book on public welfare reform in the United States, David Ellwood develops an ethical notion he calls "reasonable responsibility." What, for example, is a reasonable work expectation for a single-parent head of household?[9] His notion is helpful, and it has a biblical ring if applied consistently throughout society. The Bible instructs broadly shared responsibility for the obligations of citizenship. President Reagan's call for "a new federalism" and President Bush's image of a "thousand points of light" are important emphases in the struggle to redefine the proper roles for public and private and local and national. When it comes to assisting the poor, the Bible prefers local and private action. But when the local and private response is not possible and forthcoming, a public and more centralized response is in order. Urban ghetto realities in the latter decades of the twentieth century should force a serious rethinking of the established mix of public/private and local/national in order to save the United States from losing in a murky wave of hopeless despair a number of its poorest (and historically most disenfranchised) citizens.

EDITOR'S PERSPECTIVE

By addressing ghetto poverty in the context of the biblical principle emphasizing a decentralized approach to working for a solution to poverty, John Mason took on what is probably the toughest nut to crack, next to the problem of drugs, in our entire social system. The seven areas he identifies that need to be worked on if real progress is to be made in bringing public justice to bear on ghetto poverty are incredibly complex and diverse: (1) the need to restore the desire for and existence of a strong nuclear family (the Bible's first line of defense); (2) the need to find a constructive way to hold parents responsible for their children; (3) the need to see that paternity benefits are paid by the absent parent when a one-parent family exists; (4) the need to create surrogate families that provide mentors and models when the natural parents are incapable or unwilling to serve in those capacities; (5) the need to provide housing for the poor that is not isolated or concentrated but is scattered throughout the community where jobs and the social infrastructure are available to reinforce the positive benefits realized when one emerges from poverty; (6) the need to provide meaningful education and remediation for the poor; and (7) the need to involve all segments of society—private/public and local/national—in efforts to redress ghetto poverty.

Probably the greatest difficulty in tackling such a problem (next to the fact that we are dealing with the ongoing consequences of the Fall) is its size and complexity, which can cause those concerned about it to feel overwhelmed and helpless as they attempt to cope with it. For example, I was listening recently to a man from Baltimore, Maryland, who had spent over twenty years working to reverse the cycle of poverty in that city only to find himself moving backward in the last five years because of the onslaught of drugs in the neighborhoods. The emerging drug problem threatens to undo everything he and others have accomplished. He continues to labor, but he is becoming discouraged. This kind of reality brings to light a whole different dimension of the problem of poverty that I believe is critical and needs to be integrated into any thinking about a search for a solution. We need to step back a moment and reexamine the problem from a somewhat different perspective.

I am thinking about our need to face and address the dynamics of *motivation*, its source, and its role in the lives of those experiencing poverty and in the thinking of those outside poverty who are called on to promote a solution for the problem. Apathy, hopelessness, and discouragement devastate persons in poverty. Few of the poor dare believe they can emerge from it. And people who want to help do not know exactly what to do. What can be done to correctly motivate all concerned and not merely result in a feeling of guilt (probably false guilt) that leaves its possessor resigned to the helpless inevitability of progressive poverty when no solution seems to be at hand?

Christians need to remember that success, as the world measures it, is not promised those of us who respond to the plight of the poor. As Cal Beisner reminded us in his chapter ("Biblical Incentives and an Individual's Economic Choices," volume 2, pages 191-201, of this series), four categories of incentives may motivate Christians in response to Christ: (1) to act for Christ out of *gratitude* for His redemptive love in the hope that our *service* to others will both glorify God and elicit positive responses from the persons served; (2) to seek the *furtherance of God's Kingdom* (Christ's effective rule in the hearts of His children and the influence of His precepts in the affairs of human endeavors); (3) to be His *stewards in the exercise of dominion rule* over the created order; and (4) to *serve* others as we bring God's blessings to them in the exercise of our larger role as God's priests (see 1 Pet. 2:9). The Spirit of God provides a rich and full knowledge of God's love for us and our position in Christ, which frees us to follow Him wherever He calls (ministering to those in poverty, rearing children, programing a computer, etc.). The call of Christ, the memory of His acts of love, and the sustaining power of the Holy Spirit enable us to persevere in a specific calling. We need those who are called of God to minister to the poor, and the Church must recognize and support such ministries.

But what of persons caught in the clutches of poverty who have not been motivated by the love of Christ? Can Christians hope to help such people apart from the gospel? The very phrase, "apart from the gospel," sets up a false dichotomy. It implies that the gospel is somehow separated from ministry to the whole person, but a poor gospel is so divided. Furthermore, we have already established that public policy follows the individual, the family, the Church and other nongovernmental organizations, and businesses in assuming responsibility for the poor.

How can public policy effectively approach the problems of motivation so intricately interwoven with the entire poverty issue? Cal Beisner also addressed this aspect of motivation in another chapter of volume 2 ("Biblical Incentives and Economic Systems," pages 168-186, and most specifically in the section "Two Types of Economic Incentives," pages 172-177). He said, "Biblical precept and example reveal two chief types of economic incentives: reward and punishment." He went on to explain that while people's needs and desires vary greatly, the Bible speaks of *external* incentives (not merely internal incentives as do so much modern psychology and motivational theory). That is so because the Bible understands people as moral decision makers responsible for their choices; choices are to be functions of the intellect and will, not the feelings and emotions.

Policies must appeal to the prudent self-interest (not selfishness) of the people in poverty. This in turn must be coupled with a reasonable and discernible hope that one's response will be rewarded with success, which is particularly important when one has experienced many defeats and failures. I would like to offer three suggestions that build on the philosophy of "workfare" as described in the body of John Mason's chapter.

Human capital (the economic equivalency of human value) is a precious resource that we cannot afford to waste. From an economic viewpoint, only human activity has the capacity to produce a multiplication of economic benefits. When a human is successfully integrated into the economic system, he or she produces benefits for the entire system that transcend the mere economic output and consumptions of that individual. In other words, it is in everybody's best interest to see to it that everyone who possibly can should be fully incorporated in the economic processes. To help accomplish this, I would like to see public policy that develops incentives to stimulate the *private sector* to seek solutions to the pervasive problems associated with poverty. I do not believe government programs can be personalized to the degree necessary to bring about their success, nor do I believe centralized efforts, in this case, can do the job as effectively. I want the government to offer tax incentives to the broadest possible group of potential problem solvers.

First, I would like to see businesses given a meaningful tax incentive to find, train, and employ persons living in poverty. They could be given tax shields equivalent to a multiple of the actual costs incurred in finding, training, and employing the poor (as defined and identified). Restrictions would be needed to safeguard the practice by limiting the number (absolutely or as a percentage of a firm's work force) of such people that could be employed by a firm, by not allowing the poor to replace others already employed, and by requiring a good faith commitment on the part of the employer to a time of employment that will require the employer to persevere in solving the problems that will be encountered in any effort to integrate the poor (especially those who may have inappropriate self-concepts and attitudes). Then, as an extra inducement, businesses that demonstrate genuine success in helping those ensnared in poverty to escape will be provided additional economic rewards—tax refunds, extensions in the lengths of time the tax shield will be allowed to run, and so on.

Second, as a part of the training incorporated in the first option, everyone employed under such an incentive program should be required to view and demonstrate comprehension on sixty thirty-minute videos (run during an appropriate time at work) covering a wide array of subjects dealing with "life management skills" and basic social values that foster a prudent, productive, and responsible life. Most of us who have grown up in middle-class (or upper-class) America have no notion of the basic deficiencies in training and comprehension of many of the poor in the most rudimentary principles governing social interactions in the marketplace. I am thinking of basics, such as the benefits derived from punctuality, dependability, effort, civility, manners, honesty, and similar traits that are learned and generate rewards. Then there are many skills that can be learned to enhance one's sense of "being in charge of my life": budgeting skills, prudent purchasing decisions, planning, time management, self-discipline, and so forth.

Videos covering a number of such topics and skills need to be produced so that socially rewarding behavior can be stimulated. Our self-identity is in part wrapped up in a multitude of little things that, when done poorly or well, affect our sense of well-being. These things influence how others see us and respond to us, which in turn reinforces good behavior or elicits antisocial conduct. Some Christians will object strenuously to these suggestions on the grounds that the family should play this role in life. I agree with that, but I am working at the fourth and fifth levels of help here because the first three (individuals, families, churches and other nongovernmental organizations) have failed to provide adequate support and training.

Finally, I would attack the problem of housing the poor through tax incentive programs that would make it feasible for the private sector to construct single-family and duplex housing units scattered throughout urban areas (made possible through legal means, if necessary). To qualify to live in such housing, the poor would have to be employed in the "economic recovery" program outlined in steps one and two above. To qualify for the tax breaks that would be given the builders, the families would have to be involved in the purchase of their homes—an additional incentive for the poor to seriously assume responsibility for themselves as quickly as possible.

The three steps noted above may be unworkable in some specific details, but I believe the concepts are fundamentally sound. Surely more serious thinking about them can yield workable improvements.

What has been outlined does not change the human heart, however. The power of the gospel—the Holy Spirit using God's Word—is the only thing that can bring about that kind of desired change. But that is not the role of public policy. Public policy is to seek justice in the public arenas. I believe justice is served by seeking (even through prudential means) the participation of more people in the rewards of a behaviorally wholesome life—maintaining nuclear families, absorbing education and training, working hard, being prudent, and so forth. The redistribution of wealth that occurs through this effort elevates everyone and takes from no one. I believe these are appropriate ends.

PART V

MONETARY POLICY: AN INSTRUMENT FOR JUSTICE

This is the first of two sections dealing with the twin instruments of monetary and fiscal policy—those governmental activities most directly affecting economic variables, such as the levels of production, the level of employment, price levels, inflation, interest rates, economic growth, foreign exchange rates, level of foreign trade, and distribution of wealth. This section considers monetary policy; Part VI looks at taxation, a major component of fiscal policy.

As we prepare to read Dr. Douglas Vickers' chapter applying biblical principles to a national policy on money and banking, two things should be noted. First, Christians who are professional economists do not all agree on the most basic issues. Should there even be a national monetary policy (Israel did not have one) that goes beyond the efforts to see that a free market exists where a metallic-based (gold, platinum, etc.) currency is used and limited by the physical quantity of the base metal? A number of Christians believe the answer to this question should be a resounding NO!

Subscribers to the "NO" theory believe that monetary integrity can be maintained only by the physical restrictions of limiting the supply of money to an amount equal to the value of a scarce metal, which provides a backing for the circulating medium. It is not generally made clear, however, how the value of that scarce metal is itself to be specified, what may cause or permit changes in it, and how such variations may in turn impact the monetary system. As Dr. Vickers points out, for these scholars (he and I are not of their persuasion), money is only a "veil" behind which real economic activity takes place. Money does not embody any economic content in itself; money is merely a symbol or shadow of real economics. From this perspective, any publicly fostered alterations in the money supply (or its attendant trappings: interest rates, reserves, etc.) can create only disruptive and unjust side effects contrary to biblical intentions.

Dr. Vickers and those of us who join him in his understanding of both biblical and general revelation as they apply to this issue believe, as do those with whom we differ, a fundamental concern of Scripture is that the integrity of any money base be diligently guarded and preserved. We believe, however, that the use of a metallic base for determining the quantity and value of money is just as subject to the consequences and ravages of sin as any other system. The debasement of metals has and will occur; perfect markets have never existed that were beyond the manipulative ploys of governments, businesses, churches, families, and individuals.

More important, though, money has a vital and real economic function, which transcends the view that it is solely a symbol and veil. For example, money has both a time and a place value—you can spend it now or save it for the future; you can take it wherever you go and buy whatever is there. Money is, if you will, a "warehouse of value" where economic time and place choices are stored. When this economic reality is coupled with human psychology, the management of money—personal and institutional—impacts buying and selling decisions, which impact inflationary pressures, employment, and so forth.

The second thing to be noted is that Dr. Vickers did not write his chapter for professional economists who, for example, may be looking for the appli-cation of Scripture to a Federal Reserve Board decision to lower interest rates in the face of a weakening economy. He is writing to defend the position that Scripture does not *prescribe* a metallic-based monetary system just because coins and barter were the prevailing medium of exchange in biblical days; to say that when Christians find themselves living with a monetary system such as ours (he is not treating the Federal Reserve System as if it is normative, but as a reality), they are to work with it because God has established governments for the purpose of seeking justice for all people, and Christians are to promote the most successful working of the system possible in a fallen environment; to review the necessary elements of any monetary system; to lay the theological foundations on which we should examine and build a just monetary system; to relate biblical principles to monetary and banking policies; and to tie this concern for public justice to considerations of human welfare and economic and civil righteousness, and relate them to God's creation mandates.

[A personal note: Almost two decades ago when I was struggling with what it meant to responsibly integrate Scripture with the discipline of busi-ness, Doug Vickers' work integrating Scripture with economics came to my attention. I was greatly heartened to discover a fellow pilgrim, especially one who was demonstrating integrating skills. I corresponded with him (he was in Australia at the time) and received much encouragement in return. His participation in this series is, therefore, especially pleasing to me because he has been a pioneering spirit in this endeavor to integrate Scripture with public policy.]

CHAPTER 5

BIBLICAL PRINCIPLES APPLIED TO A NATIONAL MONETARY AND BANKING POLICY

Douglas Vickers

Dr. Douglas Vickers is Professor of Economics at the University of Massachusetts, having served previously as Chairman of the Department of Finance, University of Pennsylvania, and Dean of the Faculty of Economics, University of Western Australia. He graduated (B.Sc., Econ., Ph.D.) from the University of London (England).

Dr. Vickers has written numerous papers in theoretical and applied economics and the history of economic thought, in addition to Studies in the Theory of Money, 1690-1776, Money Capital in the Theory of the Firm, Financial Markets in the Capitalist Process, *and* Money, Banking, and the Macroeconomy. *His writings in apologetic theology include* Man in the Maelstrom of Modern Thought.

No single issue conducts us more effectively to the complexities we face in these studies of public policy than the fact that we live in a monetary economy. Money finds its way into every corner of our economic lives. Earning and spending, borrowing and lending, saving, investing, accumulating, and bequeathing—all in one way or another find expression in monetary terms. Poverty and wealth, affluence and security, indigence and distress—all have monetary dimensions. It is true, of course, that neither money itself, the idolization of which is the "root of all evil" (1 Tim. 6:10), nor the materialism that the notion of money conjures up is the whole of life. There are other issues that the gaining of the whole world cannot supplant (see Matt. 16:26). But in the wholeness of our lives the economic dimension of things has crucial significance. And within the scope of economic realities the question of money keeps clamoring for attention. On the level of basic life patterns the prophet of old brought up the question of money in his charge: "Wherefore do ye spend money for that which is not bread?" (Isa. 55:2). Money brings to sharpest focus the implications, the trust, and the liabilities of the stewardship that our creaturehood imposes on us.

But the problems of money, and its place in the national economy and the aggregate scheme of things, are not easily or frequently understood. No economic issue has been more diversely interpreted than that of the nature, the function, and the significance of money. The ferment of ideas in this area has led to major advances in economic thought, but developments have not always been soundly based and the problem of money has been the hunting ground of adventurers and cranks.

The very title we have assigned to this chapter opens a question of historic concern. It suggests that if left to itself the monetary economy will not always function at a high degree of efficiency and that a maximally attainable level of economic welfare will not necessarily and automatically be realized. It suggests that there are reasons for a "national monetary policy." Of course many economists at the present time, among them some distinguished Christian commentators, have argued that money is simply a "veil" beyond which real economic activity takes place, and that money itself does not exert a unique and independent effect on the economy. The complexities of our economic system, however, make the creation and circulation of money not only necessary but also a potentially disruptive and disequilibrating force as well as a corrective and enhancing influence when the economy tends to dislocation. If there are demonstrable reasons why the aggregate economy will not necessarily and automatically equilibrate at a level at which all those willing to work find work to do, some part of the explanation may be found in a malfunctioning of the monetary system, or some adjustment to the amount of money available and the terms on which it can be acquired may contribute to correcting the situation.

If our thought is captured by the economic notions of *laissez faire* and assumptions of automatic harmonies in the market economy, everything can be expected to work out for the best, and there could never be any work for a "national monetary policy" to do. In the absence of any need for national economic policy there would be no need to spend very much time explaining how to do nothing. But in conditions of less than full employment or less than stable monetary values, and in the absence of automatically equilibrating markets, counteracting policy at the level of monetary and other economic affairs may be desirable. The biblical ethic addressed to our responsibilities to the poor and the disadvantaged has pressing relevance in this age. It is true that the Scriptures lay down the responsibility to work, and they make it clear that "if any would not work, neither should he eat" (2 Thess. 3:10). But what does the Christian ethic say to those, and to us in relation to those, who do not work simply because, as a result of the instabilities and malfunctioning of the economic system, there is no work for them to do? Should they not eat?

THE ESSENCE OF THE MONETARY SYSTEM

Two preliminary issues call for comment as a background to our fuller argument. First, money is not of the essence of economic relations; and second, money is created in our contemporary economy by a complex and highly interdependent structure of banks and other financial institutions. The first issue concerns the essential functions of money. The second directs our attention to the form of money. It is necessary to keep function and form distinct and also to see the logical dependence of the latter on the former. Function precedes form. The form that money assumes depends on what is widely acceptable as performing the functions of money in the economy.

When we say that money is not of the essence of the economic problem, we mean that it is possible to conceive of an economic system in which money did not exist at all. But such a system would not be very efficient in an aggregative sense. The production of goods would still occur, but exchanges of goods produced by one individual would be made directly for goods produced by another individual. Considerable economic costs would attend such a barter exchange system. In a monetary economy, on the other hand, goods do not exchange directly for goods. Money intervenes as a medium of exchange. The fact that produced commodities now exchange for money implies that the possession of money is a means of transporting purchasing power, or command over goods and services, over time and distance. The expectation that whatever is produced will be able to be exchanged for such generalized purchasing power permits and facilitates a high degree of specialized production activity. This "division of labor" allows each individual to contribute to the national output by concentrating on that line of production in which his skills and endowments give him the greatest comparative advantage. Specialization of production and indirect monetary exchange point to the maximization of the economy's aggregate income and the possibilities of generalized economic welfare.

But in this arrangement of things money functions not only as a medium of exchange. It functions also as a store of value. Money received in exchange for produced commodities may not be spent immediately in the purchase of other commodities. It may be held and thus lie idle. The holding of money, it has been said, is a means of transporting purchasing power over time. This, apart from the benefits of production for indirect exchange, is the essential difference between a monetary and a barter economy.

In the logic of barter economic arrangements, there obtains what became known in classical economic thought as Say's Law, which rested on the proposition that production took place only to be able to acquire other goods. Production was the means to the end of consumption. When this notion is extended to a monetary economy, it implies that the total value of what is demanded in the markets of the economy will necessarily be the same as the total value of what is produced. Put in another way, it implies that the total incomes generated in producing the national product will be spent and respent in purchasing the national product. There cannot, therefore, be any deficiency of demand for the goods and services the economy is capable of producing. There cannot, therefore, be what economists have referred to as a general glut or a general overproduction of goods and services. There cannot, therefore, be any deficiency of demand for the economic resources necessary to produce goods and services. Notably, there cannot be any involuntary unemployment. Any individuals who remain unemployed are unemployed because they choose to be unemployed. The only unemployment is voluntary unemployment.

It is unfortunate that such a mistranslation of Say's Law from a barter to a monetary economic system has perverted much of contemporary economic thought. It is doubly unfortunate that much of contemporary Christian economic commentary has similarly been based on the assumption of the applicability and the explanatory competence of Say's Law. In short, to the extent that part of one's income is set aside or saved rather than spent, to that extent the level of the aggregate spending stream, and thus the aggregate demand for goods and services and for the labor necessary to produce those goods and services, is reduced. It may be argued that what is saved does, in fact, find its way back into the spending streams of the economy and, therefore, to the overall demand for goods and services. This, it may be imagined, necessarily happens because what is saved will be made available for borrowing, and will, therefore, be transformed into investment or further consumption expenditure. The proposition that saving will be automatically transmuted into investment was made famous by Adam Smith in his classic *Wealth of Nations* in 1776. It became known in economic literature as the Turgot-Smith saving-investment doctrine.

In this proposition we have the further significant monetary implication of Say's Law, the notion that an automatic mechanism in the economy guarantees that savings will flow into investment. In our complex system of financial institutions, unfortunately, there is no inevitable guarantee that that will be the case. On the contrary, the high degree of instability and the cyclical fluctuations in investment expenditure are a principal cause of generalized economic fluctuations, and with them the varying levels of involuntary unemployment and price disturbances that have been experienced in the past.

Such an understanding of economic institutional structures in no sense argues, as some Christian economists have claimed, against the Christian ethic of prudent provision for the future in the form of saving and the avoidance of excessive or conspicuous consumption. It is simply to recognize the realities in the monetary economy, to recognize that investment and planned expenditure streams in general are subject to high degrees of uncertainty and ignorance. The determinants of investment expenditure necessary to fill the savings gap are multidimensional. It is as the Apostle James responded to the merchants who said, "Today or tomorrow we will go to this or that city, spend a year there, carry on business and make money" (James 4:13, NIV). "Why," James observed, "you do not even know what will happen tomorrow." Such is the context of ignorance and uncertainty in which business and economic decisions are made. Such realities are at the foundation of the economic instabilities that make monetary policy meaningful.

The remaining preliminary point we noted, one that conducts us to the heart of the question of banking policy, has to do with the form of money. Historically, many different substances have circulated as money, principal among them being metals of one kind or another. Indeed, throughout the late nineteenth and into the early twentieth century, there existed a reasonably freely functioning international gold standard. It is true that in Old Testament times and in the economic arrangements of God's theocratic people, money took a metallic form. In fact, the adulteration of the metallic monetary unit was invoked by the prophet Isaiah as an analogical reference to the corruption and sinful dissipation of God's people. Isaiah's complaint that "Thy silver is become dross" (Isa. 1:22) is echoed in Ezekiel's condemnation that "the house of Israel is to me become dross: all they are brass, and tin, and iron, and lead, in the midst of the furnace; they are even the dross of silver" (Ezek. 22:18). One highly respected Christian economic commentator has found in Isaiah 1:22 the "key verse" for his entire economics, and in his extended argument for money of a form "backed" by gold or some other hard asset he has concluded bluntly that "unbacked paper money is immoral." Similarly the entire structure of the contemporary American banking system, with its practices of lending and "multiple indebtedness," has been labeled "immoral"; the Central Banking System, the Federal Reserve System to which we shall refer, is claimed to be "immoral," and calls are heard for its abolishment. Every man should then, it is suggested, be his own banker and the issuer or creator of his own money.

But to observe that money was of metallic form during the earlier theocratic administration of God's people in no sense argues that form is the necessary or the only admissible one that money must assume at this time. It is true that we are required to do as Ezra did at a critical juncture of Israel's history. He "prepared his heart to seek the law of the LORD, and to do it" (Ezra 7:10). We insist, in other words, on the sanctity and perpetuity of the moral law. However, to insist on the sanctity and perpetuity of the moral law is in no sense to insist on the sanctity and perpetuity of the institutional forms in which the mandates of that law first came to expression. To do so is to fall prey to the current theonomic confusion of the moral and civil law or to its error in failing to understand the "schoolmaster" (Gal. 3:24) function of the civil and ceremonial law. As the apostle argued, "After that faith is come, we are no longer under a schoolmaster" (Gal. 3:25).

Certain biblical principles that were clearly promulgated in those earlier times continue, however, to have force and determinative significance in our contemporary monetary arrangements. The biblical ethic requires justice, equity, and evenhandedness in all economic activity and monetary transactions: "Ye shall do no unrighteousness in judgment, in meteyard, in weight, or in measure. Just balances, just weights . . . shall ye have" (Lev. 19:35-36; see also Deut. 25:13-15). The prophets returned repeatedly to complain against God's people that they were guilty of violating the law, and were "an abomination unto the LORD" (Deut. 25:16), on precisely those grounds. Micah referred to "the scant measure that is abominable" and continued, "Shall I count them pure with the wicked balances, and with the bag of deceitful weights?" (Mic. 6:10-11).

These principles come to pointed relevance for contemporary monetary and banking policy in their insistence on the preservation of the value of the monetary unit. In other and more familiar terms, the problem of inflation, or of a diminution in the purchasing power value of money or, that is to say, a rise in the general commodity price level, is in need of urgent and continual address within the orbit of monetary and banking policy. Those Christian economists who see in the Eighth Commandment, "Thou shalt not steal" (Exod. 20:15), a condemnation of inflation and inflationary economic policies are on thoroughly sound ground. Whatever is understood to constitute the nation's money supply, it must be subject to those regulations that maintain a close relation between the needs of the economy for money or a circulating medium and the amount of it that is brought into existence.

In our contemporary economy the principal form of money is technically referred to as debt money or credit money. For the main part, the money supply, apart from the notes issued by the Federal Reserve Banks and the coins issued by the Treasury, consists of deposits held by the public at the banks and other so-called depository institutions. The latter, in addition to the commercial banks, are the mutual savings banks, savings and loan associations, and credit unions. These financial institutions all "create" money by placing amounts to the credit of the deposit accounts of individuals and business firms. The deposits are then transferable from one individual to another by means of checks. The deposits come into existence mainly as a result of the institutions making loans to, or purchasing assets (notably securities) from, individuals, business firms, and nonfinancial institutions. When a bank loan is made, the transaction is effected simply by the bank's crediting the loan amount to a deposit account in the borrower's name. Thus money is created.

There are constraints or limits on the extent to which the depository institutions can go in creating money in this manner. The Central Bank, the Federal Reserve System in the United States, is empowered by relevant acts of Congress to specify the magnitude of the "reserves" that the depository institutions must maintain against the deposit liabilities they have created. Such reserves are held principally in the form of accounts at the Federal Reserve Bank. By varying such reserve requirements, or by taking action to change the amount of reserves possessed by the depository institutions, the Central Bank discharges its responsibility for monetary policy. Monetary policy should be implemented in such a manner, of course, as to take account of the economic conditions that exist and are expected to exist in the time period ahead, notably with respect to price levels, unemployment, interest rates, international exchange rates, and achievable rates of economic growth.

Against this background we shall look in the following sections at certain foundational theological considerations and a number of biblical principles that can structure our approach to monetary and banking policy. We shall then conclude with a comment on some specific questions that might well engage our further consideration.

THEOLOGICAL FOUNDATIONS

The theological foundational propositions, or the issues of biblical doctrine, in which our analysis is grounded intersect with those that are relevant to many other parts of this series of studies. Our thought structures in relation to monetary and banking policy are tethered to the revelatory moorings that can be summarized under the headings of Creation, creaturehood, and the implications of economic stewardship; human solidarity; the Fall and the ravage of sin; and the institution and the implied economic functions of the state.

Creation—Contemporary thought is not hospitable to the idea, certainly not to the fact, of Creation and the sovereignty of the Creator-God. The broad movement of humanist-evolutionist thought of the late nineteenth century consolidated the assumptions of human autonomy and led to the exclusion of externally provided norms. Holding, however, to the revelatory datum that "the worlds were framed by the word of God" (Heb. 11:3), the Christian acknowledges the createdness of reality and the covenantal obligations that man's creaturehood imposes on him. The structure of creation reality implies that integral to it was an economic dimension of human awareness, which is evident in the earliest creation mandate: "God created man in his own image . . . male and female. . . . And God blessed them, and God said unto them, Be fruitful, and multiply, and replenish the earth, and subdue it: and have dominion over . . . every living thing" (Gen. 1:27-28). Here man is established as a viceregent under his Maker, and the task is entrusted to him of expanding, unfolding, and working out the meaning-potential of the entire created reality or environment in which he was placed.

The economic obligation under which man came to self-realization and which is implicit in the creation-developmental mandate is summarized under the heading of stewardship. Man was constituted a steward under God, charged with the right and responsible administration of the property of God entrusted to him. This stewardship in the economic realm carries along with it obligations that are best summarized under the headings of work and development. The ordinances of work and of property stewardship were supplemented by two features that have come to significant expression in the post-Fall state of human affairs. We may refer to these under the headings of differential endowments, on the one hand, and solidarity or interdependence on the other.

Cain, for example, was an agriculturalist, and Abel was a pastoralist (see Gen. 4:3-4). Jabal, one of the sons of Adah in the line of Cain, was again a pastoralist, "the father of such as dwell in tents, and of such as have cattle" (Gen. 4:20). His brother Jubal, on the other hand, engaged in the cultural activity of the provision of music, being "the father of all such as handle the harp and organ" (Gen. 4:21). Tubal-cain, his half brother, specialized in metalworking; he was "an instructor of every artificer in brass and iron" (Gen. 4:22). The gradual expansion of the economic implications of such differential endowments can be observed throughout the early chapters of Genesis until, by the time of the attempted construction of the Tower of Babel, a remarkable and highly developed and diversified industrialization had been achieved (see Gen. 11).

The contemporary relevance of these considerations rests not only in the development of a complex, interdependent market and exchange system of the kind we have already mentioned. Their implications protrude to larger questions of economic organization and policy. The creation mandate imposes on us the obligation to conserve the economic resources entrusted to us, including, most notably, the resources of employable manpower, and to dedicate them to the development of reality to the glory of God and to the benefit of the population at large. In regard to our present subject we may thus make at least two statements. First, the blessing and the sanctity of work call for profound respect, and the wastage of men and the violation of their dignity that results when the functioning of the economic system leaves them involuntarily unemployed cannot be easily countenanced by Christian consciences. Second, the objective of economic growth and development, taking along with it a rational evaluation of the true economic costs of growth, cannot be easily set aside in the light of the distress and anguish and blight in which too large a proportion of the population is bound.

The efficient functioning of the market system and the effective employment of men and other resources, on the one hand, and the ongoing development of economic systems and production possibilities, on the other, take up two central issues of monetary policy.

Solidarity and individuality—The theological doctrine of the sanctity of the individual is to be held in tension with that of human solidarity. The demands of solidarity are not exhausted by a simple cognizance of the federal headship of Adam or by the fact that in his fall he dragged the race into sin (see Rom. 5:12). The implications of the latter will engage us in the following section. Inherent in the creation structures was a solidarity of social relationship that clearly projects its imperatives to economic affairs.

The principle of solidarity is starkly apparent in God's address to Cain. The blunt interrogation, "Where is Abel thy brother?" (Gen. 4:9), expands its meaning to a broader social and cultural level than that of simply a familial relationship. The notion of solidarity is projected in the apostolic injunction, "Bear ye one another's burdens" (Gal. 6:2), and in the warrant that we are to "do good unto all men," though that is expanded by the significant "especially unto them who are of the household of faith" (Gal. 6:10). "Look not every man on his own things," the same apostle observed, "but every man also on the things of others" (Phil. 2:4). For economic affairs, the fact of human solidarity comes to expression on an initial and minimum level in the necessity we have observed for efficiently functioning markets and exchange procedures. In this direction, and in the degree of interdependence it envisages, each individual's economic self-realization is warranted, but it is to be countenanced and protected in the light of the parallel creation reality of the sanctity of individual worth and property.

The responsibilities of individual stewardship and of personal activity and development are intrinsic to the creation mandate. It would accordingly be an inversion of the created order to permit the rights and prerogatives of individuals on the economic level to be usurped by collectivities or by institutions of a governmental or quasigovernmental kind. Nevertheless, the functioning of the economic system in its present fallen state will not always be such that, if left completely to itself, every individual's personal welfare will be automatically guaranteed. It has been observed already that the malfunctioning of the system may give rise to involuntary unemployment, even at times to prolonged and structural unemployment in certain geographical areas and among certain demographic groups. In such instances the biblical considerations of solidarity point to the need for remedial or compensatory economic policy action, and at precisely that point, issues of a national monetary policy again come into focus.

These conclusions, and the biblical imperatives from which they derive, bear on the condition of the poor and the ameliorative measures that might be addressed to it. Our comments on this point can be minimal in view of John Mason's brilliant and definitive discussion in his "Biblical Teaching and Assisting the Poor," *Transformation* (April-June 1987). But plenty of reason exists to conclude that poverty can be expected to result from the failure of the economic system to adjust rapidly enough to changes in the economic environment and to variations in the demands for commodities and employment.

There are more reasons than might have been imagined to give credence to our Lord's observation that "ye have the poor always with you" (Matt. 26:11). A particularly keen comment of one Old Testament writer is that "when the righteous are in authority, the people rejoice: but when the wicked beareth rule, the people mourn" (Prov. 29:2). The same focus on the condition and the status of the poor has structured in many instances the complaints of the prophets against the economic practices of the time. Isaiah, for example, presses the economic need to "loose the bands of wickedness, to undo the heavy burdens, and to let the oppressed go free . . . to deal thy bread to the hungry, and . . . bring the poor that are cast out to thy house" (Isa. 58:6-7). The writer of Proverbs asserts, "The righteous considereth the cause of the poor: but the wicked regardeth not to know it" (29:7), and "The poor and the deceitful man meet together: the LORD lighteneth both their eyes. The king that faithfully judgeth the poor, his throne shall be established forever" (29:13-14).

Provision was made in the Old Testament theocracy for interest-free compassionate loans to the poor (see Exod. 22:25). The Proverbs observes again, "He that hath pity upon the poor lendeth unto the LORD; and that which he hath given will he pay him again" (Prov. 19:17). Moreover, the reinterpretation of the Old Testament ethic in the teaching and parables of our Lord has left a similar deposit of concern for the poor. The biblical ethic projects its imperatives forward to the present time, and monetary policy has clear responsibilities in this connection. It needs to take action to provide the economy with a sufficient and sufficiently flexible money supply to permit the highest possible level of economic activity and employment, a stable rate of economic development, and a rate of interest that permits and facilitates sustained investment and other expenditures. It thereby makes a highly important, if indirect, contribution to the prevention of the distress and indignity of poverty or to its alleviation when it occurs.

The Fall and the ravage of sin—The fact of the economic dimension is due to our finitude; the form of the economic problem is due to our sin. The fatal breach, Adam's fall that brought man into a new relation with God, has profound implications for a right view of our economic affairs. Now, as a result of Adam's fall, we live in a fallen and sinful society. Therefore, we have to work with the economics and with the scope and objectives of monetary policy of a fallen society.

At this stage we do not have the luxury of legislating for an economic structure or an economic policy that would be suitable to the administration of a theocracy, such as that under which God's people of old existed. Nor do we have the luxury of legislating for the economics of a contemplated millennium in which righteousness abounds and where economic relations are impeccably determined by the mandates of the law of God. We live, quite simply, in a fallen society. As Christian thinkers and Christian participants, we must understand the economics of a fallen society and address our analysis to it. With all of its incongruencies, complexities, and institutional structures, it nevertheless affords the Christian scope to explain the manner in which it may be continually reformed to bring it into closer accordance with the requirements of the law of God.

To attempt to understand contemporary society or its economic dimension and expressions without the benefit of the biblical doctrine of sin is intellectual criminality of the highest order. The implications for our present inquiry of the fallen societal conditions lie precisely in the shattering of the primeval harmony, for that is the meaning of sin. Sin is always the shattering of harmony, always the inversion of God's order. In our economic affairs, harmony can no longer be naturally and automatically expected to exist. The considerations and expression of self-interest and of selfishness, though self-interest does not necessarily imply selfishness, call in serious question the possibility of automatic harmonies and the inevitable realization of maximally attainable economic welfare and benefits. Of course, it is vital to take account of the operation of God's providence and the working of His common grace in the economic sphere. Some authors, writing from a purportedly Christian perspective, have gone so far as to base virtually their entire economic and market theory on the proposition that the common grace of God so harnesses and directs the self-interested actions of sinful men that harmonious outcomes do inevitably occur. Adam Smith's "invisible hand" is here baptized in theological terms.

It may be thought preferable to conclude, on the contrary, that if left completely to themselves, in the traditions of what we referred to previously as *laissez faire*, economic arrangements may well produce concentrations of exploitable economic power. Such concentrations of power, and the exploitation of them for narrowly conceived self-interests, may occur, and have occurred, in industrial corporations, in trade unions and similar combinations among the suppliers of labor, and in the government in the exercise of its economic functions. Such exploitations are capable of producing, and have produced, significant inequalities and inequities, though again inequality does not necessarily imply inequity, in the distribution of income and wealth. Such inequalities may be thought to be, on every reasonable ground, unrelated to the basic inequality of individual endowment and opportunity that we noticed previously when we referred to the differential endowments inherent in the creation structures.

The institution of the state—In considering the prerogatives and responsibilities of the state, we understand that it exists for the right ordering of affairs in the economic as in other spheres of societal experience. But our argument in no sense depends on a humanistic or an elitistic viewpoint that claims some kind of abstract superior competence, in some relevant economic sense, of a social collectivity. We do not begin our thinking about the state and its economic administration from the standpoint that a government bureaucracy can achieve, by some form of socioeconomic engineering, a maximum good for society as a whole, however that may be defined, superior to what could be realized in any other way.

We observe quite simply that following the Adamic fall, it was necessary that God should ordain, as part of the expression of His common grace, a method of organizing and ordering human affairs in accordance with His precepts of right behavior. Here we find the origin of the state and its delegated possession of power. The state does not exist by virtue of a contract between men in the manner of Rousseau, or as an agreed means of preserving certain rights of personal property in the manner of Locke. Nor does it exist, as Thomas Hobbes said, as a means of making tolerable the societal life of man, without which his life is "solitary, poor, nasty, brutish, and short." The state, to the contrary, exists because it has been ordained by God (see Rom. 13:1), and it exists for the right ordering of human affairs under the enlightenment of the precepts God has clearly set forth.

Israel of old was established as a theocratic nation, as the Pentateuchal evidence clearly indicates. But Edward Young points out that the book of Judges "serves to show that the theocratic people need a righteous king. Without a king who reigns under the special authority of God, confusion follows." (*An Introduction to the Old Testament* [Grand Rapids, Mich.: Eerdmans, 1964], page 170.) The concluding statement of the book of Judges observes, "In those days there was no king in Israel: every man did that which was right in his own eyes."

We are here concerned not to develop a political theory but simply to note that the "confusion" to which Young has just referred had a demonstrable economic dimension. This, unfortunately, continued to be the case, as the prophets were forced to observe repeatedly (see Isa. 5:8; Amos 8:4-6; Zech. 7:9-10). It follows that the proper responsibilities of the state are not exhausted until their economic aspects are adequately considered. It remains for Christian thought to wrestle rigorously with understanding the manner in which the societal "confusion" to which Young has referred comes to expression on the economic level. And it remains, then, to consider with corresponding care the manner in which, in the light of the biblical imperatives, the Christian doctrine and the Christian ethic point to ways in which ameliorative and corrective action might be taken.

POLICY PROBLEMS AND BIBLICAL PRINCIPLES

We are now in a position, in view of our understanding of the structure of the monetary economy and the biblical-theological foundations we have examined, to consider directly the task and compass of monetary and banking policy and the relevance of biblical principles to it.

In the United States the locus of responsibility for monetary policy or, as economists refer to it, the monetary authority is the Federal Reserve System (generally referred to as the Fed). This legally and technically independent body, constituted by an act of Congress, in effect functions as a quasigovernmental institution. This follows from the power of appointment of the members of its Board of Governors that is vested in the President and from other provisions related to the Boards of Directors of the twelve regional Federal Reserve Banks making up the system. At times, the policy actions of the Fed appear to have been influenced by national political considerations. But in general, the independence of the Fed has been jealously guarded.

Leaving aside the technicalities of its operations, the general scope of monetary policy can be defined by saying that it refers to any action taken by the Fed to influence the cost and availability of money. The Fed's actions can influence the terms on which bank and other financial institutional loans are available. In the course of doing this, it has an impact on the rate of interest in the money market. When the Fed buys or sells securities in the market, it influences their market value and the yield or rate of interest implicit in that value. The Fed can vary the rate of interest at which it is prepared to lend funds to the depository institutions. The Fed can also use its regulatory authority to designate the level of reserves that the depository institutions are required to maintain against their deposit liabilities.

Monetary policy is designed to have an effect on at least six important economic variables: (1) the level of economic production and activity; (2) the level of employment or unemployment in the economy; (3) the general commodity price level or the purchasing power value of money; (4) the rate of interest; (5) the achievable and maintainable rate of economic growth; and (6) the international exchange rate, or the international value of the country's currency, and the international capital flows and the balance of payments associated with it. The following minimal comments on these questions, while they will take up issues we have already raised, are designed to open the way for more expanded discussion and the application of relevant biblical principles.

We have observed the potential instabilities, dislocations, disequilibria, and the absence of automatic harmonies in the national economy, and we have noted the relevant biblical concept of solidarity. Monetary policy needs to be alert to the requirements of the economy for money supplies at a cost and on terms that will be likely to correct instabilities. That the market economy is capable of, and has in the past exhibited, quite serious fluctuations, and that it can generate, and has in fact generated, unconscionable levels of involuntary unemployment is clear on the briefest inspection of the relevant data.

The relevance of monetary policy for the general commodity price level and its impact on the purchasing power value of money bring to sharp focus the biblical requirements of justice and equity we have considered in this connection. Here, most notably, we confront the problem of inflation. By this we mean a rise, and at times a continuing rate of increase, in the price level. The causes and the costs and the possible cures of inflation have engaged the best economic minds at seemingly inordinate length without the achievement of a clear consensus. For many, inflation is thought simply to be "always and everywhere a monetary phenomenon." Many Christian commentators appear to have been captivated by such thought forms. The argument follows that if inflation is a purely monetary phenomenon, it can be corrected by purely monetary means. If the excessive creation of money is arrested, it is claimed, inflation will be arrested. Some authors have argued from this starting point that a return to the gold standard is required as a means of imposing what they consider the necessary monetary discipline. The Old Testament phenomenon of metallic money forms is at times invoked in this connection. But leaving aside the technicalities of the gold standard and the reasons for its ineffectiveness, we can find the deeper meaning of inflation and the relation of the money supply to it on other levels.

Commodity prices in large and quantitatively significant sectors of the economy are not determined by the freely functioning forces of supply and demand in atomistically competitive markets. They are set by producers, primarily with reference to their costs of production and possibly with reference to price levels set by dominant or "price-leader" firms in their industries. The biblical injunctions directed to justice, equity, fairness, and integrity impinge on the industrialist's setting of his profit margin markup over costs that determines his selling price (see Exod. 20:15; Lev. 19:13; Mal. 3:5; Luke 16:13; Col. 4:1; James 5:4). The prophet's complaint against monopolistic concentration (see Isa. 5:8) also touches the issue.

The responsibility of monetary policy, therefore, is not as simple as that of restricting the creation of money on the grounds that it directly determines the price level. Indeed, any abrupt reduction of the money supply is likely to impact most directly not on the price level at all, but on the level and strength of the expenditure streams in the economy and thereby on the level of economic activity and employment. Money, we can say, comes into existence substantially in response to the demand for it. That demand may, it is true, be the result of the desire and the attempt to make excessive expenditures, such as the excessive government expenditures in the United States in the 1980s. At that time federal government budget deficits on the order of $200 billion per annum were realized, and during the first eight years of that decade, the total national debt increased to almost three times its previous level. Excessive expenditures imply a demand-induced inflationary pressure. But the causal explanation is to be seen in those expenditure decisions, not primarily in the creation of money that follows from them.

Similarly, inflationary price pressures follow from an increase in industrial costs, such as those that result from an increase in wage and income payments in excess of the increase in industrial productivity. The biblical ethic directed to greed and inequity is relevant to such developments. But again, an increase in the money supply will follow from the increased demands for money that such phenomena make necessary. Such an increase must occur if the industrial economy is to have sufficient money to finance the previously existing level of production and employment at the new, higher, cost-induced price levels that result from the wage pressure. Monetary policy is then faced with the question of whether action should be taken to permit an increase in the money supply to accommodate the increased demand. If the choice is made to constrain rather than increase the money supply, the cost of money, or the rate of interest, can be expected to rise, expenditure streams will be diminished, and lower activity levels and higher unemployment will ensue. The complexities of the economic structure are such, and the scope at numerous points for the application of the biblical ethic is such, that no simple or short answer setting out the biblical prescription for monetary policy is possible.

Comparable complexities protrude their significance for monetary policy when we consider the remaining objectives we have referred to. Questions directed to the appropriate rate of interest, which is implicit in the preceding comments, the preservation of growth rates that will satisfy the biblical mandate for economic development, and the appropriate international exchange rate can be evaluated in the light of the biblical data. How, for example, do policies on these various levels affect the welfare and benefits of individuals or classes of individuals in different sectors of the economy? How do they influence the distribution of income, wealth, and welfare? Do they point to inflationary increases in prices and thereby offend against the Eighth Commandment? Do they cause such redistributions of income and wealth, from fixed income earners to variable income earners, from the old to the young, from the private sector to the public sector, from the future to the present (by reducing saving and investment and increasing present consumption), that offend against the prohibition of theft, against the ethic directed to the state and condition of the poor, against canons of equity and economic justice, or against the mandate for balanced and sustainable economic development?

Not all expressions of economic theory countenance the need for intervention by responsible societal and governmental authorities to correct imbalances or to preserve an economic climate in which the market mechanisms can function to maximum advantage. For those economists whose perceptions of the world see automatic market harmonies at work, and for those Christian commentators who subscribe to their analysis, economic and monetary policy of the kind we have referred to is unnecessary and irrelevant. For them, market adjustment forces work with high velocity, and interventionist action at the policy level is calculated to do more harm than good. For the so-called new classical economics, with its arguments for rapid adjustment velocities generated by what are referred to as rational expectations, and its claim that a natural rate of unemployment exists and is not able to be dislodged by monetary policy, the policy concerns we have referred to are irrelevant. The technical arguments cannot be rehearsed at this point. But doubt can be cast on their robustness and their adequacy to enlist the unswerving support of Christian sympathies.

In fact, the need for monetary policy action to contribute to economic stability has come very much to the fore at the time of this writing (August 1989). In the United States the Chairman of the Board of Governors of the Fed has observed in congressional testimony that an easing of the monetary situation, an increase in the money supply, and a lowering of the level of interest rates may now be necessary to offset a possible slackening of economic activity and a lowering of the rate of economic growth. In England at this time monetary policy discussion has similarly envisaged a lowering of interest rates, although the recent evaluation of Britain's economic position by the Organization for Economic Cooperation and Development has suggested that it might not be advisable to lower interest rates there too far too soon, in the light of certain international and exchange rate implications.

Our discussion to this point has focused principally on the meaning and scope for a biblical critique of the issues of monetary policy. It should be noted, also, that on more detailed and technical levels, issues arise in the matter of banking policy. By that we refer to two points. First, the Congress has from time to time passed legislation that impacts on the competitive structure of the banking and financial institution industry, and it has thereby influenced the mechanisms by which the creation of money can occur. Second, the Fed and other agencies such as the Federal Deposit Insurance Corporation and the Comptroller of the Currency have authority to regulate the activities of the banks in several ways. They can and do make regular inspections of the books and the lending activities of the banks to determine the appropriateness of the risks they are undertaking in view of their responsibilities to their depositors; they regulate the conditions under which banks and other financial institutions may merge, possibly by forming holding companies and diversifying their activities; they have had authority from time to time to regulate the terms on which bank loans can be made, in connection, for example, with stock exchange security purchases, real estate investment, and retail sales credit. Room exists for consideration from Christian perspectives of the rightness of preserving or encouraging a high degree of competitiveness in the banking and financial industry at the same time the authorities discharge their responsibility to maintain order and equity in economic-financial arrangements and market potentials.

THE OVERRIDING ISSUE

Biblical data and theological principles—and Christian thought securely informed by them—need urgently to be brought to bear on the structures and practices of the highly complex monetary-financial economy. At the most basic level we have seen the relevant issues to expand from the biblical doctrines of Creation, stewardship, solidarity, the Fall and the ravage of sin, and the data pertaining to the institution of the state and its implied economic function and responsibility. The issues that protrude from these foundational principles point to deep considerations of human welfare, economic and civic righteousness, and the proper development of the meaning of creation reality God has mandated.

These issues impinge forcefully, in turn, on the preservation of righteous cultural and economic constructions so that by the grace of God the interests of His Church in the world will be protected and advanced. If it is true, as the biblical data attest, that the Lord of history eventuates all things by His grace in such a way that the destiny of His Church will be secured and His name will be honored and glorified, we are called to the high office of participating in understanding and developing economic affairs to this end. Relying on the apostolic acknowledgment (see 2 Cor. 3:5) that we are not "sufficient of ourselves to think anything as of ourselves; but our sufficiency is of God," may we be, by His grace, in mutual humility and forbearance, worthy of that task.

EDITOR'S PERSPECTIVE

Doug Vickers was right when he noted at the beginning of his chapter that its very title raises perhaps the most fundamental question of all: Should there be a set of national policies governing monetary and banking concerns, or should we follow a *laissez faire* policy where only the free market forces are in effect? There is a normative aspect to the question, and a pragmatic dimension to it as well. From my perspective, one should desire (normative) and seek (pragmatic) a full-blown *laissez faire* environment only in a utopian, pre-Fall set of conditions that do not exist.

The fallacy I perceive in the extended logic—logic not constrained by other equally true realities—of those who press hard for a truly *laissez faire* environment lies in the fact that the natural forces they rely on and speak of in the marketplace are *not* natural forces governed in the same manner as the laws of physical nature. Moral laws and physical laws—both being real and self-corrective—do not operate in the same way. Physical laws are not contending with fallen, perverted, self-oriented, and multifaceted personal wills capable of purposefully rejecting the normative boundaries designed for them. Moral laws, while existing under God's sovereign rule, are not subject to ultimate change but are pervertible by human choice. The laws of physics have no personal will and cannot choose to set themselves aside. People, on the other hand, can act both with and against God's expressed intentions. I do not wish to labor the point, but I believe this distinction is critical to the matter before us.

I have previously stated (*Biblical Principles and Economics: The Foundations*, pages 97-100, 113-115) that those who support a *laissez faire* philosophy certainly point us in a biblical direction when they remind us that we are moral choice makers, and that we should be given as much freedom as possible to exercise those choices. The phrase, "as much freedom as possible,"

120

however, should be understood to mean something short of absolute freedom or "unconstrained freedom." I believe that people in a community must impose some constraints on themselves for the public good. Accepting and realistically dealing with our fallen nature embody this necessity as far as I can determine.

If we accept the above argument, then let us have our honest differences regarding which government policies and actions do not go far enough and which ones go too far. No one else is authorized by God to finally speak for the public but those in the seats of government—the Church speaks *to* the public but not *for* the public.

Even if one rejects what I have said in the previous four paragraphs, it seems that the pragmatics of living in a pluralistic society as we do dictates that we ought to try to bring the operations of the existing public structures into as much conformity with God's revealed principles as possible. To be in the world but not of the world means we are to have and act upon a different set of values, principles, and truths. It does not, I believe, demand noninvolvement in the affairs of government. Joseph, Esther, and Daniel, I think, would agree with me.

Probably the biggest problem facing persons who sincerely desire to foster justice in the public arenas and marketplace is that of "guessing" how the market will respond to any intervention. A few people make a policy and see to its implementation. Millions of people evaluate it in light of their own perceived best interest and then act in their own best interest. The fundamental problem of predicting outcomes flows from the fact that human psychology manifests a mixture of personal perceptions entwined with a host of external events and forces of both a natural and a manmade character. The reactions of people and final outcomes are sometimes bewildering.

For example, even as I am writing this, the events currently taking place in the Communist bloc of nations would have been the stuff of absurd dreams if someone could and would have predicted them five years ago. The nature, rate, and force with which these philosophical, political, social, and economic changes have occurred are still too much for me to take in and digest so quickly. What do they mean for our domestic economic output, foreign trade, national defense, international banking, and other domestic public policies? What demands for change will they bring? Will those set free from state oppression know how to self-regulate their freedom?

Even closer to home, and a bit more historic, who would have believed in 1979 or 1980 that the next eight years would see the U.S. debt soar by $200 billion a year without its causing enormous inflation, bringing about a shortage of capital in the private sector, fostering high interest rates, and generally producing many economic problems, even in the short run? Hindsight provides us with many reasons why we got by during the 1980s with what we did, but foresight would hardly have encouraged such a "soft landing." (Some economic "prophets" still sing of doom in the wings, and it may come, but by the classical economic wisdom of twenty-five years ago, the predicted doom should have already been here and passed.) The point is simple. Bull and bear philosophies in the stock market, pessimistic and optimistic outlooks, panic and calm, and other outlooks reflect the state of our psyche, and that psyche serves as an accelerator and brake on the economic affairs of a nation (and the world). This very truth is one of the heaviest arguments used by persons supporting the *laissez faire* philosophy to justify their contention that the government should stay out of public policy insofar as it intervenes in the free exchanges of the marketplace.

Even as I face in the same direction as my *laissez faire* friends—toward personal freedom of choice—I still desire public policy that addresses justice in the marketplace because, as stated before, fallen people by their sin nature cause many of the economic injustices that occur in the freest of markets (and in the most controlled markets, too). It is not wrong, therefore, to seek justice whether we as Christians find ourselves operating in a controlled or a free market. Christians are called to seek justice first.

In closing this section, I want to comment on what I believe is the most fundamental biblical principle to be kept before us as we seek justice through public policy, and give one illustration of a publicized complaint registered by private parties when the principle was ignored and injustices resulted. I am referring to the principle of not being "respecters of persons," or of not giving certain people special advantages. This very fundamental aspect of justice is equity. If public justice is not fair, evenhanded, and equitable, it sheds the garb of justice and puts on the robe of legal privileges for the favored few—an abuse of public power. Favoritism and similar unfair activities are incompatible with public justice.

The complaint is against the Board of Governors of the Federal Reserve System and the Securities and Exchange Commission, arms of the federal government dealing with the specifics of monetary and banking policy, the subject of Dr. Vickers' chapter. The comments are drawn from a one-page statement developed by Davenport & Co. of Virginia, Inc., from advertisements placed in the *Wall Street Journal*, the *New York Times*, and the *Investor's Daily* by Neuberger & Berman in October 1989. The Davenport statement was entitled "Stop the Numbers Racket on Wall Street" and contained the following material, which is representative of the entire document:

INSIDER ADVANTAGES
The American people have always believed in fairness, in the idea that laws and regulations should apply equally to all. Program trading, however, is blatantly unfair and inequitable:

• Its players are allowed to buy and sell on a 5 percent margin. The margin for the average investor buying common stock is 50 percent.

• The program traders are hooked up directly to the New York Stock Exchange computers, enabling them to get their massive transactions in ahead of anyone else. The average investor has to stand in line.

• The program traders don't need to abide by the uptick rule when selling short. Anyone else who sells short can only do so when the stock has gone up a beat, not when it is down. This prevents economic avalanches. Program traders, on the other hand, can sell short on the way down, which is the equivalent of pressing the accelerator of a runaway truck to the floor.

WE RECOMMEND THAT:

1. The Securities and Exchange Commission immediately revoke the exemption from the uptick rule that it inexplicably gave program traders in 1986, and
2. the Federal Reserve take responsibility for index futures margin requirements and immediately increase them to 50 percent, the same level as for common stocks.

The more basic question is, Should the federal government be involved in the regulation of the securities markets? Do we need a public policy in such an area of economic activity? In an area as important to the overall economic health of a people as its opportunities to invest in the capital markets of the world, and where position, proximity, financial size, information, and other factors make such a difference in peoples' opportunities to compete on a level playing field, public rules and oversight are justified. The same could be said for each of the six public policy areas Dr. Vickers outlined in his chapter—the level of economic production and activity; the level of employment; and so on. A communitywide interest in each of these areas as well can be enhanced—justice fostered—through public policy.

PART VI

TAXATION: AN INSTRUMENT FOR JUSTICE

Modern governments not only create and regulate monetary policies but also formulate and execute fiscal policies—policies relating to the taxation and redistribution of wealth in a political entity. Taxation, the revenues dimension of fiscal policy, is the subject of this section. The aspect of fiscal policy concerned with the redistribution of wealth is subsumed (part of it) in other chapters dealing with public welfare, agricultural policy, national security, and so forth.

Taxation (and all public policies) should *first* have a regard for justice—equity, righteousness, fairness, and rights. The concern for the *rights* of the people is somewhat tougher to define, protect, and provide than some other aspects of justice, especially when we are wrestling with the rights of the disadvantaged people in a population. It is tough because our emotions can get ahead of our deeper understanding of needed biblical truths, and the compassion of individual (and collective) public servants can usurp the role of justice in the public areas. Dr. Henry called this problem "the hoax of the welfare state."

On the other hand, justice and compassion are not incompatible attributes of character and behavior. After all, God is always just, and He is filled with compassion. Justice does not require compassion. Compassion, on the other hand, cannot set aside justice or ever create an injustice, either directly or indirectly, and be genuine, godly compassion. Public policy may have a compassionate consequence—meet a true need of the beneficiary—but justice, and not compassion, must be the touchstone of public policy.

Dr. John Anderson has done an outstanding job of keeping the concept of compassion, as it relates to fiscal policy, subordinated to the more fundamental requirements of justice. He has not ignored the tension possible between justice and compassion, but neither has he forgotten compassion as if it is inherently incompatible with justice. His careful placement of compassion under the banner of justice is important for two reasons.

First, people in public office should not assume that they are compassionate because they are involved in the process of taxing the general citizenry and redistributing the proceeds to others. No personal righteousness or personal compassion is associated with such an act. No "Robin Hood" ethic in Scripture stores up treasures in Heaven to the credit of the tax collector and those who redistribute wealth. The public official who is just and fair to all citizens is the righteous governor.

Second, compassion that is not circumscribed by justice in the public arena can quickly bring about new evils as repugnant as the wrong the so-called compassionate behavior purports to rectify. Empathy, sorrow, sympathy, pity, and compassion are heartfelt affections that manifest aspects of the human potential wonderful to behold, but they are not innately endowed with the capacity to address issues of comparative equity and fairness.

John Anderson's chapter is beautifully balanced and needs to be read carefully because most of us generally come to the subject of taxation with strong negative biases. We are not, for example, in the habit of thinking about whether or not a tax is efficient and nondistorting—a tax that does not cause people to take actions distorting economic decisions in an effort to avoid or take advantage of the tax laws. Issues like these need to be thought through if we are to evaluate the equity of a tax system, though. The chapter is intellectually stretching but vital to the whole proposition that public policy is a legitimate dimension of any government's overall responsibility as set forth by the Scripture.

CHAPTER 6

BIBLICAL PRINCIPLES APPLIED TO FEDERAL, STATE, AND LOCAL TAXATION POLICY

John E. Anderson

Dr. John E. Anderson is Professor of Economics at Eastern Michigan University where he teaches public finance and urban economics. His scholarly research and publications have focused on issues of property and income taxation and urban development. Professor Anderson has been active in the policy arena as well, having served as Deputy State Treasurer of Michigan. His responsibilities in that role made him the principal adviser to the Governor and the State Treasurer on issues of tax policy. He earned his Ph.D. in Economics at Claremont Graduate School in 1977. He has also been a visiting Associate Professor at Michigan State University.

I t has been said that the only sure things in life are death and taxes. But that is surely not true from the Christian perspective. We know that Christ has triumphed over death. That leaves us with one sure thing in life—taxes. Taxes must be paid to the federal government, making April 15 an important date on our calendars—perhaps eclipsing Easter in importance if measured by the time we allocate to preparation for the two events. Taxes must also be paid at various times of the year to the state, city, county, school district, water district, library district, and a host of other governments. With such a complex and overlapping system of governments, what basic biblical principles can be applied to the design of tax policy? That is our question and the focus of the comments in this chapter.

The following discussion attempts to integrate biblical principles with sound tax policy in the context of a well-developed Western economy with several levels of government. This task is difficult since tax policy alone, aside from integrating biblical principles, is a complex and controversial topic. The Bible has very little to say directly about taxes, but it has much to say about justice and equity. As a measure of the difficulty of these issues, consider that the U.S. Catholic Bishops, who have shown little reluctance to make controversial policy suggestions, refrained from citing specific tax policy recommendations in their Pastoral Letter. They said, "We recognize the extreme complexities of tax policy and do not wish to offer extensive policy suggestions in this area."[1] They did, however, identify two principles they felt should be incorporated in any tax reform proposals. First, taxes on the poor should be eliminated or offset, and second, the principle of progressivity (taxes as a fraction of income rising with income) should be a guiding norm. I will begin with a broad overview of the public sector and the role of taxes and then proceed to specific policy recommendations motivated by biblical principles.

First, we must consider this question: Does the biblical witness specify a certain set of tax policies that are optimal? I believe not. What about the more general question of whether the Bible prescribes one economic system as normative? John Stott has said that the biblical witness balances realism between humanistic optimism and existential pessimism. Capitalism attracts Christians because it takes the Creation seriously—people take initiative and create wealth in this system. But capitalism is repulsive to Christians as well for its focus on greed and its minimal interest in the weak and poor. On the other hand, socialism takes the Fall seriously—priority is given to the poor and concern focuses on equitable distribution. But socialism repels Christians as well due to its focus on government that chokes human inventiveness.[2]

Does the Bible specify a normative economic system? I think not. Stephen Charles Mott has put the difficulty of interpretation in this context this way:

> [A] form of anthropological insensitivity to the concreteness of Scrip-
> ture is to force it to answer questions brought to the text which are
> culturally foreign to it. The apologies which locate capitalism or social-
> ism in the Bible make this mistake.[3]

Rather, the Bible provides guidance for Christians engaging in economic roles and transactions, regardless of the specific political-economic institutional setting in which they find themselves. The Christian counterculture disfavors all modes of social and economic organization in a fallen world.[4]

Given that no clear preference is provided in Scripture for the broad form of an economic system, we will probably not find specific tax policies described— much less a full "theology of federal-state-local fiscal relationships." Rather than look for such a comprehensive theology, my comments focus on fundamental biblical principles that can be used to guide the design of tax policy.

WHY HAVE TAXES?

The existence of a tax or system of taxes presupposes the existence of a government or system of governments. As we consider biblical principles applied to taxation, we are operating within a presupposed system of governments—federal, state, and local (in the United States). But prior questions must be considered. First, what roles will government play in the economy? Second, which duties will be assigned to the various levels of government? In Western economies the traditional roles of government have come to include the functions of allocation, distribution, and stabilization.[5] The allocation function involves the decisions of allocation of resources to the production of goods, both public and private. Private goods are those we encounter in the marketplace—cars, VCRs, and clothing. Public goods are different in nature, being nonexcludable and nondepletable, and are consequently provided by governments. For example, a lighthouse is a public good since it is nonexcludable and nondepletable. If we build a lighthouse, we cannot exclude some sailing ships from using it while others use it. Also, its use by one sailor does not diminish its remaining usefulness to other sailors. When goods are nonexcludable and nondepletable, the private market mechanism will fail to allocate resources properly and will provide too few lighthouses. A role for government is clearly to provide goods that society values but the private market mechanism allocates too few resources to provide. Other examples of public goods include a clean environment, national defense, and education. Public goods are provided by all three levels of government—federal, state, and local.

The second role of government is the distribution function. This role involves changing the distribution of income and wealth to conform with an acceptable standard set by society. The economic system may reward some people (owners of factors such as land, labor, and capital) and fail to reward other people (the unemployed or subjects of various forms of discrimination) in ways that society finds unacceptable. If so, government may alter the distribution of income through various measures including progressive taxation of income or wealth. This function of government is generally assigned to the federal level since state or local policies to affect the income distribution have the effect of distorting economic activity, diverting resources into tax avoidance activity.

The third and final function of government is that of stabilization—assuring an economic situation with high levels of employment, stable prices, and adequate rates of economic growth. The federal government generally is assigned this role through its tools of macroeconomic policy. Fiscal and monetary policies are designed to accomplish economic stabilization and growth. Increasingly, however, state governments are playing a role in this area.

Given these functions, the role of a tax system is to enable the governments to provide public goods, alter the income/wealth distribution, and stabilize the economy. The level and the form of taxation are secondary. The tax system should be equitable (complying with our notions of fairness) and efficient (nondistorting to the economy). Equity involves both horizontal fairness (similar individuals are treated similarly by the tax system) and vertical fairness (different individuals are treated differently). A given tax is defined by both the tax base (what is taxed) and the tax rate (what proportion of the base is taken in tax). Consideration of a tax will involve both issues.

Christian views vary widely on the precise roles of government and the extent of activities justified in fulfilling these roles. From minimalist government roles advocated by conservative (speaking in economic terms) Christians to interventionist roles advocated by liberal Christians, years of debate have not resulted in a consensus among Christians any more than in the general populace. This investigation begins with the assumption that some government is needed, indeed ordained by God (see Rom. 13:1), and hence must be financed by taxes.

The focus is then on the biblical principles that guide tax policy, given that governments fulfill desired functions. In these matters, as well as others, we must avoid arguments from silence. For example, just because the Bible says nothing about value-added taxation does not mean that this form of taxation cannot be consonant with biblical principles.

BIBLICAL PRINCIPLE—RENDER TO CAESAR[6]

The first question to be examined centers on the payment of taxes. Is it biblical for a Christian to pay taxes to a secular government? Or does the Christian's "otherworldly" focus preclude the payment of taxes?

A principal scriptural passage used in conjunction with many discussions of Christian stewardship describes Jesus' encounter with the Pharisees when He said, "Render to Caesar the things that are Caesar's, and to God the things that are God's" (Mark 12:17, NASB). The issue dealt directly with the matter of taxation. The Pharisees wished to trap Jesus on an issue of taxation. Would He support such a graft-ridden system where the tax collector was the epitome of a sinner (see Luke 19:7)? The Pharisees asked, "Is it right to pay taxes to Caesar or not?" (Mark 12:14). Why was this such a difficult question for the Pharisees? Why was this the question they posed to trap Jesus? Jesus' reply tells us something about taxes; it also tells us something about Jesus.

The Romans had divided the kingdom of Herod the Great, king of the Jews, in 4 BC. The partitioned kingdom was then ruled by his three sons who received tax payments from Jewish citizens, just as Herod the Great had done. Although no one liked paying taxes, then as now, there was no religious issue involved since Herod's sons were Jewish. The area of Galilee, where Jesus lived, was ruled by Herod Antipas until AD 39. Archelaus was given authority, and his rule in Judea was very oppressive. In fact, when Joseph heard that Archelaus was reigning in Judea upon his return from Egypt with Mary and Jesus, "he was afraid to go there" (Matt. 2:22, NASB). After nine years the Roman emperor removed Archelaus and established Judea as a Roman province with a political appointee as governor. That meant the Judeans had to pay taxes to Caesar, the Roman emperor. The Roman equivalent of a millage election, a census, was held in AD 6 to determine the tax yield for the new province.

Jewish teaching had always held that it was right and proper to pay taxes to government officials. The prophets had taught that such tax payments acknowledged the divine will (see Ezra 7:21-23). A new teaching had begun to circulate about the time of the AD 6 census, however. The new teaching asserted that Yahweh alone was King of Israel and payment of taxes to a gentile ruler amounted to high treason against Him. This teaching is attributed to Judas the Galilean (see Acts 5:37). Payment of taxes to gentile rulers was not an issue for Jews in the lands of the Dispersion, but for those in "God's country" it was another matter. F. F. Bruce asks the question this way: "Was it right for God's people, living on God's land, to give a proportion of its produce to a pagan ruler? When it was framed in those terms, the obvious answer for many was 'No.'"[7]

Now it is clear why that was such a difficult question to ask Jesus. To answer that payment of the tax was appropriate would mean that Jesus would offend the followers of Judas the Galilean and others in Judea. He would appear to be unpatriotic. On the other hand, to answer that payment of the tax was inappropriate would mean that He would run up against the Roman authorities who would not appreciate His seditious teaching. The Pharisees had Him. Or so they thought.

Jesus' response was wonderfully simple yet tremendously profound. He asked for a coin—a Roman denarius with which such a tax would have been paid. He asked whose face and name appeared on the coin. The answer was Caesar's. Jesus' response was to say that the coin with Caesar's name and face on it was obviously Caesar's. Therefore, it should be given back to Caesar. F. F. Bruce notes that the verb usually translated "render" has the meaning of "giving back to someone that which belongs to him."[8] Jesus' answer could have implied implicit acknowledgment of Caesar's sovereignty. Did He mean that it was wrong to use money with a human likeness since it violated the commandment not to make graven images? Probably not. Jesus' teaching always held money in light enough regard that that is unlikely to have been His main point. More likely, Jesus was saying that for the people of God, intent on keeping God's law, that money was inappropriate. Use Caesar's coins to pay Caesar's taxes. What is important is to discover God's claims and assure that they are met. Jesus' primary focus was on God's Kingdom, not on an earthly kingdom.[9]

The above analysis describes payment of a civil tax, but Scripture also records Jesus' reaction to an ecclesiastical tax. Matthew 17:24-27 presents the account of the collectors of the Temple tax asking Peter whether Jesus paid the tax. He answered, "Of course" (v. 25, TEV). Jesus later posed the question to Peter: "Who pays duties or taxes to the kings of this world? The citizens of the country or the foreigners?" (v. 25, TEV). And Peter responded, "The foreigners" (v. 26, TEV). The implication drawn from his response was that Jesus and His disciples did not owe the tax since they were citizens of the king's country, but to avoid offending the Temple tax collectors, Jesus sent Peter to a nearby lake and instructed him to fish. He assured Peter that the first fish he would catch would contain a coin of sufficient value to pay the tax for both of them. The force of the argument is about citizenship in God's Kingdom, not about tax payment. But the event illustrates that Jesus paid the tax, perhaps even though He felt it was unjustified. Some observers of Jesus, however, interpreted His response as encouragement to avoid paying taxes (see Luke 23:2).

The biblical record provides evidence that Jesus paid both civil and ecclesiastical taxes. Of course, Scripture also teaches that God's laws are supreme, and when asked to violate God's law by obeying man's law, the Christian has no choice (see Acts 4:19). Nonviolent resistance, including tax resistance, may be appropriate. As an alternative, many Christians support legislative efforts to establish the World Peace Tax Fund into which tax payments may be made but out of which only nonmilitary expenditures may be appropriated. This approach enables Christians to fulfill their civil responsibility without supporting the misplaced trust of our government on military weaponry and nuclear arms (see Ps. 20:7; 44:6-7).

If Christians are generally to pay their taxes and participate in government structures that design tax systems, what biblical principles can be applied to tax policy issues? This is the question to which we now turn.

BIBLICAL PRINCIPLE—JUSTICE

Justice, and only justice, you shall follow, that you may live and inherit the land which the LORD your God gives you. (Deut. 16:20, RSV)

He has showed you, O man, what is good.
    And what does the LORD require of you?
To act justly and to love mercy
    and to walk humbly with your God. (Mic. 6:8)

"Woe to you, teachers of the law and Pharisees, you hypocrites! You give a tenth of your spices—mint, dill and cummin. But you have neglected the more important matters of the law—justice, mercy and faithfulness. You should have practiced the latter, without neglecting the former." (Matt. 23:23)

The preeminent biblical principle guiding the design of a tax system, indeed society in general, is the concept of justice.[10] Fairness is a first priority in establishing a Christlike policy of any type. Isaiah the prophet was given the message that the Lord had "looked for justice, but saw bloodshed; for righteousness, but heard cries of distress" (Isa. 5:7). Justice can be defined only in terms of a standard of righteousness. The Lord's standard is perfection. His justice is perfect and is consistent with His standard of righteousness. By His justice God is exalted (see Isa. 5:16). He requires Christians to follow His example and act justly as well. We must be just in our economic relationships, including tax policy and public service provision, and require justice of our leaders.

Psalm 72, written by Solomon, contains a vivid description of the characteristics of the ideal ruler:

Endow the king with your justice, O God,
  the royal son with your righteousness.
He will judge your people in righteousness,
  your afflicted ones with justice. (Ps. 72:1-2)

Such a ruler would levy taxes with fairness as a major component of their design. The problem, of course, is to define what is fair. The tax system and the distribution of services provided with those tax moneys should reflect a concern for justice. It is pointless to have a tax system that reflects biblical concerns for justice if the services provided by government are available only to the wealthy. For example, higher education could be funded through a flat rate income tax with a substantial exemption making the structure of the tax mildly progressive. But if access to universities is limited in ways that prevent children of low-income households from matriculating, injustice is done.

Modern public finance theory has several standards by which to judge the equity of a tax system. Those standards include measures of horizontal equity (treating equals equally) and vertical equity (treating unequals unequally). A good tax system should accomplish both goals, making sure that citizens with similar incomes pay similar taxes, but those with very different incomes pay very different levels of tax. However, policies designed to make a tax horizontally equitable may have the effect of making it vertically inequitable and vice versa. It is difficult, if not impossible, to have it both ways. For example, a homestead property tax exemption, advocated for reasons of vertical equity, poses problems from a horizontal equity point of view since it treats homeowners and renters differently.

Ronald Pasquariello has written a fivefold standard for evaluating a tax system from a Christian perspective.[11] He suggests that tax justice requires that we should (1) tax all income, (2) redistribute income, (3) be progressive, (4) be efficient, and (5) be simple. Each criterion is designed to coordinate with biblical principles of justice and *shalom*. Each principle needs further consideration, and the combination of the five principles must be studied as a whole. While I will not attempt a comprehensive critique of these principles, I list them to suggest that Christian thinking on taxation has provided a set of principles that can function as a benchmark against which proposed tax policies can be judged. These principles, in some ways redundant and in other ways self-contradictory, nevertheless provide a standard.

Another perspective on biblical justice involves viewing the individual within community. Dignity is found and nourished in the community of Christians, not in isolation (see James 2:1-13). As a result, my view of a just tax system must be incorporated in my view of the community, not simply in the size of my individual tax bill. We struggle with this balance between individual freedom and corporate responsibility both in economics in general and in tax policy in particular. John Maynard Keynes has said, "The political problem of mankind is to combine three things: economic efficiency, social justice, and individual liberty." Certainly the political difficulty in tax policy is just that. How do we design a tax system that is efficient (causing the least distortion to economic decision making) and just (meeting our collective standard of fairness and equity), and preserves individual freedom (not sacrificing the rights of the individual)? The Christian's specific concern is that biblical principles be applied in the challenge—applying biblical principles of efficiency related to stewardship of the earth's resources, biblical principles of justice in a clear regard for the poor, and biblical principles of human freedom in the design of a tax system.

WHAT STRUCTURE OF TAX RATES SHOULD BE USED?

Nowhere does Scripture specify the optimal tax rate that should be used to tax income, wealth, consumption, capital gains, or any of the other things a modern economic system taxes. What, then, can we cull from Scripture regarding tax rates? The magic number that first comes to mind is the 10 percent tithe. Since God specified that the tithe should be 10 percent, should we advocate a flat rate tax system wherever possible, further advocating that the optimal rate, regardless of base, be precisely 10 percent? Clearly not. Although some Christians take the tithe as a model for the policy recommendation that taxation should be the flat rate with the highest possible rate of 10 percent, this view is not an appropriate application of the scriptural principle.[12] The focus of the scriptural admonition to tithe (see, for example, Deut. 14:28) is that the community should support the weak and those lacking the means of production. The Levites lacked land—a primary factor of production in an agrarian society. The objective of tithing was that they may "eat and be filled" (Deut. 14:29, RSV). The further objective was that blessings of God would flow to those obedient in tithing. Mott suggests that the economist deduce from this passage "a principle that an adequate portion of private production be gathered for the needy rather than to focus upon the particular proportion appropriate for the Hebrew village."[13]

Aristotle suggested a taxation method providing proportionate geometric equality. Arnold McKee describes Aristotle as "somewhat the victim of the mathematical mysticism of his day" on this issue, however.[14] McKee recalls that Aquinas specified different forms of proportionate equality for an aristocracy, an oligarchy, and a democracy. Given our democratic context, he concludes,

> In modern mass democracy, where each person has an equal say in electing government and where accumulation of economic power subverts the system, it seems appropriate that taxation be levied in an approximately equal manner and that public goods be equally available to all.[15]

The challenge is to apply the traditional rules of ability to pay and the benefit principle to taxation. Here we run into difficulties in transforming the general principle to a specific policy prescription. If we require equal sacrifice from both low- and high-income persons, how do we measure the degree of sacrifice involved for each? If the tax being considered is an income tax, is a $100 reduction in income due to the tax worth more or less to a wealthy person than to a poor person? By whose estimation? Their own? If we assume that the marginal utility of that $100 is smaller for the wealthy person, a rough form of progressive taxation is justified. We should take a larger share of that person's income than a poor person's. But how progressive should the tax be? These are very difficult and complex problems. As an alternative, if we assume equal marginal utility of a dollar for all persons, equal sacrifice would mean equal proportions of income should be taken in tax. A flat rate tax would be prescribed.

Economic research on taxes is heavily shaped by the classical utilitarian theories. The fundamental objective from this point of view is to design tax policies that enhance happiness or well-being. Ultimately, income is the standard of measurement with a link assumed between income and happiness. Since taxes reduce income, which reduces utility in this framework, the focus centered on developing theories of equal, proportional, and minimal sacrifice.[16] Sacrifice was to reduce utility equally or by the same proportion for all taxpayers under the first two standards. The third standard, that of minimal sacrifice, was to reduce aggregate societal utility by the smallest possible amount for a given level of tax revenue raised. All three standards were investigated in the classical literature, but the minimal sacrifice standard became dominant.[17] It was subject to criticism on many counts, however, including the impossibility of measuring utility.[18] The most crushing blow to the minimal sacrifice standard comes not from its own inherent weakness; the problem is that when we combine such a concern for equity with a concern for efficiency—minimal disruption to the economy in terms of its output—we face a difficult tradeoff. Equity requires minimal sacrifice, which calls for highly progressive taxes, but efficiency requires equal sacrifice, which calls for highly regressive taxes. In modern economic theory the optimal taxation literature has tried to incorporate both concerns by focusing on the labor-leisure choice problem, acknowledging that leisure provides utility and that taxation of income involves a disincentive to work. The resultant policy prescriptions from this literature recommend mildly progressive tax structures.

From the Christian perspective, such models lack relevance since Christ calls us to be disciples and find our fulfillment in Him and in Him alone. We enjoy material blessings that provide some measure of happiness or utility, but to model our objectives as solely consisting of income or wealth accumulation is to ignore the tenets of Scripture. Does this mean that classical or neoclassical theories of taxation are irrelevant in discussing biblical principles of tax policy? Certainly not. We live in a fallen world in which the truth has been exchanged for a lie (see Rom. 1:25). Utility maximization is a good characterization of the fallen objective functions we collectively have as a society.

BIBLICAL PRINCIPLE—COMPASSION

The ideal ruler described in Psalm 72 would also be compassionate:

> For he will deliver the needy who cry out,
>   the afflicted who have no one to help.
> He will take pity on the weak and the needy
>   and save the needy from death.
> He will rescue them from oppression and violence,
>   for precious is their blood in his sight. (Ps. 72:12-14)

It is clear from Scripture that God has, and requires Christians to have, a special regard for the poor. The biblical concept of justice includes compassion—an extraordinary concern for the poor.[19] God is not biased in favor of (or against) any person or group of people.[20] An economic system takes care of the wealthy, however, and disregards the powerless, the widow, the sojourner, and the alien (see Lev. 25:35; Deut. 26:12). God's concern for these people is evident in Scripture.[21] As a result, tax policy should provide such concern as well. Does that mean the poor should pay no taxes? Not necessarily. Scripture also teaches personal responsibility and requires each individual to be account-able. It may mean that a poor person is asked to contribute a modest amount toward supporting the public programs benefiting all while a wealthy one is asked to contribute a more substantial sum. John Mason has studied the Old Testament system of assistance to the poor and concludes that reciprocity was an important element of those programs. The needy were obligated to work, and members of the community—the wealthy in particular—were obligated to provide assistance.[22] The design of a tax system should be just and embody compassion. The subsequent enforcement of such a tax system should then be perfectly just. Once compassion is built into the tax system, it is sufficient to be just (giving people their due) in its application.

If a tax system is to require lower rates of taxation of the poor than of the wealthy, this objective can be accomplished in two specific ways—through exemptions and credits. First, an exemption provides tax relief by reducing the taxpayer's tax base. The exemption of a flat amount of each person's portion of the tax base (whether it is real estate, income, consumption, or any other tax base) offers relief disproportionately to the poor. For example, a homestead property tax exemption of $10,000 of assessed value for all homeowners pro-vides greater tax relief to the low-income family with a $30,000 home (reduc-ing their tax by one-third) than to the wealthy family with a $300,000 home (reducing their tax by one-thirtieth). Second, a tax credit reduces the taxpayer's tax liability. For example, the state can grant an income tax credit for local property taxes paid. This credit can be expressed as a percentage of the dif-ference between the property tax paid and a designated threshold and has the effect of making the income tax more progressive and the local property tax less regressive.

A tax system should be just, reflecting fairness and compassion, and it should also be efficient—wasting few resources. The discussion now turns to issues of efficiency as required in our role as stewards of God's earth and its resources.

BIBLICAL PRINCIPLE— STEWARDSHIP OF EARTH'S RESOURCES

Another major biblical principle that should guide the design of tax policy from the Christian perspective is God's call to us to be stewards of His earth and its resources (see Ps. 24:1). From the Genesis account onward in Scripture, the responsibility given humans created in God's image is to be wise stewards of the resources provided (see Gen. 1:26-30). That stewardship includes the wise use of all resources—land, labor, and capital. Land is the broad term used by economists to include all landed resources: minerals, water, soil, air, and so on. Labor involves the use of time for market production. Its complement is time used for leisure activities. Capital includes both human (experience, knowledge, training) and nonhuman components (machinery, equipment, and buildings).

Within the broad command to be stewards of God's earthly resources lies the responsibility to not waste those resources. The economist likes to refer to that waste as an inefficient use of resources. We are to use resources efficiently, in harmony with the command of God to act justly. For example, a tax policy must be just in the senses already discussed, and it must not result in wasted time (labor) or other resources (capital or land) devoted to tax avoidance activity. To the extent that a tax policy encourages people to spend their time finding ways to evade the tax (legally), labor resources are being wasted. For example, if a state permits local governments to levy a property tax on inventories, merchants have an incentive to load their merchandise on a truck and drive it across the state line for Tax Day so that their assessment will be lower. The next day the truck can be driven back and unloaded. The tax has been avoided. Such a tax is clearly inefficient. Resources are used in tax avoidance activity rather than in productive use. Of even greater concern would be a tax policy that encouraged individuals to withhold their labor from the market, denying their God-given abilities from finding expression in creative activity (in God's image).

Of course, policies enhancing both equity and efficiency are welcomed. Robert Haveman has suggested that the efficiency-equity tradeoff concept may be inappropriate for many public policy questions since the presumption of a tradeoff precludes consideration of policies that improve both equity and efficiency.[23] A good example is the Tax Reform Act of 1986, which improved the equity of the federal personal income tax by closing numerous loopholes and improved the efficiency of the tax by lowering marginal tax rates, reducing the incentives to divert resources into tax avoidance rather than productive activity. The Tax Reform Act of 1986 has many flaws, but it represents a policy change that, on balance, improved the tax both ways.

Another aspect of doing justice in tax policy is requiring people and firms to be accountable in their actions that affect others. Within the allocative role of government lies the responsibility to discourage negative externalities and encourage positive externalities. Externalities, or spill-over effects, are economic effects that flow from one person's (or firm's) activity to another's. For example, when a person makes the private decision to drink alcoholic beverages, the result may affect others—when the drunken person decides to drive. Consequently, the private market fails to allocate resources properly, and we have too many drunks killing innocent people on the highways. One solution to the problem is to tax alcoholic beverages to force the consumers of the products to internalize the external costs otherwise imposed on others. A recent study of alcoholic beverages in particular suggests that the present level of taxation is about one-half of that needed to fully control the social costs of drinking.[24]

The Scriptures teach that the Christian is not to be drunk with wine but to be filled with the Holy Spirit (see Eph. 5:18). A Christian view of tax policy would then agree that external costs from drinking wine should be internalized with the appropriate tax. But this example can certainly be generalized. The broader principle is that activity generating external costs should be taxed while activity generating external benefits should be subsidized (a subsidy being a negative tax). An extension of this policy would suggest that honesty and fidelity should be subsidized by government while dishonesty and infidelity should be taxed. Such policy is an application of biblical principles but runs into administrative problems.

Business firms should also be held accountable for their externalities, or spill-over effects. Tax policy is surely part of the necessary solution in reducing negative externalities that occur as part of the production process. If an Exxon tanker spills millions of gallons of crude oil in Prince William Sound as part of the process of producing gasoline, then a tax increasing the firm's private marginal costs of production to equal society's marginal cost (including the cleanup expenses) is needed to bring about the proper allocation of resources. Such a tax would be only part of a comprehensive solution to the problem but is nevertheless part of the solution.

We must be careful, however, that such taxes are not used selectively, having disproportionate burden on specific groups of people. For example, a state lottery is a form of taxation that may be justified on the grounds of gambling's external effects, but it may have other consequences. For each dollar spent on lottery tickets, an average of forty-five cents is paid out in prizes in Michigan. That is a tax of 55 percent. In practice, lotteries are our most regressive forms of taxation. In Michigan, for example, the lottery has been estimated as being more than twice as regressive as the state's second most regressive tax—the sales tax.[25] Arguing that such regressivity is acceptable because the tax is voluntary is vacuous. The gasoline tax is voluntary, too. Earmarking the revenues from the lottery for school aid makes no difference since the state budget shell game does not assure that additional revenues will be allocated to schools. Since poor inner-city blacks bear the burden of the lottery tax, we must be concerned about its effects.

ANOTHER VIEW OF TAXATION—TAX EXPENDITURES

A discussion of taxes should consider what is taxed as well as what is not taxed. Tax expenditures are specific forms of exempt income or activity that reduce tax liability. The effect of exempting these forms of income and activity is equivalent to a direct expenditure for these items. A full view of the expenditures in the federal budget would include these tax expenditures, also.

The Congressional Budget Office estimates that tax expenditures amounted to some $361 billion in the 1988 budget compared to official budget receipts of $900 billion and outlays of $1,069 billion.[26] The major tax expenditures are (1) personal deductions on the income tax for state and local taxes paid, charitable contributions, medical expenses, and interest paid, (2) exclusions from taxable income for state and local bond interest, employee benefits, social security payments, veterans' benefits, and welfare, and (3) investment incentives in the form of tax credits and accelerated depreciation schedules.[27] For example, the deductibility of mortgage interest for homeowners reduces their tax liability by $19.9 billion.[28] This tax preference is equivalent to a direct federal expenditure in the amount of $19.9 billion to homeowners.

The distribution of benefits flowing from these tax expenditures merits attention. John Witte cites unpublished U.S. Treasury estimates of the benefits concluding that "the first obvious and overwhelming conclusion . . . is that the well-off benefit from tax expenditures is much more than those in lower income brackets."[29] Although half of the tax expenditures benefits were received by those with incomes in excess of $30,000 in 1977, that same year individuals with incomes of $30,000 or less accounted for 95 percent of the tax returns filed. While measures of the share of benefits received by a particular group are sensitive to the standard of comparison (whether benefits are measured relative to income, taxes paid, or other measures), Witte computes the shares several ways and notes,

> A very plausible set of conclusions is that: (1) the highest-income taxpayers get relatively more from tax expenditures, regardless of the equity standard; (2) the poor do very well relative to the taxes they pay; and (3) the middle class is disadvantaged by the aggregate tax expenditure system from any perspective.[30]

TAX REFORM ISSUES AND EXAMPLES

Henry Aaron and Harvey Galper summarized the state of the U.S. income tax system prior to the Tax Reform Act of 1986 as follows:

> The U.S. tax system has become a swamp of unfairness, complexity, and inefficiency. The accumulation of credits, deductions, and exclusions designed to help particular groups or advance special purposes conflict with one another, are poorly designed, and represent no consistent policy. The tax system causes investors to waste resources on low-yield investments that carry large tax benefits, while high-yield investments without such benefits go unfunded. The result is a shrunken

tax base that requires needlessly high rates on wages, salaries, and other taxable income. Overall the system undermines the faith of citizens that tax burdens are shared fairly. The time has come for basic reform.[31]

This dismal view of our income tax structure was accurate. Reform was needed. The Tax Reform Act of 1986 (TRA) made fundamental changes in the system by broadening the tax base substantially (for both individuals and corporations) and reducing marginal tax rates dramatically. The effects have been to improve the tax system from a horizontal equity point of view, making the tax more fair. The reduced rates and closed loopholes have also improved the efficiency of the tax system. Less economic activity is wasted in pursuing tax writeoffs than before, and the tax rate distorts economic decisions less due to the lower marginal rates. The TRA also shifted a share of the tax burden, at least nominally, from individuals to corporations. It is anticipated that over the first five years $125 billion in tax burden will be shifted from individuals to corporations. This effect surely clouds the real impact of tax reform, however. The increased tax burden on corporations is shifted to consumers, employees, and shareholders in some combination, resulting in higher individual tax burdens. In tax incidence, as elsewhere in life, things are not always as they appear.

Tax reform removed many low-income taxpayers from the tax rolls by raising the personal exemption and the standard deduction. Prior to tax reform, a single person began paying tax at the threshold of $3,590 while after reform that threshold was $5,000. For a married couple the corresponding figures were $5,870 and $9,000. A family of four hit the taxable income threshold at $8,030 prior to tax reform but did not have to pay taxes until an income of $13,000 after reform. Those changes in the tax law were beneficial in bringing a greater degree of justice to the tax system.

This solution is a temporary fix, though, unless the tax system is indexed. Without indexation, as inflation raises nominal income over time, the poor will once again be subject to taxation. Politicians can again take millions off the tax rolls at some future date by raising the personal exemption or the standard deduction and claim political credit for doing so. The real solution is to index the personal exemption and the standard deduction to retain their value in real terms, net of inflation. This has been done since 1985 at the federal level, but most state and local income tax structures are not indexed.[32] It should also be noted that while the federal income tax is exemplary in having indexed brackets, personal exemptions, and standard deductions, many other aspects of the tax structure are not yet indexed. Most notable is the taxation of nominal, rather than real, capital gains. Full indexation should be our objective in the design of an income tax structure, but it can be a very expensive proposition.

As an example of the policy options states faced in the wake of tax reform, consider the simulation of the effects of two particular options Michigan confronted. The state could either raise the personal exemption or lower its tax rate in response to federal tax reform's base-broadening effects to avoid unwanted new revenues.[33] The distributional effects of the two policies are summarized in table 6.1.

Table 6.1
SIMULATED EFFECTS OF TAX POLICY CHANGES

AGI*	Savings from Personal Exemption Increase	Savings from Tax Rate Reduction
< 10	19.9%	3.8%
10 to 20	20.4	11.2
20 to 30	19.0	17.6
30 to 40	17.7	21.0
40 to 50	11.6	17.0
> 50	11.3	29.3

*AGI indicates federal adjusted gross income measured in thousands of dollars.

The policy choices have different distributional effects. Nearly 30 percent of the benefits from the rate reduction go to those with incomes in excess of $50,000 while 40 percent of the benefits from the personal exemption increase accrue to those with incomes less than $20,000. Given the other efficiency effects of tax reform, the clear choice from a biblical perspective is to increase the personal exemption. Justice is enhanced in this specific policy change.

SUMMARY AND CONCLUDING COMMENTS

Three biblical principles should guide the design of tax structures: justice, compassion, and stewardship. Tax laws should treat people fairly, requiring people of similar means to pay similar taxes. Compassion is required in taxation, relieving some of the tax burden on the poor and powerless. The design of tax structures should minimize the incentives to waste resources—especially human resources. These guiding norms are biblical and can be used to consider tax policy proposals of all types. Their coordinated fulfillment may be difficult, and tradeoffs may have to be made, but the focus brought to policy questions by these principles is that required by Scripture.

A remaining question is, To what extent can Christians impose their views on appropriate tax policy on others in a pluralistic society? Biblical values belong to the whole world, but people vary in their preparation to receive them.[34] Here, we have the responsibility of finding the highest point at which our social and economic structure can respond to these principles and of implementing them accordingly.[35]

EDITOR'S PERSPECTIVE

John Anderson has provided a solid biblical foundation on which to build an equitable and compassionate tax structure. There is a massive potential danger lurking in the background, though, that I want to bring forward and address now that we are deeply involved with the overall subject of public policy. I will surface the danger in stages and then speak to it pragmatically.

Readers who are digesting the entire CHRISTIANS IN THE MARKETPLACE Series are by now familiar with the hermeneutical (interpretive) and philosophical world view that has shaped these four volumes. In the first two books that set forth the theological foundations for business, economics, and public policy, the finest evangelical scholars who could be assembled were asked to write on specific topics with which they had been previously and positively identified. That meant they were presenting a view they deeply believed in. Each of their topics, however, represented one side of a pair of topics that embody an historic point of difference in the Church that theologians have discussed for centuries, without resolution.

The selection of these particular topics held in tension was intentional because how people resolve them has an enormous impact on their world view and subsequent behavior. Furthermore, I believe that most of us select a particular hermeneutical perspective for the reasons I outlined in considerable detail in the "Editor's Perspective" at the close of Dr. Henry's chapter: (1) our inherent propensity to seek resolution, psychological comfort, and security (needs emanating from the Fall) rather than remain open to an inscrutable and never-ending effort to balance the tensions; (2) our self-perpetuated ignorance of the Scriptures; and (3) our substitution of a knowledge about God for a relationship with Christ. What these identified tensions are, how our beliefs about the positions represented in them shape our world views, and why we hold particular hermeneutical views escape, I am convinced, the notice of the vast majority of Christians. We are often sheep following a trail simply because it is comfortable and familiar.

I am also persuaded that the truth of Scripture demands a "both/and" holding of the biblical truths embedded in the tensions we have been examining and not an "either/or" stance. This belief has shaped the content of the "Editor's Introductions," "Editor's Reflections," and "Editor's Perspectives." But such a belief places its holders in a precarious position of trying to balance those truths that only someone with infinite knowledge and wisdom could keep in proper balance. Precisely!

God alone has such perfect knowledge and wisdom. His imparting of them to us is only partial—sufficient, but partial. When we set out to balance the tensions between the scriptural revelations about our individual responsibilities with the biblical truths about our collective nature and responsibilities, we need the Holy Spirit's help. Furthermore, if both biblical history and general history are to be believed (I believe they are), God is more likely to work out His sovereign will through the tugs and pulls that occur in and between the competing factions than He is through a single voice or even a few voices. We are responsible to state our individual positions, though, so that they become part of the larger body of shaping influences. That is what this series is trying to accomplish.

The issue at hand is no exception. Those of us who believe that Scripture places the primary responsibility for our individual and family economic well-being on us as individuals and families, and who simultaneously acknowledge that the state has a legitimate role to play in the community life of its citizens, find ourselves immediately faced with an enormous tension. How are we to balance these truths?

Libertarians (they are not a homogeneous group, either) are going to pull our thinking toward minimizing governments, enlarging the role of individual choices in a free market, and emphasizing personal obligations and rights. They are more likely to subscribe to a view of collective connectiveness that should be governed, constrained, or enlightened by natural laws that lead the way to reasoned solutions to individual/collective problems.

Egalitarians will be inclined to balance the tensions very differently, although they, too, are not uniform in their thinking about problems and solutions. They will enlarge the role of government and speak of the unfair consequences emanating from human inequality, hurtful (sinful) social mores (sex, race, age, disability discrimination), abuses of power, and so forth. People who lean in this direction have less confidence in the sufficiency of natural laws and believe more in the intervention of the community to redress the negative consequences of the natural order and humanly generated troubles.

I am afraid that the perceptions of "natural and personal observations" often start to dominate the thinking process from this point forward, more than the special revelation of Scripture. The libertarians have a rightful distrust of decision making by the few for the many. History supports their fear; natural observation supports their logic. The egalitarians have a righteous concern when they observe that history and the natural order have produced a number of conditions—depressions, droughts, etc.—where there were dislocations in an economy and when in the immediate and near future there was no solution in sight to the human suffering. The libertarians' dependence on long-run solutions leaves too many people suffering injustices or shortages in the short run. Both are right! Therein lies a mystery of our reality, as God designed it—*a constant reminder of our true dependence on Him.*

The relationship of this truth to the issues surrounding taxation is direct. Once we have accepted the legitimacy of government's having some role through public policy—to provide "public goods" the private sector will not voluntarily provide, to be involved in some form and to some degree in the creation and redistribution of wealth, to make attempts to stabilize the economy when it is dislocated—then the need to tax and finance the government's efforts is before us. How deeply should a government interject itself into the economic affairs of a community? How much taxation should be allowed? These questions surface when we work on the continuum of choices that confront us when we abandon the comfortable zone surrounding the polar position of absolute *laisez faire* or absolute socialism.

I said earlier that I would address this issue pragmatically. The answer must be pragmatic because we are on the tightrope seeking a balance between two biblical realities—the individual and his or her relationship to the community—that only the Spirit of God can sovereignly reconcile, but for whom no one can speak authoritatively on matters of specific policy. (So these four books join the efforts of others who wish to responsibly influence the debate on public policy and be part of God's sovereign solution. None of the scholars who participated in these four volumes knew beforehand how their personal perspective would be used and integrated with the editor's perspective.)

Our forefathers were extremely wise, I believe, when they sought to establish a nation "under law" rather than a nation "under men." Without getting embroiled in the discussions of why our forebears perceived this to be sound, I will simply say that I would not trust myself with the absolute authority to govern others, so I do not believe it is wise to give such power to others who share my nature. But believing that the government must be prepared to seek justice for those who, for whatever reasons, become economically and politically disenfranchised, I am nevertheless bound to seek solutions.

Remembering that our forebears would not allow the national government to levy a tax on income in 1789, and only did so in 1913 with the passage of the Sixteenth Amendment to the Constitution, I am of the persuasion that the greater error occurred in 1913. The error, in my judgment, was not so much in opening the door to taxation but in opening it into an arena without bounds or limits. That opened us up to far more government "under men" than ever before because access to the purse brings with it massive power. Public leaders were removed from the constraints of the Constitution and allowed to rule by a set of laws much easier to change than the Constitution.

I believe, therefore, that a *constitutional limit* should be placed on the power of the federal government to tax the people. I have much less concern for the powers of the states or local governments, for they will experience "competitive" advantages and disadvantages (market forces) according to their taxing choices. The wisdom of a particular constitutional limit is not as clear to me. A limit of 10 percent has many logical appeals and links itself to a natural comparison with the "tithe" given in Israel to those who served the people under the direction of God. But I am not positive the principle is directly transferable. The warning Samuel gave the people when they were asking for a king, however, clearly indicates they could expect to pay their tithe to God and a tax to the king (see 1 Sam. 8:11-18). Pressing Samuel's points, where he indicated the king would take a tenth of their seed, grapes, and flocks (vv. 15, 17), this would amount to a 20 percent reduction in income—10 percent to the priests, 10 percent to the king. Samuel considered that onerous. I would, therefore, conclude that the constitutional limit, in a pluralistic society where *few* tithe, should be allowed to run no higher than 20 percent for all the affairs of the various levels of government. Those who have rejected the God of Israel as their King, and the only One who can produce the fruit of self-control to help reduce the need for so much public policy, must then accept the consequences of being governed by other humans who share their own nature. And those who govern must have access to the economic means necessary for instituting and carrying out public justice—the power to tax.

PART VII

PUBLIC JUSTICE AND GOVERNMENT REGULATION

Regulations are very much a part of our lives. They exist because we need direction, we are unrighteous, and they foster justice, when properly conceived, in a world where people struggle over the rights of individuals and the good of the community. Our families regulated us when we were children (if they loved us; see Heb. 12:7-11); the schools we attended enforced regulations; the Church places requirements on its members when it functions in a biblical manner; the institutions we work for provide us with job descriptions and policies.

Before the Fall, a set of positive regulations (the creation mandates—family, work, and worship) and one negative regulation ("from the tree of the knowledge of good and evil you shall not eat" [Gen. 2:17]) gave Adam the directions necessary to function in accordance with God's purposes. Following the Fall, more regulations were announced. Those regulations were eventually encapsulated in the Ten Commandments and explained by the prophets, priests, kings, scribes, Sadducees, and Pharisees for centuries. The Law was given because of our unrighteousness (see Gal. 3:19), with the intent that it would be our tutor and lead us to Christ (see Gal. 3:24). But persons who reject Christ and are not being led by the Spirit to develop the characteristic of righteous self-control (see Gal. 5:23) surely need some form of external, consequential regulation to foster justice in the marketplace.

Fundamentally, the unrighteous hate restrictions—both righteous and onerous ones. For this basic reason, businesspeople grouse about government regulations being imposed on them.

These opening comments are not to be interpreted as a blanket endorsement of government regulation of business, but it is utterly naive to think that we can be surrounded by people who are dead in sin, self-centered in their focus, and infected with greed, materialism, and covetous attitudes and not need a goodly amount of regulation. The miracle is that God's common grace was so

147

strong and pervasive for such a long period of time in our history. Free markets pull businesspeople toward prudent behavior, but competition is no substitute for the constraining powers of the Holy Spirit. Free markets, with and without God's blessing on them, will produce monopolies, positions of power, special "opportunities" (inside information, for example), and other situations where people will act either righteously or unrighteously. Only God's common grace, not free market forces, can ultimately keep the marketplace from being heavily peppered with unrighteousness. Christians need to be careful that they put their confidence in God and not in the market mechanisms or government regulations.

In the chapter before us, Dr. William Wood describes the three primary regulatory issues encountered in the marketplace: (1) the role of the state in the face of economic monopolies and other power problems; (2) the role of the state in achieving justice in the pricing structures of state-authorized private monopolies—utilities, trash collection, and so forth; and (3) the state's role regarding matters of health and safety as they relate to workers, customers, and the public. The standards of efficiency and equity, two components of public justice as it relates to government regulation of business, are then discussed with the acknowledgment that economists are generally more comfortable dealing with the efficiency questions than the equity ones. The equity issues, though, are equally important and constitute a major stimulus for our interest in discovering godly principles that address government regulations. Finally, Dr. Wood names six biblical principles pertaining to the fundamental issues encountered in public policy debates on government regulation of business. He concludes the chapter by applying these principles to specific situations in the three areas he initially identified.

CHAPTER 7

THE POLITICAL ECONOMY OF REGULATION: BIBLICAL PRINCIPLES AND MODERN APPLICATIONS

William C. Wood

Dr. William C. Wood has conducted a wide range of research in regulation and antitrust. The author of two books on nuclear regulation, he has advised the House Subcommittee on Energy and the Environment, the National Association of Insurance Commissioners, and the Environmental Policy Institute on nuclear regulatory issues. Dr. Wood, a former Associated Press reporter, received his Ph.D. in Economics from the University of Virginia. He has held faculty appointments at Virginia, Bridgewater College, and Vanderbilt University. Currently he is Director of the Center for Economic Education at James Madison University.

B iblical times were much different from our own in the relationship between commerce and the state. Today the state is actively involved in regulating prices and profits, health and safety. Then the state, powerful as it sometimes was, had a much less developed role in regulating commerce. Questions of government regulation that might arise today simply did not arise in biblical times, and so direct guidance for public policy from the Bible will naturally be limited.

Questions of public policy, however, often come down to questions of how people behave and the policy maker's conception of the good. On such questions, the premise of this volume and of this chapter is that the Bible is authoritative. Therefore, the task at hand is to interpret biblical wisdom in terms of modern policy questions.

MODERN ISSUES IN REGULATION

Although hundreds of regulatory issues could be identified and studied, the most important questions in regulation are small in number. Three of the leading ones are these:

1. What role, if any, should the state take in seeing that monopoly and market power are not exercised?
2. What, if anything, should the state do to assure that pricing structures result in goods and services being delivered efficiently and justly?
3. What role, if any, should the state take in promoting the health and safety of the customers and employees of private firms?

Question 1: Market power—The two standards commonly applied to economic institutions are efficiency and equity.[1] Economics, taken as a social science, has much to say about efficiency. However, practicing economists are often reluctant to render judgments on equity, since social science methods can say little about matters of equity.

Competitive market outcomes generate certain kinds of efficiency. Costs are held down by competitive markets because producers with high costs will be penalized by low profits. Service to all customers willing to pay the costs of providing a product likewise is encouraged. The equity or fairness of free market outcomes is another matter, subject to considerable debate in the conventional secular economics literature.[2]

The efficiency of noncompetitive markets is more in dispute. Judged by their delivery of existing goods and services today, noncompetitive markets fail in basic ways. They may leave unserved some customers willing to pay the costs of being served. Costs may rise out of control in the absence of competitive pressures. However, the argument has been made that efficiency *today* is too narrow a criterion, and that firms in noncompetitive markets may be better innovators over the long term.[3] Also, in some industries (such as the telephone industry) large firms may be better able to offer service than small firms.

As a society, we have attempted to get the benefits of private enterprise even where markets are likely to be noncompetitive. For firms designated as public utilities, regulation extends to prices, profits, and service. For other firms, the regulation is generally limited to enforcement of the antitrust laws. In any case, the regulation is aimed at preventing the exercise of monopoly power. It is worth considering whether our regulation of monopoly power can be enlightened by application of biblical principles.

Question 2: Pricing structure—Regulation of market and monopoly power has been aimed at keeping the overall, or average, level of prices within bounds. Less attention has been paid to the structure of prices to different customers. Among price structures that raise the same amount of revenue, there are many different ways of dividing up the burden.

One possibility to divide up the costs of public utility operations is to base prices on the costs of serving individual customer classes. Under such plans, customers who are costly to serve pay more than others. Although determining the costs of serving customer classes is quite difficult, the principle is straight-forward.

Other possibilities involve using rate structures to generate fair outcomes, with little regard to the costs of serving customer classes. One such possibility is the use of "lifeline" utility rates, which provide a low level of essential utility services (such as a basic telephone connection or a very modest amount of electricity) at low rates. Additional usage is at much higher rates to subsidize the universal provision of "lifeline" service. Since fairness is more a concern than efficiency in many of these decisions, we need to consider what biblical concepts of fairness can tell us about them.

Question 3: Health and safety regulation—In historical terms, a very new development in our society is the extension of governmental authority into health and safety regulation. Even as regulation of prices and service has been declining with the deregulation of major industries, health and safety regulation has held steady or even expanded. Even the so-called unregulated industries, whose prices and profits are not scrutinized by government, are subject to health and safety regulation.

Health and safety regulation affects relationships other than the firm-customer relationship that traditionally has been the subject of regulation. It also affects the firm-employee relationship and relationships between firms and their communities. Because health and safety regulation attempts to protect lives and health, rather than simple material well-being, it is an especially sensitive area for public policy.

As a society, we still are groping for the proper ways to approach issues of health and safety regulation. Thoughtful and well-informed observers can take very different positions on questions such as the classic "How safe is safe enough?" Health and safety concerns are timeless; here, too, an intelligent application of biblical principles can usefully illuminate public policy.

SOME GUIDING BIBLICAL PRINCIPLES

Although the Bible does not directly address regulatory issues, it provides some principles highly relevant to regulation. Here is a survey of some of the most significant ones.

Principle 1: In arm's length business transactions, a provider of capital is to be allowed a just return—The Law of Moses is sometimes taken as forbidding interest in business transactions. For example, Exodus 22:25 directs, "If you lend money to one of my people among you who is needy, do not be like a moneylender; charge him no interest." However, Deuteronomy 23:19 states,

> Do not charge your brother interest, whether on money or food or any-
> thing else that may earn interest. You may charge a foreigner interest,
> but not a brother Israelite, so that the LORD your God may bless you in
> everything you put your hand to in the land you are entering to possess.

In context, it is clear that the prohibition on interest applies among the children of Israel but not in arm's length transactions with foreigners. When, as today, corporations are owned by people of all faiths and serve customers of all faiths, the transactions can be regarded only as arm's length in nature.

The New Testament expands on the injunction to give freely. Jesus calls on His listeners to make compassionate loans without return of interest or even principal:

> "And if you lend to those from whom you expect repayment, what
> credit is that to you? Even 'sinners' lend to 'sinners,' expecting to be
> repaid in full. But love your enemies, do good to them, and lend to
> them without expecting to get anything back. Then your reward will be
> great, and you will be sons of the Most High, because he is kind to the
> ungrateful and wicked." (Luke 6:34-35)

Those who would grow spiritually, then, should give freely; but for public policy purposes, when people of all faiths are lending to provide goods for others of all faiths, a return on capital is indicated.

The Scriptures also appear to sanction application of present-value methods, which have been elaborated into today's financial valuation models. In such models, the value of an asset today is seen as the present value of the asset's future stream of earnings. A future dollar is worth less than a dollar today, both because a present dollar can be earning interest and because a future dollar may not be received after all. The description of the Year of Jubilee in Leviticus 25 pointed out that after "seven times seven years" land would revert back to its original owner. Therefore, a sale of land was to be regarded as only the sale of the land's services until the next Year of Jubilee:

> You are to buy from your countryman on the basis of the number of
> years since the Jubilee. And he is to sell to you on the basis of the
> number of years left for harvesting crops. When the years are many,
> you are to increase the price, and when the years are few, you are to
> decrease the price, because what he is really selling you is the number
> of crops. (vv. 15-16)

The final sentence of this passage is in striking accord with the modern concept of the present value of an asset's income stream.

The New Testament parable of the talents speaks of the return on assets. This parable of Christ contrasts the faithful servants who put their master's money to work, doubling it, and the lazy servant who hid the money in the ground. Less noted is the master's statement about what the lazy servant should have done if he were unwilling to put the money to work: "Well then, you should have put my money on deposit with the bankers, so that when I returned I would have received it back with interest" (Matt. 25:27).

This parable reflects what would be recognized today as the risk-return tradeoff in invested assets. By taking the risks of employing the master's capital, the two faithful servants achieved returns of 100 percent—one on five talents, the other on two talents of money. The lazy servant should at least have deposited the one talent of money, earning a smaller amount of money that reflected the lesser risk. Figure 7.1, showing the risk and return of the servants' investments, represents a tradeoff like that identified by modern asset pricing models.

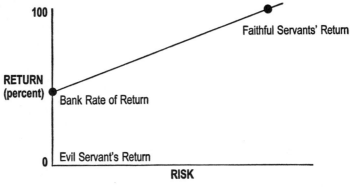

Figure 7.1
RISK AND RETURN IN THE PARABLE OF THE TALENTS

The risk-return tradeoff is not the focus of this parable, but the master is cited approvingly, and the parable does not question his right to earn a return on his invested money. The parable establishes the rate of interest as a floor rate of return that the master could expect, even from a lazy servant who would not work to increase the capital. Both Old and New Testament passages recognize the legitimacy of earning a rate of return on arm's length business transactions.

Principle 2: God abhors concentration of wealth and power when it is used to take advantage of others—Although the first principle calls for a just return on capital, the Scriptures make clear that economic power is not to be abused. The Old Testament Jubilee provisions can be interpreted as a built-in mechanism for preventing an unhealthy concentration of owership of land, the primary productive factor in ancient Israel. In addition, the prophets cried out against a concentration of wealth and power (see Isa. 5:8; Mic. 2:1-2). Isaiah specifically addressed woes to those "who add house to house and join field to field till no space is left and you live alone in the land" (5:8). The penalty for such behavior is severe:

> The LORD Almighty has declared in my hearing:
>> "Surely the great houses will become desolate,
>>> the fine mansions left without occupants." (5:9)

Wealthy oppressors are warned in the New Testament Epistle of James:

> Your gold and silver are corroded. Their corrosion will testify against you and eat your flesh like fire. You have hoarded wealth in the last days. Look! The wages you failed to pay the workmen who mowed your fields are crying out against you. The cries of the harvesters have reached the ears of the Lord Almighty. (5:3-4)

Thus there is in the Bible a general presumption against concentration of wealth, particularly when it is used to oppress others.[4]

Principle 3: Ours is a fallen and imperfect world in which good intentions by imperfect men and women will not by themselves lead to good steward-ship of resources—A recurring and pervasive theme in the Scriptures is the consequences of sin. In the first instance of sin in Genesis 3 and in the Final Judgment in Revelation 20, sin separates mankind from God, with terrible consequences. The consequences are not just spiritual, however; all human institutions fall short of their potential because of sin. The Church, the home, the workplace—no institution is free of the consequences of sin.

Modern opinion polling tells us that the public distrusts the ethics of policy makers in business and government.[5] Much has been made of these polling results, but the same results reflect a decline in faith in all institutions, including the Church. If there is a lack of ethics in our modern institutions, it surely comes as no surprise to those familiar with the consequences of sin.

Academic economics has not always reflected the failings of mankind and mankind's institutions. For example, at one point public interest theories of regulation were common.[6] The theories showed how private markets could fail and how a more powerful party *could* intervene to correct the market failure. The theories, almost unwittingly, assumed that government *would* perform the necessary corrections. The assumption was that government would protect the public interest. The public interest theories today are under attack from rent-seeking theories, whose foundation is that all agents, including government officials, seek their own interests instead of the public interest.[7] The rent-seeking theories have many implications, but among them is the idea that neither governments nor businesses should be assumed to be consciously promoting the public interest. Because of rent-seeking behavior, the challenge is to channel self-centered motives to serve the public good—with the public good usually defined as economic efficiency.

Rent seeking becomes especially troublesome when the rent seekers obtain governmental powers such as taxation. In such positions of authority, the rent seekers' burden on the citizenry can be quite large. James Gwartney interprets the time of Israel's kings as showing specifically a scriptural warning against rent seeking by governments.[8] Samuel's warning in 1 Samuel 8:10-17 is comprehensive: If Israel insists on a king, that king will take everything from flocks and vineyards to sons and daughters for himself. "When that day comes, you will cry out for relief from the king you have chosen, and the LORD will not answer you in that day," Samuel concludes (v. 18).

Today the powers and programs of governments have grown to the point that rent seekers need not be government officials but can instead be individuals using governmental power to their own advantage. Therefore, the modern analyst must not assume that rent seeking will be limited to officials within governments.

A biblical view of the failures of mankind is quite compatible with a rent-seeking view of economic activity. Rent seeking becomes just one more aspect of mankind's fall.

Principle 4: The material goods of this world are not to be revered; Christians are not to worship them or give up really important things to seek them—The ultimate end of regulation today is consumption. As a society, we are not so much concerned about the price of water for its own sake as we are concerned that customers be able to afford to consume at least a modest amount of water. Although the Scriptures recognize such needs, they firmly disapprove a reverence for material goods. A powerful statement of the proper attitude toward material goods is found in the Sermon on the Mount:

> "Do not store up for yourselves treasures on earth, where moth and
> rust destroy, and where thieves break in and steal. But store up for
> yourselves treasures in heaven, where moth and rust do not destroy,
> and where thieves do not break in and steal. For where your treasure is,
> there your heart will be also." (Matt. 6:19-21)

These comments leave no doubt about the outcome of one's preoccupation with possessions:

> "No one can serve two masters. Either he will hate the one and love the other, or he will be devoted to the one and despise the other. You cannot serve both God and Money." (vv. 24-25)

Consumption may be a suitable end for a secular government deciding how to regulate its businesses, but the New Testament warns against a single-minded focus on material goods.

Principle 5: Although human life, health, and safety are to be revered, there are higher values than health and safety in this world—Biblical teaching, especially in the New Testament, shows that God intends mankind to revere human life, health, and safety. "You shall not murder" (Exod. 20:13) is, of course, one of the Ten Commandments. This commandment was made much more stringent by Jesus, who extended it to include not only actual cases of murder but cases of being angry with a brother (see Matt. 5:22).[9]

Even in cases of accidental death—today's involuntary manslaughter or an entirely unintentional accident—the Old Testament makes it known that the loss of life is to be taken quite seriously. Numbers 35:22-25 specifies the procedure for dealing with an accidental death in the context of blood feuds that might break out if surviving family members sought vengeance by killing the person responsible for the accidental death:

> "But if without hostility someone suddenly shoves another or throws something at him unintentionally or, without seeing him, drops a stone on him that could kill him, and he dies, then since he was not his enemy and he did not intend to harm him, the assembly must judge between him and the avenger of blood according to these regulations. The assembly must protect the one accused of murder from the avenger of blood and send him back to the city of refuge to which he fled. He must stay there until the death of the high priest, who was anointed with the holy oil."

In today's terms, the penalty specified in Numbers for such an accidental death would be considered severe. Modern interpretations of the "fellow servant" rule would make the employer rather than the worker liable for the accident. The penalty in Numbers amounted to an enforced exile to another city for an undetermined time until the death of the current high priest. The exile was all the more severe because the refugee could legally be killed by the victim's family if he ever left the city of refuge before the high priest's death (see Num. 35:26-28).

The Bible goes beyond teaching a reverence for life to other teachings, two of which are especially relevant today: (1) fatal accidents and illnesses are not necessarily to be regarded as judgment for sin; and (2) there are spiritual values far more basic than health and safety.

In the teachings of Jesus, fatal accidents and illnesses do not necessarily represent judgment for sin. The Gospel accounts indicate that Jesus was correcting a commonly held misconception at that time. Jesus said, "Or those eighteen who died when the tower in Siloam fell on them—do you think they were more guilty than all the others living in Jerusalem? I tell you, no! But unless you repent, you too will all perish" (Luke 13:4-5). The nature of the accident is not elaborated further in the Bible. However, the circumstances allow us to infer that equivalent modern accidents—whether involving construction or even structural failure of an airplane—do not represent judgment for sin. Assuming that a man's blindness was caused by sin, Jesus' disciples asked, "Rabbi, who sinned, this man or his parents, that he was born blind?" "Neither this man nor his parents sinned," said Jesus, "but this happened so that the work of God might be displayed in his life." Jesus then restored the blind man's sight (see John 9:2-7).

The primacy of spiritual values over health and safety is directly stated in Matthew 5:29. The teaching of Jesus there seems severe: "If your right eye causes you to sin, gouge it out and throw it away. It is better for you to lose one part of your body than for your whole body to be thrown into hell." Although this is not a direct and literal recommendation for self-mutilation, it makes quite clear the relative importance of spiritual health over physical health and freedom from injury.

The biblical view of life, health, and safety, then, is rather complex. The Bible teaches that we are to regard life with reverence and that we are not to endanger others. We are not to take accidents and illnesses lightly by just brushing them off as deserved consequences of sin. Neither are we to forget that spiritual health is so essential that it matters more than having eyesight from both eyes or the use of both hands.

Principle 6: The poor of society are to be provided for, even at the cost of some interference with private production and consumption decisions— Avoiding distortion of production and consumption decisions is a recurring theme of modern welfare economics.[10] In a number of diverse policy areas, this general principle means structuring taxes and regulation so that decisions about consumption and production are left up to individuals and firms. For example, providing rental subsidies to poor families is considered better than providing public housing because of the distortion of housing patterns that may occur with the in-kind housing benefit. Tax analysts seek out taxes that extract revenue with minimum changes in production and consumption. Regulators seek rules that limit profit without distorting production techniques.

In this strand of modern welfare economics, keeping regulation from interfering with the production technology of a firm has become elevated to the status of a first principle. However, this approach is not necessarily biblical. Leviticus 19:9-10 cites specific obligations for those who grow grain and grapes:

> "When you reap the harvest of your land, do not reap to the very edges
> of your field or gather the gleanings of your harvest. Do not go over
> your vineyard a second time or pick up the grapes that have fallen.
> Leave them for the poor and the alien. I am the LORD your God."

The modern welfare economist's recommendation to maximize efficiency in growing grain and grapes would be to let the grower choose harvesting techniques. Then, welfare would be paid for by a tax designed not to distort harvesting techniques, so that the grower would continue to produce large amounts. God's law is different; in this case it sanctions explicit interference with harvesting techniques as a provision for the poor. This plan is striking in its simplicity, providing for food and the terms under which it is made available to the poor.

In a similar way, a modern welfare economist might recommend that injured travelers be cared for through specialized travelers' aid services funded by structured taxes and transfers. That was not the way of the good Samaritan, who became personally involved with the injured traveler on the road from Jerusalem to Jericho (see Luke 10:30-37). No doubt there was considerable interference with the Samaritan's production and consumption plans, not to mention the unanticipated expense of the two silver coins left with the innkeeper for the injured traveler's bill. Yet Jesus' direction to the listener at the end of the parable is clear: "Go and do likewise."

PUBLIC POLICY APPLICATIONS

Subject to the ever-present limitation in applying scriptural teachings to a society so different from that of biblical times, there seem at least three areas in which a biblical perspective could provide especially useful guidance in modern regulation: (1) the antitrust laws; (2) regulation of public utilities; and (3) cost-benefit analysis.

The antitrust laws—God's abhorrence of concentrated wealth and power might at first seem to directly justify strong antitrust policy. If strong antitrust policy led directly to reduced concentrations of wealth and power and better results for workers and consumers, the link would be straightforward. However, there are a number of obstacles in moving from the scriptural principle to laws on the books.

The first obstacle is that monopoly can actually be more favorable to consumers than competition under some circumstances. The controversy over the breakup of the Bell System leaves considerable doubt whether consumer interests actually were well served by the court-ordered divestiture.

A second obstacle is that monopoly power possessed may not be misused, particularly if the firm recognizes that abuse of its monopoly power would invite competition and a loss of its dominant position. Under certain circumstances, so-called limit pricing (a monopolist's low-price policy designed to limit entry of competitors) may be in consumers' interests. U.S. antitrust law, reflecting this concern, has typically drawn a distinction between the mere possession of monopoly power and its exercise. Unexercised monopoly power, while not presumptively legal, has been very hard to attack under U.S. law.

A final obstacle is that firms can actually turn antitrust policy against their competition—reducing the degree of rivalry in a manner counter to the intent of antitrust policy. This obstacle is especially apparent in private antitrust. As opposed to actions filed by the government itself, private antitrust actions are filed directly by firms that feel injured against the firms that damaged them.

Today it seems likely that the public interest is not being served well by having private firms take each other to court on antitrust grounds. The "new antitrust strategy," as it is labeled by Arthur D. Austin, is more concerned with intimidating competitors than it is with the traditional goals of antitrust.[11] The shortcomings of private antitrust enforcement are now documented. Purely strategic antitrust cases have increased to the point that a majority of total cases may well have nothing to do with maintaining competition.[12]

The perspective the Bible adds to this problem is that in a fallen world, public policy cannot be constructed on the assumption that individual self-interest will automatically lead to the public good. Rather, that individual self-interest must be carefully channeled by policy makers who act as clever stewards of resources.

Proper response to the abuses of private antitrust depends on a clear understanding of the differences between self-interest pursued through the market and self-interest pursued through the power of the state. There are built-in limits to firms seeking through markets to increase their profits at the expense of their customers and workers. The firm that charges too high a price loses market share; the firm that pays its labor too little may find it difficult to attract suitable workers. Indeed, the channeling of self-interest into consumer interest is the genius of the market system. However, the exercise of self-interest in the legal sphere can be quite damaging to consumer interests, since a strategic firm can have the coercive power of the state on its side.

That firms use the antitrust laws against each other is no surprise to the analyst with a clear-eyed view of the nature of man. The real surprise is that private antitrust policy proceeded for so many years under the assumption that private firms would bring cases promoting the public interest and not just their own strategic interests.

One proposal to reform private antitrust is to limit the conditions under which a suit can be brought, so as to reduce the tendency of firms to sue their competitors when no consumer interest is being harmed. A realistic public policy approach would not consist of asking enterprises to "be good" and serve the public interest by refraining from strategic lawsuits, even though Christian business managers clearly have such an obligation not to exploit the legal system. Rather, a realistic approach recognizes the necessity of continuing to allow businesses to seek their own interests—while structuring incentives to align those interests with the public interest.

Design of utility rates and rate structures—After a stormy period in the 1970s and early 1980s, utility regulation has settled into a period of calm. A return of energy market disturbances, however, could well thrust utility regulation back into an adversarial setting. The regulator who would be true to biblical teaching could bring keen insights to utility regulation.

One insight would be that a return on capital at least equal to opportunity cost is not immoral. The parable of the talents, as discussed earlier, contains an implicit opportunity cost concept. Therefore, if energy prices rise suddenly, threatening utility returns, adjusting rates to prevent a confiscation of owners' capital would seem justified.

The Bible also teaches concern for the poor, however, and the poor would certainly be hurt by such increases in utility rates. Low "lifeline" rates for basic service subsidized by higher rates for those with greater consumption would be one possibility for cushioning the blow.

A standard objection to lifeline rates would be that such rates distort production and consumption decisions. The recommendation of modern welfare economics might be to set up a nondistorting utility rate structure and then use a tax-and-transfer program to ensure at least survival levels of public utilities to all consumers. Totally refraining from distortion of production and consumption decisions is not a biblical concept, however, and there may well be a role for lifeline rates as a modern implementation of Old Testament gleaning. A biblical perspective at least prevents the regulator from approaching the problem entirely as a problem in production and consumption.

Cost-benefit analysis—A major theme of regulation in recent years has been the trend to assign specific dollar values to costs and benefits in decision making.[13] Policy makers are increasingly more likely to insist on numbers to back up an assertion that a policy has benefits greater than costs. The debate becomes especially sensitive when, in health and safety regulation, the benefits involve life and safety while the costs are dollar outlays by businesses to comply with regulations. For policy makers, the underlying issue is how to weigh the relative values of dollars saved and available for increased consumption, as opposed to accidents and illnesses or even deaths avoided. The debate over lifesaving regulations is sometimes even reduced to this question: What is the value of a life?

At first glance, it might seem that biblical guidance on this question is that the value of a life is infinite. Jesus asked, "What good will it be for a man if he gains the whole world, yet forfeits his soul? Or what can a man give in exchange for his soul?" (Matt. 16:26). Interpretation of this verse is complicated by the fact that the Greek for "soul" can also be interpreted "life."[14] The point is that no price is high enough to compensate a person for the loss of his or her eternal being.

However, the loss of one's eternal being is not the focus of regulation, nor typically is the loss of an identifiable person's human life. Since our human bodies do not have infinite lives, the issue is rather greater or lesser survival time on this earth. Moreover, the loss of an identifiable person's life is almost never at stake in regulatory decisions. Rather, what is at stake is small changes in survival probability, measured in tiny fractions of a percentage. For example, an occupational safety standard expected to save two lives in a population of two million workers amounts to an increase in survival probability of 0.0001 percent for members of the affected population. This is not a life-and-death decision to the policy maker but a decision about survival probabilities. When we cross the street against a traffic light, incurring a small decrease in survival probability in return for a finite benefit, we show that we value changes in survival probability at less than an infinite amount. A less-than-infinite value on the life of this world—but in an entirely different context—is consistent with the teaching of Jesus, as in Matthew 16:25: "For whoever wants to save his life will lose it, but whoever loses his life for me will find it."

While life and safety in this world are not to be valued as infinite, it also appears from biblical teaching that the scales are not to be tipped too far in the other direction. In the most unsophisticated forms of cost-benefit analysis, a dollar's worth of anything is equivalent to a dollar's worth of anything else. A program that costs poor people $4 million and benefits wealthy people $5 million has a favorable benefit-cost ratio. Safety equipment that costs $2 million but avoids only $1 million worth of injury cost has an unfavorable benefit-cost ratio. Such an unsophisticated form of cost-benefit analysis is not biblical, since the underlying values place such an emphasis on dollar benefits of consumption. This emphasis is directly at odds with the teaching of Jesus Christ on the relative unimportance of the goods of this world.

None of this is to imply that regulators should forsake quantitative analysis.

At the very least, cost-*effectiveness* (as opposed to cost-*benefit*) analysis can show where resources can be used most effectively. A cost-*benefit* analysis tries to reduce all effects to dollar terms, whereas a cost-*effectiveness* analysis reduces only the costs to dollar terms. For example, in occupational regulation, a policy maker might conclude that a particular regulation would cost $3 million and that the summed increases in survival probabilities were worth only $2 million—so that the regulation should be denied on cost-benefit grounds. (Note that saying "summed increases in survival probabilities" are worth $2 million is very different from saying that the lives are "worth" only $2 million. "Value of a life" is an unfortunate term to be applied when the debate concerns changes in survival probability for a large population rather than the life of a specific identifiable individual.)

In contrast to a cost-benefit analysis, a cost-effectiveness analysis would calculate only the cost of increasing survival probability under the regulation and then compare that cost with the costs of alternative ways of increasing survival probability. By ordering first the more cost-effective lifesaving methods, the regulator can save more lives for any given level of resources devoted to lifesaving. The regulator who would be a good steward of resources must at least consider cost effectiveness to avoid making decisions that reduce the number of lives that can be saved by regulation. Regulation faithful to biblical principles gives due attention to the resources committed by regulation as well as the great value the Bible places on individual human life and well-being.

CONCLUSIONS

The Bible certainly cannot be considered a policy handbook for modern regulators and businesses subject to regulation. Still, application of biblical principles can bring a new perspective to the field of economic regulation. The regulator is not just arranging incentives to maximize production and consumption. Consciously or unconsciously, poorly or effectively, the regulator is directing the employment of God's resources and affecting the well-being of humans created in God's image. Regulation is a serious calling that can be usefully informed by biblical perspectives.

EDITOR'S PERSPECTIVE

Dr. Wood has clearly set forth the link between biblical principles and public policy in the area of government regulation of business. He has covered three areas of regulation with great proficiency while acknowledging at the Scholars' Colloquium, where all the chapters were discussed, that other subjects like the regulation of financial markets (discussed briefly in the "Editor's Perspective" following Dr. Vickers's chapter), the function and ethics of "speculation" in carrying out the creation mandate regarding work, and the matter of the "corporate veil"—managers hiding behind the legal and personified skirts of the corporate entities to avoid personal accountability—could also be examined with beneficial results. The space allotted to Dr. Wood's topic precluded such an exhaustive study.

The very idea of calling for some public regulation of business, however, is so foreign to the thinking of most people associated with business that I want to expand on the legitimacy of some form of business regulation by building on the third biblical principle Dr. Wood noted: "Ours is a fallen and imperfect world in which good intentions by imperfect men and women will not by themselves lead to good stewardship of resources."

It should be obvious to us all by now that some form of regulation and accountability is necessary for everybody. It was for Adam before the Fall; it is for us after the Fall. More frequently, the form or extent of the regulation causes us concern, not the necessity for some degree of it. It seems apparent to me that the consummation God is moving His children toward is that of *self-control*. But even His mature children live and work in either formally or informally regulated structures. The family, church, and business institutions all have some written or unwritten regulations by which they operate. Furthermore, Christians are unmistakably told to live under and obey the governing authorities. When we are genuinely righteous, though, we seldom chafe under truly just regulations, especially in a free society where the governing authorities are eventually accountable to the people.

This last statement, implicitly endorsing freedom of choice, is a major building block in the argument of those who want a free market with as little regulation as possible. They contend, and I agree with them, that the dispersion of decisions, and the power associated with those decisions, is a major preventer of problems that so frequently occur when only a few people in a centralized governing body are allowed to rule the decision-making processes—and particularly when they also have the coercive power to enforce their own rules and regulations. Government regulators, for example, are often perceived as wearing as many as five hats: (1) legislators—writing the operating rules after Congress established the "general authority"; (2) prosecutors—bringing charges against those working under the rules; (3) judges—hearing and interpreting the charges brought against those accused of violating the rules; (4) jury—deciding on the guilt or innocence of those charged; and (5) enforcers—levying the fines and policing the judgments.

In summary, we have those who look to self-control, those who desire market mechanisms to effect controls, those who support some level of state control, and those who look to a combination of the first two alternatives or all three. I fall into the last group. People can grow in their ability to exercise self-control. Giving people as much latitude in a free market *as is reasonably prudent* (a moral judgment) is good. But governments still need to regulate businesses. (It is also true that governments need to be constrained by the workings of a free political system, for they suffer from the ravages of sin as well.) In the "Introduction" to this section, it was stated that it is naive "to think that we can be surrounded by people who are dead in sin, self-centered in their focus, and infected with greed, materialism, and covetous attitudes and not need a goodly amount of regulation." At least five additional factors support the conclusion that justice in the marketplace mandates the establishment of reasonable regulations to serve the rights of the individuals and guard the legitimate concerns of the community.

ECONOMIC POWER

Dr. Wood rightly observed that occasionally God has expressed a fundamental concern about the concentration of economic power—connecting field to field; the principles behind the establishment of the Jubilee; and so on. Businesses with enormous financial resources have the financial strength to make an individual's efforts to redress a personal injustice almost impossible. We need to ask if it is any wiser to trust those who manage institutions with large concentrations of economic power than it is to trust those who run the state. If concentrations of power must exist, is it not better to opt for countervailing power? Using a boxing analogy, is it not wiser to put two heavyweights in the ring together than to pit a lightweight against a heavyweight? I, for one, would be delighted to have smaller governmental entities, with little government regulation, if we would insist that our economic institutions are to be small, also.

TECHNOLOGY

As communications and transportation seemingly shrink the world and allow businesses to dispense the benefits and potential hazards of their technology more rapidly and widely, the potentials for negative side effects grow so large that it is imprudent to allow those driven by profit motives to plunge ahead in a competitive market without some public constraints regarding the safety of their products. The temptations are massive to get to the market first with new drugs, chemicals, bioengineering technology, and so forth because the greatest share of the market is often captured by the first innovator. Managers strive to be first—often a measure of success—and their self-identity may be on the line when making decisions to market technically sophisticated products. Surely the past fifty years have revealed enough health and safety problems emerging through the existing screen of government regulations to indicate that the incidents of harm would be far more numerous if no regulations were in place.

URBANIZATION

Over 70 percent of the North American population lives on 1 percent of the land. This statistic has enormous implications for the community and people's need for public restrictions. Throwing one's garbage on the street is no longer acceptable behavior. Every home can no longer have its own well or septic system. Pollution in its many forms—burning trash, automobile emissions, smokestack pollutants, industrial waste, and so forth—suddenly constitutes a community concern. God set forth rather elaborate regulations for the Israelites pertaining to health matters in their camp, even though those concerns were related to other specific problems (see Lev. 13:1-59; 14:1-57; 15:1-12; Num. 5:1-4; 19:11-22). A person's opportunity to undermine the health or safety of a neighbor, though, is not to be regarded lightly. The generation of nuclear energy, the production of toxic chemicals, and other humanly generated outcomes that produce great benefits, with concomitant potentials for harm, are legitimate concerns for the community to regulate. Our mere proximity to one another alters the extent and sometimes the very nature of our freedom.

RETRIBUTION

Justice requires personal retribution, not merely institutional retribution. Biblically, it is unjust for a person to do harm to a neighbor and then be excused from making personal restitution. The establishment of nonpersonal "legal beings" (corporations) that are allowed to bear the economic penalties for human misconduct has permitted our society to drift away from personal accountability and the basic biblical principle of retribution that was so clearly discussed by Dr. John Sparks in "Business Law and Biblical Principles" (volume 3, chapter 13). Society has been content to let those who work for corporations hide behind the corporation's personified legal veil for over one hundred years, but we know that God will call everybody to a personal accounting (see Rom. 14:12). Love requires us to do no less in this life. We discipline those we love and seek their long-term good by holding them personally accountable for their inappropriate conduct. This course is essential for personal growth to take place. Christians should seek to establish systems where accountability and retribution are maintained and where some standards for determining retribution are enunciated in the governing regulations.

FEAR

Not only is the fear of the Lord the beginning of wisdom (see Prov. 1:7), but fear of properly constituted and correctly administered public authority is also good (see Rom. 13:3-5). Perfect love casts out fear (see 1 John 4:18), but where love is missing, where people think more about themselves than their neighbors, it is healthy to establish and maintain just processes that strike fear in the minds of those who willfully ignore properly constituted and appropriate community constraints. Paul's question in the Romans 13:3-5 passage, "Do you want to have no fear of authority?" assumes the answer is self-evident: "We want to have a proper fear of God's governing authorities when we are tempted to do or have done evil." The unrighteous hate fear; the godly understand and respect the appropriateness of godly fear. Fear is a wholesome part of God's economy, and we should properly incorporate it in a balanced community.

In summary, government regulations are a legitimate part of God's overall design. He put regulations on Adam both before and after the Fall; He is renovating His children so they can assume more and more self-control; He has provided those who do not earnestly desire His discipline and direction with governing authorities they can rightly fear, for their own good. The balance between having freedoms and regulations is a function of God's common grace, with greater freedom (when it is being exercised healthily) being a mark of God's sovereign pleasure in administering the benefits of godly conduct to the general population that they might taste the benefits of righteousness, even though they do not acknowledge it as a gracious gift from Him.

PART VIII

STEWARDSHIP
OF THE ENVIRONMENT

How are Christians to positively influence society to take a wholesome interest in environmental issues in a manner reflecting the principles and standards of Scripture? Is it possible to achieve such a goal in a pluralistic community? The answers are not easy to come by, but the chapter before us offers the best possibility of doing so that I am aware of.

Dr. P. J. Hill identifies five biblical principles that should undergird the thinking of Christians called on to address today's many environmental issues. These principles are relevant to our discussions because they draw us forthrightly into the biblical tension between mankind's use of the environment and our responsibility to care for it. Many secularists point an accusing finger at the Christian community and blame our forefathers for being extremely anthropocentric (conceiving of man as the central fact and final aim of the universe). These accusers believe Christians promote the biblical mandate, calling for mankind to exercise dominion over the earth, without restraints. Or in effect, Christians are accused of letting a tiger out of the cage without then controlling it. The principles Dr. Hill identifies ask us to more faithfully consider and articulate our obligation to care for the environment.

Dr. Hill also examines three of the critical determinants governing how people will respond to various opportunities to economically benefit from the use of the environment. These determinants are (1) the person's ideology or world and life view, (2) the fullness of the information people have available and implement when making decisions about the environment, and (3) the incentives that come to bear on the decision maker when opportunities are present to profit by using the environment.

The core of Hill's work, however, focuses on property rights. Property rights determine who can take action regarding the use of property, and who will be able to participate in and influence the outcome of actions regarding the environment. The proper structuring of property rights is, therefore, critical to operationalizing the biblical principles and environmental ideology. Dr. Hill discusses the attributes of property rights—exclusivity, liability, and transfer-ability—that must be present if society's efforts to deal with environmental issues are to have a fighting chance of reflecting the concerns contained in the intent of the biblical principles. In expanding on this concept, he relies on concrete examples to promote understanding of his thesis.

It is enlightening to discover how our United States structure of property rights mitigates against many of God's principles and yet encourages the respect of others. Those of us who manifest the assumptions of our culture, believing we have and are embracing a sound concept of property rights, have much to contemplate as Dr. Hill's chapter unfolds.

CHAPTER 8

BIBLICAL PRINCIPLES APPLIED TO A NATURAL RESOURCES/ ENVIRONMENT POLICY

Peter J. Hill

Peter J. Hill is the George F. Bennett Professor of Economics at Wheaton College, Wheaton, Illinois. He is a coauthor of two books, The Birth of a Transfer Society *and* Growth and Welfare in the American Past, *and has published articles in the fields of economic history, property rights theory, and environmental policy. Professor Hill received his Ph.D. in Economics from the University of Chicago. Prior to his appointment at Wheaton College, he was at Montana State University and held visiting appointments at Purdue University and the University of Iowa.*

In today's world, one does not have to search very hard for news of environmental problems. Massive oil spills, depletion of the ozone layer, air pollution, tropical deforestation, toxic wastes, and numerous other issues confront us daily. How should Christians react to such situations? Can we in good conscience use up natural resources? How do we trade off the needs of future generations against the use of resources to feed today's hungry around the world? Just what is a responsible environmental ethic? This chapter searches for biblical principles that apply to these and other resource issues and then discusses the application of those principles in the light of modern environmental problems.

The logical place to begin in any discussion of Christian perspectives on resources is the Creation. The fact that God is the Creator of the universe gives a special value to all of nature. Even before the creation of man, God honored other parts of the order by calling them good (see Gen. 1:4, 10, 12, 18, 21, 25). This point is important because some authors have labeled Christianity extremely anthropocentric and ultimately responsible for the environmental crisis.[1] They have held that Christianity's teaching of man's dominion over nature has led to a low view of nature and to its exploitation. However, a full reading of Scripture conveys a very different picture.

Thus the first principle is that the creation has worth and stature completely apart from man's involvement in it. One of God's purposes in creation was for the created order to give glory to Him: "The heavens declare the glory of God; the skies proclaim the work of his hands" (Ps. 19:1). Nature serves something beyond human purposes and as such must be respected and honored. The significance of creation is amplified in passages such as Job 38–41 where God depicts dramatically how vast and mighty creation is in relationship to man's understanding.

The worth of nature is further emphasized by Christ's redemptive activity, which involves creation as well as mankind:

> The creation waits in eager expectation for the sons of God to be revealed. For the creation was subjected to frustration, not by its own choice, but by the will of the one who subjected it, in hope that the creation itself will be liberated from its bondage to decay and brought into the glorious freedom of the children of God. (Rom. 8:19-21)

One must be careful, however, in honoring creation not to lapse into pantheism. The Bible makes it very clear that God is separate from the created order and our worship is to be reserved for Him alone. There are distinct elements of pantheism in much of modern environmental ethics.[2] In an attempt to create an appropriate reverence for nature some modern thinkers have called for worshiping the natural order and speak of that order in terms of a unity and purpose not allowing for an external creator. Christians must remember that the physical universe we observe does not represent all of reality. We live in a physical world worthy of our respect, but much beyond it is of consequence.

The second principle concerns the usefulness of creation to mankind. Even though nature has intrinsic value apart from its relation to man, one of its purposes is to serve man. The creation account itself outlines this:

> Then God said, "Let us make man in our image, in our likeness, and let them rule over the fish of the sea and the birds of the air, over the livestock, over all the earth, and over all the creatures that move along the ground." (Gen. 1:26)

> God blessed them and said to them, "Be fruitful and increase in number; fill the earth and subdue it. Rule over the fish of the sea and the birds of the air and over every living creature that moves on the ground." (Gen. 1:28)

Man's dominion over nature is emphasized by the verbs in these passages, *radah* (to rule) and *kabash* (to subdue), which have a firm, almost harsh ring.

One can translate *kabash* as "to tread under foot" or "to conquer." Likewise, *radah* can mean "to tread" or "to prevail against." God further explains man's relationship to creation when He tells Noah: "Everything that lives and moves will be food for you. Just as I gave you the green plants, I now give you everything" (Gen. 9:3). On the basis of these and numerous other passages it is evident man has responsibility for ruling and maintaining nature, and the use of creation is very much a part of God's plan for mankind.

If one looks only at the passages just cited, one can see why some commentators feel that a biblical view of nature leads to exploitation and overuse. However, the relationship between man and nature must be informed by the rest of Scripture. Genesis 2:15 records the command that man in the Garden of Eden was "to work it and take care of it," a concept that softens somewhat the dominion passages of Genesis 1. Psalm 8 reasserts man's dominion over nature but very much in the context of wonder and awe. It implies that we have been given responsibility for God's creation, but it is a responsibility not to be taken lightly. We are to be careful, considerate managers of nature, always remembering that God is the Creator. Specific passages also detail how man is to be a careful manager of the land (see Lev. 25:1-5), wildlife (see Deut. 22:6), and domesticated animals (see Deut. 25:4).

Thus the dominion that God has assigned involves responsibility. In the Old Testament, dominion was often used to describe the rule of a king over his subjects, but the rule entailed both privileges *and* responsibilities. Rulers who exercised their dominion wantonly, without appropriate care of those under them, are condemned throughout the Scriptures.[3] In the same way man is to be a careful steward over that which God has given him dominion. We have an even deeper understanding of what dominion means in Christ, in that our dominion over nature is to be as His over the universe, one of sacrificial service, not cruel subjugation.[4]

A third biblical principle is God's ultimate ownership of all of creation. This is implicit in the previous discussion of man's dominion over nature but needs to be made more explicit. We are charged with being careful managers of nature, but we must never think that we are the ultimate owners. Stewardship implies that we are managing the resources on behalf of the owner, the Sovereign God of the universe. Numerous passages make this relationship clear:

"Although the whole earth is mine, you will be for me a kingdom of priests and a holy nation." (Exod. 19:5-6)

"The land is mine and you are but aliens and my tenants." (Lev. 25:23)

The earth is the LORD's, and everything in it,
    the world, and all who live in it. (Ps. 24:1)

"Yours, O LORD, is the greatness and the power
     and the glory and the majesty and the splendor,
     for everything in heaven and earth is yours." (1 Chron. 29:11)

This principle of stewardship means that arrogance toward nature is never fitting. We are to be careful managers of God's resources, always recognizing that we have but temporary control of them and that servanthood is an essential aspect of godly stewardship.

The concept of stewardship leads to the fourth principle, that of accountability. Being a responsible steward means there are standards by which one is held accountable for what one does with the resource being managed. Both Old and New Testaments assert that we are responsible, moral creatures with the capacity for choice. God holds us accountable for the quality of our choices in all areas of life; our management of natural resources is only one of them.[5]

Finally, the last biblical principle asks, For whom is the earth created? Who should be included in our calculations when we consider optimal rates of resource use, just the present generation or future generations as well? Again, Scripture affirms that God is the Lord of all generations, that He does not value one generation above another, and that, as His stewards, we must have the same attitude. It is appropriate to include the needs of the present generation in our calculations, but we must also recognize that future generations count and that their needs must be acknowledged.

Thus we have five basic biblical principles relevant to natural resource policy: (1) the creation has worth apart from its usefulness for mankind; (2) nevertheless, one purpose of nature is that it is to be used by man; (3) man's control over nature is one of stewardship, not ultimate ownership; (4) man is held accountable for how he manages creation; and (5) future generations must not be ignored in resource decisions.

How does one make these principles operational? Are they anything more than nice-sounding rhetoric to create appropriate warm, fuzzy feelings about the environment? Surely they represent far more than that, but to discover specific guidance on natural resource policy, much more analysis is in order.

This chapter started with the suggestion that not all decisions about our natural environment have been good ones. To improve the quality of our decisions and bring to bear the principles developed here, we need to understand the decision-making process. All decisions are a function of three basic elements: the *ideology* of the decision maker, the *information* that individual has when making a decision, and the *incentives* the decision maker faces.

The term *ideology* is used as shorthand for an individual's world view. Every person has a value framework through which he or she processes information about the external world. This set of beliefs will determine how one weighs different facts and even what one considers relevant information. If we want better decisions about the environment, developing a strong environmental ethic is fundamental. Belief structures can be altered, as evidenced by the environmental movement of the last several decades. Casual empiricism would indicate that at least some people are less likely to litter, more inclined to regard polluting activities as socially unacceptable and to have a greater respect for nature, because of the "consciousness raising" that has taken place. Needless to say, any ethic not fully grounded in Scripture will not be completely true, and the modern environmental movement is a good example of that. As pointed out earlier, much smacks of pantheism among many environmentalists, particularly those of the New Age variety.

The Christian has every reason to embrace an appropriate environmental ethic, one that honors creation but distinguishes it from the Creator. The principles outlined in the first part of the chapter form the basis for a scriptural ethic that respects nature but also allows for mankind's interaction with it. Decisions affecting natural resources will be improved to the extent that they are based on an appropriate ideology, or belief structure.

However, simply recommending reformation of our world view is not sufficient. Our ability to act responsibly toward nature has been hindered by our alienation from God. The original Fall and our continued rebellion mean that we act selfishly, that we have limited knowledge, and that we often fail to recognize the full magnificence and glory of the natural order, a magnificence and glory reflecting God's character. In view of these failings we must not rely on ideology alone to lead us to good decisions about creation but must also examine the other influences on decision making, namely, information and incentives.

Information and incentives are very much affected by the institutional order of a society. The social institutions pertinent to resource issues are the rules that assign responsibility; that is, they determine who can take what actions and who gets a hearing with regard to those actions. These rules, sometimes called property rights, are crucial determinants of what information is generated and what incentives the decision maker faces.

These property rights generate appropriate information and incentives to the extent that they embody three characteristics: exclusivity, liability, and transferability. Exclusivity means the owner of a resource is able to capture a return from using the property in a way advantageous to other people, and it also means that owner can exclude others from benefiting from the use of the property unless they have secured the owner's permission. If exclusivity does not exist, a resource will be overused. For instance, on the American frontier there were no exclusive rights to live North American buffalo. If a buffalo hunter decided to postpone the shooting of any particular animal, he had no assurance that he would have the option to exercise that right in the future. The only way he could be assured of an exclusive right to a buffalo was to shoot it. Live buffalo were owned by everyone; dead ones belonged to the person who killed them. Is it any wonder that such a property rights system led to the near extermination of the species?

Liability forces a resource owner to bear the costs of actions that harm others. If property rights fully embody liability, costs are not imposed on others without their willing consent. For instance, I will allow you to impose harm on me, that is, use up some of the grass on my cattle ranch for your livestock, only if you adequately remunerate me. If liability were not fully attached to your property, that is, your cattle, you could drive them across my land, allowing them to remove some of the grass without compensating me. Pollution is a notable example of an incomplete property right, of liability not being present. It is exactly analogous to the cattle example in that individuals can use up some of another's resource, for instance, the clean air, without appropriate compensation.

Transferability encourages owners to look for ways of using property that benefit others. The fact that a piece of property can be bought or sold means that a resource owner who ignores the wishes of other people does so at a cost, a reduction in wealth. If rights are not transferable, no such wealth loss is associated with ignoring the wishes of others.

An excellent example of the problems of nontransferability occurred in the summer of 1987 on the Ruby River in Montana. The Ruby is one of the prime trout fishing streams in the nation, but it also supports substantial agricultural activity through irrigation. Because of the severe drought in 1987, irrigators drew out so much water that a sizable fish kill resulted. Why could not farmers be convinced to leave enough water in the stream to maintain fish? Was the value of water for irrigation higher than its value for supporting trout? That was not the case. Instead the problem was an institutional impairment to the transfer of water rights, in that Montana law does not allow for any instream holding of rights.

A private organization, Trout Unlimited, was willing to purchase from farmers enough water to sustain the fish. And farmers, despite the drought, did not value *all* of their water so highly that they would have been unwilling to engage in such a transfer. In other words, the potential existed for a mutually beneficial trade, one that would force farmers to take account of an alternative use for their resource. However, the lack of transferability of water rights meant that farmers faced no wealth loss from ignoring the wishes of conservationists and fishermen.

Thus the attributes of exclusivity, liability, and transferability are essential for a well-functioning property rights system, one that fulfills the biblical mandate of holding individuals accountable for their decisions. If any one of those attributes is missing, people can act irresponsibly with regard to creation, at least in part because they do not have adequate information or appropriate incentives to make sound decisions.[6]

The information available to a decision maker is very much a function of property rights because people, in the process of trading property rights, generate indexes of value for various uses of property. For instance, a landowner who knows there is coal on the land can readily obtain information through the price system about how others in society value that coal. If that individual also holds rights to the coal, that same information contains incentives for the owner to take actions that satisfy other people, namely, make coal available for them. Since part of the biblical mandate with regard to creation is to use it for mankind, it would seem to be appropriate to be aware of and respond to people who desire to use coal as a fuel source.

But is mining the coal the only use for that land? What if mining leaves ugly scars on the earth's surface, permanently reducing certain individuals' aesthetic enjoyment of that land? How does a price system take those desires into account? Will coal be mined while aesthetics are ignored? The price system does not adequately represent all desires, and its failure to do so is caused by a lack of appropriate property rights. If the landowner had exclusive control over view rights to her land, she could charge an appropriate fee, and the price system would communicate to her whether the land was more valuable left in its pristine state or mined for coal.

The fact that property rights are not well defined and enforced is at the heart of the environmental crisis. The lack of a full rights structure means decision makers do not have appropriate incentives and information. Therefore, it is not surprising that resource misuse occurs when property rights are incomplete. Of course, simply pointing out the lack of adequate property rights is not a solution to the environmental problem, but it provides some general guidance. We do not necessarily want to fully define rights to all resources; in some cases the transaction costs of doing so are too high. For instance, defining exclusivity in view rights would be extremely difficult. But many other property rights problems are not so intractable, and the property rights framework is a useful way of looking at environmental issues.

For instance, air and water are the major resources suffering from pollution problems because they are usually treated as common property, that is, property where no one has exclusivity. Any individual who uses a particular airshed or watershed to dispose of waste does not face the full cost of his action; instead the costs are spread over all the potential users of that resource.[7] The answer is to attempt to restructure property rights so that exclusivity, liability, and transferability exist. Sometimes there are legal barriers to property rights definition and transfer, as in the case of water law in many states, and they can be removed. In others, the government must take positive steps to force decision makers to bear the full costs of their actions. For instance, a tax per unit of air or water pollution increases the costs of using the air or water as a waste disposal mechanism. If the tax is set at the correct level (if it represents the cost of pollution to other users of the resource), the decision maker faces the correct incentive structure. He can continue to pollute if he is willing to pay the cost, and if he does, the additional benefits to society from the polluting activity exceed the additional costs. In all likelihood under such a tax the polluter will decide to reduce emissions—but not to zero.

Another useful way of altering property rights in air is through "the bubble concept." Under such a structure, people residing in a particular airshed, through some government entity, would decide how much pollution they are willing to live with. Rights to the pollution would then be available to producers in the area. The rights could be either handed out on the basis of historical production or auctioned off to the highest bidder. An important element of such a system would be transferability; for the rights to result in the greatest production at the lowest cost, each pollution right would need to be fully transferable among firms in the airshed. Then each producer would face an appropriate incentive structure and could decide if it would be cheaper to purchase pollution rights and continue polluting at its historical rate, to adopt pollutant-reducing technology, or to shut down.

Each of these proposals involves government action of some sort. Because the definition and the enforcement of property rights are at least in part a function of government, an alteration of those rights will probably also involve government. However, one must carefully specify the type of action appropriate when suggesting that government is the answer to environmental problems. Seeing the problem as one of inadequate property rights gives positive guidance about how government can be most effective—through the clear specification of rights and the fuller defense of them. Unfortunately, too often government's involvement in resource issues has not been framed in a property rights context and hence has not been as effective as possible.

For instance, in terms of air and water pollution, the common governmental response has been through command and control. Under such a system, government specifies the amount of pollution that can occur from each source and, in many cases, also specifies the technology to be used in reducing emissions. Numerous studies have shown that for any goal achieved through command and control, a bubble concept with transferable rights could achieve the same level of pollution reduction much more cheaply.[8]

The oft-repeated suggestion that government ownership and management of resources are solutions to environmental problems might seem to be appropriate when private property rights and markets have failed to lead to sound resource management. However, it ignores the fact that under government ownership, it is very difficult to construct property rights so that decision makers face appropriate incentives and receive correct information.

The United States Forest Service is an example of incentives and information gone awry. Created by federal legislation in 1891, this government agency has responsibility for some 188 million acres. It is charged with managing these lands in an environmentally and economically sound manner, but unfortunately fails to meet either goal. Much of the acreage for which it has responsibility has conflicting multiple uses: logging, wildlife habitat, and recreation, to name but a few. However, bureaucratic incentives are structured so that each district manager finds it to his or her advantage to maximize that district's budget. Thus commercial timber production takes precedence over other uses, since such production requires massive Forest Service road building and other budget-intensive activities.

Logging of Forest Service lands is not necessarily bad; private forest managers who face appropriate incentives engage in logging activities. However, the Forest Service carries logging far beyond what makes economic sense and in the process encourages massive environmental disruption. To provide access for timber companies that have successfully bid for logging rights, the Forest Service prepares subsidized roads. Approximately 342,000 miles of roads have been built by the Forest Service, more than eight times the total mileage of the U.S. Interstate System. The Service plans to build another 262,000 miles over the next thirty years.[9] These roads encourage erosion, which harms trout streams, and also permit motorized vehicles to enter previously inaccessible areas, causing deterioration of wildlife habitat. Perhaps more dramatic is the actual logging, which often results in ugly clearcuts and further erosion.

Again, not all logging activity is bad, but the tragic thing about Forest Service activity is that it encourages harvesting of timber where, even aside from aesthetic considerations, the commercial value of the timber does not cover the costs of the timber sales. From 1974 through 1978 over half the timber sales in the national forests did not cover the costs of timber management and reforestation.[10] The Northern Rockies and Alaska, areas where timberlands are ecologically fragile, have an even worse record. In the states of Colorado, Wyoming, Utah, Montana, Idaho, and New Mexico the Forest Service generally receives less than twenty cents back for each dollar it spends on timber management and road building.[11] And in the Sitka National Forest in Alaska, the return is seven cents on the dollar.[12] The point of all these comments is not that the Forest Service is staffed by bad people, but that the incentives are such that environmentally destructive and economically unsound policies are favored. Numerous other examples abound of government mismanagement of resources, all of which attest to the difficulty of appropriately structuring incentives in the public sector.[13]

But even if government action takes the appropriate form, that is, to better define and enforce property rights, will we get the right rate of resource use from a biblical perspective? How do we know that the desires represented through property rights and markets are truly scriptural? Is it not possible to have a well-functioning market system and still have resources put to ungodly uses? At this point the biblical environmental ethic must inform the private property system. An institutional structure that embodies exclusivity, liability, and transferability in its property rights will accurately represent the desires of members of society and will also encourage resource owners to respond to those desires. Full accountability, a biblical concept, will be in place. However, one must remember that Scripture most often discusses accountability in the context of responsibility to God, and the accountability being discussed here is accountability to other people, an entirely different concept.

All of this reaffirms the need for a biblically based view of nature and of man so that the desires represented in the marketplace will come closer to God's desires. At the same time, however, it is not clear that any alternative democratic institutional structure would lead to a more godly environmental policy. The biblical mandate of valuing nature but making use of it does not offer much guidance in the particulars of resource use. Evidently God has allowed man to work out those details on the basis of his own perceptions of needs, with those needs appropriately informed by an awareness of God and His principles.

We are stuck with human desires, as imperfect as they might be, as our standard to measure how resources should be used. God has given us the opportunity and responsibility to manage His creation, and it therefore seems appropriate to have an institutional structure that reflects human desires and holds individuals accountable as to whether they use their resources according to those desires. Such a structure is the system of property rights described earlier. If this seems a weak defense of property rights, that may be because it is.[14] One can conceive of many cases when a system of well-defined and enforced property rights results in resource use that seems to violate God's standards. However, it is difficult to conceive of another property rights structure that does better at making sure God's standards are not violated. The two most obvious alternatives, common property and government ownership, suffer from such obvious faults that they are clearly inferior choices.

Despite this rather lukewarm endorsement of private property rights as the correct mechanism for controlling resource use, several facets of such a system deserve some approbation. Such a rights structure allows for expression of certain aspects of the biblical principles outlined at the beginning of this chapter.

First, a private property system will not produce zero pollution in the sense of stopping all alteration of the environment; but neither will it allow growth at all costs with material desires superseding all others. If property rights are fully defined and enforced, some emissions will still foul our air, not all water will be of pristine quality, and the use of nonrenewable resources will not drop to zero. However, the significant difference between that world and the one we presently live in is that actions altering the environment would take place only if all users of the environment were convinced that those actions were to everybody's mutual advantage. In other words, there would be no uncompensated losers. A person who valued an unspoiled view more than someone else valued a factory smokestack in the middle of that view would win out. The factory smokestack would not exist, at least not at that location. Such a property rights system would not stop economic growth but would allow it to occur only if the benefits were valued more highly than what was given up to get that growth. Such an approach to resource use seems appropriate in view of the first two principles outlined at the beginning of the chapter, that we are to appreciate and value God's creation but also see it as usable for human purposes.

Another component of a private property rights system is that it does not depend on complete social agreement for action to take place. Diversity is permitted by virtue of the fact that a person who has strong feelings about resource use that differ from the group consensus can, under such a system, express those feelings through prices and markets. This can be of particular importance to Christians who find themselves at odds with prevailing wisdom about the environment. If such beliefs represent a minority position, they are much more likely to find expression in a system of private property rights than under alternative rights arrangements.

An apt illustration is found in an incident dealing with different bird species. During the 1920s a leading conservationist, Rosalie Edge, became concerned that conservation groups gave little attention to the preservation of nongame birds.[15] She felt that the Audubon Society and state game departments were more concerned with songbirds and game species than raptors. She was particularly incensed over the wholesale slaughter of those raptors as they migrated down the Appalachian Mountains. One place in eastern Pennsylvania, Hawk Mountain, was an especially popular spot for killing falcons, eagles, ospreys, and hawks.

In an effort to stop the slaughter Mrs. Edge tried to get the Hawk and Owl Society, an affiliate of the National Audubon Society, to purchase the mountain. Failing that, she took matters into her own hands, purchasing the property herself and hiring a young naturalist to manage it. Today, the Hawk Mountain Sanctuary stands as a monument to Rosalie Edge's farsightedness, with as many as three thousand people in one day using the lookouts in the fall to observe the large numbers of migrating birds.

If control of resources had been totally under political control, it is doubtful that, even in a democratic setting, Mrs. Edge could have succeeded in convincing a majority of the population that Hawk Mountain should have been off limits for persons hunting raptors. To protect poultry and game birds, many states had a bounty system to reward hunters who killed hawks. In 1934, the year Rosalie Edge purchased Hawk Mountain, Pennsylvania law permitted the shooting of all hawk species and paid a bounty on goshawks. The Audubon Society was ambivalent about raptors. Mrs. Edge said,

> The indifference of the Audubon Association to hawk protection, the fact that in certain of its publications it recommends the pole-trap and that it uses steel-traps on its chief sanctuary; that it believes in the "control" of many valuable species and in general urges the protection only of the "birds of lawn and garden" makes it undesirable that the Audubon Association shall have a controlling voice in the policies that shall regulate the sanctuary at Hawk Mountain.[16]

However, given the system of property rights that prevailed, Mrs. Edge did not have to convince the majority of the wisdom of her position; rather, she had to secure agreement from only one other person, the owner of the property. He sold her the land, she acted on her distinctly minority view of the future, and her vision has turned out to be valuable for the rest of us.

But can we be assured that future generations will have a place in a market economy? Are not the Rosalie Edges of the world few and far between? What of God's concern for all people of all times? Is there not a chance that a system based on private property rights will cater exclusively to the desires of the present generation compared to the needs of future ones? Again, the appropriate question to ask is, Compared to what? What alternative institutional arrangement will do a better job than one that embodies transferable property rights? It would be nice to posit a theocracy headed by an omniscient saint, and if that were a realistic alternative, markets would come out second best. However, if we stick to real world possibilities, well-defined rights that can be bought and sold look quite good indeed.

Contrast for a moment a resource being managed under two alternative regimes. It is exhaustible, hence it is important to give future generations some voice in the choice about the appropriate rate of use. Under the first regime, a pure democracy controls the use of the resource. With different expectations by members of the population about the resource's future value, the average perception will dominate. In other words, if the present generation thinks that, on average, the resource has a future value (discounted to the present) greater than its value in present consumption, it will be preserved. On the other hand, if the average expectation of the resource's future value is less than its value in present consumption, it will be consumed.

Now take the same resource, the same population with the same set of preferences and expectations, but make the present/future allocation on the basis of transferable property rights. In this case the resource is more likely to be preserved for the future because it is not the *average* perception about the future value of the resource that counts, but instead the perception of those *most* optimistic about its future value who express themselves in the marketplace. These individuals will purchase the resource in the expectation of a high future value, hold it out of consumption, and in the process preserve it for future generations. In fact, for any resource to be used in the present, all who believe it has some value in the future must be outbid.

All of this is not to say that altruistic feelings for future generations are unimportant. Under either system such sentiments will result in greater preservation for future generations. Notice, however, that the political system depends entirely on altruism, or people caring for future generations, while the market order allows those preferences to be expressed but also rewards individuals who, for selfish reasons, decide to withhold resources from present consumption.

Giving future generations a voice is a bit awkward. Their preferences will be expressed only in people who exist presently, so it is useful to have someone stand in for them today; they need agents to represent them. These agents cannot know perfectly the desires of people not yet born, but they can make educated guesses about these desires. In the market arena these agents are either unselfish contributors to the future or speculators acting on their perception of future demands for resources. If their perceptions are correct, their wealth increases; if they guess incorrectly, they suffer a wealth loss. Thus these agents have strong incentives to be well informed and to correctly predict the needs of future generations.

In a world where Christian charity and concern for others are sometimes in short supply, it is useful to have a mechanism that allows for the needs of the future to be met, by those acting charitably *and* those pursuing profit. Again, institutional design is a fundamental component of a system that satisfies God's desire that we think not only of this generation.

CONCLUSION

A Christian perspective on the environment is not an easy one to come by. Although God gives us some overarching principles in Scripture, the issues are complex and often emotion laden. The modern environmental movement, while reacting to a previously unscriptural exploitation of nature, is rife with paganism. Thus the Christian must truly desire the mind of Christ in dealing with these questions and must think long and hard about the particulars of the various issues.

This chapter has argued that three elements are crucial to good decisions, and that a society without all three will have little hope of developing and maintaining a natural resource policy that reflects the Christian's concern for both the creation and the Creator.

The three elements that must be in place are (1) an appropriate belief structure or ideology, (2) a system that generates adequate information, and (3) an incentive structure that holds individuals accountable for their behavior. Under such a system we have at least the hope of managing the earth in a way pleasing to the Sovereign God of the universe.

EDITOR'S PERSPECTIVE

Dr. Hill's discourse identifies the five biblical principles that should guide our thinking on environmental matters and discusses how these can be undermined or fostered by the impact of people's ideology, the information they have available when making environmental decisions, and the incentives they encounter in the economic arena where property rights embodying (or failing to embody) the attributes of exclusivity, liability, and transferability determine the operationalization of God's revealed principles. I must ask again, How are Christians to positively influence society to take a wholesome interest in environmental issues in a manner reflecting the principles and standards of Scripture?

Christians can influence society in such matters in two ways that remain faithful to both righteous conduct and godly motives. (This latter emphasis is a reminder that our motives and intentions for doing something are as important to God as are our specific acts [see 1 Cor. 4:5].) First, the Holy Spirit's application of the gospel message to someone's heart will of necessity bring about profound changes in the life of the convert, in matters of conduct and purpose. The gospel is not to be presented to the world with this as its primary purpose, however, but it is nevertheless a fact that people's world view is reshaped when Christ becomes their Lord and Savior.

The gospel has as its primary goal the salvation of sinners, which is a past, present, and future process, not a one-time event. (I was saved; I am being saved; and I will be saved.) This process has seven facets to its completeness. In its entirety, salvation embodies (1) the *calling* of each person to a right relationship with God in accordance with His terms of reconciliation; (2) *regeneration* (rebirth) by the Holy Spirit empowering the individual to see and enter the Kingdom of God (see John 3:3-6); (3) *conversion* through which the sinner truly repents and by faith lays claim to the finished work of Christ on his or her behalf; (4) *justification* by which Christ's righteousness is imputed or ascribed to the credit of the convert so that he or she can be accounted righteous by the Eternal Judge; (5) *adoption* into God's family so that one is removed from Satan's family and returned to God's family, becoming an heir to eternal life with its infinite benefits; (6) *sanctification* whereby one is renovated and truly becomes more and more like Christ in intentions and conduct; and (7) *glorification* whereby God will finally and eternally perfect the entire being.

The only visible impact of the gospel on us is manifested in our sanctification, the sixth facet of the salvation process. Sanctification transforms our ideology from a man-centered one, as the Spirit writes the Word of God on our hearts, so that we begin to see God, ourselves, and others (including the world) from God's perspective. This basic reshaping of our understanding and meaning of reality can (should) spill over into every aspect of our lives, which is precisely what P. J. Hill is interested in when he talks about environmental issues with Christians. He calls us to think about this matter in the light of God's expressed interests.

The second way Christians can influence the process of making environmental decisions in the larger community, especially among groups that reject the Christian perspective, is to find and employ biblically sanctioned incentives that appeal to the public and produce the best system of property rights that will encourage sound environmental policies. Does this imply that Christians should engage in planned manipulation? It does not. It means we acknowledge and have the conviction and courage to do this based on the biblical evidence substantiating this conclusion. Three arguments support the appropriateness of identifying these kinds of incentives.

First, the human potential of knowing the difference between good and evil was activated with the Fall. This ability to know good and evil, a universal characteristic of humans, is nevertheless subject to being repressed, rationalized away, or perverted by those whose personal desires oppose their knowledge of God and what He desires (see Rom. 1:18-23). But as long as Christians know God's desires, we can go to the marketplace and appeal to the general knowledge of good and evil in the name of the well-being of everybody's neighbors, in the name of fairness that looks to mutually serve all affected parties. We can also act in the name of prudent self-interest (not selfishness) that reflects practical, sound, discreet, circumspect, wise reasons for improving concepts of property rights in the areas of exclusivity, liability, and transferability as explained by Dr. Hill.

Second, Christ declared, "You are the salt of the earth . . . [and] the light of the world," and you are to "let your light shine before men in such a way that they may see your good works, and glorify your Father who is in heaven" (Matt. 5:13-14, 16). Biblically, salt is both a preservative and a savoring element. The preservation concept most directly applies in this context. Christians need to point to the practices destroying the environment and call for their cessation while offering positive alternative courses of action (lights in the marketplace). The cry to stop is best heard when a constructive alternative accompanies the plea.

Finally, God created an ordered universe and instituted both internal and external incentives to stimulate us to good works. The incentives are many in number and diverse in character. Scripture even goes to the length of explaining that something as basic as hunger pangs is part of God's system of incentives (see Prov. 16:26). Two chapters (8 and 9) of volume 2 in this series were devoted to external incentives (rewards and punishments) and internal incentives (subjective psychological drives) that stimulate people to act in specific ways. The gospel's impact on the individual's ideology and view of environmental issues was discussed at the beginning of this "Editor's Perspective." The gospel is God's instrument to alter the internal incentives and motives of people. One human cannot, however, purpose to invade the internal incentive structure of another person. Thank God! If we could, the temptation to "play" God would be enormous.

Individuals and communities (businesses, governments, etc.) have the right, even the obligation, to provide external incentives to persons subject to their influence. Such incentives should be broad enough to encompass both rewards and punishments. Those in the public arena responsible for the maintenance of public justice ought to be encouraged to develop a publicly sanctioned system of property rights that will carefully take into consideration the necessary restructuring of the exclusivity, liability, and transferability attributes so that they will foster better environmental stewardship. For example, Dr. Hill discussed the fact that air and water are resources that really suffer from pollution problems because they are normally treated as common property. That is fair enough, so long as no particular member (person or institution) uses the common property as a place to dispose of waste. When one does, the old property arrangements will no longer work.

Governments represent the community. When dealing with certain problems, such as air and water pollution, should governments alter the rights to common property through addressing the attribute of exclusivity, liability, or transferability, or some combination of them? The logical point at which to alter property rights in the case of air and water is in the area of liability. That is, those who dump pollutants in the air or water that adversely impact those downwind or downstream should pay for the negative consequences they create that affect their neighbors. A sufficiently high tax should be levied on a graduated scale reflecting the level of pollution that allows the revenues to cover the "after the fact" pollution cleanup or that provides the proper incentive for the polluter to spend the money on emissions control procedures rather than pay the tax. Determining proper tax rates will be easier said than done, for information on the consequences and costs of pollution rectification is not readily available. The concept set forth by Dr. Hill certainly points us in the direction to move as we seek to cope with this growing problem.

Governments also compete against one another across both state and national boundaries, and getting governments to agree on pollution taxes will be no easier to achieve than trying to get individuals to agree on voluntarily restructuring property rights. Those that have the current advantage, those that seek an advantage, and all others that suffer the consequences of existing policies have their own incentives to seek and their own self-interests to protect. Nations, too, must be offered incentives by the community of nations to seek what is just for the world.

PART IX

AGRARIAN JUSTICE

The next chapter, "Biblical Principles Applied to a National Agricultural Policy," is particularly significant for this series because it affords us the opportunity to affirm the particular process that has been followed throughout the construction of the volumes: discovering biblical principles and applying them to specific marketplace problems instead of falling prey to the age-old temptation to look for specific how-to procedures, rules, and techniques. Why is this chapter so important in this regard? Because the most frequently heard comment questioning the application of Scripture to the solution of practical problems in the modern-day marketplace is that it was delivered to people living in an agrarian economy and it is therefore doubtful that Scripture's assertions transfer adequately to problems encountered in a high-tech society.

If people perceive that God gave His Word to His people as rules and regulations for application in specific and rather narrow contexts, they will conclude, in all probability, that much of Scripture is not transferable to situations in this century. Christ never held such a narrow view of Scripture, though. In fact, His authoritative expounding of the Word in the Sermon on the Mount (see Matt. 5–7) is delivered with the opposite understanding in mind. He taught that the law of God was not to be construed as having application in only the narrowest and most technically conforming situations where the letter of the Law—"Thou shalt not kill," for example—was being limited to its narrowest application—murder. The law in the case of "killing," as defined by Christ, covered anger and a condemning, disdaining attitude (see Matt. 5:21-26). Its application was to reach the deepest attitudes of the heart as well as specific situations. Principles at work in the Law are sometimes referred to as the spirit of the Law.

The third book (*Biblical Principles and Business: The Practice*) applied biblical principles to twelve specific disciplines of business (marketing, management, accounting, information systems, etc.). The book went to great lengths to make the point that Scripture does indeed speak to modern-day technologies, as well as ancient ones, because it always addresses the state of the human heart (character, intentions, thoughts) and human behavior as it affects our neighbors.

Since the topic of the forthcoming chapter is agriculture and the Scripture was delivered to people living in a society where the economic system was dominated by agriculture, would it be logical to expect more biblical commands and rules applying to this area of public policy than, say, the topics of money and banking or foreign trade? Readers who expect this to be the case will not be encouraged by the findings of Dr. Paul Wilson. There is almost as great a distinction to be made between the agrarian system of biblical times and that of modern times as there is between manufacturing and agriculture in modern times. The differences are enormous. Biblical principles by their nature compel us to move away from the narrow, constrictive perceptions of the Word that can so easily beset those who prefer to walk by rules rather than by the Spirit. The Holy Spirit has come to set us free from a regimen of "rule keeping" and to form the mind of Christ in us, whereby biblical precepts reflect the larger intent of God's revelation.

We must shoulder the responsibility of making some hard moral choices—hard in the sense that they will be unpopular with those who will be required to give up special privileges (unjust privileges?). Paul Wilson recognizes this reality in his work as he identifies four dominant driving forces that influence agricultural policy today and acknowledges how hard it will be to interject new ideas or perceptions of justice that emanate from the biblical principles composing the body of *covenant economics* with its subprinciples of charity, stewardship, and justice. The solution, from the human side of the "God and man" equation, must be found in making and following through on moral judgments derived from biblical principles, not a few rules or how-to procedures. The difficulties of implementation will be discussed in the "Editor's Perspective."

CHAPTER 9

BIBLICAL PRINCIPLES APPLIED TO A NATIONAL AGRICULTURAL POLICY

Paul N. Wilson

Paul N. Wilson is an Associate Professor in the Department of Agricultural Economics at the University of Arizona in Tucson. Dr. Wilson earned his Ph.D. in Agricultural and Applied Economics from the University of Minnesota. His teaching and research responsibilities are focused in the areas of production economics, agricultural business management, and agricultural finance. He has published in economics and agricultural science journals. Dr. Wilson is the recipient of several teaching awards, and he has recently developed a new course in ethical considerations in agricultural and natural resource policies.

The Bible shows us God working in an agricultural society. From the semi-nomadic times of Abraham, Isaac, and Jacob to the farms of the first century AD, agriculture dominated the economic lives of the people of the Bible.[1] Agricultural products, both crops and livestock, formed the basis of the national economy, and herders and farmers represented the majority of the population. Wealth and capital were measured by herd and farm size. Crop production depended highly on adequate rainfall. And rain variability produced a dynamic and sometimes contentious border between the cropped and the grazed regions of Palestine.

Two of the most frequently cited agricultural policies in the Bible are the Jubilee and Sabbatical years in the Old Testament. These policies encouraged the reallocation of capital, a period of renewal for depleted soils, and a community food bank for the less fortunate. The most striking references to agriculture in the New Testament are the herding and farming metaphors of shepherd and sheep, wine and wineskins, seed, plowing, pests, pruning, and fruit-bearing trees, to name only a select number. Jesus' parables are agricultural analogies because they were directed at the everyday experience of the people.

In some ways this agrarian society of ancient times reflects modern agriculture in the United States. Markets worked, and food was available at a price to villagers, urban dwellers, and religious and government leaders who did not have a direct link to the farm. There was a growing gap between the wealthy and the poor in rural areas. The Romans developed infrastructure, roads, aqueducts, water sources, and new agricultural lands, but levied significant taxes on the beneficiaries. Roller mills and beam presses represented important technological advances for grinding corn and producing olive oil. And finally, world markets were being developed for high-value commodities, which could be stored and transported by ship at a reasonable cost.

But what does this ancient agricultural society, and the Bible in particular, have to offer to agricultural policy makers at the end of the twentieth century? This chapter attempts to answer this question. First, after a brief overview of the history and status of U.S. agriculture, four major forces driving agricultural policy today will be discussed: agrarian fundamentalism, rent seeking, technologicalism, and internationalism. The second major section of this chapter will explore the biblical principle of covenant economics and the subprinciples of charity, stewardship and justice. Finally, the implications of covenant economics will be used to redirect U.S. agricultural policy along a more biblically compatible path.

MAJOR FORCES DRIVING U.S. AGRICULTURAL POLICY

A major, if not the primary, objective of U.S. agricultural policy is to maintain a dependable, low-cost supply of food and fiber to the citizens of this country. Although there are other policy objectives like reducing soil erosion, maintaining the family farm, increasing competitiveness in world markets, and developing rural areas, the bottom line in all these efforts is food security. This emphasis on a secure food supply has its philosophical and political roots in two historical periods: the colonial period of Thomas Jefferson and the economic depression of the 1930s.[2] The Jeffersonian position—that the traditional values of independence, thrift, stewardship, private property, and neighborhood were best developed on family farms—is an important part of the agricultural policy debate today. Likewise, vivid memories of the Dust Bowl and a severe farm depression in the decade prior to World War II kindle fears of similar events in the 1990s. The emotional and political force of these fears is evident in the fact that major federal farm legislation and the policy tools used to implement these laws have changed very little since the 1930s.

Yet radical structural changes have occurred in the U.S. agricultural sector since the end of World War II. Recognition of this historical development is critical in designing effective and efficient agricultural policies consistent with

Scripture. The best allocation of our resources as Christians is toward efforts that will shape a future for agriculture compatible with society's goals and biblical directives. We cannot turn back the future.

An overview of these historical trends is necessary before a biblically based agricultural policy can be developed.[3] Table 9.1 illustrates that only 2 percent of the citizens in the United States now live on farms or ranches. This figure has been under 10 percent for nearly three decades. Three million people are employed on the nation's farms, providing direct employment to 3 percent of this country's work force. These downward trends likely will continue through the 1990s. Although subject to wider fluctuations over the years, farm income has been comparable to nonfarm income since 1970. In 1987 farmers earned 22 percent more than their nonfarm counterparts. Farms also are becoming larger and fewer in number. The most rapid structural changes came between 1950 and 1970. These adjustments continue to occur today but at a slower rate.

Table 9.1
INCOME, POPULATION, EMPLOYMENT,
AND SIZE OF U.S. FARMS, 1950-87

	1950	1960	1970	1980	1987
			Percentages		
Farm population (mil.)	23	16	10	6	5
As a percent of U.S. population	15	9	5	3	2
Total farm employment (mil.)	10	7	5	4	3
As a percent of U.S. employment	17	11	6	4	3
Average farm income as a percent of U.S. average household income	68	72	102	88	122
Farms in the U.S. (thou.)	5,648	3,963	2,949	2,433	2,160
Acres per farm	213	297	374	427	461

The preceding text paints a rather bleak picture of the importance of agriculture in the U.S. economy. Although this analysis reflects the status of production agriculture, it does not adequately describe the overall situation of the food and fiber system. When agricultural employment is measured by economic activities from the producer through the retailer, a different picture emerges concerning the significance of the agricultural sector. Nearly 20 percent of the U.S. labor force is actively involved in the system of providing food and fiber to the nation and the world. These activities contribute 20 percent of the gross national product. In addition, an average American spends 25 percent of income on food and fiber. Therefore, although production agriculture has undergone some radical changes, the agricultural system remains a vital part of the economy.

But who is producing our food and fiber? Table 9.2 demonstrates that in 1970, 98 percent of the farms had individual gross sales of less than $100,000 but contributed 69 percent of total sales. By 1987, this same classification of farms represented 86 percent of all farms but only 30 percent of all sales. By 1987, 4 percent of the farms in the United States produced commodities that represented close to 50 percent of gross sales. But we must be careful with these figures. Inflation has contributed to this measure of bigness by inflating the nominal sales categories and boosting producers into "larger" categories. Also improved technologies such as greater milk production through improved dairy herd breeding and management have shifted producers into higher sales categories without changing their absolute size. The bottom line, however, even with these adjustments factored in, is that U.S. agriculture is characterized by many small farms producing 25 percent of the output while 1 percent of the farms produce over 30 percent of the food and fiber for this nation.

Table 9.2

NUMBER OF FARMS AND DISTRIBUTION OF GROSS FARM SALES
BY SALES CLASS, 1970-87*

	1970		1980		1987	
Sales Class	% of Total Farms	% of Total Gross Sales	% of Total Farms	% of Total Gross Sales	% of Total Farms	% of Total Gross Sales
Less than $19,999	82	29	63	11	63	10
$20,000-$39,999	10	19	12	7	10	5
$40,000-$99,999	6	21	14	18	13	15
$100,000-$249,999	1	10	7	18	20	23
$250,000-$499,999	0.4	8	3	19	3	17
$500,000 and over	0.1	14	1	28	1	31

*Percentages may not sum to 100 due to rounding.

We must not lament the demise of the small farm without analyzing the data in table 9.3. Today part-time farming is an income-generating and stabilizing influence in American agriculture. People opt for commuting to jobs in the commercial and industrial sectors while living on farms. In 1987, 86 percent of the farm families in the United States earned more than 50 percent of their income from off-farm employment. Only the largest farming operations now are nearly totally dependent on the sale of food and fiber for their income. Again these figures illustrate the bimodal nature of U.S. agriculture: many farm families choosing a rural lifestyle supplemented by off-farm income, and two hundred thousand large farms producing the majority of the agricultural commodities.

Table 9.3
OFF-FARM INCOME AS A PERCENT OF NET HOUSEHOLD
FARM INCOME FROM ALL SOURCES BY SALES CLASS, 1970-87

Sales Class	1970	1975	1980	1985	1986	1987
			Percentages			
Less than $19,999	72	92	107	105	101	99
$20,000-$39,999	24	47	97	86	74	75
$40,000-$99,999	17	23	59	57	49	53
$100,000-$249,999	16	15	27	24	22	26
$250,000-$499,999	0	9	14	10	10	13
$500,000 and over	0	2	4	3	4	5

Agrarian fundamentalism—A significant, and growing, portion of the rural and urban population would like to see the agricultural production sector return to the structure and agrarian values of the pre-World War II period. Agrarian fundamentalism, the first major force driving agricultural policy, takes on many forms and is hardly monolithic in its attempt to restructure American agriculture.[4] The Jeffersonian branch of agrarian fundamentalism argues that family-operated farms represent the moral and political strength of the nation. Large, corporate farms hiring nonfamily labor exploit the land and mine the soil. Farm life is the ideal lifestyle since it creates the values on which this nation was founded. Therefore, government policy makers should act to reverse the movement toward bigness and support policies that ensure the competitiveness and long-term viability of middle-sized family-operated farms.

A second branch of fundamentalism, although not considerably different from the Jeffersonian branch, is represented by the land ethicists. These individuals believe we should hold the land (i.e., soil, trees, prairies, animals) in sacred trust for present and future generations.[5] Land ethicists argue that the federal government and land grant colleges have a very limited ethical obligation toward the land; therefore, the policies they promote and the technologies their researchers develop disturb the harmony between man and the earth. To counter this modern disregard for "biotic communities," the individual farmer and landowner must become the nurturer, husbandman, and steward of the land. Land ethicists argue that individual action will ensure the long-term productivity of the soil for future generations.

Although some people would argue against the following classification, sustainable, regenerative, and low-input agriculture represents a third, and politically powerful, branch of agrarian fundamentalism. Proponents claim that modern agriculture is too dependent on chemicals. These manmade additives, combined with intensive cultural methods, create serious probabilities for surface and ground water pollution as well as increased soil erosion. Research and policy efforts, according to its proponents, should be redirected toward ecologically sound agricultural technologies, which support long-term values rather than short-run profits. Modern technology should be placed in a position subordinate to the long-term viability of the land resource.

Rent seeking—Profit, or economic rent, is the return to resources that exceeds the resource owner's opportunity cost, or return in the best alternative use. Temporary rents are earned by entrepreneurs, innovators, and progressive managers as they reallocate resources to economic activities with relative higher returns. This normal profit-seeking incentive is critical for the operation of our capitalist economy. Market signals indicate relative prices and potential rents, thereby inducing economic agents to take advantage of favorable supply and demand conditions.

But rent seeking in U.S. agriculture does not pertain only to temporary profits. Government policy since the 1930s, influenced by the lobbying efforts of farm commodity groups and organizations, has encouraged rent-seeking behavior where long-term rents are obtained from the U.S. Treasury. This phenomenon exists when output is fixed in some way. In agriculture, acreage reserve programs, set-aside acres, cross-compliance acres, and acreage bases are supply control techniques supporting higher commodity prices to the farmer. In fact, the entire commodity price support program can be viewed as a payment for idling crop acres. This successful rent seeking does not yield additional products for society. Instead, resources are taken from individual A and given to individual B to produce nothing.[6] These returns in excess of opportunity costs are capitalized into the land. Also, lawyers, lobbyists, and even economists earn rents from their support of the rent-seeking behavior of commodity groups and farm organizations.

But who receives these agricultural rents? As shown in table 9.4, government payments reflect a normal distribution between the low to high sales-category farms. However, the distribution of farms by sales category (table 9.2) is highly skewed toward the smaller farms. Combining the information in these two tables, we can conclude that larger farms receive a higher percentage of the government payments. For example, in 1987 the largest farms, representing 4 percent of all farms, received 20 percent of all government payments. This situation is logical since most government payments are tied to production levels and the number of base acres, two criteria favoring the larger producer. At the other end of the spectrum we see that 73 percent of the farms, mostly small operations, received 20 percent of all payments. This payment bias has been particularly apparent since 1980.

The incidence of these government payments across states is evident in table 9.5. States with diversified agricultural sectors, such as California, Florida, and North Carolina, depend very little on government payments. For every $1.00 of net farm income received by California producers between 1983 and 1987, these same farmers received only $.08 to $.12 in government

payments. But other states, particularly those dependent on feed grain production such as Iowa, Nebraska, and Minnesota, rely on government payments.
Significant economic rents appear to be permanently institutionalized in these
states. For example, in 1987 Illinois farm operators received $.94 from the U.S.
Treasury for every $1.00 earned in net income. Because of the Payment-In-Kind
(PIK) program in 1983, Nebraska producers that year received $2.04 from the
government for every $1.00 of net income. Total government payments nation-
ally have averaged 35 percent of net farm income during the last five years.

Table 9.4
PERCENT DISTRIBUTION OF GOVERNMENT PAYMENTS
TO FARMERS BY SALES CLASS, 1970-87*

Sales Class	1970	1975	1980	1985	1986	1987
			Percentages			
Less than $19,999	44	26	12	5	7	8
$20,000-$39,999	22	17	11	9	10	12
$40,000-$99,999	19	28	32	25	26	27
$100,000-$249,999	7	13	22	33	32	32
$250,000-$499,999	4	8	15	17	15	12
$500,000 and over	3	7	7	11	9	8

*Percentages may not sum to 100 due to rounding.

Table 9.5
GOVERNMENT PAYMENTS AS A PERCENTAGE
OF NET FARM INCOME

Top Ten States by Net Farm Income—1987	1983	1984	1985	1986	1987
			Percentages		
1. California	12	9	8	9	8
2. Texas	114	36	34	42	39
3. Iowa	*	34	41	50	72
4. Florida	1	2	2	1	2
5. Nebraska	204	36	29	48	62
6. Minnesota	83	34	41	48	60
7. Wisconsin	17	15	15	17	23
8. Kansas	102	61	47	59	57
9. Illinois	*	33	31	60	94
10. North Carolina	8	5	4	8	13
Total U.S.	58	24	25	32	36

*Net farm income was negative in the state for the noted year.

These economic rents exist because of political will to transfer tax and treasury funds to rural areas. By supporting the continuation of commodity programs,
the argument goes, the federal government is maintaining and promoting the
economic welfare of rural America. Government subsidies indirectly support

fertilizer and seed dealers, truck and barge operators, and the food- and fiber-processing industries. Although some of these arguments have the familiar ring of agrarian fundamentalism, the data indicate that large farm operations receive an amount of government payments far beyond their relative numbers. These are the very operations that agrarian fundamentalists claim are exploiting the land rather than nurturing the soil.

Technologicalism—A third driving force in the evolution of agricultural policy is the belief that modern science and improved productivity will ensure the survival of American agriculture. Land grant colleges and the U.S. Department of Agriculture have successfully created a research and extension establishment that has transformed agricultural production over the last fifty years.[7] Today, a single American farmer produces enough food to feed eighty people. Crop yields are higher, labor productivity compares favorably with other high technology industries, and rates of gain for beef cattle and average milk production for dairy cows are the highest in history. Science applied to agricultural production is one of the outstanding success stories of the twentieth century.

This supply-side research, and its emphasis on technical efficiency, has lowered average production costs. Yet since agricultural technology is a readily traded international commodity, continued research is needed to maintain and expand U.S. agriculture's share of world markets. Other nations rival the United States in grain, beef, and vegetable production, and proponents of technologicalism argue that we cannot afford to remove ourselves from the research treadmill. Without continued support for agricultural research the agricultural sector will lose its competitive advantage. The United States will become a net importer of agricultural commodities, and our food security position will be vulnerable.

Many analysts see this increased dependence on technology as an irreversible and upward trend.[8] A specific example of a technology with a bright future is biotechnology. With synonyms ranging from genetic engineering and recombinant DNA to plant breeding, these new tools for biological research will produce safe, quality food products, enhance plant and animal productivity via reduced costs, and conserve vital resources. But concerns arise with the direction of some biotechnology research. Should researchers develop plant varieties resistant to pesticides or plants resistant to pests? What would be the position of large agricultural chemical firms like Dupont and Monsanto? Which type of research would the agrarian fundamentalists or rent seekers support? Which type of research is in the best interest in the general public?

Another technological example is the development of bovine somatotropin (BST), which when injected into, or fed to, dairy cows can increase herd productivity by 10 to 30 percent. As this research progresses in the private sector and in publicly supported land grant universities, the federal government is spending millions of dollars each year to bolster the price of milk received by dairy producers. In recent years the government has even purchased entire dairy herds to reduce the production capacity of the U.S. dairy sector. So as a society, we simultaneously are investing in output-increasing technologies and federal programs to buy this surplus output from the producers. Technology does not appear to be solving the economic adjustment problems in rural areas.

Internationalism—A final force in shaping agricultural policy is the realization that U.S. agriculture has been internationalized. Domestic agricultural policies can no longer be developed and implemented without regard for international commodity and financial markets. Monetary, fiscal, and trade policies in Japan and the European Economic Community have the same magnitude of importance to farmers in Iowa or Wyoming as domestic programs. Exchange rates influence the competitiveness of exports, interest rates dampen or encourage capital investment, and trade regulations restrict the movement of commodities. The recent emphasis in the GATT (General Agreement on Tariffs and Trade) negotiations concerning crop subsidies illustrates the interdependence of agricultural policies throughout the industrialized world.

COVENANT ECONOMICS

The Bible does not outline clear choices for agricultural policies in the final decade of the twentieth century. A biblical framework for analyzing the complex forces of sustainable agriculture, price subsidies, and technical change is not explicitly discussed. Nevertheless, the overriding biblical principle of a covenantal relationship between God and mankind can provide inspired guidance toward a new direction in agricultural policy.

Covenants generally are thought of as solemn agreements or bonds between two equal, willing parties. In modern society most covenantal agreements are written and signed by both parties. Unwritten covenants do exist between friends and to a lesser extent between employers and employees. A second type of covenant is made between nonequal parties. These are generally gifts or promises by the stronger party. The weaker party is asked to respond in such a way, based on the covenant. There is no force involved. Each party is free to make the covenant.

The biblical concept of covenant represents a nonequal-type arrangement where God stipulated all the covenantal requirements.[9] God made the commitment and then asked the Israelites to commit themselves to Him. God made unconditional promises for the future, and man's role in the covenant was one of obedience. The covenant implied a special relationship between God and a community of faith, and a covenantal relationship between individuals. Mankind was and is viewed as both communal and individual.

The first covenants between God and humankind were with Noah (see Gen. 9:8-11), Abraham (see Gen. 15:18-21), and Moses (see Exod. 19:5-6; 24:3-8). Israel agreed to be a covenant people in the Sinai by following God's commandments (see Exod. 20:1-17). According to Christian theology, Israel did not remain faithful to the covenant, but God did.[10] That faithfulness was revealed in the life of Jesus Christ. The Second or New Covenant was sealed by the death and resurrection of Jesus (see Luke 22:20; Heb. 8:9). These events in human history produced, through the lives of the apostles and believers, an appeal to internalize the Second or New Covenant into the lives of all men and women. Christian beliefs were to become an integral part of the very life and value system of the people.

Based on this biblical foundation, covenant economics is defined as the study of the allocation of scarce resources among competing wants subject to the spirit of Christian values. Self-interest is not the sole driving force behind economic decision making in covenant economics. Human behavior is influenced by spiritual values, thereby making people and community more important than property. With this definition, the principle of covenant economics can be divided into three operational subprinciples: charity, stewardship, and justice. In a Christian economic ethic these subprinciples are overlapping and interdependent and must be lived out in a simultaneous fashion.[11]

The economics of charity—Charity is the willingness to share something of value to improve the life of another person. Conventional economic theories have difficulty modeling charitable impulses in the resource allocation process. Traditionally, individuals are viewed as having insatiable wants and desires that are not affected by the wants and desires of other people. Although this simple utilitarian paradigm provides a powerful tool for explaining a large portion of observed human behavior, it does not model the concept of biblical charity.

The Scriptures state that the rich and the poor are God's creatures and the care of the poor is a religious duty (see Prov. 22:2, 9; 14:31). Not only does the oppression of the poor lead to economic and spiritual disaster (see Amos 4:1-2), but the abuse of any person is an affront to God (see Prov. 17:5). The New Testament in turn argues for an ordering of human desires that ranks the well-being of the poor above the accumulation of additional wealth. Wealth is not evil, but people will be judged by how they use their wealth (see Matt. 6:19-21; 19:23-24). Idolatry of riches is sinful (see Mark 10:17-22). Jesus commands that people give to the poor in a spirit of love (see Matt. 6:1-4) and not flaunt their wealth before men and women (see Luke 16:19-31). Humankind is reminded that concern for the poor must show itself in action (see 1 John 3:17-18).

The individual Christian and the Christian community are challenged to demonstrate a radical set of preferences where the welfare of each individual is interrelated. The concept of the tithe (see Lev. 27:30-32; Deut. 26:1-15) challenges the Christian to live more simply and attach a greater weight to the suffering of the needy, which in turn is converted into voluntary actions of sharing time and wealth. Families, neighborhoods, churches, schools, and voluntary associations facilitate social closeness and charitable behavior.

The economics of stewardship—Stewardship, from a Judeo-Christian perspective, is the covenantal responsibility to develop and share productive resources for the benefit of present and future generations. Whereas charity deals with the relatively more static concept of the giving of wealth and time, stewardship is a dynamic process that optimizes societal welfare over time. This principle has been used to criticize or support capitalism, argue against or for economic growth, and speak out in favor of or against environmental protection.

Although the Scriptures are quite clear concerning the spirit of Christian stewardship, specific courses of action are not prescribed for our modern world. The weaker party (i.e., humankind) in covenant economics must recognize that God is sovereign over all the world (see Ps. 50:7-15). Resources are represented not only by material possessions or renewable and nonrenewable natural resources but also by time and talents. Humankind is only a caretaker of these resources (see Matt. 25:14-30). For example, the Sabbatical Year was meant as a time to take stock of these blessings, rest and rejuvenate these resources, and share blessings with those less fortunate (see Lev. 25:2-7, 20-22; Exod. 23:10-11). Profit was recognized as a means to a higher goal.

Private property rights can be a means of encouraging stewardship and promoting productive economic activity. The early Church held some of its property in common, but this action was not mandatory and was agreed upon due to the prompting of the Spirit (see Acts 2:44; 4:32-37). Jesus Christ never condemned private property (see Matt. 21:33-46; Mark 12:1-12; Luke 20:9-19). But because of human sin, modern economic man emphasizes his selfish interest in private property while minimizing the sovereignty of God over these resources.[12] Yet covenant economics demands a more equitable tradeoff between the expected welfare of present and future generations. In keeping with the economics of stewardship, short-term selfishness should be sacrificed for the long-term welfare of society.

The economics of justice—Of all the economic issues in the Christian community, the principle of justice generates the greatest degree of disagreement and animosity. Commutative justice, concerned with the transactions between two individuals, is directly related to charity and produces a relatively minor strain on the Christian ethical fabric. However, distributive justice creates significant disagreements regarding how a community should relate to its members. Discussions relating to wealth redistribution through taxation, land reform, support of the family farm, and the pros and cons of a market-oriented economy all deal, at least in part, with distributive justice.

The Jubilee Year is the biblical teaching most often cited in support of distributive justice (see Lev. 25:8-34). Resting the soil and recognizing the Lord's dominion over the land are important objectives of the Jubilee Year. The ancient commandment requiring the reversion of landed property to its original owner every forty-nine years is used often in modern times as an argument for increased public ownership of property or a redistribution of wealth. Although this policy may have been designed to prevent the growth of economic classes, there is no evidence that the Jubilee Year was ever practiced by the Israelites.[13]

Then what does the Jubilee Year mean for modern society? A redistribution of land to its original owners is highly impractical, if not impossible. And such a redistribution scheme would surely make most individuals in society worse off. However, the spirit of the Jubilee Year in a modern context is economic opportunity, not the explicit redistribution of productive resources. Members of each generation must have the opportunity to reach their productive potential (i.e., develop human capital) as human beings, while recognizing the imperfectibility of man because of the Fall (see Gen. 3). This opportunity ethic promotes equity in economic relationships but does not guarantee equality.

Yet biblical justice goes beyond the Jubilee Year. Other biblical mandates for economic justice include a warning against the abuse of authority (see 1 Kings 21:1-26; Isa. 10:1-14), an appeal to employers to pay their laborers in a timely manner and treat them as images of God (see Lev. 19:13; Jer. 22:13), a condemnation of a legal system that does not treat individuals fairly (see Exod. 23:2-3; Deut. 16:19-20), and a call for wealthy nations to assist low-income countries (see Matt. 25:31-46). What is critical about all these biblical directives is that quantitative guidelines are not proposed or established. The spirit of justice is proclaimed. Few concrete, prescriptive solutions to injustice are offered. It is the believer's responsibility, and the responsibility of the faith community, to take this spiritual guidance and promote greater justice in the world through specific policy choices.

APPLYING COVENANT ECONOMICS PRINCIPLES
TO AGRICULTURAL POLICY

Christian scholars, including economists, often expound on what they perceive as morally correct policies without regard for the managerial, technical, and political feasibility of their proposals. Although our society needs idealistic prophets, increased emphasis on realistic plans of action is necessary if the Christian segment of our society is to have a role in the public policy arena. The danger is that what is a realistic plan to one analyst, Christian or nonChristian, may be "pie in the sky" to another. Therefore, political risks to supporters of a significant redirection in agricultural policy will be enormous. History has shown that there is a direct correlation between the outrage directed at proposed policy changes and the economic rents received by the affected group.

A scripturally based agricultural policy is guaranteed to create controversy. With the goal of ensuring an adequate and safe food supply within the constructs of a covenant economics framework, redirected agricultural programs will create gainers and losers in the agricultural sector and society at large. In covenant economics the gainers must be the poor and the land. The losers will be the rent seekers who have "farmed" the agricultural policies for at least the last decade.

A farm income/stabilization insurance program—The biblical principle of charity applies to actions toward people who have fallen on hard times caused by drought, cataclysmic events in their lives, or the lack of educational and employment opportunities. In these cases the Christian's welfare is diminished due to the suffering of the less fortunate. However, there is no indication that a significant portion of taxpayers' dollars is directed to the needy through the present price support and loan programs administered by the U.S. Department of Agriculture. In fact, the convincing evidence in this chapter indicates that megafarms, native American farms, and state governments mine the U.S. Treasury because of their ability to maneuver through the agricultural laws and take advantage of legal loopholes. This is a perverse type of charity. In addition, under the present programs consumers pay higher prices for food and fiber and "support" rent-seeking behavior through their federal income tax payments.

The first policy action based on covenant economics would be the gradual elimination by the year 2000 of the current price support and loan programs that have been in existence in one form or another since the 1930s. There are numerous reasons for this decoupling-type proposal. Price subsidy programs create surpluses, which the government must store and manage at a cost to the taxpayer. Also input subsidies obscure real production costs. Combined, these government policies distort market signals in domestic and international markets and create a misallocation of resources by the decision maker and society. By tying price subsidies to output, current policies ignore the heterogeneity of U.S. agriculture. An adequate policy for a corn/soybean farmer in Illinois most likely will not be appropriate for a cotton farmer in the San Joaquin Valley of California due to the differences in farm size, technologies, water availability, and crop mix.

But what should replace the current programs? Consider the following scenario. A nationwide mandatory farm income/stabilization insurance program would move the management of risk in farming away from the government and more toward the farmer.[14] Farmers would insure themselves against an income level lower than the average net cash income for the last five years. When income fell below this level, the farmer would receive a cash payment that would be 80 percent of the loss in net cash income or $50,000, whichever was lower. The federal government would pay half the insurance premium. Premiums would fluctuate based on claims made the previous year. A stabilization fund also would be established as a financial reserve. Farmers would invest part of their profits in this fund, and their contributions would be matched by the federal government. These private contributions would be tax deductible. Reserves from the fund would be used prior to receiving benefits from the income insurance program.

A major problem with this proposal is the fact that we live in an international agricultural economy. If the United States removes the price and export subsidies on agricultural commodities and the European Economic Community does not, American farmers may lose valuable export markets to French, English, and German growers. This scenario reveals the importance of trade negotiations and the lowering of subsidy levels throughout the world. Without trade reform, social resources will continue to flow into the pockets of the wealthy. However, Australia and New Zealand are preparing to take this radical step of eliminating price subsidies.

But why would this insurance program be superior to the present policy? First, the proposed program would be commodity-neutral, thereby giving managers the freedom and flexibility to respond to market signals without sacrificing income. Second, the proposal would eliminate the skewed expenditures from the U.S. Treasury to large, high-income farms. A portion of these "saved" funds could be used to develop programs for the farm and nonfarm rural poor. A third advantage is that this program would eliminate the need for ad hoc disaster assistance programs—favorite sources of rent-seeking activity in the past. Finally, this proposal would require that the Federal Crop Insurance Corporation (FCIC), the Agricultural Stabilization and Conservation Service (ASCS), and the Soil Conservation Service (SCS) merge into one administrative unit to fully coordinate their activities in serving the agricultural sector. The next policy action will make the need for this merger clearer.

Natural resource management practices—Stewardship of the land resource is a critical concept in covenant economics. Natural resources are to be enjoyed and cared for by society, not idolized or destroyed. Future generations have a right to enjoy God's bountiful grace and beauty as revealed in our environment.

The Conservation Reserve Program (CRP) of the 1985 farm legislation has been successful in removing highly erodible acres from crop production for ten years. The success of this new program and the willingness of the Congress to target the economic assistance contained in the drought assistance legislation of 1988 indicate that targeting or recoupling farm programs to sustainable land management practices is managerially, technically, and politically feasible. Increased efforts should be made, particularly through tax regulations such as investment tax credits, to induce farmers to adopt profitable cultural practices and production technologies that ensure a safe food and water supply for the nation and reduce soil erosion to sustainable levels. The FCIC and SCS would have to work closely together to certify compliance with the new policies, and the ASCS would evaluate farm budgets and income at the county level for the income insurance program.

Rural education and development—The covenant economics principle of justice emphasized the opportunity of all individuals to obtain an adequate standard of living to ensure a healthy and productive life. Poverty in rural America is more serious with the nonfarm population than with small-scale farmers. Farmers, as a group, have done relatively well economically in the last two decades (see table 9.1). But farm work is seasonal and very dependent on commodity prices. Local rural businesses and industry hire few people. Those whose skills are poorly developed find themselves at the mercy of the weather and the economy, with very few employment options. In many instances migration to urban areas is the only alternative.[15]

An increased emphasis on education in rural areas is a necessary component of any rural development program. Poorly paid teachers, dilapidated schools, and a lack of money for new programs in science, math, and computers place many rural areas at a basic disadvantage to their urban counterparts. More federal resources should be targeted through state agencies to rural areas. As a result of the proposed modifications in current agricultural policies, several billion dollars should be available each year.

Although the proposed policy alterations will slow the structural changes in the agricultural sector, technological advances and relative wage rates will continue to draw resources out of farming. Persons who want to remain on the farm must have alternative employment opportunities to supplement their farm incomes. Therefore, a percentage of the resources saved from the elimination of the price support and loan programs should be redirected to the states to promote the development of rural-based industries. The existence of modern production and service industries near large rural populations is an essential condition to stem the consolidation of farm units and preserve the agricultural culture that many citizens value so highly. And more important, industries in or near rural areas provide an economic opportunity for the rural poor.

CONCLUDING REMARKS

There needs to be a convergence of the forces of problem recognition, political will, and policy analysis for changes in public policy to take place.[16] In recent years and months the problems in rural areas have become more and more evident due to financial stress, ground water pollution, budget deficits, food safety concerns, and the increasing consolidation of the agricultural production sector. Public recognition has managed to catch up, in terms of emotion and concern, with the rigor and depth of existing policy analysis. In many states, the political will also has responded to these challenges. However, the Congress has not had the political courage or will in fifty years to alter, in any significant way, the national agricultural policies.

The Scriptures establish clear priorities in the allocation of resources; few tradeoffs exist in the framework of covenant economics. The poor and the land have priority. Ministry to the poor and stewardship of the land are critical conditions in God's Kingdom. Yet the courage to oppose special interest groups and political action committees is found wanting in most public officials. Only a Christ-motivated and -centered faith is strong enough to propose policies that will fulfill our covenantal relationship with God.

EDITOR'S PERSPECTIVE

Dr. Wilson was asked at the Scholars' Colloquium why he did not recommend the complete elimination of all government help in the arena of agriculture and opt for a pure market-driven solution. He reminded us that the biblical principles he identified sponsored a concept of covenant economics, a relational rather than market system concerned with loving one's neighbor, stewarding God's possessions, and seeking public justice. This concept is in contrast to the utility theory and creation of wealth proposed by worldly economics. Given this fact, and given that the existing agricultural system is deeply influenced by special interest groups oriented toward economic wealth, he believed it was prudent to seek the kinds of solutions he explained as workable intermediate goals to encourage a directional change. He considered these recommendations preferable to a full-blown model reflecting an idealized state quite beyond near-term solution. In my judgment, this approach represents true wisdom, not compromise.

Discussing distributive justice and the Jubilee Year, Dr. Wilson comments, "Although this policy [establishing the Year of Jubilee] may have been designed to prevent the growth of economic classes, there is no evidence that the Jubilee Year was ever practiced by the Israelites." He attributed this assertion to R. de Vaux in *Ancient Israel, Volume 1: Social Institutions.* The claim that the Jubilee was never practiced is heard frequently (I made the same statement in volume 2, page 245), and while in one sense it is technically accurate, it does not wholly reflect Scripture. I point this out now for two reasons.

First, the implications of the full biblical account, not just the observation that specific Jubilee years were not designated by the leaders of Israel, need to be considered. Second, all fifty scholars who participated in the creation of this four-volume series agreed that circumstances allowing wealth to be concentrated in the hands of a minority (or majority for that matter) in a way that creates artificial barriers excluding those without wealth from opportunities to help themselves economically constitute a primary issue of economic justice that needs to be faced by the Christian community. These two subjects will be addressed, therefore, once again.

There is no evidence that a designated year (one common year for everybody to observe) was ever established for the Jubilee as outlined in Leviticus 25:8-17. There is a lot of evidence, however, that one of the central tenets of the Jubilee principle was not forgotten but remained in operation for hundreds of years. Which principle was honored? The principle of redemption that was to operate during the years between the Jubilee years (see Lev. 25:23-28). (Archer Torrey brought this fact to my attention, for which I am very grateful.)[1]

The evidence is simply this: For hundreds of years after the Law was given, and after the Israelites entered the Promised Land, the Scripture tells of people honoring the redemption principle. I will cite just a few examples. (1) Moses was called on to settle the question of which tribe would get the land in the Year of Jubilee if daughters of one tribe married men of another tribe (see Num. 36:1-13). (2) At the conclusion of the war that broke out between all the Israelites and the tribe of Benjamin, in which Benjamin was thoroughly defeated (see Judg. 20–21), the remnant of Benjamin was allowed to return to its land inheritance, and *every man* from the other tribes returned to his inheritance (see Judg. 21:23-24). (3) Who can forget the account of Elimelech and Naomi fleeing the famine in Bethlehem (having abandoned their inheritance) and then Ruth and Naomi, upon returning home ten years later, seeking the help of Boaz as Naomi seeks a buyer for her land, which obviously remained her inheritance while she was gone (see Ruth 4:3). (4) And finally, King David was also aware of a family's land inheritance when he, because of his great love for Jonathan, restored Saul's land to his grandson Mephibosheth (see 2 Sam. 9). Such evidence convinces me that for hundreds of years, the tribes of Israel and the families in those tribes were aware of and practiced (to a meaningful degree) the law as it pertained to the redemption rights of families. The principle was an integral part of the institution of the Year of Jubilee and should not be overlooked as we seek to discern the importance of the original mandate.

Little discernment is needed to conclude what is involved in the principle of redemption and the Jubilee. From the time God removed Adam from the Garden of Eden and required him to live in a hostile natural environment, it has been evident in both the biblical accounts and the experiences of mankind that individuals and family units are primarily responsible for their own physical well-being. Furthermore, the biblical accounts reveal the prophets (Amos, Habakkuk, Isaiah, Malachi, and Micah, for example) crying out against marketplace injustices and the oppression of the poor. The "land rights" were obviously given to make sure that every family had an opportunity to provide for itself, and to supply a mechanism whereby those rights could be protected generation after generation. That was done knowing that circumstances, poor judgments, and sin would cause some people to become disenfranchised. The consequences of such realities were not to be perpetuated from generation to generation among God's children, though.

The time has come for the Christian community to address the issue of wealth distribution in modern times in the light of these principles. A few comments have already been made about this issue (in this series, see volume 1, pages 179, 201, 269-272; volume 2, pages 118, 207-246; and the "Editor's Perspective" following chapter 2 in this book). The solution, it seems to me, is at least comprehensible. Its accomplishment, though, does not rest in the power of man alone. Only God, through His acts of special and common grace, has the ability to set in motion the activities necessary to redress the problem. It is a worthy goal for Christians to labor for, however, because God has revealed that it is His general will for people to care for themselves, and that it is not His will for one economic class of people to structure things so that another group is denied access to opportunities to provide for themselves.

Two fundamental realities must be acknowledged and embodied in any solution undertaken to seek a just distribution of the world's wealth. If they are ignored or perverted, we will come out of the starting gate with an impossible handicap. First, we must understand that the availability of economic wealth is elastic, not fixed. Believing that the economic pie is expandable is the first line of hope for those who desire to improve their economic condition, and the first line of defense against the belief that the only means of redressing the problem is to confiscate and redistribute the existing wealth. Confiscation is at best a short-run solution. In fact, it can lead only to the destruction of the models and incentives necessary to find a just way out of the difficulty. (This important truth—the economic pie is elastic—was discussed briefly in volume 2, pages 19-20.)

The second reality concerning wealth redistribution is that any effective solution must be patiently pursued; real and lasting results must be sought through personal discipline and sacrifice over a long period of time. There is no quick fix. That is one reason the problem is so difficult to deal with politically. The solution is fundamentally long run in nature. There is no quick and easy way to materially expand the economic pie. It takes two generations under the best conditions because of the complex nature of the barriers that must be overcome and the solutions that must be instituted if a just and true reallocation is to occur.

The barriers are generally found in the minds of those who already have the lion's share of the wealth, control the institutions (legal, economic, political, etc.) that are in place, and possess the power to restrict or alter access to opportunities that reshape and redistribute economic rewards. The real barriers are generally discovered in the defensive mechanisms of the old nature where it is assumed that "your gain is my loss." Envy, greed, pride, and covetousness are grounded not in a set of logical, long-term realities but in short-run, self-centered perversions of reality.

Persons who already have wealth must be persuaded of the truth that if they will invest wisely in the "means" necessary to set free the creative potential locked up in the latent skills and intellectual powers of the disadvantaged segment of society, *both* they (those who already have wealth) and those who are set free from their captivity will prosper more and more. What are the "means" being referred to?

Three complex ingredients make up the prerequisite "means" to expand the economic pie, to reallocate wealth (not by taking and giving, but by the disenfranchised earning a healthy share of an expanding economic base), and to include the economically disenfranchised members of society. These elements are (1) an abundance of *moral capital*, (2) a social infrastructure that fosters and develops the potential of the community's *human assets*, and (3) a legal, economic, and political structure that offers all segments of the population equitable access to economic *opportunities* (work, saving, and owning private property). These three ingredients are clearly promoted in the Scripture.

Moral capital encapsulates one's world and life view, one's self-identity, one's capacity to be committed to "right" in the presence of strong short-run self-interests, and one's attitudes and thoughts about God and others. Moral capital is reflected in one's capacity for self-denial and self-sacrifice. It is contained in one's ability to be committed to the true well-being of one's neighbor. It is one's value system. It is what is embodied in the second of the two great commandments (see Matt. 22:34-40). Christians, of course, know that the commandment to "love your neighbor as yourself" is made possible only as the first commandment ("love the Lord your God with all your heart, and with all your soul, and with all your mind") is made operative in the lives of God's children under the tutelage of the Holy Spirit.

Moral capital must pervade a large enough segment of a community to become the basis for its social mores before the society can establish the values foundation that will support a wholesome community infrastructure. This infrastructure will promote the development of latent human abilities and skills necessary to draw from the raw materials of creation the wonders God has stored up for us. Family structure, the educational and training programs, the arts, literature, and the media must all teach, uphold, and reward imaginative and creative endeavors. God is the Author of all human talents and skills. He designed us with artistic and intellectual capabilities to build and craft from the original order those things that serve and enrich mankind and glorify Him (see Exod. 31:1-6). But the opportunity and encouragement to develop these personal abilities and capacities must be promoted and sustained in the community infrastructure if those who are likely to be disenfranchised economically in future generations are to have a reasonable prospect of being delivered from such a waste of human resources.

Finally, the elevation of human expectations that accompanies moral enlightenment and the awakening and development of the human potential will create a worse state of social and political affairs unless they are provided genuine opportunities to be rewarded: "Hope deferred makes the heart sick, but desire [expectation] fulfilled is a tree of life" (Prov. 13:12). That is the way God has made the human spirit, and whenever a hope is raised in the human breast, it is not a genuine, realistic hope unless a reasonable expectation of its being fulfilled is also present. That means genuine opportunities must be present for all to share in the bounty of God's created abundance if the governing systems are to be just.

Sin and the rebellious spirit of the world fight the creation of moral capital. Human assets are all too often wasted as we seek personal advantages, pleasures, and our own will at the expense of helping our neighbors. And opportunities to earn a share of the potential wealth are frequently denied those who are outside looking for a door through which to enter the established structure. Man's side of the curative prescription is relatively easy to define, but we are helpless to bring it to fruition apart from overcoming the curse of sin with the power of love. The power, however, to do even this is not inherent in us; the power is God's alone.

PART X

EDUCATION: WHO IS RESPONSIBLE FOR WHAT?

Five authors in this volume (Marvin Kosters, Bruce Wilkinson, John Mason, Paul Wilson, Dick Chewning) have already noted in substantial ways the relationship between the development of human capital and education. They have focused on the essential need to develop human capital, though, and have not elaborated on how education is to be carried out in doing this beyond indicating its role as a means to that end. The time has come to examine this critical component of stewardship in detail.

As Dr. James Skillen leads us through this incredibly complex public policy matter, we realize the magnitude of the philosophical issues involved. He outlines some examples of why education is important in the context of the larger community, including its effect on the moral health of a community (related to the mutual confidence and respect between parents and the schools) and its role in helping a nation to be economically competitive in a world market. Skillen reminds us that the list of both personal and national needs related to education is enormous.

Dr. Skillen raises seven penetrating questions about the government's involvement in education. In the process, the significant role of government is not denied. But he shows us that the answers, formulated in the light of the nine biblical principles he presents (four main principles, with one having five subprinciples), lead to the conclusion that the government's primary responsibility in education should be radically refocused. Governmental and parental responsibilities are confused and inverted in our current public policy.

The heart of Dr. Skillen's chapter is the section "The Illuminating Power of Biblical Principles for Contemporary Public Policy." Here he thoroughly discusses the real conflict between contemporary public policy and the Scripture's assignment of the primary responsibility for education of children to parents. Once again, though, Jim Skillen does not seek to remove government from

211

the educational equation. He argues instead that the role of government should be that of establishing an "agency relationship" with the community (representing the parents and the broadest needs of a pluralistic society) rather than being the foremost "principal party" determining every facet of the educational process in the public arena. This section will be demanding for persons who have not thought through these complex issues, but it is full of insights that need to be taken seriously.

His concluding section, "A New Direction for Education Policy in the United States," is incredibly practical, principled, and balanced. In it he sets forth a reasoned argument and approach (he modestly emphasizes that it is a *suggestion*) for establishing a "public pluralistic system of free schools." If his suggestions were accepted, the entire population would be offered many more educational choices, without sacrificing standards (unless raising them is considered harmful), and the government would return the "value issues" to the marketplace for adjudication. The people who control the existing educational oligopoly (a small number now control the "product" offerings) would have something to lose, but the public would have much to gain.

CHAPTER 10

BIBLICAL PRINCIPLES APPLIED TO A NATIONAL EDUCATION POLICY

James W. Skillen

James W. Skillen is the Director of the Center for Public Justice in Washington, D.C. He has edited the Center's Public Justice Report *since 1977. The Center is seeking to develop a Christian perspective on civic responsibility and to promote a more significant approach to political action on the part of Christian citizens.*

A graduate of Wheaton College (A.B.) and Westminster Theological Seminary (B.D.), Skillen completed his Ph.D. at Duke University in Political Science. He taught at Messiah College, Gordon College, and Dordt College before moving to Washington in 1982.

Dr. Skillen lectures throughout the country on political responsibility and public policy and writes regularly in popular and academic magazines and journals. He is coauthor of Disestablishment A Second Time: Genuine Pluralism For American Schools *(Eerdmans, 1982) and the author of numerous articles on education policy.*

THE CONTEMPORARY CONTEXT

The multidimensional importance of education seems to manifest itself with increasing urgency everywhere in the United States today.

• The economic competitiveness of the United States in the world depends on whether our children can learn better and faster than they have been learning in the recent past.
• Meeting the needs of the ghetto underclass depends on job training for lifelong work and not merely on temporary public welfare.
• The growing distance between the poorest and the richest Americans is due, in part, to different educational opportunities and achievements.

• The moral health of the country is, to a significant degree, a function of the cooperation and mutual confidence between parents and the schools to which they send their children.

We could expand almost indefinitely this list of personal and national needs related to education. Surely there can be no doubt about the seriousness of education policy today.

Before we can talk about a national policy, however, we must look carefully at the topic under investigation. What is involved in public policy for education? What are the chief issues and questions to be addressed?

1. Certainly one of the first questions concerns the very nature of government's responsibility for education. This overarching question then divides into at least two basic parts:

A. What should be the *proper distribution of responsibility* for education among families, schools, and governments? Which of these holds the principal responsibility for the education of children? How should these three different institutions be related to one another? Should government even be involved in the education business? Should it be the preferred or exclusive provider of educational agencies for children? According to what constitutional or other principles should disputes and conflicts between these institutions be adjudicated?

B. Depending on the answers given to the questions in 1-A, how should the responsibilities that properly belong to government (if any) be distributed within our *federal* political system? Should education policy be set primarily by federal, state, or local governments? What about the public administration of education policy? What about funding? Should we even have a "national" education policy?

On the basis of our judgments about the proper role of government in education (1-A) and about the "federalist" question (1-B), we must then press on to a number of particular questions within the public policy realm.

2. How should government establish justice and equity in the educational arena with respect to race, gender, handicapping conditions, and religion—differences that are not, in themselves, necessarily educational distinctions? Or does government have a responsibility here?

3. Should education be supported by means of public taxation, and if so, what is the best (just) means of taxation? Property tax? General income tax? Sales taxes? Lotteries?

4. If government distributes funds for the support of education, what is the most equitable manner of doing so? By local districts to government-run

schools only? By voucher or partial voucher for students to use at any school?

5. If parental choice of schooling is judged to be an important ingredient in 1-A above, then what are the proper means for government to recognize those choices?

6. Given the multiple concerns of government for local, state, and national well-being (including the benefits of high employment, a high rate of literacy, international competitiveness, and civic respect for law and government), what are the best means for the government to encourage educational improvement where it may be needed? If American children appear to be falling back from an earlier standard of educational achievement, how, if at all, should public policy address the need for educational improvement?

7. Closely related to 1-A and 2 above, how should public policy for education deal with religious freedom? Here we face the long and very specific history of First Amendment disputes over American schooling.

BIBLICAL PRINCIPLES

If the seven points just noted provide a short list of enduring questions that have arisen in the course of the development of American education policy, what are the biblical principles with which Christians should approach these questions?

We live today in a highly differentiated society made up of many institutions and relationships. Moreover, we live in a country that is quite unlike ancient Israel or even the earliest modern states where a uniform faith was enforced or taken for granted. The New Testament authors were, for the most part, addressing the Christian church, the people of God, not the public policy issues of a particular political order. Thus, a quest for biblical principles that can shape our judgments about education policy must proceed very carefully and with deep historical sensitivity.

1. The first biblical principle that should guide our thinking about education policy, I would argue, is that human beings are God's creatures, made in His image, living with a mandate to develop the creation in obedience to His commandments and directions (see Gen. 1–2 and countless other Scripture passages). Under this general heading I would then distinguish several dimensions:

A. Creaturely development of the creation is governed by a "stewardship responsibility" under God, the Creator. To be able to serve as good stewards, *we must learn to know the creation*, care for its many creatures, and discern its boundaries and purposes. The growth of our knowledge under the guidance of earlier generations is crucial here. Education, broadly understood, is fundamental to the fulfillment of such stewardship.

B. *Knowledge stems from wisdom*, which begins with the fear of the Lord. True education is not manufactured out of thin air or out of autonomous human wishes. It is education fit for human beings who have been made for life with God in God's world. This world functions on God's terms. Its order and destiny originate with the Creator.

C. Human disobedience rooted in the disregard of God has brought darkness to human understanding and leads us all toward foolishness, educational errors, and failure in the performance of our stewardship responsibilities. *Sin, and not simply a lack of learning, stands at the root of ignorance.*

D. *The final Judge and Redeemer of the creation is Jesus Christ.* Thus, the principle of creaturely stewardship is fulfilled in its educational as well as its other dimensions only in relationship to Christ's lordship. To ignore this is to misunderstand all of history and the very condition of the creation under God, according to the Bible.

E. The point made in 1-D does not imply, however, that education can function only within Christian communities or in Christian schools. Jesus Christ is not a private, gnostic god. He is Lord of the whole creation, and through Him all things were created in the first place. By God's grace and patience in the present age, human creatureliness has not become the closed preserve of confessing Christians. Moreover, Christians remain sinners who are being saved by grace; thus they often perform (both in education and in other areas) in disobedience to God's revelation in Christ. The chief point here is that on biblical terms *the possibility of good education in God's creation*—the possibility of distinguishing truth from error, of learning how to be good stewards of the creation and to participate in its meaningful historical development—*hangs upon God's judgment and redemption of the creation in Jesus Christ.* There is no other ultimate principle or means of enlightenment.

2. Within this biblical framework of general principles, I would then point to the particular creational principle that parents bear the first and chief responsibility for loving, nurturing, and raising their children. They are the "principals" in their children's education even if they use "agencies" outside the home for schooling and apprenticeships.

3. In the third place, the Bible recognizes "differentiated responsibilities" for the fulfillment of many divine mandates, surely including the education of children. Individuals, homes, extended families, farms, shops, congregations of believers, and so forth are not self-sufficient and closed entities. Rather, they function interdependently in ways allowing for the historical differentiation

of numerous "offices" of particular, limited accountability. (For example, consider the appointment of lower judges under Moses [see Exod. 18], the establishment of deacons in the early Church [see Acts 6], and the recognition of many divine callings among the people of God such as teachers, prophets, etc. [see 1 Cor. 12].)

Without in any way erasing or thwarting the "principalship" of parents for the care of their children, the Bible allows for the differentiation of what today we would call apprenticeships, schools, and other educational agencies that have as their particular and limited purpose the education and training of children. I would identify these extrafamilial educational institutions and relationships as "agencies" in the service of parental "principalship" (up to a certain age), which must then fulfill particular educational purposes in keeping with the wider range of human responsibilities before God. Socially differentiated "schools" then express their unique callings of providing job training, developing knowledge, fostering wisdom, and so on as complements to the learning that goes on in homes under parental love and care, in businesses that pursue economic productivity, and in many other institutions and social relationships.

4. Finally, I would point to the biblical principle of justice to which God holds all human beings accountable. This far-ranging principle touches every person and human institution, but it comes to special focus in the responsibility of public officials appointed to govern and judge entire communities. From many details of the Mosaic covenant and from particular prophetic denunciations and admonitions, we hear how God holds governing officials responsible for "giving each its due"—for punishing the evil person and rewarding the good person (see, for example, Job 29:1-17; Rom. 13).[1]

Today in our society we must then ask how civil government ought to "give each its due" in the educational arena. What does public justice demand for families, for schools, for individual citizens, for the marketplace, for public health and well-being, for religious freedom? How should public law be shaped so that the particular responsibilities of parents, teachers, students, employees, consumers, citizens, and government itself receive just treatment? How can each of these arenas of human responsibility best be held accountable?

THE ILLUMINATING POWER OF BIBLICAL PRINCIPLES FOR CONTEMPORARY PUBLIC POLICY

The first way to illustrate how these biblical principles apply to education policy is to show their power in helping to explain some of the dilemmas or contradictions in current policy. They serve as a light on today's path as we seek answers to the seven questions posed at the outset.

For example, consider the question about principalship in education. If parents should be recognized as the principals in the education of their children, and if government should do justice to parents by means of its education policy, then one reason we have conflict and contradiction in American education today is that these principles are not adequately heeded. Why?

Two incompatible assumptions have controlled education policy in the United States at least since the nineteenth century. The first has its roots deep in Greek and Roman traditions that were revived in the West during the Renaissance and the Enlightenment. That assumption is that the government of a city or state holds the *primary and direct* responsibility for educating its citizens. To whatever extent government recognizes the authority of other institutions (such as families, independent associations, churches, etc.), those authorities are nonetheless viewed as subservient to government in the area of education.[2]

A second assumption, in conflict with the first, is the biblical one that parents hold primary responsibility for the education of their children. Some governmental responsibility for upholding justice in schooling may be legitimate, according to this tradition. And a variety of agencies outside the home may be required for the education of young people. But laws governing schooling should be built on respect for the priority of parental principalship in the education of children.[3]

These two assumptions have been operative in the development of American schooling. During the colonial period and up until about the 1840s, the second assumption was predominant. From the 1840s to the present, the first assumption has predominated. The two assumptions continue to struggle in tension with each other. But it is not possible to act on both at the same time without contradictions and anomalies showing up in public policy.

Today, state and local governments (with federal and judicial support) take for granted their principal responsibility for schooling. Governments then seek to fulfill that responsibility by means of their own state-established agencies—the common public schools.[4] Within this legal framework the authority of parents is generally incorporated into the civic governing structure of the local public school. That is to say, parents may exercise educational responsibility for their children *indirectly* by means of their membership in the political community. They can vote for school board members as well as for local, state, and federal officials. They may join the PTA and express personal opinions to school officials. Parental principalship in education, in other words, is swallowed up in government's principalship. Thus, by definition, public agencies (government-run schools) are treated as belonging to the parents by way of their citizenship.

At the same time, parental authority may still be exercised in another way in the United States. Parents may choose to opt out of the public system of education and select another agency of education—a nongovernment school or perhaps home schooling. This choice does not deprive parents of their civic rights; therefore, they can continue to exercise responsibility in the public arena, even serving on the local public school board, for example. Nor does the choice to opt out of the public system relieve parents of the responsibility to pay taxes for the public schools.

However, the parental choice of any agency other than the local common school has negative consequences. That choice is treated today as a *private* choice, which must be supported at additional personal expense. Choosing to opt out of the government-run system will mean missing out on many privileges attached to the publicly supported system of schools. In sum, we may say that parental primacy does not rule in America today even though parental initiative has not been eliminated altogether.

Exposing this inner tension in the American laws that govern education also helps to show why the debate over federalism concerns a totally different matter from the debate over parental principalship and choice. Whatever the merits of locating authority for education at the local, state, or federal level of government, if the law is based on the assumption that government is the principal in schooling, then parental principalship will be denied or subordinated to that of government. This will be true whether the schools are run by the local, state, or federal government. If, on the other hand, public law would establish the primacy of parental principalship in education, then the responsibility of government would change at every level. This is not to say that the federalist question is unimportant; rather, two different issues are at stake here. Many people who desire greater parental involvement in schooling will argue for more local control and less state or federal control. "Localism" might reduce the number of people involved in the public control of local schools, but it will not in itself shift principalship from the local government to parents.

A second illustration of how the application of biblical principles helps to illuminate the arena of education policy is found in the current debate over "religion." As I have explained in an earlier article, Americans now take for granted not only the primacy of government over parents in education but also the "secularity" of the public order and the confinement of "religion" to a private sphere. This mode of thought depends on a modern Enlightenment point of view closely connected with the assumption that government has the principal responsibility for education. "Religion," from this point of view, is private, personal, and ecclesiastical. The "secular" is assumed to be the domain of the state, embracing all of the state's operations and institutions, including its schools.

From about the middle of the last century, state and local governments in the United States have assumed the prerogative of setting up and running schools for citizens on the grounds that they, the governments, are trustees of the secular public trust, which includes basic education. Parental (and other) authorities must acknowledge their subservience to government's prior rights and responsibilities in this regard. If parents want to exercise the right to organize the education of their children directly, then, by definition, they must opt out of the public secular order. Naturally, from this point of view, a private or religious choice must be paid for by the private party, not by government.[5]

Beginning in the 1940s, with major decisions such as *Everson v. Board of Education of Ewing Township*, 330 U.S. 1 (1947), and *McCollum v. Board of Education*, 333 U.S. 203 (1948), the U.S. Supreme Court sought ways to handle particular education disputes within the context of the philosophy and assumptions just described. To the present day, one can hardly find a reference to parental rights and responsibilities in education except within the context of presumed governmental principalship, which entails favoritism toward government-run schools. And the Supreme Court almost always frames the circumstances in terms of the religious/secular dichotomy.

The three-part test the Supreme Court now uses in school decisions involving religion is applied generally to evaluate the government's compliance with the establishment clause of the First Amendment:

> First, the statute [a state or federal law] must have a secular legislative purpose; second, its principal or primary effect must be one that neither advances nor inhibits religion . . . ; finally the statute must not foster "an excessive government entanglement with religion." (Chief Justice Burger, *Lemon* I, 403 U.S. 602 [1971], pp. 612-613)

Burger believes this test can justify state aid to "church-related" schools by means of "secular, neutral, or nonideological services, facilities, or materials" (*Lemon* I, pp. 616-617).[6]

In an earlier decision, *Abington School District v. Schempp*, 374 U.S. 203 (1963), the Court ruled against a Pennsylvania law that had required Bible reading in the public school. That law violated the establishment clause of the First Amendment according to Justice Clark who wrote the majority opinion:

> The place of religion in our society is an exalted one, achieved through a long tradition of reliance on the home, the church, and the inviolable citadel of the individual heart and mind. We have come to recognize through bitter experience that *it is not within the power of government to invade that citadel, whether its purpose or effect be to aid or oppose, to advance or retard. In the relationship between man and religion, the state is firmly committed to a position of neutrality.* (pp. 226)

Notice how Clark assumes that religion is unambiguously private, having its identity entirely outside the state. Partly because of this unproven and unquestioned assumption he overlooks one of the central institutions in society that has promulgated our "exalted" religious traditions, namely, the schools. He refers to the home, Church, and individual heart as the great centers of religion. But this dogma distorts and hides the simple fact that schools were the centers of Christian training for decades into the nineteenth century, and even by the end of last century, Protestantism, in both its pietistic and its republican religiosity, thoroughly penetrated the so-called nonsectarian, public schools.

Even in the case of *Wisconsin v. Yoder*, 406 U.S. 205 (1972), where the Supreme Court granted a partial immunity from compulsory school attendance to an Amish group in Wisconsin, the majority opinion followed the well-established lines of the prevailing mind-set. Chief Justice Burger stated that the Court's evaluation of the Amish claims has to determine whether "their religious faith and their mode of life are, as they claim, inseparable and interdependent." He continued,

> A way of life, however virtuous and admirable, may not be interposed as a barrier to reasonable state regulation of education if it is based on purely secular considerations; to have the protection of the Religion Clauses, the claims must be rooted in religious belief. (p. 215)

Burger assumes that religion is so distinguishable from life that it is possible to differentiate a life (or part of a life) guided by religion from a life (or part of a life) guided by purely "secular considerations." He also assumes that the First Amendment defines religion in a way sufficient to keep it from being misused by irreligious or nonreligious persons. And the chief justice is convinced, finally, that if the religion clauses cannot be appealed to, then "secular" people with "secular" claims have no grounds for escaping the majoritarian educational requirements imposed on all citizens, no matter how virtuous and admirable may be the education they might prefer to give their children. The very concept of ordered liberty, says Burger,

> precludes allowing every person to make his own standards on matters of conduct in which society as a whole has important interests. Thus, if the Amish asserted their claims because of their subjective evaluation and rejection of the contemporary secular values accepted by the majority, such as Thoreau rejected the social values of his time and isolated himself at Walden Pond, their claims would not rest on a religious basis. Thoreau's choice was philosophical and personal rather than religious, and such belief does not rise to the demands of the Religion Clauses. (pp. 215-216)

Clearly, Burger believes that the "secular values accepted by the majority" ought to have moral authority over "society as a whole." No adequate account is given of families and schools and churches in this judgment. Only if a person or group can appeal to the religion clauses of the First Amendment in a way that the justices accept can that person or group find relief from (and a chance to opt out of) the requirements of majoritarian governmental control within the public domain. Burger's entire argument presupposes the religious/secular qualification of the private/public distinction.

Notice, however, what is overlooked and distorted here. Simply ask these questions: "Are families religious or secular institutions?" "What makes a school 'private' if it truly educates students to become mature, competent, and employable adults and respectful citizens?" "What if a parent chooses to send his or her child to a nongovernment school that makes no religious claim?"

Obviously, in the case of a parent's choosing a nongovernment school for nonreligious reasons, the religious/secular distinction cannot apply. But why, in that case, should government withhold equitable funding and recognition from the school and from those parents? If the answer is that government has the primacy in selecting schools for its citizens, then is it not relegating parental choice to second place even without appeal to the religious/secular distinction? And is that not discriminatory unless one argues consistently that all educational responsibility resides with the government without exception? Such a conclusion, however, would call into question the Supreme Court's decision in *Pierce v. Society of Sisters* (1925) where the Court upheld the right of parents to choose nongovernment schools (at their own expense). If *Pierce* is not overturned, then the conflict between parental principalship and government principalship ought to be resolved in a manner that brings equity and fairness.

By granting full public recognition and funding only to its own schools, government denies justice to teachers, parents, families, and nongovernment schools. It thereby fails in its obligation to give each its due, namely, to treat all citizens with fairness. A little financial help for the secular parts of private-school children may help, but it only underlines rather than resolves the continuing inequity of the private/public, religious/secular dualism.

Now ask these questions: "On what grounds does the government have a right to grant itself a monopoly over the secular?" "May the government claim sovereignty over everything secular, without limits?" "On what grounds does government have the right to decide that religion belongs primarily, if not only, to individual conscience, churches, and church-related institutions?"

Notice what the misguided private/public, religious/secular framework does to obscure reality. If parents choose, on self-confessed religious grounds, to educate their children in a school established by an organization that is *not* a church, does that create a religious question for the courts? Not so if religion is identified with churches, because there is no church connection here. If some parents choose not to send their children to a public school because they do not like its philosophy of education, is that a religious choice or a secular choice? It could, of course, be either religious or secular depending on the parents. If parents choose to teach their children at home, no matter what they teach them, is that a religious choice or a secular choice?

The point of these questions is to show that the use of the First Amendment in school issues is frequently misleading. The First Amendment does not mention families and schools. In fact, it does not even refer to churches. The way the amendment is usually interpreted, however, is to identify religion with churches or with private conscience and then to say that government enjoys a monopoly over what is secular. Families and schools are not treated by the courts as having independent identities separate from Church and state or from the religious and the secular.

But surely family life, education, and business can be as secular as politics. The government has no right to claim a monopoly over everything secular, does it? Likewise, the life of some families, schools, and businesses can be as religious as church life. Churches do not monopolize religion. Clearly, if the states and federal government are to establish a just policy framework for education, then some revisions will be needed in the most basic assumptions and legal definitions related to present-day education law.

We could select many other issues of concern in contemporary American education—issues that would help to illuminate additional problems and questions raised earlier. The discussions of principalship and religion are sufficient, however, to show that national education policy from a Christian point of view requires a reconsideration of fundamental matters related to the very identities and responsibilities of government, schools, and families.

A NEW DIRECTION FOR EDUCATION POLICY IN THE UNITED STATES

Taking seriously the biblical principles summarized in this chapter and looking carefully at the responsibility of government for education in the United States today, how might we begin to formulate a national education policy?[7]

We should begin, I believe, by seeking a change in the dominant assumptions about principalship and agency in education. This cannot be done, however, without giving serious attention to the importance of government's responsibility for justice and equity in society. The ongoing ambiguity and contradiction in American education policy will never be satisfactorily resolved until we recognize that government has a legitimate and proper concern for public justice, including the just treatment of citizens in their educational development, *and* that government cannot do justice to everyone involved in education until it recognizes that parents hold the *principal* responsibility for the education of their children. The change in assumptions at this point leads, of necessity, to changes in assumptions about the meaning of public versus private and sacred versus secular.

Let us begin with the family. As long as children are minors, parents should be held accountable for their children's well-being. This is not to say that parents have to do everything for their children and that government may do nothing. To the contrary, children are also citizens with basic rights that need to be protected by government. But the rights and responsibilities of parents to care for their children should not be taken away or infringed by a governmental mandate that destroys their responsibility as principals in the nurturing and care of their children.

True parental principalship cannot be acknowledged, however, without rejecting once and for all the claims of educational principalship by government. Even where government fulfills principal responsibilities for some of its minor citizens (orphans, for example), it should do so *in loco parentis*, not as if it holds *original* parental principalship.

This fundamental change in assumptions, namely, rejecting government's principalship and acknowledging only parental principalship for the education of minors, does not mean the complete privatization of education. Recognizing the rights and identity of the family as family is what is crucial here. The family is neither an individual person nor a department of state. Government should not swallow up family members by treating them simply as citizens, thus abrogating their rights and identities as family members. Nor should government accept the total isolation and autonomy of those persons as if their individuality gives them some right to absolute privacy and public unaccountability.

The proper response is for government to acknowledge the family, with its inherent parental responsibility for the care and education of minor children, and at the same time accept its own responsibility for the public protection of all citizens, most of whom happen to be members of families.

Second, we must change the focus of our attention, if not our fundamental assumptions, about the nature of educational agencies—the schools. Throughout our entire history we have had many kinds of schools. The establishment of government-run schools has never eliminated all other schools, nor has the public system ever educated all children. Before the 1840s most schools were independent of direct government management. Even after the 1840s a significant percentage, from 5 to 20 percent, of American schools were nongovernment schools. This fact alone bears testimony to the reality that educational agencies need not be government owned and operated in order to function as agencies of education. It also tells us that the reality of a school is not simply an extension of the government's standard bureaucracy for enforcing rules and providing general services. Even government schools usually possess a degree of autonomy, ranging from independent budgets to separate elections for school board members. The "public" character of those schools does not mean the absorption of the educational process into general governmental administration.

A school is a differentiated agency for education. It is built on a philosophy of education; it hires teachers who have the talents to train students in different disciplines; it must stand *in loco parentis* and thereby deal amicably and in a trustworthy fashion with parents; it takes in *students* who then take on a role that can be distinguished from the more general role of *child* in a family and *citizen* in the civil community. In other words, schools are schools and not simply extensions of families or the government. They have a life of their own with a peculiar identity and quality to them.

To do public justice, therefore, governments should acknowledge the full reality of schools just as they should recognize the full and distinct reality of families. Government does not deal merely with individual citizens-in-general; it deals with citizens who are at the same time family members and school participants, among many other things.

The rightful recognition of schools as distinct social entities does not mean that the government should relinquish all concern for education. It does not even imply that the government should close down all of its own agencies of education. Instead, the government should begin to look upon schools, including its own, as distinct agencies of education rather than as mere departments of state. When this is connected with other changes suggested here, it will make all the difference in the world.

Government *does* have responsibility to secure public justice for all its citizens, which among other things should mean recognizing the rights and responsibilities of various institutions and associations that are *not* departments of state—such as families, churches, schools, business enterprises, and so forth. It is, indeed, government's responsibility to see that individual citizens, families, and schools are not unjustly discriminated against. The Greek Orthodox church should enjoy the same public rights and protection as the Presbyterians or Baptists or any other church. A black child should have the same rights and privileges as a white or an oriental child.

When it comes to education, a government might well decide (as our states have done) that fairness, equity, and equal opportunity for its citizens require that each child should enjoy formal education, or at least that each should achieve a certain level of proficiency by different ages in life. The debate about the details of this type of public concern and responsibility can take a number of directions and embrace a host of legitimate "public health and welfare" concerns.

Many questions cannot be answered abstractly and once and for all: Should schooling be required up to a certain age, or should the government merely require the passing of certain tests? Should every child be required to learn English? To master some American and Western history? To participate in driver's education? The questions can go on and on. Though these and many similar questions might not meet with easy resolution or universal public consensus, they are legitimate questions, I believe, for governments (state, local, and federal) to be asking and resolving *for the sake of the equitable well-being of all citizens*.

Nevertheless, all these questions should, in the future, be asked within a framework that *takes for granted both the principalship of parents in the education of their children and the right of all schools to receive fair and equitable treatment as they offer their services to the public*. How, in this case, will public law have to change?

The first major consequence of this shift in assumptions will be to open up genuine *parental choice* of schooling for children. The present form of choice for parents is either to use the district public school or to opt out of that system at their own expense. This choice simply is not viable for many with low incomes, and it is an unfair choice even for those with sufficient income. If parents are truly the principals in the education of their children, then the only way government can do justice to them is to recognize their principalship and to treat all parents fairly. No matter how much good the government wants to do for its citizens through education, if it tries to perform that service while denying parental rights, it will end up doing injustice. How, then, can parental choice be respected properly and equitably?

Genuine parental choice from among different educational agencies can be realized only if public law no longer gives unjust privilege to its own public school agencies. In other words, the recognition of parents as the principals in the education of their children must coincide with the public recognition of those agencies parents choose. Every school must have the same legal and financial opportunity to open its doors to the public to offer its services.[8]

Tremendous discrimination now exists in that nongovernment schools receive neither public funding nor public recognition (except as private schools). By contrast, the means by which a genuine diversity of schools can be treated equitably in public law are manifold. We need not discuss all the options here. What is clear from this argument, however, is that tax credits or vouchers to alleviate some of the financial burden for parents who select "private" schools will not be enough to do full justice under present circumstances. These benefits might provide a first step in the direction of greater equity. But as long as government schools are treated in privileged ways, public moneys for "private" education will never be distributed in truly proportionate amounts, nor will those expenditures ever be fully legitimate.

In fact, I would argue that it is illegitimate for public funds to be spent for private purposes. The reason that tax credits or vouchers are even considered today is that most citizens realize there is a public purpose being achieved in nongovernment schools. The way to deal with that fact, however, is to give full recognition to all schools that perform the public service of training young people for adulthood. And that means treating all such agencies, both government and nongovernment schools, as eligible for parental selection without disqualification or financial inequity.

Now, at this juncture, let us bring in the issue of religion. What if some parents select a school that happens to be run by the Catholic church? If the government supports such a school, whether directly or indirectly, does it become illegitimately entangled in religion or run the danger of establishing a religion? To the contrary, within the framework I have outlined here, it would be discriminatory of the government *not* to allow parental choice of religious schools. The only establishment danger would arise if the government decided to give special benefit to those who attend Catholic schools over against those who attend Presbyterian or government schools. A fair and equitable distribution of funds for all educational choices would establish nothing more than the high value of education in the context of parental choice and freedom for all schools.

In the Supreme Court's words, the "secular" (I would rather say "general public") purpose of education legislation should be to promote education for every citizen. If that legislation properly recognizes parental principalship as well as the independence of educational agencies, then its "general public" purpose is fulfilled if all parents are free to choose a school for their children's education. If the conscience of some parents requires a Catholic parochial school, or a school with a philosophy of education that is Christian or Jewish or Muslim but is not connected with any church, or a school that claims to be nonreligious, then the government would be doing justice both to the parents and to the schools by treating them all equitably with the same degree of public recognition and public funding.

Government would run the danger of "entanglement" only if it interfered with parental choice for reasons other than protection of the general public good. No religion would be established; in fact, this is the only way for the government to keep from establishing either religion or irreligion in its own specially privileged agencies. Parents should choose, and schools should offer services; the government should not mandate or monopolize the school agencies for education.

In this respect, the entire issue of religion versus secularity is removed from the arena of education. That was a mistaken connection in the first place.[9] It might never have become an issue if the nineteenth-century Protestants had not tried to remove Catholic schools from public recognition on the grounds that they were "parochial" and "sectarian." It would never have become an issue if Americans had not misidentified religion with privacy and with churches alone. Religion is not simply what goes on in churches and in some individual consciences; it also embraces the way many people choose to live, including the way they choose to raise and educate their children.

Government should have no constitutional right to predefine the limits and scope of religion. Nor should it have the concomitant right to give itself a monopoly over the so-called secular world. We have already tried to show that families and schools are important actors in both the so-called secular world and the religious world. Government must give full attention to the welfare of the entire public and always mandate, through law, what is in the public interest. If its mandate happens to include the mandate of education for every citizen, then government must see to it that the mandate is carried out in ways that do justice to all the children, parents, teachers, schools, and other persons and organizations involved in education. If some citizens choose to make education part of their religious practice while others prefer to identify schooling with something irreligious or nonreligious, then so be it. That is not government's concern.

Now, finally, let me examine a few of the implications for government's responsibility in all of this. If government no longer claims principalship in education, and if it recognizes with full equity all the agencies that offer educational services, and if it treats education as education rather than as something divided between religious privacy and public secularity, then how can it still assure that every child will receive the public protection and assistance needed for the sake of public justice?

Until now, state governments have held major responsibility for the legal structuring of education. Neither local governments nor the federal government has held that primary legal responsibility. A new national education policy can be built on this foundation, even if some slight changes in funding occur. The following suggestions take for granted the centrality of the states in making education laws. At the same time my suggestions presuppose a fundamental revision of the laws at all levels to recognize parental principalship.

The first thing government will have to do is to make very clear the essentials of public fairness for every citizen. These essentials will almost certainly include such things as "free" education for all, no racial discrimination, no undue hardship for persons with handicapping conditions or for new immigrants, and so forth.

Many of these characteristics of a just society have not been adequately implemented within the present framework of public education. A new pluralistic system can probably do a much better job. But there is no way to guarantee ahead of time an error-free system. An ongoing commitment will have to be made to pursue justice for every citizen as well as for families and schools and other communities. Local, state, and federal governments, along with the courts, will have to keep busy updating laws and changing policies to make sure that education is offered in an equitable manner to every citizen. Without attempting to prejudge all future government decisions, and without implying that each of the following suggestions is exactly what is needed, let me, nonetheless, list a few things that government might do to fulfill its role in a new pluralistic system.[10]

State governments might, for example, invite any school that wishes to do so to become part of a new "public pluralistic system of free schools" on the terms that each will be allowed to receive a proportionate amount of public funding (proportionate to the number of students each educates) either directly from the government or indirectly through student vouchers. The terms of entry into this new system might include the following (among others):

1. Freedom for each school to define its own philosophy of education.

2. Freedom to maintain its own form of governance.

3. Freedom to hire and fire teachers in accord with its own philosophy and behavioral standards.

4. The requirement that any child who wants to come to that school (whose parents choose it) may not be turned away, though retention is to be determined on the basis of the school's discipline code and curricular and behavioral standards. Such a requirement could not be used to eliminate the right to establish various specialty schools such as all-boys or all-girls schools, vocational training or college preparatory schools, and so on.

5. The requirement that the school must either participate in an independent accrediting agency (at its own level of schooling) or meet state standards for basic educational competencies and testing.

6. The requirement that a school may not, as a condition for entrance, charge additional tuition beyond the basic per-student amount given by the government. This requirement would not prohibit a school from raising additional private funds for its program.

This six-point suggestion is only that—a suggestion. If something like it were adopted, it would not require the closing or elimination of schools that chose not to participate in the new system. Some schools still might have reasons for not wanting to participate in the public pluralistic system. They would, naturally, forgo the benefits of public support and funding. But that would be their choice rather than the government's discriminatory exclusion.

If something like the system just described were to be funded through student vouchers given directly to parents, then government would also have to establish a fair and equitable means whereby school buildings and other capital investments would be built, distributed, and used proportionately among all schools.

If the American people can achieve a new consensus that government should promote educational well-being among all its citizens by granting consistent freedom of choice to parents and an equitable freedom of opportunity to all schools, then the other details can be worked out case by case, from year to year. The proposal made here is designed to do justice to all—including justice to America's wide diversity of families and schools—so that they can train up children in accord with their deepest beliefs and moral convictions. This proposal, it seems to me, allows parents, schools, and governments to fulfill their unique responsibilities in accord with biblical principles.

EDITOR'S PERSPECTIVE

Can Dr. James Skillen's "public pluralistic system of free schools" become a reality? The answer depends on a number of factors, but regardless of the ultimate historical answer to this question, Christians in the United States need to think about how they can best live and serve God in a pluralistic society. At the very beginning of such a discussion, it should be recognized that many Christians reject anything that appears to either accept or normalize pluralism as a social model. Normalization is not the object of this "Perspective." The object is to live in a godly way in the midst of an existing reality.

God's children are engaged in spiritual warfare every day in the marketplace and arenas of government: "Our struggle is not against flesh and blood, but against the rulers, against the powers, against the world forces of this darkness, against the spiritual forces of wickedness in the heavenly places" (Eph. 6:12). The "ruler of this world" (John 12:31; 14:30; 16:11) is not in the same league with Adonai (the "Lord," emphasizing God's sovereignty as King), but neither are God's people inherently strong enough to purpose and will matters into existence according to our own desires. The world is as it is today because our Sovereign God chooses to work His will out through the current conditions, and those conditions for us are discerned in the middle of a pluralistic society. Dr. Skillen has simply accepted this as fact. He is wise to do so, in my opinion, for that is the environment in which we must work.

Accepting pluralism as the current reality, and seeking to alter its internal judgments about how to justly accommodate the diverse groups in it, is much more likely to bear fruit than purposefully seeking to bring into existence a whole new social structure. I know of no civilization in history that has plotted a move in the political environment that has allowed it to move rapidly from one set of cultural presuppositions to a new set, apart from an invasion or a physical revolution. God worked for centuries to prepare the descendants of

231

Abraham for the Promised Land, and God took centuries to firmly establish the Christian Church as a significant shaper of the culture in the West.

Furthermore, the influence of the Church in Western Europe and North America has been very much on the wane for over a century. Futurists, in whom I put no stock, are saying the Church's influence in the West will in fact continue to diminish in the foreseeable future.[1] Such predictions merely reflect trends (not prophecies), but the trends are apparent to those who observe such matters.

Surely it can be said that pluralism is an improvement over the other world systems of political monarchism or totalitarianism that have so often been the alternatives in history. Command systems and representative/democratic systems have very different track records in economic/political spheres, but even acknowledging that, the work of this editor in these four volumes has never endorsed a particular economics or political system, for our purpose has been to let Scripture reform our thinking, not to justify existing operations. Nevertheless, Scripture reveals that God created us with the power and responsibility to exercise moral choices in an environment where the stewardship principle of property management under the aegis of family-denominated units was the basic prescription (the principle being that everyone has access to the resources necessary to provide for the family).

With the establishment of the New Covenant, where the scattered Church became the new Israel (the new nation of God) and Christ sits on the throne of the hearts of His subjects, a free and open public pluralistic system is probably the best economic/political environment Christians should hope to enjoy. If this is true, then we must be very gentle and wise as we seek to positively influence society. Confused thinking can only hurt God's cause, and that is what Dr. Skillen alludes to when he discusses the tragic and mistaken confusion on the issue of religion versus secularity:

> [The mistaken connection between religion and secularity] might never have become an issue if the nineteenth-century Protestants had not tried to remove Catholic schools from public recognition on the grounds that they were "parochial" and "sectarian." It would never have become an issue if Americans had not misidentified religion with privacy and with churches alone.

Christians must act justly and wisely if we are to be heeded in the public arenas. When we—Protestants, evangelicals, Christian "right," Catholics—seek to gore another's ox, it must be done only when it is possible to demonstrate clearly that we are seeking the good of the *entire* community—true public justice—and not merely trying to protect or promote our private interests.

Probably the biggest objection to being in a pluralistic society given by those who oppose it (those who want a Christian nation) is that Christians who labor in the political/judicial arenas in this kind of environment are constantly confronted with the pressure to compromise biblical principles. That is certainly one way to perceive the situation, but from my perspective, this view is grounded in a set of false assumptions. It assumes Christ's Kingdom is to be an earthly one, prior to His physical return. Even those who are persuaded of this through the biblical accounts need to acknowledge, though, that their beliefs should compel them to work in the existing pluralistic system for its transformation, and this work must be carried out step by step (each step being a compromise with the ultimate desired goal).

Another way to perceive the situation is to believe that Christians are called to be salt and light in the world and that we are not being compromised when we are less than totally victorious, but the Enemy is being restrained and driven back every time we can persuade the system to take one more step in a godly direction. I believe Jim Skillen's proposal to work for a "public pluralistic system of free schools" fits beautifully into this latter understanding of our calling.

PART XI

A NATIONAL HEALTH CARE POLICY?

In the Preface to this book is the following statement:

> The chapters deal with two different kinds of public policy issues.
> The first kind involves issues that the government itself controls
> directly—regulating the money supply and organizing the military
> and the police, for example. The second kind concerns the relation of
> government to nongovernmental institutions and organizations whose
> responsibilities do not originate with government, but the government
> seeks to encourage, discourage, regulate, or protect them, depending on
> the circumstances.

National health care policy clearly falls under the heading of the second type
of public policy issue mentioned. With somewhere between 11 and 15 percent
of our gross national product devoted to the care of our physical health, it is one
of the most important public issues in sight. Our government is deeply involved
with the issue, rightly or wrongly, and Christians need to clarify in their own
minds what this role should be. The predictions all point to continually increasing costs that cause more and more political pressure on those who govern.

The pressures driving up medical costs are many and complex, but at least
five major ones are worth noting as we prepare to read Dr. James Henderson's
chapter. First, we live in an extremely litigious society where medical suits
are filed at every turn. As a result, persons in the medical profession practice
what could be called defensive medicine, which generates a second round of
pressures. Doctors now ask that more and more tests be run on their patients
to avoid being second-guessed with the hindsight of 20/20 vision. Expensive
technology is also being made available to the medical profession, and that is
being employed, at very high costs, in the defensive battle.

A third force in the marketplace is the so-called third-party payment concept. (This concept was discussed at some length in volume 3, *Biblical Principles and Business: The Practice*, in the "Editor's Perspective" following chapter 11, "Biblical Principles Applied to Insurance.") When those who receive medical treatments do not have the burden of paying for the services because either government or third-party insurance programs provide the resources to pay, there are no cost savings incentives placed on the users. These third-party payment programs generate enormous upward cost pressures in the system.

The humanist's world view rising in the minds of more and more people in society, replacing the older Judeo-Christian world view, places a distorted value on resisting terminal illnesses that afflict the very elderly and infirm. (For example, Dr. Henderson states that 25 to 35 percent of the Medicare payments are made on 5 to 6 percent of the enrollees who die within one year of the treatments.) When one does not have the hope of eternal life, the value of one's temporal life assumes convoluted value.

And finally, individuals in the medical profession are not above manipulating all these forces to generate income for themselves. With the advent of Medicare and Medicaid, an entire "health industry" suddenly became visible in the marketplace. National hospital chains and health care organizations blossomed, and their stocks began to appear on the major stock exchanges. The government's involvement (pumping in large sums of money generated through an increase in payroll taxes) stimulated enormous interest in the health care industry. When huge sums of federal money flow, smart business minds dart to the scene like fish to water that has been chummed.

CHAPTER 11

BIBLICAL PRINCIPLES APPLIED TO A NATIONAL HEALTH CARE POLICY

James W. Henderson

James W. Henderson is Associate Professor of Economics at the Hankamer School of Business at Baylor University. He has worked alternatively as an economic consultant, business analyst, and market research specialist. Prior to joining the Baylor faculty in 1981, he was Vice President of Finance and Development at the Dallas Minority Business Center, a Department of Commerce-funded business development organization. Dr. Henderson completed his undergraduate work at the University of Houston where he majored in Finance. He then received both M.A. and Ph.D. degrees in Economics from Southern Methodist University. His publications include articles in the Journal of Development Economics, Economics of Education Review, Journal of Financial Education, Journal of the Southwestern Society of Economists, Baylor Business Review, Cashflow, Journal of Cash Management, *and the JAI Press series* Research on Income Inequality. *He has authored* Obtaining Venture Financing: Principles and Practices *(Lexington Books, 1988),* Strategic Financial Planning *(Prentice-Hall, 1990), and coauthored* The Financial Analyst's Deskbook: A Cash Flow Approach to Liquidity *(Van Nostrand Reinhold, 1989).*

> As for the days of our life, they contain seventy years,
> Or if due to strength, eighty years,
> Yet their pride is but labor and sorrow;
> For soon it is gone and we fly away. (Ps. 90:10)

SCOPE OF THE PROBLEM

The size of the health care industry is indicative of the scope and nature of the problem facing policy makers. In 1986, Americans spent over $1.25 billion per day on health care, totaling over $458 billion for the year. That figure can be compared with spending on national defense that year of $277 billion, less than two-thirds the health care outlays. In relative terms, health care spending represents 11 percent of U.S. gross national product and is projected to reach 15 percent of GNP by the year 2000. In contrast, most developed countries (Great Britain, West Germany, Canada, and Japan included) spend from 6 to 9 percent of their gross products on health care.

For all the money spent on health care, Americans are virtually no healthier than citizens in other advanced economies. According to almost any measure of health (e.g., life expectancy or infant mortality), the U.S. population is no healthier as a result of its higher spending. Life expectancy at birth in the United States is 71.2 years for males and 78.2 years for females. In Canada, the same measure is 71.9 and 79.0 years for males and females, respectively. Similar comparisons can be made for Japan (males 74.8 years and females 80.5 years) and the United Kingdom (males 71.8 years and females 77.8 years). Infant mortality data provide much the same picture (measured as number of deaths per 1,000 live births). The figure is 7.9 in Canada, 5.5 in Japan, 9.4 in the United Kingdom, and 10.5 in the United States.[1]

Thus, the major issue facing policy makers in modern developed nations is that changes in the level of health of the population depend more on nonmedical factors than on the quantity of medical care available. Victor Fuchs has observed, "When the state of medical science and other health-determining variables are held constant, the marginal contribution of medical care to health is very small in modern nations."[2]

Current evidence seems to indicate that variations in the level of health among individuals and groups are due largely to nonmedical factors, that is, hereditary, lifestyle, and environmental factors. This indication is not to imply that the overall level of health of a population is not influenced by medical care. The impact of medical care is determined mainly through advances in medical research and not the quantity of care.

Gross spending on health care and the general level of health purchased are only two aspects of the problem. Another important issue is how the high cost of medical care affects access to care for individual members of society. In 1986 there were over thirty-two million admissions to hospitals, representing one person for every three U.S. families. The average cost per inpatient day was $499.19; coupled with the average length of stay of 7.1 days, that represents an average expenditure of over $3,500 per hospital patient. It is not surprising that over seven million individuals had medical bills totaling over 15 percent of their annual income, or that five hundred thousand of them had bills representing over 50 percent of their annual income.

The staggering realities of the health care system in this country make it easy to question the efficacy of current policy and wonder just how we are going to get out of this dilemma. My concern is based on my role not only as a consumer and taxpayer but also as a Christian in my desire to know and understand what is pleasing to God. What biblical principles should guide the development of a national health policy? I believe some overriding principles can help us establish a God-pleasing national policy that focuses our perspective on the "big picture" and minimizes our reliance on sometimes ill-advised, short-term solutions.

The goals of this chapter are modest. The primary objective is to consider the broad implications of a biblically based vision of health care. It is beyond the scope of this study to prescribe a full policy plan for collective involvement in the health industry. However, identifying the guiding principles revealed in the Scriptures is an important step in establishing a detailed set of priorities for action along with suggestions for allocating resources oriented toward achieving our national goals for the health and welfare of members of our society.

The major aspects of a national health care policy will be outlined in the next section. Given the magnitude of the challenge facing policy makers, it will be obvious that a moral framework for a health policy is essential. The third section will discuss the biblical principles (the correct moral framework) that can guide the establishment of a national health care policy. Application of these guiding principles will be made in the fourth section, followed by a summary and conclusions in the fifth section.

IN SEARCH OF A NATIONAL HEALTH CARE POLICY

The challenge facing decision makers has always been one of attempting to satisfy the unlimited demands placed on the finite resources available to society. When dealing specifically with health policy, we must first recognize that health is not the only goal of society and may not be the most important goal. Individuals validate this claim daily in deciding to smoke cigarettes, inject drugs, operate a motor vehicle while under the influence of alcohol, and ride a motorcycle without wearing a helmet.

Health care must be placed within the context of other goals considered vital by society: national defense, education, economic competitiveness abroad, environmental protection, poverty relief, and a balanced federal budget. To a large extent these are competing goals. The single-minded pursuit of one goal can lead to ever larger expenditures in that area. In establishing spending priorities, health care has a considerable advantage over other goals. The needs of this sector can be readily dramatized by citing individual cases where human welfare is involved, and consequently spending priorities are easily shifted.

The issue of resource allocation among competing goals is beyond the scope of this chapter. However, the policy of open-ended health care spending cannot continue, and a better understanding of our policy alternatives will enable us to make better decisions in determining resource allocation within the health care sector.

Three areas for health policy will be explored: (1) the general level of health of the population, (2) access to medical care, and (3) the cost of medical care.

The general level of health—Public health care policy has as one of its goals the promotion of good standards of the population's health, which means promoting activities and procedures that enable individuals to avoid illness, disability, and premature death whenever possible. The dilemma facing policy makers is that we want all suffering to end and it will not; we want to conquer all disease (including the disease of aging) and we cannot.

The new possibilities afforded by advances in medical science force us to cope with issues our forefathers never faced. We must have a realistic perspective on what medicine can and cannot do. Our ability to prolong life well into the seventies and eighties has benefited many people, but it has also brought on pain and suffering to many. As we age, the incidence of many chronic conditions, such as Alzheimer's disease, arthritis, dementia, and stroke, increases dramatically.

We can expect continued improvement of life-extending technologies, such as mechanical ventilation, artificial resuscitation, antibiotics, and artificial nutrition and hydration. Along with these improvements, we can also expect their use on ever-sicker categories of patients. Is death an enemy to be fought off at all costs, or is it a condition of life to be accepted? The issue of death cannot be dealt with until we accept the fact that our temporal lives are finite, bounded by conception at one extreme and death at the other (usually preceded by a decline in capacities).

Thus, death is not something to be postponed indefinitely, an evil to be avoided at all costs. The goal of medicine cannot be the promotion of health and the prolongation of life, because to be alive and to be healthy are often mutually exclusive. When we are instructed in the Bible to number our days, we are being told to make them count. The issue is not necessarily an extended life, but a better life. (See Psalm 90:12.)

Access to medical care—The issue of access to medical care must be examined within a specific moral framework that correctly distinguishes between individual rights and social responsibility. The individual's right to medical care has never been explicitly stated in this country. Although the U.S. Declaration of Independence states the rights of "life, liberty and the pursuit of happiness," nowhere does it state that access to medical care is a necessary condition of those rights.

A rights-based formulation to access to medical care is usually framed in terms of equality. The policy dilemma, if we use a rights-based formulation, is that we have no way of ensuring equal health care outcomes. If, instead, we ensure a right to health care, the relevant question is, How much? Equality would dictate that everyone be given the same amount. If determined by the requirements of the sickest members of the society, it would be extremely wasteful. If determined by the healthiest, it would be unfair.

Equitable access for all members of society requires that we adopt a standard of medical care politically acceptable, morally responsible, and economically affordable. The solution might be simple if we had a clear way of distinguishing between "needs" on the one hand and "wants" and "desires" on the other.

Access according to need will lead in one of two directions. If need is self-defined, it will mean that all people will have access to all the medical services that they desire. If need is narrowly defined, it will lead to access only to the minimal requirements necessary to prevent death.

To solve this dilemma, we must come up with an acceptable definition of an "adequate" level of medical care. The economist's concept of adequate is determined by the familiar marginalist's rule of thumb: The optimal level of care is defined as that level where the benefit from the last unit of care received is just equal to the cost of that care to society. Within this framework, the question of allocation is ultimately one of valuation of outcomes. What value do we place on life? On reduced pain and suffering? How do these values change when we are the ones receiving medical care? What about a relative? A friend? A total stranger?

The economic approach alone may not be an adequate guide to public policy. If the level of adequate care can be defined as the level necessary "to achieve sufficient welfare, opportunity, information, and evidence of interpersonal concern, to facilitate a reasonably full and satisfying life,"[3] then we recognize that society is not responsible to provide all the care that a person might want. In other words, justifiable restrictions may be placed on the exercise of certain medical options to assure the wise use of resources as long as those restrictions are applied uniformly across society without bias.

The issue of access to medical care is usually one of affordability. While most will agree that the ability to pay must not determine life and death, we must also recognize that some incentives for economizing must be preserved. Any other position would be very expensive as the number of people calling for medical attention increased without limit.

The cost of medical care—The recent focus been on cost containment. With the increased concerns over the cost of care, there is some evidence that the major objectives of a health policy may be fundamentally at odds. The problem is to provide for the health of the population in a manner accessible to everyone without pushing utilization beyond the point that the delivery of medical care is no longer considered cost effective.

A place to begin evaluating the cost effectiveness of our current health care delivery system is high tech medicine, particularly life-extending technology. Current medical practice is driven by the "technological imperative"[4] that has transformed our medical philosophy from caring to curing and our individual perspective on good health from aspiration to expectation.

According to this philosophy, when someone is faced with a medical problem, everything that can be done ought to be done. If the service is available to anyone, it ought to be available to everyone. If it is available to everyone, it ought to be available regardless of one's ability to pay. Thus, it becomes society's responsibility to provide the service to all who demand the service. Medicare studies have shown that 25 to 35 percent of the program's expenditures in any given year go to the 5 to 6 percent of the enrollees who die within that year. This high expenditure on nonsurvivors is a major reason that spending on health care is rising so dramatically.[5]

A national health care policy cannot provide every person with all the health care he or she may desire. Such an open-ended policy is inappropriate in an environment where health care is not the only objective. A national policy must be able to establish reasonable priorities and devise acceptable means to allocate resources sensibly.

GUIDING PRINCIPLES FROM THE BIBLE

If we are serious about the Apostle Paul's instructions in Ephesians 5:1 to "be imitators of God," we must know what God is like and what we need to do to please Him.[6] In God's infinite wisdom, He provided us with a detailed reference manual to His character and nature—His inspired Word. That same Word also supplies the information we need to organize our lives and activities—both individually and collectively.

Within that context certain biblical principles are available to help us organize our thoughts for the task at hand, namely, the establishment of a national health care policy. The principles are as follows:

1. We are made in the image of God.
2. As a result of the Fall, we have acquired a sin nature.
3. Because God is a respecter of liberty, we are accountable to Him for our actions.
4. We are to be productive in our pursuits and at the same time reject materialism.
5. We are to be good stewards of the resources God has given us.
6. We are to show compassion for others, especially the poor.

7. We are responsible for the care of members of our own family.
8. Not all poor health is the result of specific sinful acts.
9. Life is short, and death is inevitable.

This list is not meant to be all-inclusive. However, it provides the basis for our initial exploration. We will now examine these principles in more detail, along with their respective policy implications.

We are made in the image of God—The principle that we have been made in God's image is taught throughout the Bible in various contexts (see Gen. 1:26; 5:1; 1 Cor. 11:7; James 3:9). Although this image has been somewhat clouded by our sinful nature, it nonetheless exists. As image bearers, we are each important to God.

God's attitude about the value of a human being is far different from that seen in the world. The world tends to equate value in terms of status and productivity—good looks, credentials, income, and wealth. In contrast, Christ's teachings about people provide a clear picture of value in God's sight (see Matt. 6:26; 12:12). In fact, the cross of Christ is the ultimate proof of the value of all human-kind (see Mark 10:45).

Taking God's view, we begin to understand the meaning of the expression "the sanctity of life." In God's eyes we are all equally valuable. Each of us is uniquely significant and has the responsibility to live in a manner pleasing to Him, showing respect for all of God's creation including ourselves and others.

As a result of the Fall, we have acquired a sin nature—The fall of mankind described in Genesis 3 not only brought on physical death but also excluded us from the benefits of Eden. Prior to the Fall, the earth gave up her fruits more or less automatically. But because of sin, the earth has been cursed; it grows thorns and thistles as well as grain.

Thus, we are forced to make difficult choices. This is the purview of economics and one reason that economics has been referred to as the "dismal science." Due to the Fall, resources are scarce, but we have unlimited wants. We must reach decisions involving the allocation of these scarce resources. People who think that we have the resources to solve all the world's problems have not accepted the harsh reality that we, along with Adam and Eve, were evicted from the Garden many years ago.

Even though the Fall corrupted our nature, it did not completely erase God's image from us. The doctrine of total depravity teaches that we are corrupt in our intellect (see Rom. 1:28; 2 Cor. 4:4), conscience (see 1 Tim. 4:2), will (see Rom. 1:28), heart (see Eph. 4:18), and total being (see Rom. 1:18–3:20). This sin nature extends to all mankind and into all aspects of our existence; nevertheless, we are not necessarily as morally perverse as we could be.

Because God is a respecter of liberty, we are accountable to Him for our actions—God created mankind with a free will, with the freedom to make choices (see John 8:36; 1 Cor. 8:9; 1 Pet. 2:16). Even though it is His will for all to acknowledge Him and lead blameless lives, in His infinite wisdom He gives us the freedom to accept or reject Him and to pursue His will or our own desires.

As free agents, we are also held responsible for our actions (see Gal. 5:13). Eventually, we will be accountable to God for our choices here on earth (see 1 Cor. 3:12-15). Accountability thus indicates that we have certain guidelines we are to follow in the decisions we make. When we freely agree to follow God, we also agree to accept some limitations on our individual behavior. These limitations are defined by the Ten Commandments (see Exod. 20:3-17), explained in Christ's teachings in the Sermon on the Mount (see Matt. 5–7), and summarized in the great commandment (see Matt. 22:37-39).

We are to be productive in our pursuits and at the same time reject materialism—We are repeatedly told that there is virtue in being productive and working hard. However, this virtue is not an end in itself. God expects us to act responsibly since even the ability to gain wealth comes from Him (see Deut. 8:18). The more richly blessed a person, the more is required of him (see Luke 12:48).

The abundant life that we are promised (see John 10:10) is not a promise of material prosperity. However, hard work and productivity often lead to material well-being. We must be careful that our material prosperity does not become a stumbling block. God does not condemn wealth as such but judges the way it is accumulated (see Prov. 13:11; 15:16-17), the way it is used (see Luke 12:16-21; 16:19-31; 1 Tim. 6:17-19), and the priority it assumes in one's life (see Matt. 19:16-24; 1 Tim. 6:9-10). It is impossible to serve both God and money (see Matt. 6:24).

We are to be good stewards of the resources God has given us—In a free market society, ownership is a social function and raises the questions of sovereignty and stewardship. Ownership is limited to God; He owns all that we possess, and we are merely caretakers of what is rightfully His. Moses writes that the land belongs to God and that we are but aliens and travelers here on earth (see Lev. 25:23; see also Deut. 10:14; Ps. 24:1; 50:12).

The owner-steward relationship is developed more fully in the New Testament parable of the talents (see Matt. 25:14-30). Here and in Mark 4:25, it is clear that faithful stewardship brings rewards just as surely as unfaithful stewardship is punished.

Genesis 1 states no fewer than seventeen times that God is the Creator. As created beings, we are responsible to God for our actions. Interestingly enough, the theory of evolution receives popular acclaim because it relieves mankind of all responsibility to any higher authority.

We are to show compassion for others, especially the poor—Not only has God commanded us to love one another (see 1 John 4:7), but He has placed a special responsibility on us to show compassion to the poor (see 1 John 3:17). Throughout Scriptures we are instructed to provide assistance. The book of Proverbs is full of references to our responsibility for those less fortunate (see 14:31; 17:5; 21:13; 22:2, 9, 16, 22-23; 28:27; 29:7, 14; 31:8-9).

New Testament references include the writings of Paul (see 2 Cor. 8:8-15; Gal. 6:2-10; Eph. 4:28; 1 Tim. 6:18) and the teachings of Jesus Christ (see Matt. 22:37-39; Luke 6:32-36; 14:12-14). In fact, our helping someone in need is the same as helping the Lord Himself (see Matt. 25:40).

We are responsible for the care of members of our own family—God has established the family as the most important institution for the caring and nurturing of individuals. Parents are to bring up their children in an atmosphere of discipline and instruction (see Eph. 6:4). In return, children are to show respect for their parents (see Eph. 6:2-3).

This command goes beyond mere courtesy and obedience. It requires providing financial assistance to parents in need (see 1 Tim. 5:4). Anyone who refuses to follow these teachings and provide for the family is considered worse than a pagan (see 1 Tim. 5:8).

Not all poor health is the result of specific sinful acts—One result of our sin nature is that sickness and death were introduced into God's perfect creation (see Gen. 3:16-19). However, the Bible also teaches that sickness and poor health are not the results of specific sinful acts (see the story of Job; Luke 13:1-5; John 9:1-3). In other words, God does not punish us for specific sins that we commit. Granted, some illnesses are self-imposed, due to our lifestyle decisions. Chronic smoking increases the risk of acquiring lung cancer; IV drug use increases the chance of getting AIDS. However, these and other specific instances are actually exceptions to the general principle. For the most part, illness and other calamities are the result of sin nature and not specific sins.

Life is short, and death is inevitable—In contrast to the timelessness of eternity, our sojourn here on earth is short and is even compared to a water vapor that vanishes in an instant (see James 4:14). Our temporal fate is no different from that of the animals (see Eccles. 3:19); there is a given time to live and an appointed time to die (see Eccles. 3:1-3; 8:8; 9:12). Some may live for as long as seventy to eighty years (see Ps. 90:10), but the reality of death is inescapable. All of us will die someday.

APPLYING BIBLICAL PRINCIPLES
TO HEALTH CARE POLICY MAKING

In the nineteenth century, a system of political economy emerged in Western society based on the teachings and writings of Adam Smith, Edmund Burke, and Alexander Hamilton that stressed individual freedom and personal responsibility. The system that we call free enterprise was superimposed over a religious system emphasizing hard work and prudent management. While the results were harsh and brutal for some, the overall outcome was an unprecedented expansion in material output and wealth and a rapid improvement in the standard of living for the average citizen.

One reason that free enterprise works as well as it does is that few resources are expended in an attempt to change human nature. In other words, public policy makers must recognize mankind's moral limitations and identify reality-based options rather than fantasy-based solutions. Thus, public policy is more a matter of establishing incentives and tradeoffs than itemizing goals and intentions.

Application of the biblical principles described earlier can be of a general nature (with application to more than one policy goal) or more specific to one policy goal. The three major areas for health policy will be presented below along with the applicable principles.

The general level of health—How do the principles outlined here help us understand the appropriate way to view our health? The fact that we are made in God's image is a good starting place. Since every human being has God's imprint, our bodies can be used to glorify Him and His creation. Good health is important in fulfilling our mission on earth, but it is not to be pursued at all costs. When it was time for Christ to experience the ultimate in poor health for another goal, He recognized where His priorities were and pursued them wholeheartedly.

The lessons for us in a secular world that worships life and fears death are clear. We need to deal more realistically with imminent death, or what may be medically diagnosed as terminal illness. When death is imminent, especially at the end of a long life, it is not a respect for life that causes us to pursue lifesaving technology without considering the quality of the life extended. It is our enslavement to that same technology and our inability or unwillingness to accept the plan authored by God before the world began.

For decades medical ethicists have given attention to this point. It seems that when an individual's life is at issue, morality becomes relevant. Several biblical principles have some indirect applicability here, also. Under these circumstances, the well-informed patient must be allowed some input into the decision. Second medical opinions are also extremely important (see Proverbs on the use of wise counsel), and peer review (medical accountability) should be added into the process.

Even though the use of life-extending technology (including resuscitation) may not always be in the best interest of the patient, we must be careful how we apply these principles. It does not mean that the use of life-extending technology is a bad thing under all circumstances. However, we cannot pretend that we can overcome death or that life has meaning only if it can be extended indefinitely. The obvious cost-saving solution is to withhold life-extending technology from those with the lowest probability of survival.

This solution may not be as simple as it seems because of the uncertainty of correctly diagnosing probabilities of survival. We currently spend the most resources on patients with unexpected medical outcomes: the survivor who had a low probability of survival, and the nonsurvivor who had a high probability of survival.

The improvement in our ability to accurately diagnose illness and predict survival probabilities should make the establishment of a policy on the use of life-extending technology an option in the future. As long as the policy is not used to terminate unwanted lives (abortion and euthanasia) and is uniformly applied without bias, it can be carried out in a manner that respects biblical principles.

Access to medical care—The issue of access to medical care is usually discussed within the context of affordability. Several biblical principles help us understand how policy should be developed within this area.

Individual life is to be respected for its own sake, not in terms of its narrowly defined value to society. This is not meant to preclude the evaluation of cost effectiveness in the distribution of health care resources, only that they should not be distributed on the basis of wealth or some definition of social merit.

Since the incidence of illness and thus the need for health care services is largely an undeserved phenomenon, the cost of illness and its treatment should be broadly spread among members of society without regard to its actual or probable use. This argument counters the principles of experience-rated health insurance premiums and is more compatible with community ratings.

One perplexing and related issue concerns what to do about the influence of lifestyle and environment on health. To a certain extent, individuals contribute to their own medical care requirements by the lifestyles they lead and the environments they inhabit. Smoking leads to lung cancer and heart disease. But not everyone who smokes is affected in the same way, and choosing not to smoke does not guarantee that one will not die of lung cancer or heart disease. While it makes financial sense when dealing with the individual policyholder that insurance premiums are experience rated, in the name of fairness and equal treatment, community rating for health insurance seems the only reasonable choice.

In our society, health insurance, or rather the lack of it, is a major barrier to access to medical care. The United States is the only developed nation in the world without some form of a national health system, but that does not mean national health insurance or socialized medicine is the only way, or even the best way, to fulfill society's obligation with respect to this issue.

Two economic issues must be addressed within the context of health insurance: moral hazard and the free rider problem. The relevant definition of moral hazard, when dealing with medical care, is the tendency for an individual to desire more care when the direct out-of-pocket cost is lowered.

Conventional health insurance coverage changes the nature of the price system (Adam Smith's invisible hand) and changes the incentive structure completely. Individuals and providers have no incentive to compare the cost against the expected benefits of the proposed care, which leads to a phenomenon that Mark Pauly refers to as "flat-of-the-curve medicine,"[7] where additional expenditures provide minimal benefits.

While it can be argued that society has a moral obligation to provide access to an adequate level of health care, it should also be recognized that the individual has the responsibility to pay a fair share based on some measure of ability. The phenomenon of the free rider happens when individuals, recognizing society's obligations for access, intentionally fail to take reasonable steps to provide for their own health care, even when they can afford to do so.

With respect to both phenomena, it is clear that sinful mankind will find a way to take advantage of the situation and exploit it for his own good, often at the expense of other members of society. We cannot change mankind's sin nature, but we must try to minimize the opportunities to manipulate the system. Thus, it is appropriate to hold people responsible for a fair share of the cost of their own care and that of their families.

As the government's role in the provision of health care has steadily increased, the family's role has substantially diminished. The prominent government role has brought into question the moral obligation of adult children to supply funds for the welfare of elderly parents. Although the Bible is clear on this subject, we still "need to have some sense of what we can legitimately, in the name of filial obligation, ask and expect of families in the care of their own elderly, and what the reasonable limits of such expectations ought to be."[8]

In 1983 the Reagan administration, as part of the Medicare program, enabled states to exercise the legal option of requiring children to contribute to the support of elderly parents. "Family responsibility" laws were adopted in only a few states (Virginia, Indiana, and Mississippi) and are rarely enforced.

There are two dilemmas here. More and more of the elderly are reaching old, old age (eighty plus). That age group is the predominant user of long-term institutionalized care. As the price of long-term care increases along with the number of elderly requiring the service, the need to widen the scope and acceptability of family care increases.

In addition, over 70 percent of the elderly poor are female. Currently, the requirement for receiving Medicaid (Medicare does not pay for long-term care) is impoverishment, that is divestiture of all resources. This legally imposed dependence on the federal government of one of the most vulnerable segments of society is not only unconscionable but is taking away (in the financial realm) something God gives all His children (in the spiritual realm)—a sense of security. This policy obviously needs to be reconsidered.

The cost of medical care—A harsh economic reality is that a program promoting the general level of health and providing easy access to care is also extremely expensive. As medical care has taken a larger share of gross national product, concerns over the mounting cost of care have become central in the policy debate. Clearly, the issue is one of promoting the general welfare of the population by providing equitable access to medical care without pushing utilization beyond what could realistically be viewed as an appropriate level of care (i.e., what is socially optimal and thus cost effective).

Our call to good stewardship demands that we efficiently manage the resources God has entrusted to us. We have the freedom to use those resources in furthering God's purposes here on earth, assuming that they are not wasted. Thus, public policy ought to promote cost-effective medical care. That is to say, our definition of appropriate care must take into consideration the cost of care in relation to its expected benefit.

We must also be careful that our preoccupation with wealth does not result in an unresponsive attitude toward the needs of individuals. Our call to reject materialism means that we are to use our wealth to promote a fair allocation of health care resources apart from considerations of ability to pay.

Is it appropriate, then, to expect that people pay a fair share of the cost of their own health care? While it may be a societal obligation to provide fair access to health care, it is also an individual obligation to pay one's fair share. Both obligations rest on the principle of fairness.

Based on what we know about human nature, the free rider problem severely challenges policy makers. When individuals know that others will come to their assistance in the event of a medical emergency, and thus fail to take reasonable steps to provide for their own health care, they are taking advantage of the rest of society.

By implication, then, steps should be taken to reduce the likelihood that those who can afford to insure against medical emergencies will fail to do so.

One possibility may be some form of mandatory health insurance plan or, at least, an effective and affordable means of providing health insurance to the uninsured and uninsurable.[9]

Finally, at least part of the high and rising cost of medical care is due to the extensive reliance on the third-party payment mechanism. With government-subsidized care through Medicare and Medicaid (about 40 percent of total expenditures) and private insurance coverage (about 30 percent of total expenditures), the incentive for individual economizing is weak because of the relatively small out-of-pocket cost of care.

Incentives for economizing may come from a shift in the method of payment from a retrospective one to a prospective one. The federal government has already moved in this direction with the implementation of diagnosis-related groups (DRGs) for hospital payment. Currently, the Congress is considering the form of a new way of paying physicians for covered services called a resource-based relative value scale (RBRVS). With the ballooning costs of outpatient services, studies are under way to develop ambulatory visit groups (AVG) similar in theory to DRGs. Under all three plans, the shift is from individual fee-for-service to payments based on treatment groups.

SUMMARY AND CONCLUSIONS

Even under the best of circumstances, economics cannot provide solutions to the problems of medical care. But economics can offer a decision framework within which we can study the implications of individual choice behavior and define the alternative approaches available to us. We know from economics that growth in output is essential; otherwise, health care will take an ever-expanding share of our output and result in an increasing concern with the distribution of income.

We also know from a policy perspective that we cannot give every person the level of health that he or she may desire. But we can provide a direction based on sound biblical principles whereby coherent goals can be set and rational priorities can be established. A goal of conquering all disease is unrealistic and is a prescription for ever-increasing expenditures on health care.

To quote John Adams: "Ours is a system designed for moral men, it will work for no others." Any system works best in a Christian environment because of the moral responsibility brought about by the Christian influence. The same is true for the free enterprise system. It is not inherently moral in itself; it simply functions most productively in the same environment that Christianity functions most productively. Thus, any medical care system that we develop must rely on the same basic principles that we as Christians rely on in guiding our daily lives—the revealed Word given to us in the Bible.

EDITOR'S PERSPECTIVE

It shocked me to learn from Dr. Henderson's work that we spent more on health care in our nation, during a period of rapidly increasing military expenditures, than we did on national defense (in 1986, $458 billion versus $277 billion, or $1.25 billion per day—almost $5 per day for every living soul in the country). Surely something is askew in the society—not that health care is less valuable than national defense, but that so much is spent on it in absolute terms. What is wrong, in my opinion, is what is ignored—*prevention*. An old nonbiblical proverb says, "An ounce of prevention is worth a pound of cure." It is easier to prevent an illness than it is to cure it. This line of reasoning also reflects an area of concern discussed in considerable detail in Scripture.

The medical profession is an old one. Its practice is mentioned both favorably and disdainfully in the Scripture. Charlatans, magicians, and witch doctors were to be driven from the society and avoided at all costs (see Lev. 19:31; Deut. 18:10; 2 Chron. 33:6), but doctors like Luke (the author of Luke and Acts) were respected men (see Col. 4:14). Job referred to his comforters as "worthless physicians" (Job 13:4), and Christ referred to a proverb of His day when He said to the people at Nazareth that they would no doubt say to Him, "Physician, heal yourself!" (Luke 4:23). Physicians were unquestionably a visible part of the society in biblical times, but the teaching of Scripture is predominantly on prevention.

The prevention concept appears in four forms in Scripture: (1) a concern for diet, (2) matters of stress and fatigue, (3) diagnosis and quarantine, and (4) physical safety. We will look briefly at each one. Christians should take the biblical accounts to heart and note their intent, especially the explanation made by Christ and others that the dietary laws were given primarily for reasons other than the sake of righteousness (see Mark 7:14-23; Acts 10:15; Rom. 14:1-4; Col. 2:16).

Why were the dietary laws instituted? Was it for the sake of the people's good health? Scripture does not say explicitly. But modern studies affirm the sensibleness of the Old Testament dietary concerns, and Christ and His apostles made it clear that their purpose was something other than the people's personal holiness (apart from heeding the law in obedience to God's expressed will, an obvious act of holiness).

The following excerpt taken from a lengthy Bible dictionary note on food was written by Dr. K. A. Kitchen as he outlined the various Old Testament dietary laws:

> Leviticus 11:1-23, 29ff. (cf. 41ff.), and Dt. 14:3-21 record the law on animals allowed or forbidden as food. In addition to the ox, sheep, and goat, it was permissible to eat seven kinds of venison (Dt. 14:5), and all other cloven-hoofed animals that chewed the cud. Those animals which failed to fulfill both demands were forbidden as food and listed as "unclean," together with more than a score of different kinds of birds. With regard to fish, etc., only those with both fins and scales might be eaten. A very few specified insects might be consumed (the locust-family). Some of the creatures forbidden were simply unfit for human consumption; others (e.g. swine) were unsafe in a hot climate; still others may have been too closely identified with surrounding idolatry.[1]

Grains, fruits, vegetables, honey, dates, and nuts were all commended and enjoyed. Milk and its derivative products of cheese, butter, and curds were a staple along with olive oil. Evidence suggests the people of Israel were not big meat eaters despite the size of their herds and their frequent animal sacrifices. Certainly Daniel did not want to eat "the king's choice food," and he "sought permission from the commander of the officials" to be allowed to eat vegetables and drink water for ten days before the decision was made to require him and his friends to drink the wine and eat the richer foods (the appearance of Daniel and his friends was better than the others following the test; see Dan. 1:4-16).

The purpose here is not to talk about what constitutes a healthy diet, but to understand that God thought the matter important enough to tell His children about it in a day and age when there was no scientific way to determine what was healthy. No one should be surprised by the fact that the information given still stands the test of time, science, and natural revelation. Many an American would prevent further health problems from occurring if the food prescriptions of the Old Testament were followed and the more popular table fare of our day was altered to reflect the biblical diet.

Fatigue and stress are acknowledged killers in modern society, especially in the West. Although no scientific study has been done that will validate my perception, there appears, on the surface at least, to be an inverse correlation in our society between the decline in the observance of the Lord's Day for worship, rest, and acts of mercy and the rise in hypertension, stress, and illnesses closely related to these body-destroying realities. Furthermore, when people do not know the Father, Savior, and Advocate (who authored their existence, knows their every need, and is willing to be so fully involved in their every experience in a loving way that trust, peace, and joy may supplant their fear, anxiety, stress, and depression), they face the full consequences of the Fall with only their limited personal resources.

Knowing that God loves us and is *absolutely sovereign* (truly no event takes place in our lives outside His foreknowledge and plan to incorporate it into the glorious renovating work He undertakes as He restores us, degree by degree, to the image of Christ) brings security, confidence, peace, and hope to our minds. Anxiety, at its heart, is a care (caused by a thwarted will, blocked desire, unwanted outcome, or frustrated expectation) that draws our attention away from God (leaving Him out of the picture), reveals our disbelief (distrust) with respect to His will and plans, or shows our misunderstanding of God's ways. The cure for anxiety is to *rest* in God, not in man or circumstances.

The third preventive process is to be observed in the procedures established in Scripture to provide diagnostic attention to potential health hazards and the practice of quarantining those who manifested the signs of threatening diseases. The laws governing the diagnosis and treatment of leprosy (all skin rashes, swellings, scabs, bright spots, and sores were to be considered potential leprosy) and body discharges illustrate this (see Lev. 13–15; Deut. 24:8-9). Once again, the point is not really to draw attention to the particular practices of diagnosis and quarantining, but to highlight the biblical concern for preventing problems from intensifying. Prevention was clearly the biblical way of trying to contend with potential health problems.

Finally, public health and safety are also addressed in Scripture from the perspective of prevention rather than cure—do it correctly at first so it will not have adverse consequences later. The examples are not contemporary in character, but they are as applicable in principle as they were when first given. For example, the need for industrial safety (safety of mines, machinery, and working conditions) is not any different in character from the Israelites' construction of protective fences to keep people from falling off buildings (see Deut. 22:8) or their response if their capital assets (oxen) brought about the death of a worker (see Exod. 21:28-29). Other examples could also be cited (see Exod. 21:33-34; Deut. 23:12-13), but the point is clear, I believe. God told the people through the recounting of specific illustrations what they were to prevent. He also revealed the consequences if they failed to prevent injury or loss of life. The call of God is to act before the potential problem has a chance of overtaking anyone.

Part of the problem in our society is that far too many people want to live and act as they please, without regard for their health (food, drink, care of teeth, drugs, etc.), and then have the group (fellow workers, society at large) share the burden of their neglect. This attitude is irresponsible. True responsibility is exhibited in prudent behavior that seeks to prevent the difficulties before they materialize. That is the biblical approach.

PART XII

TRADE AND INTERNATIONAL JUSTICE

Probably no area of public policy reflects more clearly than foreign trade the all-too-present spirit of retaliation and its self-serving, self-justifying compatriot, the spirit of blame shifting, deep in the heart of each person. This latter attitude is sometimes called the Adam and Eve principle. Adam's statement after the Fall shifting blame to God and Eve, and away from himself, is the first instance of this principle in operation ("The woman whom Thou gavest to be with me, she gave me from the tree, and I ate" [Gen. 3:12]). The attitudes of blame shifting and retaliation are likely to spring to the fore whenever people are experiencing real or imaginary difficulties that can be tied (rightly or wrongly) to the conduct of others in the marketplace. Troubles easily stimulate a search for a substitute target on which to heap responsibility in an unconscious effort to avoid personal responsibility. The inherent propensity to protect and defend positive self-identity (pride?) is so strong that most people rationalize or justify their conduct and decisions while shifting blame for troubles or failures to others.

The frequent workings of the Adam and Eve principle in the world become apparent when Dr. Grinols points to the surge in the desire of many political and business figures to substantially modify or even move away from free trade. They instead call for the adoption of new forms of protectionism so that the federal government will intervene in the market and shield domestic business from foreign competition.

As Dr. Grinols exposes this resurgence of protectionism, he in no way denies that other nations with whom we trade are acting unfairly or even in ways that contradict the very trade agreements they have signed. He simply draws our attention to our tendency to ignore unfair trade practices when the balance of payments was overwhelmingly in our favor. The fact that we have become a debtor nation—an embarrassing discomfort—stimulates and drives us to focus on the unfair trade practices of those who now enjoy trade surpluses. Dr. Grinols is quick to note, however, that "no change in foreign behavior has occurred that is large enough to explain the observed swing from a surplus to a deficit position." Then what is the problem?

The causes for this momentous shift in our trade balances are to be discovered in domestic changes, not foreign ones, and Dr. Grinols discusses these changes. He cautions us to forgo retaliation, for that will only complicate the real problem, not solve it. He then identifies four biblical principles that ought to guide our thinking about any national trade policy and applies them to the real problems underlying our negative trade balances. Dr. Grinols reveals much about human nature in the process of guiding us toward a good integration of God's Word with the issues associated with foreign trade.

CHAPTER 12

DIRECTIONS FOR NATIONAL POLICY ON FOREIGN TRADE: REVISIONIST ECONOMICS AND THE APPLICATION OF BIBLICAL PRINCIPLES

Earl L. Grinols

Earl L. Grinols did his undergraduate work at the University of Michigan where he was a James B. Angell Scholar and at the University of Minnesota where he was graduated summa cum laude *with degrees in Mathematics and Economics. He did his graduate work at Harvard University and the Massachusetts Institute of Technology, receiving his Ph.D. from M.I.T. in 1977. Dr. Grinols has worked as an International Economist for the U.S. Department of the Treasury and as Senior Economist with responsibility for international economic affairs with President Reagan's Council of Economic Advisers. Dr. Grinols has published extensively in the field of international economics and is the author of* Uncertainty and the Theory of International Trade *(Harwood Publishers, 1987). He has taught at M.I.T., Cornell University, and the University of Illinois. He is presently Professor of Economics at the University of Illinois where he continues his work in international economics.*

These . . . came to David at Hebron . . . men of Issachar, who understood the times and knew what Israel should do. (1 Chron. 12:23, 32; NIV)

And when they say that the church should give us a lead, they ought to mean that some Christians—those who happen to have the right talents—should be economists and statesmen, and that all economists and statesmen should be Christians, and that their whole efforts in politics and economics should be directed to putting 'Do as you should be done by' into action.

—C. S. Lewis, *Mere Christianity*

T oday a debate centers on what the guiding principle of American public policy toward foreign trade should be. On one side of the debate are proponents of the self-styled "new international economics," which argues for greater interventionist pursuit of national self-interest in the international arena; arrayed on the other side are supporters of the older post-World War II consensus that emphasizes the necessity of the ideal of free trade implemented through international agreement and agencies such as the General Agreement on Tariffs and Trade (GATT). Most international economists would agree that the supporters of nationalistic interventionism are gaining ground.

The debate cannot be understood without consideration of the emotional and moral norms not too far beneath the surface rhetoric. The present chapter is addressed to these norms, for it is here that principles for setting a national policy on foreign trade are to be determined.

In this chapter, I will take *foreign trade policy* to include policy related to the setting of regulations and rules governing the passage of goods and services across national boundaries. The choice of domestic tariffs and quota levels, for example, is part of foreign trade policy, as is policy dealing with international agreements governing international trade. The choice of an international monetary system is not covered under this definition—that could be considered a separate topic in its own right. Neither is Federal Reserve Board behavior aimed at influencing the value of national currency on world markets, which is part of a national monetary policy. It might be possible to consider foreign trade policy from the perspective of using trade as a tool in achieving another primary national objective, such as caring for the needs of the poor around the world or providing debt relief to selected developing countries. I have not discussed this type of policy here because I think the principles involved are better understood as applications of national policy in the primary area. Thus, I have focused on the choice of foreign trade policy for its own sake as it relates directly to the flow of goods and services.[1]

With this focus in mind, in the second section of the chapter a diagnosis is made of the major issues facing American trade policy as they are seen by the practicing international economist (a brief description is also given of what the theoretical literature has to say on the relevant issues), and an assessment is made of some of the root causes of the change in attitude being observed. The third section considers the biblical record for guidance that can be applied to international dealings. Several principles will be presented and their economic implications enunciated. Section four suggests how the principles might be applied, and closing remarks are offered in section five.

NO MORE MR. NICE GUY

If the position of the supporters of nationalistic interventionism could be succinctly characterized in the vernacular, it might go something like this: Japan primarily but also Latin America and Europe have not been playing fair in their international trade dealings. They have been governmentally intervening in the markets to tilt competition in favor of their industries at the expense of American businesses that receive no such help. Moreover, most developing countries have never fully subscribed to or participated in the obligations of free trade, even though they have been freeloading on the benefits of open trade in the advanced world and their resulting access to developed-country markets.

As a result of their behavior, America's trading partners are getting ahead of us in crucial areas and are harming U.S. interests and security. In the past we could overlook such behavior because the United States had a large lead, and American income and preeminence were not threatened. Today, however, the race is closer, the United States has a large trade deficit, and we have been patient long enough. There will be "no more Mr. Nice Guy." From now on America should look more to its own interests by pursuing the nationalist advantage wherever it can safely be enhanced. If this gives other countries pause—perhaps inducing them to improve their behavior—so much the better. Even if it does not, America will no longer be patsy to the rest of the world.

Implications of the "new" view—Trade, whether at the individual or international level, is an activity that represents a mixture of antagonism and parallelism of interests. Trade is *mutually* beneficial to both parties, but the degree of benefit each party receives is subject to the nature and structure of the trading environment. This is true both at the individual level and at the international level. Typically, few interventions in the marketplace are mutually beneficial to both trading parties unless they are interventions that tend to enhance competition. Indeed, the typical trade intervention for purposes of enhancing the national interest is positively harmful to foreign interests. In plain terminology this intervention is usually *exploitive*. Two examples illustrate.

In the first example, an American firm and a foreign firm compete to capture the world market in a technologically advanced product produced only by the two nations. Because both firms make positive profits in the growing industry, we decide that there is room for intervention to enhance the ability of the American firm to increase its size and returns at the expense of the foreign firm. Profits are to be had, so why not have them be made by the American firms rather than the foreign one? The American government accordingly aids its domestic industry through administrative intervention to limit foreign sales of the competing product in the United States. This intervention can take many forms ranging from the imposition of duties to the establishment of performance standards or import licensing requirements to review and delay imports. This intervention will enlarge the scale of the American industry, reduce its costs of production, and therefore increase its competitiveness. Moreover, as the American industry exports more, its representatives learn how to sell to foreign markets, and this knowledge eventually diffuses to the rest of industry, providing a positive externality. The effect of this intervention on the foreign firm is that its market is reduced by the lost American demand denied to it, sales fall, and ultimately, it makes lower profits. The intervention is successful (in the national interest) while harmful to the foreign firm; it is exploitive.

In the second example, an American monopolist of a high technology product sells its product to a foreign market, charging prices well above production costs. The foreign government responds by imposing a tariff on imports of the product to collect as tax revenues some of the monopoly rents being earned by the American firm from the local citizens. The result of the intervention is that foreign government revenues increase by more than the loss in the consumer welfare corresponding to the higher internal price of the American product. On the other hand, American profits drop by more than the net gains to the foreign country, so that welfare of the world as a whole declines. The intervention is successful in the foreign country's nationalist self-interest, but again, it is exploitive since the foreign country's trading partner (America, in this case) is harmed.

The pitfalls of the above strategies, and others like them, and the role of market interventions in trade to enhance the national interests have been well discussed in the international economics literature[2] and are not the primary subject here. However, it is important to list the salient points for later reference. First, while intervention is theoretically sound from the national point of view in some cases, it is destructive to the *system* that governs international trade. In the end, it can create more harm than good for each participant. Second, the process may be co-opted or "captured" by traditional protectionist demands of individual businesses or industries, which will use whatever arguments are available to justify selfish protection at the expense of *their own* nation's interest as well as the interests of the rest of the world.

Third, in many cases where intervention is potentially in the national interest, the called-for intervention (e.g., a subsidy on exports) may be exactly reversed (e.g., the subsidy should be replaced by a *tax* on exports instead) in a similar market environment where only a few hard-to-measure but key features of the market are different. For example, in choosing an intervention it usually must be known what firms believe about their rivals' responses to their actions. Economic theory offers a myriad of possibilities that can be sorted out only by knowing the given market. If the nature of the required intervention is judged wrongly, ignorance could easily cause the intervention to be harmful to the national interest.

Finally, in certain interventions, the fundamental reason that the government is able to enhance the outcome from the national point of view is that the government is implicitly assumed to know more about the true effects of a particular firm's choice than the firm itself. Assuming that the government has more knowledge of a particular industry than the participants in that industry is often a poor assumption.

Sources of the change in sentiment—One main reason for the seemingly sudden change in U.S. sentiment is the large trade deficit that has emerged since 1982, and the presumption that foreign behavior explains a large part of lost American competitiveness. It is hard for U.S. import-competing industries, citizens, and the Congress to believe that foreigners have not changed their behavior in some way that explains the difficulty in selling abroad and the apparent success of foreign products in capturing market share in the United States. In fact, though, no change in foreign behavior has occurred that is large enough to explain the observed swing from a surplus to a deficit position. Nevertheless, the result has been a wave of protectionist and interventionist sentiment that found expression in the Omnibus Trade and Competitiveness Act of 1988 and continues to gain momentum.

There are several underlying causes of the trade deficit, including a secular change in the saving habits of Americans as a whole, but the cause generally recognized as the most important one is the large federal budget deficit—an internal event nominally under the control of Congress and the president. The failure to deal with internal fiscal matters is reflected in our need to borrow large sums of money from foreign lenders and the corresponding trade deficit needed to create the flow.

A different type of domestic failure of will is mirrored in portions of the academic and public policy community where one can attain better coverage in the public press if the message is that "new" discoveries in the theory of international trade imply that intervention in the marketplace is in the national interest after all, and that such interventions are warranted in many cases. The press is only too happy to report this revisionist "wisdom" since it makes good copy, and the result is that the message conveyed is far less restrained than the creators of the theory know it should be. That is, the received message is that (1) foreign "unfairness" does pay, (2) the response should be to fight fire with fire, and (3) the new wave of theory supports it.

I do not want to carry the psychological examination too far, but to the extent that the change in national trade policy reflects a general tendency toward a more selfish and nationalistic mode of thought in America, it is worth noting. Indeed, the emotional response to a U.S. deficit plus the fact that the rest of the world is catching up to U.S. living standards, productivity, and technology may be the true motivating force for the observed rethinking of trade policy. In working out a Christian perspective on national trade policy, we must understand some of the elements of human nature that give rise to a particular position. That is, we might be much more comfortable with a particular choice of policy if we knew that it sprang from altruistic motives. In the reverse direction we might feel uncomfortable, *ceterus paribus* (other things being equal), with a policy that appeared to spring from baser motives.

BIBLICAL PRINCIPLES FOR A NATIONAL TRADE POLICY

International trade is well known to the pages of the Bible. Isaiah 60:5-6 mentions "the wealth of the Gentiles" coming to Israel and a multitude of camels covering the land (presumably bringing goods). Details of the wealth derived from King Solomon's international trading take up long passages of the book of 1 Kings. Ezekiel and Revelation 18 talk of trading on the sea when they describe the downfall of the ancient trading city of Tyre and the destruction of the new Babylon with whom the world's merchants became rich through trading. According to the biblical record, the ancient patriarchs went to Egypt to trade for grain in the famine years of the time of Joseph. Christ Himself in the parable of the ten minas in Luke 19 speaks of the gain that each servant might have had by trading, which presumably would have included international trade.

Although there is no obvious list of policy rules in the Bible for international trade, it seems to present a favorable attitude toward commerce and trade as a way to acquire wealth. The description of the virtuous woman in Proverbs 31 comments on business and trade activities, for example. At the same time, not all trade is considered equally virtuous. Scriptures frequently discuss the need for honest weights and measures, a principle that would apply to international as well as domestic dealings.

Collecting such observations, however, does not constitute a national trade policy of the type for which we are looking. Moreover, in my study of the Bible, I am convinced that a search of this type, no matter how thorough and careful, would still fail to turn up any specifically applicable guidance on what national trade policy should be. (This might be different, say, if we were looking for a policy toward the poor.) I take it as fundamental, then, that one must first determine from the Bible the most important principles that apply to dealings between men in general, and extrapolate and apply these principles to those particular dealings that constitute international trade. In this process I take as a basic premise, for example, that individuals and corporations should deal *honestly*, and appropriate regulations and rules should apply to enforce this basic mode of conduct. The position of domestic legislation on bribery of foreign officials by domestic exporters, the use of kickbacks, and other immoral nonmarket trade-related activities, for example, would be immediately covered by this basic premise. Having said this, there remains the question of setting the other parameters of national trade policy where honest men might differ on the basic approach to trade at the national level.

Principle 1: Apply the Golden Rule—Jesus said that "whatever you want men to do to you, do also to them, for this is the Law and the Prophets" (Matt. 7:12). He also said that the second greatest commandment, after loving God with all our heart, soul, and mind, is loving our neighbor as ourselves (see Matt. 22:39). These principles, which apply on the individual level, can also apply on the national level.[3] As the parable of the good Samaritan shows, our neighbor is not just our kinsman or fellow citizen; he can be a foreigner. Moreover, if these commands of Jesus are the most important of the commands for individuals, then it is safe to enlarge them to the national level and conclude that they are significant for describing dealings between nations. From Scripture we find that God's judgment generally came upon nations for two reasons. The first had to do with turning their backs on God, but the second reason related to mistreatment of other nations. Indeed, the country of Edom is condemned even for taking pleasure in the calamity of the nation of Judah (see Obadiah). (Proverbs 17:5 asserts, "He who is glad at calamity will not go unpunished.") A reasonable implication is that a policy that in practice consistently enhances our national interest at the expense of foreign interests cannot have the backing of Scripture.

Translating this principle into a pragmatic element of foreign trade policy would not appear to be difficult. The natural application to the debate at hand is to note that a policy of nationalist intervention in trade at the expense of other trading partners is ruled out for at least three reasons.[4] First, we do not like the effects of similar interventions by our foreign trading partners when U.S. interests are the affected parties. Applying the same measures ourselves violates the call to treat others as we would want to be treated. Second, if other countries behave in this manner, we will just as often be the recipients of their actions and therefore be the harmed party. Third, as noted in the second section, there are frequently cases where the seemingly appropriate intervention may turn out to be directly inimical to our own interests as well as harmful to foreign interests. In cases where interventions are unharmful to foreign interests, of course, enhancing the national welfare is perfectly legitimate.

Principle 2: Honor the sanctity of covenants—The second biblical principle relevant to the choice of national trade policy comes from scattered passages in the Bible and a very poignant case history, described below. I refer to the keeping of covenants. According to *Webster's Dictionary*, a *covenant* is "a solemn and binding agreement," "a compact or a pledge." An international agreement is therefore a covenant. According to the Bible, the keeping of covenants is an essential component of the Christian life. Covenants with God are especially holy and inviolable, but covenants with other individuals are also to be taken seriously. The words *covenant breaker* appear only once in the King James translation (see Rom. 1:31) as a description of the behavior of condemned people deserving death. Keeping covenants is an attribute of God repeatedly noted in the Bible. Psalm 105:9 says of God, "He has remembered His covenant forever, the word which He commanded, for a thousand generations." At roughly thirty years per generation, this is over five times the length of all recorded history.

The significance of covenants between nations is well described by the Old Testament account of the treaty between Joshua and the Gibeonites. Although, in that case, the original covenant was entered into under false pretenses, the Israelites nevertheless honored its terms long after the deception was discovered.

The book of Joshua indicates that God's instructions to the Israelites when they entered Canaan were to destroy the inhabitants and appropriate all of the land for themselves (see Josh. 9). (We know from other passages of Scripture that God was judging the nations then in possession of Canaan.) The seriousness of His instructions can be inferred from the fact that God was setting up His chosen people in the Promised Land, the very people through which He would later bless the world as the message of redemption was carried to every corner of it.

The Gibeonites were aware of the instructions to the Israelites and pretended to be visiting the land from a far country. Under those false pretenses, they made a covenant with the Israelites that the Gibeonites were to be allowed to live. The Israelites "did not ask counsel of the LORD" before making the covenant, but they were honor bound to observe the covenant after the deception was revealed. And they did, although the Gibeonites were made woodcutters and water carriers for the congregation of Israel and the altar of the Lord.

The Gibeonites appear in the biblical record hundreds of years later in the time of King David. Second Samuel 21 reveals that there was a famine in the land for three years because Saul had sought to kill the Gibeonites in his campaigns. Even at that much later time (four hundred years later) it was expected that the covenant would be honored.

In the present circumstances the U.S. commitment to the principles of the General Agreement on Tariffs and Trade has weakened. In response to complaints about foreign actions, and under sanction of domestic law, the United States has violated GATT rules in unilateral retaliatory actions. Officially, the American commitment has not changed, but there is increased questioning of the extent to which American commitments should be honored in light of the failure of GATT to achieve its major objective of creating essentially what was to be a "free trading club" of nations. The prevailing opinion appears to be that adhering to this agreement is often harmful to American interests and therefore that selected unilateral deviations from GATT are acceptable. Besides, the United States is large enough and powerful enough that it can get away with such behavior. The failure of other nations to adhere to their commitments just adds support, in this line of thought, to the view that the United States should reevaluate strict adherence to GATT.

Indeed, one recurring question concerns how the United States should respond when another nation violates its GATT commitments. On one hand, GATT includes provisions for dispute resolution, but on the other hand, these procedures are frequently lengthy and often ineffective in finding just verdicts. Even when a decision has been rendered in the United States' favor, enforcement of the decision is difficult. However, it is not acceptable to fail to honor a commitment because in a later circumstance it is not in your interest to do so. God speaks through King David in Psalm 15:4-5 describing the individual who may abide in God's sanctuary as he "who keeps his oath even when it hurts. . . . He who does these things will never be shaken" (NIV).

Principle 3: Recognize the relative importance of the nation-state and the individual—Scripture teaches that the Church and the individual, not the nation, are the objects of God's love. Modern thinking often has the priority between national interest and the individual interest reversed. A charge of such a reversal, for example, has frequently been leveled against Japan, which appears to set policy from the perspective of national prestige or advantage with lesser concern for policy's effects on the individual. A widely accepted, if little stated, belief is that nation-states will live forever, while the individual dies after one lifetime. The truth, of course, is just the opposite. The regenerated, saved individual and the Church will live forever, while the nation will perish. According to Isaiah, "Behold, the nations are as a drop in a bucket" (40:15). We know from Daniel's prophecy that eventually the nations of the world will end and be replaced by God's Kingdom.

The conclusion to be drawn in the present age about national trade policy is that the policy should have as its objective the welfare of each individual and not some imagined national interest or preeminence. Moreover, because God is not a respecter of persons, the choice of policy should give equal weight to individual welfare in other parts of the world.

A case in point may help to illustrate. In the field of supercomputers, the American company Cray Research Incorporated is the world leader. Cray is a private company. Japan, through the auspices of the Ministry of International Trade and Industry, encourages a consortium of Japanese electronics firms to pool their efforts to become the leading producer of supercomputers. There are good indications that the Japanese government has intervened to prevent sales of American supercomputers in Japan. Even so, the Japanese effort may represent enormous costs that are not being recouped in sales—there are better investments in electronics than supercomputing. The Japanese effort therefore seems to be aimed primarily at some notion of nationalist preeminence rather than profitability and domestic welfare. Naturally, one can imagine many reasons why becoming a leading producer of supercomputers might eventually convert into gains for the individual, but in the present circumstances these must be of secondary importance. For example, Japan does not need supercomputing technology for national defense or security reasons (one reason that a governmental intervention into the marketplace might be legitimate), as it could be argued the United States does. The Japanese intervention thus violates principle 3.

The focus on the question of how policy affects the individual, as opposed to the group or nation, has close ties to the question of what type of economic system is most conducive to spiritual growth and freedom—and how unfettered access to foreign markets relates to that system. Christians have discussed the issue of *laissez faire* and the Bible at great length, and my purpose is not to go over that ground again. However, it seems reasonable to conclude that national policy unnecessarily restricting the individual's ability to engage in welfare-enhancing activities is inconsistent with biblical principles. In application this would mean as little intervention as possible by governmental bodies in the trade arena; the benefits of trade policy should be directed toward people, not toward nationalistic preeminence.

Principle 4: Require parity of conduct—The fourth principle is really a corollary of the first three. Just as the United States should do unto others as she would like them to do unto her, so should she expect other countries to adhere to equally high standards in their dealings with her. Exodus 23:3 admonishes, "You shall not show partiality to a poor man in his dispute." And verse 6 declares, "You shall not pervert the judgment of your poor in his dispute." The implication of these verses is that partiality of either kind is false from the biblical perspective. Applied to foreign nations, this principle would appear to say that "poor" nations or "rich" nations should not receive better treatment by virtue of their status. The United States should require of herself the highest standards in her dealings with foreign nations, but she should expect equally high standards from foreign trading partners.

Two schools of thought deviate from impartiality in opposite directions. One school says that since our nation is richer and more powerful than most of our trading partners, we should not expect them to follow the same standards that we apply to ourselves. A variation of this motif holds that since other countries' cultures are different, different notions of permissible and impermissible conduct apply that the United States should recognize in policy. When dealing with the European Community, for example, we should expect compliance with the same standards of conduct that we require of ourselves, but this need not be the case with Third World countries. The other school of thought would have the world follow a uniform set of rules, but when convenient, the United States would be allowed to violate selected norms. That is, because we have the power, prestige, and position to do as we please, occasionally we should allow ourselves the luxury of doing so. (I have, of course, painted these positions starkly. In practice any action would be camouflaged by justifications rationalizing the actions taken in a particular case.) However, neither extreme is biblical. The standards of justice and conduct that apply to one nation must apply to all. The Author of the Bible is also the Creator of the world and the God of all nations. The idea of different standards for different countries is inconsistent with His character.

APPLICATIONS AND CONCLUSIONS

In the preceding discussion we have identified several strands of thought in current thinking about trade policy. One is that foreign behavior is somehow to blame for the trade deficit; therefore, the United States must get tough to defend its interests. Another is that the United States should embrace a policy of selective intervention when such policy can raise national welfare. This course necessarily implies an abandonment of much of our GATT commitment to free trade. Finally, there is the question of how to respond to foreign misbehavior and how to balance the principles of following the Golden Rule, honoring covenants, and properly recognizing national and individual objectives in the foreign trade arena. In what follows I will touch on these issues briefly while indicating how I believe the biblical principles apply.

The trade deficit—First is the question of the cause of the trade deficit and why concern about its size should have no bearing on our choice of foreign trade policy. The root cause of the trade deficit is domestic; therefore, its solution lies in domestic policy choices. The deficit may well represent a failing of some sort, but it is not a failing caused by foreigners. A Mosaic reference is relevant at this point. Students of American history have noted that American preachers in the formative years of our nation quoted from Deuteronomy 28 more than any other single passage of Scripture. Deuteronomy 28 is the famous blessing-and-curse chapter of the Old Testament where God speaks through Moses to the Israelites before they were to enter into their new land and new relationship with Him. The promise of blessing and the warning of curse delivered by Moses were challenges and signposts to the ancient Israelites, and then to the early Americans and to us today, helping them to understand the significance of the times into which they were about to enter.

Notable among the blessings and curses were the passages relating to borrowing and lending. Deuteronomy 28:12 includes as a national blessing the statement that "you shall lend to many nations, but you shall not borrow." As part of the curse, Deuteronomy 28:44 announces, "He [the alien who is among you] shall lend to you, but you shall not lend to him; he shall be the head, and you shall be the tail." The root cause of the borrowing is attributed not to foreign actions but to actions by the Israelites.

Of course, not all borrowing is harmful. In the 1800s, for example, America borrowed from European nations, especially Great Britain, to finance the building of the railroads and the settlement of the American West. Borrowing, in response to individuals' rational needs for productive funds, does not need to represent economic decline and decay. Borrowing for current consumption, on the other hand, is different. The United States has been primarily engaged in this type of borrowing in recent years.

In the early 1980s America became a large borrower of foreign funds, due primarily to its failure to reduce its consumption sufficiently relative to income. Instead of leading the nation in an effort to reduce its overconsumption, the federal government itself is the largest single borrower, overspending its budget by many tens of billions of dollars each year. This spending is determined by the behavior of our congressmen and senators. A proper understanding of the times and the American trade deficit must therefore start from the premise that the trade deficit is the result of *domestic* choices that have led to overconsumption relative to income. Foreigners are not the underlying cause of America's change from trade surplus to trade deficit.

Recognizing that the source of the trade deficit lies with ourselves is encouraging insofar as it means that the ability to reverse the deficit lies with ourselves. Foreign trade policy need not be, and should not be, the tool used to respond to the loss of American competitiveness (which is one manifestation of national borrowing and the trade deficit).

Trade policy directions—What further trade policy conclusions can we draw? We have already determined from the Golden Rule principle that foreign trade policy should not seek to raise American welfare at the expense of foreign welfare and the effectiveness of the open trading system. In this respect, our inference must be that America should reject the basic nationalist message of the new international economics and reaffirm instead her longstanding commitment to GATT, and its strengthening. This can be done in international assemblies seeking to extend GATT as in the Uruguay Round Negotiations, and in the application of domestic trade law. Fortunately, the debate over policy has not proceeded to the point that this reaffirmation in the international arena would require an impossible reversal of policy directions now in force.

In other areas, applying of the principles identified here will require a reworking of portions of existing laws. There are five main sections. *Sections 701* and *731* of the trade law deal with the imposition of antidumping (AD) and countervailing duties (CVD). In recent years the United States has been the world leader in the use of such instruments to place levies on the imports of foreign goods. In the 1980s the use of AD/CVD more than doubled the rate that prevailed in the second half of the 1970s before the U.S. trade balance deteriorated. In the recent rounds of trade legislation, the ease of using sections 701/731 and their applicability have been greatly expanded at a cost to freedom of trade and welfare of the American buyer. That AD/CVD measures usually benefit the American import-competing industry is not sufficient reason for harming importers and buyers to a greater extent than the gain to the import-competing industry and for damaging the freedom of the international trading system.

Section 201, the fair trade "escape clause," allowing relief in the form of temporary protection from foreign fairly traded goods that are injurious to an American import-competing industry, has been relatively little used in recent years—partly due to the increased availability of protection through other portions of the law. It can probably be kept as it was left under the 1988 trade bill, with due vigilance to see that it had not become the instrument of a new industrial policy making by the government. This could happen, for example, if the new negotiating powers provided for the industry and the trade representative were to be used to set a national agenda for the relief-seeking industry. Similarly, *Section 337* dealing primarily with patent and trademark violations by foreign producers selling goods into the American market can probably be left unchanged.

Foreign misbehavior—The policy reaffirming a commitment to the free trade principles of GATT, eschewing the selfish nationalist alternative, and adjusting domestic legislation to restrict interferences in trade in the form of AD/CVD actions leaves the American response to foreign trade practices to be addressed. The response to foreign misbehavior is among the most emotional and the most difficult policy choices because America is often the aggrieved and damaged party. Moreover, no one can deny that foreign practices are egregious. Only in the past few years, for example, have new agreements been reached with Japan to provide access to Japanese markets in beef, citrus, and other agricultural products in accordance with Japan's longstanding GATT obligations. However, misbehavior by others must never be the rationale for misbehavior by the United States.

Section 301 is the portion of U.S. trade law concerned with unfair foreign trade practices, including such things as violations of trade agreements. (In the typical case such agreements might be a Friendship, Commerce, and Navigation treaty or GATT.) Many of the trade dispute cases that reach the newspapers, for example, are section 301 cases. Section 301 is a domestic law that allows the United States to respond to foreign practices by taking virtually any action that the U.S. trade representative deems appropriate to elicit the desired response from foreigners. American actions under the authority of section 301 in the form of 100 percent duties on imports of foreign products in retaliation for foreign actions have been taken in the past in violation of our GATT obligations.

Where domestic law is in conflict with our international obligations, the two must be made consistent. Either U.S. behavior must change, or the international contract must be renegotiated. In response to a foreign practice, for example, if the U.S. is a signer of an international agreement, there should be no question about the dispute procedure specified in the agreement being followed. If there is no dispute procedure specified, then the rule of law about abrogated contracts should be followed, and dispute settlement procedure should be specified for the treaty. In cases where a foreign practice is objectionable, but nevertheless not in violation of any trade agreement, the United States should respond in a manner consistent with our other agreements with that nation, such as GATT.

Most policy economists recognize that in the long run, GATT needs a much improved dispute settlement mechanism incorporated into it. The American market is still important enough to the world that a renewed diplomatic effort to reform GATT's dispute settlement mechanism could bear fruit. For example, if the United States made it clear that it would seriously reconsider its membership in GATT unless a stronger dispute mechanism is agreed to, it might make material progress in implementing needed changes. There is no question that such a policy objective would take substantial diplomatic effort and legislative effort, but it is a fairly basic requirement if foreign trade policy is to be consistent with scriptural mandates.

CLOSING COMMENTS

Our investigation has produced some general principles that can be applied to foreign trade policy but no detailed road map. Nevertheless, some clear-cut conclusions can be made from a biblical base about rejecting current revisionist thinking that advocates policy motivated by selfish nationalist objectives and about making American policy and its international commitments consistent. On both points, a growing set of voices has been urging cutting corners.

In my final remark, however, I would like to address directly the spurious argument most often used to call for the revision of American thinking—the fear that America is losing ground because she deals with foreigners who do not play by the rules. Without denying that foreigners frequently violate the rules of trade in the grossest ways, the wise response from the biblical perspective, and from the perspective of our own interest, is not to adopt their methods. As individuals and as a nation, we must remember that God does not bless those who pursue purely self-centered objectives, and He *cannot* bless those who turn from their ideals to baser conduct. Japan, in its current behavioral mode, is not likely to become a successful long-term leader of the world because it offers nothing to lead the world to. Its example appears to be one of grasping, self-serving acquisitiveness. In fact, a reasonable presumption is that Japan may be heading for an ultimate fall unless it can redirect its energies to less egocentric policy, if only because Europe, the United States, the Pacific rim nations, and the rest of the world will not long tolerate its behavior. Since Japan is not now on the road to lasting success, emulating current Japanese behavior is likely only to hasten America's decline and remove her from the sphere of God's blessing. Because America nominally professes to be a Christian nation, turning to egocentric behavior would place America at the head of the line in deserving God's judgment. Instead of traveling further down this road, America should seek to implement principles that offer the prospect of retaining the American leadership position in world trade policy that she has held since World War II because she will have something to offer the world in example and thus something to lead it to.

EDITOR'S PERSPECTIVE

Earl Grinols's concluding paragraph provides an opportunity (temptation?) to explore futuristic thinking about what nations will lead the world in the twenty-first century. He is clearly not optimistic about Japan's future in this regard: "Japan, in its current behavioral mode, is not likely to become a successful long-term leader of the world because it offers nothing to lead the world to." He believes Japan's "purely self-centered objectives" are so apparent that others, while trading with Japan for mutually beneficial reasons, will refuse to follow it in a larger sense. His thoughts are provocative, but they do not reflect much of the popular literature in our society.

Combining Grinols's perception of Japan with the political turbulence currently in the world (evidenced by the number of totalitarian regimes relinquishing their controls and the resulting struggles for those nations to regain their economic and political stability) produces a mixture of realities so far reaching that no human could be expected to project the final outcome. Either of these scenarios is plausible: (1) the world order will collapse allowing the formation of a one-world government where the Antichrist can operate as described in 2 Thessalonians and Revelation, or (2) a democratic free market will ultimately emerge allowing an explosive rise in the standard of living for the world's population. If we then mix all of this uncertainty with the rising moral anarchy and decay in the West and the rapidly emerging Church in other parts of the world, the entire situation becomes mind-boggling.

It is fair to say, however, that the world is in a state of flux unprecedented in modern times—and perhaps in all of history. In times such as these, though, guiding principles are needed, and that makes Grinols's rejection of the revisionists' thinking about foreign trade so important. Their thinking violates the four biblical principles he identified: applying the Golden Rule, honoring the sanctity of covenants, recognizing the relative importance of the nation-state and the individual, and complying with the biblical requirement for parity of conduct. Throughout his discussion of these four principles, Grinols repudiated the spirit of retaliation and called for restraint by those who govern nations offended in their trade relationships. I wish to elaborate on this matter, because I believe he is absolutely correct in calling us to this kind of self-discipline.

Scripture candidly acknowledges the difficulty humans have with the spirit of retaliation because of our fallen nature. Cain is described as having been very angry with God (his anger was transferred to Abel whom he slew) because Abel's righteousness (accepted by God) reminded him of his own unrighteousness. He hated his brother for the conviction he (Cain) experienced in his heart whenever he was reminded of Abel's godliness (see Gen. 4:3-8 *and* 1 John 3:12). Lamech (Cain's great-great-great-grandson) boasted to his wives, "I have killed a man for wounding me; and a boy for striking me; if Cain is avenged sevenfold [see Gen. 4:15], then Lamech seventy-sevenfold" (Gen. 4:23-24). Our sin nature tends to multiply the desire for vengeance and badly distorts justice. Because of this human tendency to expand retaliation, God gave the principle of the "eye for an eye, and a tooth for a tooth" to the elders so that when they administered justice, they would have a principle of equity and restraint to guide them (see Exod. 21:24; Lev. 24:20; Deut. 19:21).

The Pharisees had so badly perverted this precept of God by the time of Christ's coming, however, that He found it necessary to teach once again the principle of equity and restraint as it pertained to retribution, justice, and the individual's exclusion from the application of the "eye and tooth" principle in personal matters. (The principle was given to the elders, or court, for civil and criminal matters, not for individuals to use against their neighbors; see Matt. 5:38-42.) Individuals (not states) are also reminded elsewhere in Scripture that vengeance belongs to God and that they are to make room for God to act by not taking matters into their own hands (see Lev. 19:18; Rom. 12:17-21; Heb. 10:30).

All of this being true, what hope is there of restraining nations from retaliating against one another when they are being hurt through another nation's violation of a trade agreement? What hope is there of persuading nations that they should not violate their trade agreements when it appears to be economically to their advantage to do so, at least in the immediate future? The hope of accomplishing such self-restraint rests on the *improbability* of all parties agreeing to and remaining committed to at least five fundamental aspects of a trade relationship and the necessity for the common grace of God to be supportive of such a goal for His own larger purposes (this latter necessity being the more important). What are the five ingredients of a trade agreement for which nations are responsible?

As self-apparent as it may seem, but all too frequently missing from their intent, the signers of any trade agreement should do so only when they truly agree with the content and procedures of the document. This is the first requirement for success. Signing because of political pressures, or because of a few short-term economic advantages, will result in later defaults on the agreement. Since honoring the sanctity of covenants is essential in the eyes of God, Christians should foster and strongly encourage the honoring of all national agreements. God cannot bless sin (failure to honor an agreement), so no true long-term good can be borne from treaty violations.

Second, trade agreements must be mutually beneficial for the citizens at large of all participating nations. Too often agreements reflect the interests of the state or of favored power groups within the nation. Self-serving or narrowly conceived benefits for the few violate the biblical principle of needing to recognize that the citizens of the state are to be the interest of the state, not some personified concept of the state elevating it above the interests of the citizens at large.

The two ingredients just discussed, and the fifth one to follow later, are relatively easy to pursue. The third and fourth aspects are exceedingly difficult to agree on and harder still to effect. Each deals with accountability and punishments, and their enforcement in a voluntary environment where participants are free to retreat from earlier agreements is complicated.

Third, all parties must agree on a due process whereby they may be afforded an effective opportunity to register a perceived grievance regarding a treaty violation and hope to have a fair hearing that will result in actions to redress the problem. Justice is beyond human reach unless such a system of due process can be effected. International bodies like the United Nations and the Permanent Court of Arbitration, founded in 1899 and housed in the Hague, have been established to address issues affecting international justice. Bodies such as these are without power, except the force of world opinion, which has not proven to be effective when "big differences" are at stake.

Enforcement in a fallen world requires the acceptance of coercion, which directly conflicts with the very notion of a sovereign national interest. One nation will not voluntarily allow another nation to coerce it. (This inherent conflict of perceived interests among nations explains why I spoke of the improbability of nations agreeing to and remaining committed to the five fundamentals under discussion.) Coercion, however, is a necessary reality, ordained by God in the establishment of governments in a fallen world. There is no earthly hope for achieving justice without its presence. God can effect world justice through His common grace, but human efforts are insufficient for the task.

The fourth requirement is the will to actively pursue what Dr. Grinols called the parity of conduct. The rich and the poor, the strong and the weak, and the large and the small are all held accountable under the same standards of justice. The United States did not practice this when we had large, favorable trade balances. Our failure to demand that the smaller, poorer, weaker nations live up to their agreements promotes injustice, disrespect for due process, and a disregard for contractual agreements, all of which are absolutely necessary if unity and harmony are to prevail. Without requiring people to live up to the agreed-on standards, retribution (punishment for unjust conduct) is foregone, and one-half of God's established external motivational process (rewards and punishments) is removed. (In God's economy, if mankind decides to disregard a set of God's established consequences, another set of worse consequences is waiting in the wings to come on stage.)

Finally, it is extremely difficult to maintain a continuous national commitment to specific agreements over an extended period of time, especially when there is a routine turnover in leadership. This reality is captured in the statement, "Now a new king arose over Egypt, who did not know Joseph" (Exod. 1:8). Or putting it another way, "times change." God is unchangeable, but that cannot be said about fallen mankind. Persons who want to see a trade agreement maintained must constantly work to foster justice, stewardship, and relational values that reflect God's standards.

Some people conclude that the only way a worldwide trade agreement could ever be effectively maintained would be under the coercive pressures of a world government. They deem that the only solution to the inherent conflict between nationalism and the need for an international means of enforcing the specifics of any trade agreement. We are better off without a solution at all than to embrace that suggestion.

God's intent in scattering, dividing, and establishing many nations and languages at Babel was to divide and water down the potential effects of sin (see Gen. 11:1-9). If sin is manifested to the degree that it is through the structure of nationalism, its potential is only worse and more devastating under a one-world government. The problems encountered in trying to manage and maintain international trade agreements should be accepted as the lesser of alternative evils. We can conclude, therefore, that we should strive to accomplish as much as we can through the five steps outlined here without trying or expecting to find a utopian solution to this problem in a fallen world.

PART XIII

THE SECURITY OF A JUST STATE

Dr. Theodore Malloch stunned me with his comments that many people involved with our nation's foreign policy have been devotees of the philosophy that relationships between nations should be seen and interpreted in *amoral* terms—judged without moral criteria. That is immoral! Not only is it immoral, it is impossible. All human actions rest on motives, and they affect others—both motives and actions have inherently moral qualities. The fundamental idea that self-interest alone is an acceptable and morally valid basis on which to develop a rationale for foreign policy was repulsive to me. (It is to Dr. Malloch, also.)

Then I came to my senses, not in agreeing with the amoral philosophy, but in comprehending the tension that must be allowed in a fallen world where the "wheat and the tares" grow together (see Matt. 13:24-30, especially vv. 29-30). Neither did I come to my senses by adopting the belief that international relations should be interpreted on an amoral plane. That would be unconscionable. The fact that such a school of thought exists, the fact that people who do not know their Creator in a forgiving, redeeming, and loving personal relationship should come to such a perverted perspective, is what I needed to accept. And I must understand its consequences and seek biblical wisdom to live with it in such a way as to be salt and light in the spirit of Proverbs 15:2 ("the tongue of the wise makes knowledge acceptable").

Dr. Malloch presents the complexities of the whole notion of nationalism—the "sentiment of unity and exclusiveness," to use one of his phrases. In fact, nationalism as it exists in the modern world is a Johnny-come-lately. It has emerged since the late eighteenth century and can be described as the *state* taking over the role of God, kings, and the people. The state becomes supreme; it is viewed as sovereign. People look to the state for solutions to problems in every sphere of life. Malloch's discussion is both enlightening and disturbing, for it clarifies the magnitude of the challenges to the Christian community.

The chapter does not attack the state, though. It acknowledges that God has established the state's role to function explicitly as an arm of common grace, with regard to its authority to wield the sword and to make and administer laws in the pursuit of justice. In addition, Dr. Malloch has carefully pointed out the biblical truth that the power extended to the state is to be guided and ruled by law. The two elements—power and law—are to be balanced like a seesaw, with law as the constraint and regulator.

Dr. Malloch discusses three significant areas of national security policy in light of biblical norms that should guide our thinking. He deals with strategic policy (national defense), the use of economic sanctions to effect changes in another nation's policies, and multilateralism (diplomacy: treaties, organizations, etc.).

Recognizing that inherent pride is the greatest force undermining the ability of humans to resolve their international differences peacefully, Dr. Malloch concludes that the biggest need in the development of worldwide national security policies is a large dose of "cosmic humility."

CHAPTER 13

NORMATIVE PRINCIPLES AND NATIONAL SECURITY POLICY

Theodore R. Malloch

Theodore R. Malloch (B.A., Gordon College; M.Litt., University of Aberdeen, Scotland; Ph.D., Political Economy, University of Toronto) is presently the Principal Officer of the United Nations, Economic Commission for Europe, Geneva, Switzerland, where he lives with his wife and three sons. Dr. Malloch has served in the U.S. State Department and worked on international economic policy with the U.S. Senate Foreign Relations Committee. He has also taught at Gordon College and York University and worked in the private sector with a leading investment bank and as a managing director with an economic and policy analysis consulting firm. Active in the Episcopal church, he grew up appreciating a reformed world-and-life-view and takes seriously Christ's commands over all of life.

NORMATIVE PRINCIPLES AND THE LIMITS OF THE NATION-STATE[1]

The present situation, norms, and national security policy—National security policy makes little or no sense to many people. It is easy to be overwhelmed by the mass of news that bombards us throughout our waking hours. Radio, newspapers, television news, presidential press conferences, official communiqués, books, and magazines abound. We are inundated with sources that beg to be sorted out. However overwhelming these bits and pieces of information seem, they can become intelligible to us only when we understand how to organize them and look at them through our eyes of faith. Our faith serves us like a pair of glasses.

Making sense of international affairs, and particularly national security matters, means two things are essential: (1) learning to cope with an enormous amount of contradictory information, some of which is extremely difficult, if not impossible, to verify; and (2) learning to contextualize this information because it is not objective. It always needs interpretation. As the theologian Martin Buber said, "The greater the crisis becomes the more earnest and consciously responsible is the knowledge demanded of us. For although what is demanded is a deed—only the deed born of the knowledge of Christ will overcome the crisis."[2]

Our perceptions of international reality are formed by abstracting from the totality of our experience those parts that seem most relevant to each of us. Our perception is always selective. Everyone sees things in some order, within his or her interpretive framework. Everyone comes from someplace, with a defined cultural perspective. In this sense, facts are attached to values and can never be isolated from them for very long. Perspectives ranging from liberal to conservative, and on through Marxist and fascist in all of their variations, provide frameworks that select, systematize, and interpret the constant flow of raw data. This is what Walter Lippmann called "a picture in our mind" or what others prefer to call a "world-and-life-view." A world-and-life-view helps in three distinct ways: (1) by explaining why a particular event or set of events occurred; (2) by allowing one to understand what an event or an object is in its most basic terms; and (3) at the highest level, by determining truth—what is normative, ethical, and just.

What constitutes a nation? What makes a nation-state a state? Few questions have been more contested in modern times. The answers depend on the views of the answerers: Rousseau differs from Fichte, Mazzini from Wilson, Gurion from Nasser, Nehru, or Castro. Some have argued common language is the root of the nation; others, common history or common ideals. Hans Kohn in his seminal work, *Nationalism*, writes, "Nationalism is a state of mind, in which the supreme loyalty of the individual is felt to be due the nation-state."[3] A deep attachment to one's native soil, to local traditions, and to established territorial authority has existed in varying strength throughout much of man's history. But it was not until the end of the eighteenth century that nationalism and national security, in the modern sense of those terms, became a generally recognized sentiment, increasingly molding all public and private life.

Nationalism, and its corollary, national security, when reified (the abstract concept is treated as if it is a concrete reality), becomes an *ism*; it becomes an ideology and all that that implies. All nationalism is inseparably linked to modernity—ours has become the age of nationalisms. Only in Europe over the past two centuries, and predominantly now in the twentieth century, have people identified themselves totally with the nation—civilization with national civilization, and their life and survival with the life and survival of their particular nationality. From the late eighteenth century, nationalism has dominated the impulses and attitudes of the masses and, at the same time, been the justification for the state to use its force against its own citizens and against other nation-states. Only in England and in France, especially during the Revolution of 1789, did the state cease to be the king's state and become the people's state, a national state, a fatherland. From that point, the people were responsible for their country's destiny. Nation and state were one, hence the nomenclature nation-state.

Against the common, general universal unity arose this new nationalism that glorified the peculiar and the parochial. National differences and national individualities became more important than anything else. Nationalism is quintessentially modern in the sense that God was removed from the scene, and with His disappearance, the divine plan for *all* things was forgotten. Moreover, the will of the individual, in conjunction with his fellows (i.e., Rousseau's "common will"), became authoritative for forming political and economic units. This continues to be the basic idea of the nation. In effect, the glory of the nation has fully replaced the glory of God (or of the king) as a unifying value or agent. The nation-state, be it the collective state, Nazi Reich, Mazzini's united Italy, Communist People's China, or the federal state (as in the United States), has become the principal political reality of the modern age, the mortal god of secular culture.

Concepts of the nation-state—What is the nation-state? What beliefs make up nationalism, from which the concept of national security is derived? The literature is full of different elements and concepts of nationhood. Let us list a number that deserve special consideration:

- a certain defined area or territory, either possessed or coveted;
- a common culture, language, customs, manners, and literature;
- a set of common, dominant social and economic institutions and practices;
- an independent, sovereign government; the principle that each nation is completely separate from every other;
- a belief in a common history, even myths, and common origin, sometimes racial in nature;
- a love or esteem for fellow nationals, not necessarily as individuals but as a group;
- a common pride in achievements (military more than others) and sorrow in tragedies (particularly defeats);
- a disregard for or hostility to other groups, especially if they seem to threaten or prevent the separate national existence; and
- a hope that the nation will have a great and glorious future in territorial expansion and in supremacy (i.e., as a world power—militarily, culturally, or financially).

Nationalism is a very complex concept; it defies being captured by a short, logical definition. In essence, nationalism signifies a sentiment that unifies people and is expressed in real devotion and loyalty to the nation-state and its absolute security, whatever the government in power. In its most ardent form, it requires, as Rousseau advocated, absolute devotion to and conformity with the will of the nation as expressed by the rulers. Nationalism demands the supremacy of the nation to which one belongs to such a degree that security becomes a primary or even an exclusive focus of national behavior.

Over time, numerous illusions have grown up around the nation-state and national security, none of which are true or complete. Some people have believed that their nation is a creation of God, that they alone have supernatural powers. Others have seen nations as determined by soil, or rooted in race, blood, and tribal existence. Still others have argued that their nation is the product of a demand for markets or status, or the result of the struggle for power. All of these ideas and their historical manifestations are oversimplifications at best, the product of fanatics at worst. In fact, our present understanding does not reveal any of these differences as the basis for exclusion. To do so is to proceed at the expense of truth and at mankind's peril, as World Wars I and II amply demonstrate.

As Hans Kohn said, "In this time of mental and verbal confusion when general political terms have become so emotionally fraught that they cover disparate realities, we have to start re-thinking many concepts in the interest of human freedom and the possibility of cultural intercourse."[4] None other than Harold Laski, one of the keener political theorists of the postwar period, sees nationalism as an "obstinate virus infecting the body politic of mankind."[5] And Eric Fromm in *The Sane Society* excoriates national interest and security as "our incest, our idolatry, our insanity."[6]

As Christians, we must say that if men are not compatible, it is not because they inherently differ. That sentiment of unity and exclusiveness we have defined as nationalism, and its concrete and more subtle form—national security—does not mean that persons could not live in the world more peaceably. For there is no historical, biological, or psychological basis for believing that nationalism or the security of any one nation must or will be permanent. Far below the surface of national peculiarities, however, we are far more alike than we are different, for we all bear the image of God and even the Fall did not eradicate our common bonds. This is the transcendent truth. And some of our differences, cultural and otherwise, are actually good—that is not being questioned. We are, nevertheless, God's image bearers, and only in Him do we have eternal security.

The causes of war—Whether a political culture is liberal, conservative, fascist, or Communist, today it thinks of itself in national terms. Nationalism and security have become the most important elements in modern politics. And the most pressing matter in the entire field of national security is the cause of war.

Why is political controversy so often violent? The pages of history, from one angle, appear to be almost totally covered with blood. War has been called an international disease, a collective insanity, a gross malfunction, and a global conspiracy. Others, however, find it completely rational and just, even inevitable. According to Clausewitz, "War is not merely a political act, but also a real political instrument, a continuation of political commerce, a carrying out of the same by other means."[7]

War, that organized conduct of major armed hostilities between social groups and nations (including civil war and international conflict), has many causes from so-called power asymmetries to arms races that get out of control; from nationalism, separatism, and irredentism (the "need" to recover lost ancestral territory) to instinctual aggression; from the need to create a common enemy to relative deprivation. However one chooses to explain the causes of war, the many theories agree on one thing: There has never been a more deadly game invented by human beings. Only for the nation-state are individuals so willing to lay down their lives. No other person or ideal elicits such total commitment.

Between 1939 and 1945 more than sixty million people (over 3 percent of the world's population) died as a result of World War II. It was the greatest single catastrophe in human history. And the most destructive nuclear weapons were used only in the closing days of that war. Today, nuclear weapons have become the major factor in the arsenals of the superpowers. But even the existence of thousands of these nuclear weapons has not prevented nonnuclear wars. At least twelve significant wars have been fought since 1945, and the United States participated in two of them.

Nation-states spend a great deal of their time preparing or planning to fight wars. The total expenditures of all countries on weapons now exceed $500 billion per year and continue to rise rapidly. By one estimate, 225 wars have been fought between 1648 and 1987, or one every 1.4 years.[8] Clearly, war remains the most outstanding problem of the twentieth century. Although there is no explicit biblical reference to what share of GNP should be dedicated to defense or security, historically this percentage has grown or shrunk in proportion to perceived threats and the power of various interests, including those of a geographical nature where bases were located or production facilities founded. Normatively, the question of the proper share of GNP devoted to national defense needs to be comparatively examined in the light of other domestic considerations and global needs.

Contrast the realities of modern war and expenditures for it with what we find in Micah 4:2-3 (NIV):

The law will go out from Zion, the word of the LORD from Jerusalem.
He will judge between many peoples and will settle disputes for strong

nations far and wide. They will beat their swords into plowshares and their spears into pruning hooks. Nation will not take up sword against nation, nor will they train for war anymore.

The list of prophetic testimonies, like the Psalter and the entire Exodic tradition, sees politics and security exclusively in terms of justice and peace-keeping. In Scripture, justice and peacemaking was often first undertaken for the poor and the oppressed. It is reassuring today to remember that judgment belongs to God—He, Yahweh (the eschatologically significant name in Hebrew that says, "I will be"), who liberates His people. All justice and peacemaking are therefore a concrete embodiment of the will of God.

The state and international relations—How can we normatively approach public policy in the area of national security? A number of answers are presented and discussed in Martin Rein's *Social Science and Public Policy*.[9] For example, he suggests that we can treat policy questions as unresolved, as too ambiguous and conflicting, in what he calls the empiricist approach. We can examine policy only in its historical perspective, as do the historicists. We can distrust any orthodoxy, as the skeptics are likely to do. We can consider the political reception of various policy options as pragmatists, asking only what will work. Or we can approach national security policy as moral critics, highlighting the difference between what men believe and what they actually do. This sort of witness may be most appealing to Christians. But norms of knowledge are not simply used to influence policy. The process is more complex; as policy evolves, norms are also used to selectively justify actions. So policy and norms are interactive—being as much influenced by the current agenda. This is what could be called a norm-critical approach. Joan Robinson, the economic theorist, captured the essence of this approach when she said,

> It is impossible to describe a system without moral and religious judg-
> ments creeping in. For to look at a system from the outside implies that
> it is not the only possible system. In describing it we compare it, openly
> or tacitly, with other actual or imagined systems. Differences imply
> choices, and choices imply judgments. We cannot escape from making
> judgments and the judgments we make arise from the ethical and reli-
> gious preconceptions that have soaked into our view of life.[10]

My point is that it is not only sterile to pursue the techniques of analysis divorced from issues of purpose, but it is also misleading because techniques arise to serve purposes, and these rest on normative assumptions. Beliefs attach themselves to means as much as they do to ends; beliefs about what is normative or just are tied up with acceptable, feasible, operating procedures. So for our purposes, and using the jargon of the policy sciences, policies (including national security policies) are interdependent systems of cherished abstract norms; operating principles that give these norms form in the context of specific programs and institutional arrangements; outcomes of programs enabling us to contrast ideals with reality; linkages (weak and strong ones) between aims, means, and outcomes; and feasible strategies and tactics of change.

In other words, policies always reaffirm an ethical, moral, or religious position. As Christian decision makers, critics, or policy analysts, we must look at the base and outworkings of respective policies and recover the consciousness of *created* reality and use it as the foundation for all public policy. This call is imperative in our era of gnostic futurisms, in which the Alpha of the creation has been repudiated to make possible the realization of a "secular omega," a massive shift in eschatology. Christians must see national security issues from the perspective of "creation" and analyze all public policies from this normative point of view. If we do not, others will use their perverted world view as the point of policy departure and shape the policies for us.

The present global system is characterized by several different dimensions that need to be seen together if a complete picture is to be rendered. Externally, the state system involves international relations, the rules it employs (i.e., diplomacy), and the games (including war) it used to meet its ends. Internally, the nation-state is a reflection of a given state's domestic nature. Some states are capitalistic; some are socialistic. Some nations are developed; some are less developed economically. Some states are democratic; some are authoritarian or totalitarian. In today's world, some states are religiously fanatic; others have disestablished state religions or are blatantly secular in their outlook. Finally, national security is itself always part of a given decision-making process. Foreign policy rises from and reflects a particular domestic system that varies according to the social, economic, and political (especially constitutional) arrangements, and manifests the values of the men and women who make and execute the policies in each country. Policy often depends as much on those who administer it as it does on procedures. History records this fact for all who care to look at it.

Only by analyzing each level can we have a comprehensive view of the "games nations play." Why they play, how they play, and how they regulate, moderate, or even try to abolish the game they play differ from nation to nation. This is especially true in a policy area as critical as national security where each facet is a layer unto itself and where the stakes are so high.

The current world situation actually presents three alternative scenarios: (1) a world in constant national conflict; (2) a world of international legal conformity; or (3) a world of pluralistic and diverse social systems striving to avoid fatal collisions. As Christians, we must choose and work for the third option to show respect for the diversity God instituted at Babel and to honor Him. Our task is to live in a world community while we avoid the dangers and sin of nationalism but maintain the rich diversity of our cultures. The distinction between a patriot who loves his national culture and excessive patriotism should be borne in mind. Barbara Ward in her classic book, *Five Ideas that Change the World*, argued that the stronger the nationalism, ours or theirs, the greater the risk for all of us.[11] Is it time to consider God's admonition to love our neighbors as ourselves? What might that mean for national security policy?

Unfortunately, as Harry Blaimers suggested in his telltale book, *The Christian Mind*,

> Except over a very narrow field of thinking, chiefly touching on questions of personal conduct, Christians in the modern world accept, for the purpose of mental activity, a frame of reference constructed by the secular mind. There is no Christian mind; there is no shared field of discourse in which we can move at ease as thinking Christians by trodden ways and past established landmarks.[12]

This fact is frightfully clear when it comes to discussions on national security policy.

Embarking on this difficult path where our subject is a policy of national security demands that we realize, at the outset, that our subject involves the international relations among states. That means we must have a proper understanding of the state. The state is characterized by its unique empowerments; that is, it has a monopoly on governing in a given territory. The state also has the biblical sanction to exercise power and to make laws. Power alone does not explain these prerogatives. Because the state is sanctioned by God, "realpolitik" does not exhaust a normative understanding of power relations. Rather, the state's juridical function must guide the functions of power in a proper Christian understanding of international relations and national security. Might and right are intrinsic. Might must be guided by right. Law is the qualifying idea of the state. And law exists to order, define, and ensure justice.

I would define the state as a public, legally organized community of government and subjects with a dual purpose that embodies legal jurisdiction and legal protection, the ends of which are public justice. International relations is concerned about the relations among such states. And if states exist to bring about justice, it follows that the dominant concern of international relations ought to be the true norm of international justice. This concept has serious consequences for formulation of security policy and policies on every subject of interest to a foreign ministry or a national security council—from legitimate defense to foreign assistance, from intervention or economic relations to the conduct of diplomacy.

Christians have something to say to the world of international relations and national security policy because they have a special revealed view of the world: who made it, who sustains and preserves it, and what true justice is. Different from liberalism, and the view of individual self-interests; different from conservatism, and notions of balance of power; different from Marxism, and deterministic theories of class struggle; and different from fascism, which glorifies national expansion and aggression—Christians possess a unique idea of justice that seeks to be concretized in, not abstracted from, reality.

Following this argument, we need to focus on what could be called the principles or norms for a national security policy. As already noted, we live in a world of nation-states and must, at all costs, avoid nationalism. This distinction is imperative for the Christian, who has allegiances beyond and transcending those of a territorial definition. By "normative," I mean the quality of an action estimated by a standard of right and wrong, true and untrue, just and unjust. There are, after all, only three choices in this regard. Persons and states can purposely choose to be moral (even based on a set of biblical norms), amoral, or immoral.

Realpolitik versus normativity—Many key persons involved in guiding foreign policy and national security policy today argue that national interests (self interests) alone can be the valid rationale for policy. This position, known as the "realist school" of international relations, holds that relations among states are amoral. Realists, reacting against utopianism and idealism of earlier times, do not believe much cooperation is possible among nation-states; and they certainly do not believe morality can bring it about. Instead, they assert that conflict is the hallmark of politics, particularly world politics, and that all nation-states seek to advance their own interests, exclusive of others, and do so through the exercise of power.

As Christians, we cannot accept the realists' strict dichotomy between morality or normativity and national interest. Such thinking is not only erroneous but also dangerous and unbiblical. We can consider two alternative normative propositions for national security and foreign policy. First, normative questions cannot be separated from questions of national interest and are, in fact, an integral part of the foreign policy-making process, which implies that every policy is based on a set of principles disclosed or undisclosed. Second, policies need to be shaped and judged by ultimate principles or norms—including biblical ones such as justice, freedom, mercy, and peace. They should not be shaped in some forced majoritarian sense or through coercion. They ought to be formulated in the context of a pluralistic political culture and in a spirit of tolerance.

We must include in our discussion of national security policy a critique of the realist school, which is so dominant. Its primary theorists are George

Kennan, Hans Morgenthau, Henry Kissinger, and Reinhold Niebuhr, a so-called Christian realist. Realists argue that the center or essence of international and national security is the concept of "interest," defined in terms of power. A successful foreign policy enhances national power and national security at any cost. And the international system (and its regional parts, including the global economy) turns into a system of conflict instead of potential cooperation. To quote Kennan, "Morality must be rejected. Other criteria, sadder, more limited, more practical must be allowed to prevail."[13]

This question needs to be answered: Are national interests or are normative principles (universal standards, biblical standards) to be the bases for shaping national security and foreign policy for the world's nation-states? A real confusion fostered by the apologists of "realpolitik" is their plea for the recognition of war as a necessary arm of national security policy. By accepting war and strategies based primarily on conflict, and thereby their unquestioned legitimacy, realists in the nuclear era are involved in an absurdity. Moreover, the intellectual effort to preserve the struggle for power as the bedrock of political reality makes little sense in conditions of "total war." Zbigniew Brzezinski elaborated on this in his book *In Quest of National Security Policy*, where he quoted from a speech on the strategic implications of "Thou shall not kill," while reflecting on the concept of national security:

> Moral choices are involved in the interplay of states, and historical outcomes are infused with moral consequences. Outcomes in the interplay of power are not morally neutral. Moral choices should also affect the means used in international competition, including even the exercise of force.[14]

At the outset, the realists may be correct in pointing to the tendency of each state to identify its interest with universal principles through a rationalization process that is often self-deceptive. But this warning can be accepted while still rejecting exclusive national interest as the only, final guide for policy. Most certainly Christians must do this or risk becoming idolatrous. The idea of national interest embodies two major problems. First, empirically there is rarely such a thing as the single national interest; usually there are many interests, and often competing ones. And second, governments are comprised of individual persons, each with his or her own personality, interests, and priorities. National interest can be thought of broadly to identify with the interests of the community or narrowly to promote self-serving goals—even to serving individual leaders in a "cult of personality." National interest in this sense can be most unbiblical; relational compassion and justice are biblical. Psalm 147:10-11 sums this up well, where it suggests, "The strength of the war horse means nothing to Yahweh . . . compassion does."

In the final analysis, national interest has been used, even manipulated, to mean all kinds of things to all sorts of people. But from a biblical perspective, the preservation of any one state cannot be raised to the level of an absolute imperative. And in modernity, no nation-state is the equivalent of ancient Old Testament Israel—a chosen people. Some states historically have been more or less just than other states, about this there can be little disagreement. So, too, some states have been more belligerent than others. Only God is sovereign. Therefore, the pursuit of a single national interest as the highest responsibility of statesmen or citizens should be rejected. None other than C. S. Lewis said, "Finally we reach the stage where patriotism in its demoniac form unconsciously denies itself. We all know now that this love becomes a demon when it becomes a god."[15] This does not mean that nationals of any given country should not love their home, their place, their way of life. For as Chesterton declares, "A man's reasons for not wanting his country to be ruled by foreigners are very much like his reasons for not wanting his house to be burned down, because he could not even begin to enumerate all the things he would miss."[16]

Where does all of this leave us? Lost? Not if we think about and act on what we believe. All areas of life, not only individual behavior but also world politics, are filled with both evil and opportunity for good. Likewise, every area confronts us with a host of normative choices. Personal life and national life are full of difficult questions about the use of force, charity, discipline, intervention, allocation of resources, and so on. The fact that hard choices have to be made is no reason to ignore normative answers. Somebody's ideology or religion is going to provide these answers in the final analysis.

How, then, do we take what appear to be rather abstract norms and apply them to concrete situations in policy areas as forbidding as national security? Or how do we establish priorities for competing principles or strategies? These tentative suggestions seem appropriate. Norms can and should serve as a guide in political decision making as well as in private matters, even if followed imperfectly and unevenly. After all, every policy and goal of political action, from international security policy to domestic welfare policy, is ultimately determined by a set of values. The question is, Which values? We must enunciate Christian values (biblical norms) and see to it that political "actors" have the chance to hear these standards and consider them so they can be made part of the debate. But we must at the same time be wary of the tendency of all persons and nations (including ourselves) to elevate their own ideals, institutions, and practices to the level of immutable laws of the universe or count themselves alone as God's chosen people. There is no room for self-infused nationalism, self-righteousness, or an aggressive spirit. These are all unbiblical. Realizing that nation-states are established and called by God to "bring forth" justice, we can work to have national structures that promote and organize people in ways encouraging them to follow God's norms. In this sense, nation-states that do not practice nationalism in one of its historical excessive forms are pregnant with possibilities for the establishment of justice.

Let me now provide three examples or illustrations that briefly suggest how normative principles could possibly be applied to national security policy. These examples are developed only in skeletal fashion. They and other examples need to be worked out in much greater detail. I have chosen strategic policy, the use of economic sanctions, and multilateralism because they differ from each other considerably and deal with defense, economics, and diplomacy—vital areas in national security policy.

Just defense and nuclear weapons—I have written elsewhere, and at length, on just defense policy and *Jus in Bello*, or discrimination, proportionality, and weapons.[17] Essentially, the just war tradition, in keeping with its biblical roots, recognizes the legitimacy of national defense in cases of necessary alliances or assistance under collective security arrangements and in response to overt aggression. However, it always, and in every circumstance, calls for what is referred to as "measured restraint." Counterforce, as evidenced in National Security Policy Directive 59, and mutually assured destruction do not allow for the just restraints of proportionality and discrimination. In response to the spiraling arms race, we should instead normatively argue for (1) a no-use or no-first-use policy on nuclear weapons; (2) a gradual reorientation of defense toward conventional defenses, more fully in accord with the biblical just war criteria, against total disarmament; (3) a widening of negotiations to also focus on reduction in conventional forces; (4) treaties banning nuclear growth and testing and the proliferation of chemical, biological, and short-, medium-, and long-range nuclear weapons; and (5) a defined sense of legitimate defense—recalling the proper definition of that term and a normative understanding of the nation-state.

Reorienting strategic and defense policies to meet the demands of justice—in opposition to the use or threat of nuclear weapons, and in support of legitimate defense—would allow the application of the criteria of just war over the drives of unbridled nationalism and idolatrous faith in science and technology. Such policies would also take seriously a minimum form of deterrence and redirect it toward useful, defensive weapons and away from the primacy of offensive nuclear weapons and all that they imply.

International economic sanctions—Policy experts and economists are generally skeptical about the effectiveness of economic sanctions as a means to cause real economic dislocation and to bring about desired political change. Sanctions can prove costly to those who impose them, substitution possibilities in world markets diminish the effects of boycotts, and economic sanctions at times cause undesired political consequences (i.e., a rallying of political support to the targeted regime). Nonetheless, economic sanctions can, at times, be justifiable for their moral stance against objectionable behavior.

Sanctions, boycotts, export and technology controls, credit restrictions, and even blockades allow policy makers a certain degree of flexibility and restraint short of military engagement. These measures can create minimal (or a range of) economic hardship and hold the possibility of generating desired political change. They communicate signals or threats that can be escalated, particularly if they are designed to selectively affect appropriate interest groups in targeted countries. Indeed, the economic literature on sanctions has concluded that the lack of a significant economic effect does not mean that a particular sanction has no value whatsoever. Sanctions may have political or symbolic value as expressions of disapproval and can be an effective substitute for the use of force. The question is, Under what circumstances should economic sanctions be used? And here the answer depends considerably on the situation and on the other policy options available. But the normative value of economic measures is not unimportant, and at times they can be justly and selectively used in international relations.

Multilateral diplomacy—It is abundantly clear that international law—treaties, protocols, rules, juridical decisions—is impeded by the lack of authoritative international institutions. Ever since 1815, statesmen have sought to remedy this defect by creating a network of international agencies and organs. No one seriously thinks that these will replace the nation-state; but there is considerable and growing evidence that their presence makes a contribution in at least three ways: (1) the prevention of disputes; (2) the settlement of disputes; and (3) the facilitation of decision making on a broad spectrum of political, economic, and other problems.

World War II provided the immediate stimulus to the founding of the United Nations and other postwar international bodies. A resounding "never again" was ingrained into the minds and hearts of leaders and peoples around the world. But international or intergovernmental institutions have rarely been authorized to impose their decisions on their members. And to date, very few supranational organizations have authority over nation-states.

The system of intergovernmental organizations presently in place, and as presently constituted, does not portend to supplant the nation-state or its authority over internal or external policies. Nonetheless, the United Nations, as the centerpiece of multilateralism, remains very important to its member states, which after all comprise the world. Coping with issues across the spectrum of foreign policy—such as peaceful settlement of disputes and regional conflict resolution, human rights, nuclear safeguards, disease control, environmental protection, and economic development—the United Nations has provided evident benefits to its growing constituency. Multilateralism is not, however, world government. Its effectiveness depends on the quality and atmosphere of world politics and the degree of community spirit and communication among nation-states and their various groupings. The United Nations Charter represents an honest effort by the community of nations to establish norms of international conduct and to encourage them in the dealings among nations.

The practice of conducting relations among states through official representations, or what is called diplomacy, involves the entire foreign and national security process, policy formulation and execution. The type of diplomacy—open or secret, bilateral or multilateral, ministerial or summit—varies with states, specific situations, the political environment, and the range of issues under consideration. All have their normative uses. Diplomacy should normatively contribute to an orderly system of international relations, the peaceful settlement of disputes, and the improvement of human well-being. Multilateralism has particular normative implications in a complex world of national and economic divisions, especially where global or regional needs must take precedence over local and national interests. Multilateralism is being acted out presently on such fronts as sustainable development, disarmament, environmental and health issues, and in numerous peacekeeping activities.

CONCLUSION

In the final analysis, what is needed in national security policy is a genuine attitude of "cosmic humility" that shies away from evoking the name and judgment of God on behalf of one nation to the risk of all others. The "love ethic" laid down by Christ as the norm of interpersonal relationships also has implications for the achievement of justice *in* societies and *among* nations.[18]

Psalm 100 could be read focusing on the world of nation-states and national security in the 1990s:

> Make a joyful noise unto the LORD, all ye lands. Serve the LORD with gladness: come before his presence with singing. Know ye that the LORD he is God: it is he that hath made us, and not we ourselves; we are his people, and the sheep of his pasture. Enter into his gates with thanksgiving, and into his courts with praise: be thankful unto him, and bless his name. For the LORD is good; his mercy is everlasting; and his truth endureth to all generations.

The ideals expressed in Psalm 100 may have been good for King David and people in the primitive Middle Eastern cultures, or possibly even in the

Dark Ages, but are such hopes and aspirations possible today? A. J. P. Taylor, the noted English historian, wrote,

> Religious strength has lost its strength. Not only has church-going declined, the dogma of revealed religion—the Incarnation and Resurrection—are believed by only a small number. Our Lord Jesus has become, even for many avowed Christians, merely the supreme example of a good man. This is a great happening in history . . . few remain Christians in morality, even fewer keep the faith.[19]

I have here argued that normatively grounded moral choices must be woven into the very fabric of foreign and national security policy and policy making. Choices must be evaluated in terms of norms that the Christian understands to be those emerging from the biblical basis. We need to start connecting our biblical norms with our national security policy thinking. There is no guarantee that this task will be easy or meet with quick success. Furthermore, equally committed Christians may disagree with one another. Humility and tolerance will have to be exercised. But the Scripture tells us that war and the poor will always be with us. Scripture also calls us to be peacemakers and to attend to the needs of the poor. The vision of the Kingdom of God allows Christians to work for justice, freedom, and peace; to bring help to the poor; and to free the captives. We are required as individuals to do no less in our lives as members of nation-states.

EDITOR'S PERSPECTIVE

This chapter and the one preceding it (foreign trade) do more to point out the worldwide consequences of the Fall than any of the other chapters. Covetousness, greed, pride, anger, and selfishness are felt and seen on an even larger scale when they manifest themselves in the international arenas of foreign trade and national security. So what is to be done to address the effects of these sinful characteristics?

The concluding paragraph of the preceding "Editor's Perspective" (chapter 12) intentionally raised the possibility of forming a single world government (a frequently suggested "solution" offered by nonChristian idealistic intellectuals) and immediately rejected it. Scripture reveals that a single world government will be instituted during the reign of *the* Antichrist (see Rev. 13:7), but the biblical accounts do not favor the establishment of such a government. Scripture merely reports its coming.

As noted in the former "Perspective," God poured out His common grace on mankind at Babel when He confused the languages and scattered the people over the face of the earth. God did that to restrain evil. As ugly as the horrors of excessive and perverted nationalism can be, none can equal the eternal damage to the human soul that will be manifested when Revelation 13:8 is fulfilled: "And all who dwell on the earth will worship him [the Antichrist], everyone whose name has not been written from the foundation of the world in the book of life of the Lamb who has been slain." There is nothing in Scripture calling God's children to seek a single world government.

Then what does Scripture call us to do when we come face-to-face with the many problems on the international scene? If nations were prescribed by God (not their excesses) through His sovereign act at Babel, then what is the Christian community called to do regarding the problems that emanate from different forms of nationalism? Ted Malloch directs us toward part of the answer with his comment, "Scripture also calls us to be peacemakers." We ought to explore the context and implications of this truth and try to come away from the discussion with an understanding of how the biblical view of peacemaking and the world's view differ so profoundly. The following Scriptures will serve as the biblical building blocks for the discussion: "Blessed are the peacemakers, for they shall be called sons of God" (Matt. 5:9); "Do not think that I came to bring peace on the earth; I did not come to bring peace, but a sword" (Matt. 10:34); and "Peace I leave with you; My peace I give to you; not as the world gives, do I give to you" (John 14:27).

This verse—"Blessed are the peacemakers, for they shall be called sons of God"—is the seventh attribute and characteristic of the Christian heart that God would establish in His children. It is the seventh attitude described in the Beatitudes. It is my belief that the order of these Beatitudes is intentional, critical to a biblical understanding of the interpretation of the concept of our being peacemakers, and essential for a true understanding of all the Sermon on the Mount (see chapters 5–7 of Matthew). If we discount this perspective, the Sermon on the Mount is quickly reduced to an ethical discourse or implies a do-it-yourself form of Christianity. If we hold the view that is about to be described, the Sermon is a constant reminder of the character and behavior required of every Christian, but a standard that can become a reality only through the sanctifying work of the Holy Spirit in the life of the person who is truly the temple of God (see 1 Cor. 3:16; 6:19).

Let us examine the six marks of Christian character that underlie the quality of peacemaking, in the order of their creation by the Spirit. The first, being "poor in spirit" (v. 3), is not a psychological consequence of having poor self-esteem (otherwise it would be induced by the world rather than by the Holy Spirit), but results from the true acknowledgment to ourselves that we are not holy like God. It comes from a deep, deep awareness of our sin nature. It comes from the awareness that we are helpless to effect a change in our very nature and that only God can build the character in us that Christ described throughout the Sermon. Second, the poverty of spirit is so vivid and real that it causes the Christian to "mourn" (v. 4) his or her spiritual condition. Third, the poverty of spirit and mourning do their work and give birth to a "meek" spirit (v. 5, NIV) in the believer that yearns to accept and do God's will in every aspect and corner of his or her life. These three attitudes give rise to the fourth, a hungering and thirsting for righteousness (v. 6), which is the righteousness of Christ imputed to the believer by God (a gift, through faith—the doctrine of justification), and the actual righteousness that the Holy Spirit produces in the heart and behavior of the Christian (doctrine of sanctification). Fifth, Christ's righteousness, which is received through faith (which is of necessity accompanied by repentance and forgiveness), creates a thankful awareness of the mercy God has extended the sinner, producing a "merciful" attitude (v. 7) that will extend genuine mercy to others. The five attributes and characteristics described in verses 3-7, when formed in the Christian, give rise to the sixth, a single-minded devotion to Christ—a pure heart (v. 8)—that prepares the Christian to be an effective worker in the world.

Now we come to the "peacemaker" (v. 9). Those who are poor in spirit, mourn their spiritual poverty, become meek (accept God's perfect will), hunger and thirst for righteousness, experience mercy and become merciful, and become pure in heart (single-minded devotion to Christ) will want to be peacemakers. And what is the task of a peacemaker? A true peacemaker longs and labors (prays, talks, serves, etc.) to assist others to be reconciled with God. Reconciliation with God produces the fruit of peace (see Gal. 5:22). There is no true or lasting peace in anyone's heart, or in the world, apart from being reconciled and at peace with God. (The final Beatitude—vv. 10-12—also makes this abundantly clear. The peacemakers will be persecuted for the sake of righteousness, and people will cast insults at them and accuse them falsely because those of the world hate Christ.)

The passage, "Do not think that I came to bring peace on the earth; I did not come to bring peace, but a sword" (Matt. 10:34), is so compatible with our being called to be peacemakers because family peace, national and international peace, and any other form of worldly peace are all byproducts of being at peace with God or of God's common grace. The book of Proverbs affirms this truth: "When a man's [nation's] ways are pleasing to the LORD, He makes even his enemies to be at peace with him" (Prov. 16:7). And John 14:27 makes the same point: "Peace I leave with you; My peace I give to you; not as the world gives, do I give to you." The peace Christ gives His followers is not the peace of the world, and His disciples are not at peace with the world. God's children are at odds with the world, and the world is at odds with them.

Has the preceding discussion done away with a place for peacemaking in the international arena? It has, I hope, pointed out that the Christian should never expect lasting peace through diplomacy, negotiations, war, appeasement, compromise, or other humanly devised schemes. But it does not imply that peace in the world should not be sought after and labored for. To the contrary, it should cause us to think about both the role and the limits of government.

God established governments to constrain and punish evil, both nationally and internationally if biblical justice deems it necessary. They are to sponsor and maintain justice in a fallen world. They are arms of God's common grace. Sin gives rise to unjust governments all too frequently, but biblical history and secular history bear witness that relatively just governments have also effectively functioned for considerable periods of time. Minimally, therefore, Christians should vote for just civil servants where they have such opportunities. They should pray that God will raise up wise servants to become actively involved in government, and that those in power will pursue just laws and the just use of the government's power at every level. Every person and group that wants to pervert justice for selfish ends will hate those who pursue true justice, whether they be Christians or nonChristians. *Justice must be a higher value in international relations than peace.* Without justice, peace cannot prevail. With justice, peace may or may not be sustained for a long period of time, but the most fundamental avenue to meaningful peace in international affairs is the high road of justice. Justice is the hallmark of good government.

CHAPTER 14

BIBLICALLY AUTHENTICATED BUSINESS, ECONOMICS, AND PUBLIC POLICY

Richard C. Chewning

SERIES ACHIEVEMENTS IN PERSPECTIVE

What are God's thoughts about the issues we face as we subdue and rule the earth? How are we in the business world to cocreate, share, and distribute the wealth within the private and community sectors?

Does God, through Scripture, really address the important questions faced by the people working in [the business, economics, and public policy] areas? How specifically does God speak to issues faced by Christians involved in marketing, accounting, real estate, foreign trade, public education, national defense, etc.? Are there just a handful of biblical principles that apply to the entire range of subjects, or are there many biblical concepts that we can bring to bear on such questions?

Does the Bible prescribe a set of economic principles that are best satisfied in a particular economic system? How are Christians to resolve the tensions that exist between individual responsibility in a free market economy and society's need for some control to promote the social good? On what basis should Christians conduct business with nonbelievers: the principles of special revelation in Scripture or the principles of general revelation in nature?

These eight questions were first raised in the opening three paragraphs of the Preface of the first book in the CHRISTIANS IN THE MARKETPLACE Series, *Biblical Principles and Business: The Foundations*. The time has come to conclude the series and ask if it has answered these questions and dozens of associated ones. Has the series accomplished what it set out to achieve?

Yes, it has. The scholars have answered the questions raised in the context of their assigned topics. They have accurately, faithfully, and repeatedly brought us to the principles of Scripture. The very insistence from the outset that the scholars confine their interpretation and application of Scripture to the use of biblical principles (three or more biblical texts making the same point), rather than single texts (proof texts), has helped tremendously to clarify the truths of Scripture and avoid the speculations of men. But these revealed principles of Scripture, while being absolute in their character, frequently point us to the attributes and nature of God, fundamentally conceptual and abstract in character. For example, holiness, righteousness, goodness, justice, wisdom, faithfulness, and the like are absolute perfections of God, but they are not concrete ideas or concepts. They are discernible only when God reveals His thoughts to His creatures and acts in the way that manifests a particular characteristic.

In another sense, though, the scholars have not answered the questions raised at the beginning because believing in and acknowledging the existence of godly absolutes do not eliminate the need to make moral judgments. We must make moral judgments because the answers must embody qualities of character and conduct reflecting a God spiritual in nature. Knowing that we ought to be just in all our dealings with our customers, employers, suppliers, and so forth does not in and of itself tell us all that this concept embodies. Being just applies to a quality of relationship and action that have a rightness about them. The need to discuss rightness can be very frustrating, so many people look for rules by which to determine right from wrong.

The desire for rules that will somehow allow people to be righteous is a misguided but persistent longing in many hearts. A rule can commend rightness but cannot embody it. A heaviness comes over me when I am asked to address Christian ethics from the perspective of tell us what to do, give us some rules to follow, and explain how we are to act. I become tense when righteousness is confused with rule keeping. Righteous people will obey the law, but technical obedience falls far short of the full intent of the law and therefore short of the requirements of righteousness. Christ often made this point during His ministry. The law of God, if it is to be effective, must be written on a heart of flesh, not a heart of stone. The law, a mirror of the attitudes and conduct of God, is not a substitute for the Spirit's work of bringing the law to life in a transformed heart.

The very tendency of our old nature to want rules and principles to follow, and to substitute them for the painful work of renovation that every heart must endure under the loving discipline of the Holy Spirit, has led me to forgo listing the biblical principles identified throughout this four-volume study. Indeed, it was my intent when the series began to make such a list at its completion. In fact, the list was even begun when twelve biblical principles were outlined at the end of *Biblical Principles and Economics: The Foundations* (volume 2). At this juncture it would be easy to enumerate fifty to seventy biblical principles discussed by participating scholars, but would this faithfully portray the true essence of what this series of books has been declaring?

The answer to the question is probably no. It would be far better for all of us to continue a serious study of Scripture with the specific prayer that Christ help us to be made alive to His true character, so that our attitudes and conduct become like His in the marketplace. The study of a list of principles, while undoubtedly increasing our knowledge, could well leave us with a conclusion that falls far short of the real lessons to be learned from this series. I am convinced that these four volumes demonstrate that Scripture is always contemporary, has already addressed all moral- and value-related questions that can be raised, in any context and in any field of human endeavor, and is a distillation of revelation that truly becomes effective in and through us only when the Holy Spirit empowers it. Those are bold assertions but true ones.

THE EVER-CONTEMPORARY NATURE OF SCRIPTURE

In what sense can it be asserted that Scripture is always contemporary in its comments on business, economics, and public policy (or any other areas of human endeavor)? The authors of Scripture certainly did not have industrial capitalism, information technologies, or biotechnical societies in mind when they recorded the testimonies of God. That is true, but *The Author* of Scripture did. The Alpha and Omega, the One who has known the end from the beginning, has revealed His unchanging nature and will to us. He has expressed the eternal verities about Himself (first within the Godhead, then to His creatures) to illuminate every aspect of our nature. He has communicated His required conduct with such clarity that we are without excuse when we pursue our own desires and ignore His teaching and helping involvement in our lives.

Most aspects of designing and structuring organizations and institutions, especially in the business, economic, and political arenas, have been left up to us. We were not given the assignment of constructing a set of moral standards, however. God has provided those, and they are the eternal and universal verities of life—truths that are unchangeable. We are responsible for discerning which verities apply (and how to apply them) in specific cases, and for avoiding actions that either imbalance or bring them into conflict with one another. But these conditions—allowing eternal truths to be imbalanced or to be brought into conflict with one another—cause much trouble in the marketplace. For example, it is one thing to realize that it is morally proper to be efficient and productive (marks of good stewardship), and it is another thing to discern how we are to act justly and kindly (verities outlined in Mic. 6:8) toward our employees in view of advancing technologies that may require a reduction in our work force or cause us to seek new work skills not currently visible in those we employ.

How are we to traverse the quagmire of complex ethical problems? Undoubtedly, many people would be content to simply say to themselves that market conditions dictate what our response must be and as long as the greatest number of people are helped in the long run by our sound economic decision, regardless of its personal impact on a group of current workers, the best end is served. As true as this utilitarian statement may prove to be (it may prove to be false, too, under a more careful examination), God is just as concerned with the motives, intentions, and care with which we deal with matters like this as He is with the actual decisions and concrete consequences of our actions (see 1 Kings 8:39; 1 Cor. 4:5; 2 Cor. 5:12).

WHAT GOD REQUIRES IN THE MARKETPLACE

The quiet but persistent call of the preceding fifty-five chapters in the series is perhaps best summed up in Micah 6:8: "What does the LORD require of you but to do justice, to love kindness, and to walk humbly with your God?" This principle, in one form or another, has recurred in the four volumes and will be used here as a summarizing text. Figure 14.1, "Biblically Authenticated Business, Economics, and Public Policy," expands on the principle. The title is not to be construed to imply that God has provided us with particular systems, structures, or institutions of business and economics. The title is intended to convey that when the many biblical precepts addressing God's concern for our thoughts and behavior (as they relate to the complex array of wealth-related relationships and activities) have been manifested in our lives in a manner that meets God's interests, the processes and outcomes are biblically authentic ones. That is, they are in harmony with the eternal verities of Scripture. The diagram (figure 14.1) depicts a schema for reflecting on the diverse considerations before us as we live and work with economic realities. We will walk through the five sections of the outline as a means of reviewing and concluding the spirit of the series.

Standards for the marketplace—The world is forever asking, "How do you know what is right or wrong?" Those who do not build their answer to this question on the revealed truths of Scripture are self-consigned to the prison of human reason, volition, and emotion, all of which are incapable of bringing about human reconciliation with God, which is essential if truth is to be grasped. People will reject, ignore, or pervert the truths about God's character and conduct, resulting in substituting mankind's ideas about right and wrong for God's revealed norms. Even this truth, however, brings us only to the midpoint of Christian ethics—to the point of defining godly character and conduct.

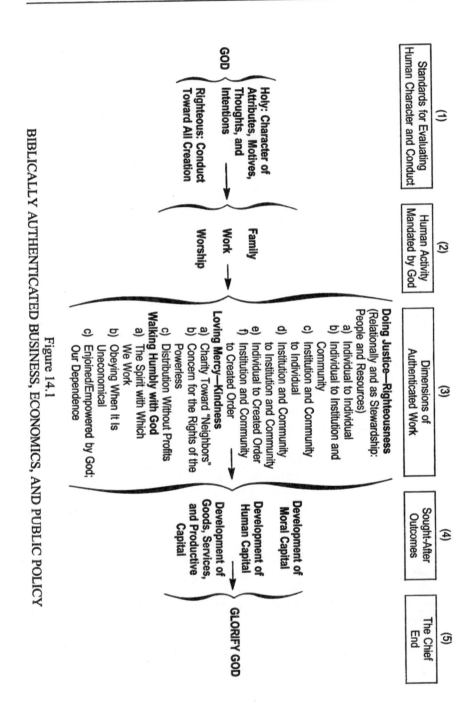

Figure 14.1
BIBLICALLY AUTHENTICATED BUSINESS, ECONOMICS, AND PUBLIC POLICY

Defining righteous character and conduct is obviously still light-years away from our being able to volitionally obey God's perfect will and do even what we profess to know. (This gap between our knowledge and ability will be examined in the last part of the third section, "Dimensions of Authenticated Work.")

Christians should always begin their contemplations about ethical and moral standards by reflecting on God. Column (1) of figure 14.1 ("Standards for Evaluating Human Character and Conduct") draws our attention to this as the first necessity for further thinking about what is most basic if business, economics, and public policy are to genuinely reflect God's purposes and not be counterfeits of His intentions. Column (1) points to two major attributes of God: His holiness and His righteousness. They both symbolize God's character and conduct. These two broad dimensions of life deal with the inherent character aspects of "being" and their outward expression. They are also the two attributes used most often in Scripture to describe God.

The attributes of God are sorely neglected today by those who preach and teach in the Church, to the poverty of our spirits. The Church often behaves as if its members are expected to discover God's character and nature through some mystical, existential experience rather than through the Holy Spirit's use of the Scripture where God's attributes are clearly set before us. Knowledge of God's character ought to be an integral ingredient in shaping and maturing our faith and conduct.

The greatness of God is unsearchable (see Ps. 145:3), but the things revealed about Him belong to us (see Deut. 29:29). And the things God has revealed about Himself ought to be the very *standards* by which we evaluate all human character and behavior, for we have been created in His image (see Eph. 4:24; Col. 3:10). God, the *unchanging* (immutable), *omniscient* (all-knowing), *all-powerful* (omnipotent), *omnipresent* (everywhere), *infinite* and *eternal spirit* (who is *just*, *wise*, *good*, *kind*, *patient*, and *faithful* in His absolutely *loving* and *sovereign* rule), is to be loved (obeyed) and emulated by us. God is the standard. We are to evaluate all human endeavors in the light of His being.

Activity mandated by God—What are the most critical or essential chapters of Scripture providing the *presuppositions* on which most of Scripture rests? The early chapters of Genesis. The first three chapters of Genesis alone contain over twenty-five statements that serve as the most basic presuppositions for the balance of Scripture. For example, if there was no historic fall of a first man and woman (Adam and Eve), we can conclude only that the perverted and hurtful characteristics in human conduct reflect a metaphysical problem emanating from the origin of mankind and not a moral problem set in motion by human choice. God is the cause of the problem in the first case (unless, of course, God is nonexistent), and sin is the result of man's choice in the other case.

Persons who discount the historic character of Genesis 1–11 cut out the very foundations of Scripture from under themselves. God's concern for the formation and maintenance of the family (see Gen. 1:28; 2:18, 20-24; 9:1, 7), the origination and continuation of work (see Gen. 1:28-30; 2:15; 3:17-19, 23; 9:2-6), and the establishment of a day of rest for the purpose of worship (see Gen. 2:2-3; 4:3-4, 26; 8:20-21) is contained in these early chapters. These three broad dimensions of life—being part of a family, working, and resting/worshiping—are not prioritized in Scripture, however. Rather, they are shown to be interrelated and synergistic. For example, we cannot really worship God in a correct way while being unjust to those who work for us (see Isa. 58:1-14; Mal. 3:1-5). God will not bless a person or family harboring known sin, for God cannot look on sin with favor (see Prov. 28:13; Hab. 1:13).

God also revealed in the first three chapters of Genesis that He, too, is part of a "family of God," when He disclosed through His self-description that He is both one and plural (see Gen. 1:1—Elohim: a plural name for God; and Gen. 1:26, God is plural in His being—"Let Us make man in Our image"). There is no implication in my statement, however, that the earliest writers or readers of Scripture comprehended the importance of these realities, but their later revelations clearly establish their significance. The first chapter of Genesis is devoted completely to God as a worker, and as noted in the preceding paragraph, His image bearers were to work. It was also God who first rested, reflecting not fatigue but the completion of a task and the appropriateness of rest in the cycle of creation (see Gen. 2:1-2). God's resting was more than a model for us, though. When He sanctified and set the seventh day apart from the other days, God established its distinctiveness (see Gen. 2:3).

Business and economics in their broadest sense (including public policy) fall under the biblical mandate establishing work. It would be a tragedy, however, if we completed this series and left the impression that working for a wage, salary, or share of profits ought to somehow be viewed as superior or more worthy than the myriad of other types of work that have no monetary rewards associated with them. God reveals no such outlook on work. We are all to serve God through our work, whether for pay or not. Scripture places no greater value on work rewarded in the marketplace than it does on work ignored by the forces of the marketplace.

One additional thing is abundantly clear. Those of us who associate the name of the Lord with ourselves through baptism and public affiliation with the Church are not to take the name of God in vain at work, or anywhere else (see Exod. 20:7). We are not to say we know Him, worship Him, and understand that He is holy and righteous (and that we are to be like Him) and then fail to reflect His character and standards in our family, work, and worship. Any breakdown on our part in these matters reflects negatively on His name, and that is what it means to take His name in vain. God has given us hundreds of examples and directives about how we are to live in a godly manner with our neighbors to help us understand His intentions and purposes for us.

Dimensions of authenticated work—The CHRISTIANS IN THE MARKETPLACE Series was begun with several objectives in mind: (1) to define, expound on, and encourage the development of a mature Christian world view; (2) to show unmistakably that God has addressed our concerns in the business, economics, and public policy arenas, and to demonstrate the application of Scripture to the functional areas of work; and (3) to call for a genuine response to God's revealed will as it applies to the marketplace. These objectives to a large degree have been met. Micah 6:8 directly addressed the second objective in its call to do justice, love kindness, and walk humbly with God in the context of the marketplace.

The outline in column (3) of figure 14.1 divides Micah 6:8 into its components and lists some points to help the reader concretize the absolute requirements for justice, mercy, and humility.

Doing justice—I still remember how startled I was when I first realized that "justice" and "righteousness" are often translations of the same Hebrew and Greek words. They are frequently interchangeable: do justice/do righteousness. We also begin to sense the importance God attaches to doing justice when we discover He has referred to the subject in Scripture over eight hundred times. While it is true that justice is used there occasionally to call for retribution in the context of civil and criminal problems, justice (as in Mic. 6:8) is generally synonymous with righteousness—a call to do what God would do.

Biblically, righteousness is used in the context of our relationships with individuals and with groups of people (family, church, community), as well as in the context of our stewardship responsibilities as they encompass work and the management of resources. The two books, *Biblical Principles and Business: The Practice* and *Biblical Principles and Public Policy: The Practice*, are resources demonstrating how God's principles of righteousness are to be understood in working in any of twelve functional areas of business and in any of twelve public policy arenas. No effort has been made, though, to exhaust the integration of Scripture with the discipline of business or public policy. In fact, the scholars were all instructed to restrict their search and application of biblical principles to several clear examples to keep the volumes from becoming too expansive.

God desires us to be righteous as we relate to our customers, suppliers, employees, competitors, government leaders, and employers. This holds true whether we work in the fields of advertising, human resources (personnel), marketing, accounting, strategic management, insurance, information systems, operations research, law, finance, real estate, or management, or in the public policy arenas of health care, income distribution, money and banking, public welfare, unemployment, taxation, government regulations, education, agriculture, foreign trade, or national defense. These functional areas are the focus in the third and fourth volumes that demonstrated the universal application of God's eternal verities and principles. They are intended to lead to the discovery of God's revealed interests in justice (righteousness) in all areas of work.

One more major consideration warrants attention before we bring the discussion on doing justice to its conclusion. Our society is enamored with utility theory in the world of business—economic decisions are judged on the grounds of their physical consequences and their generation of the most "net good." The Christian community has also embraced this concept to a large degree as the best measure for evaluating economic stewardship. Although this tool needs to be a part of one's analysis of marketplace justice, it is a tool that needs to be refined and, in some circumstances, actually disregarded. The refinement issue will be addressed in this subsection; the second issue will be spoken to in the next two subsections—"Loving Mercy" and "Walking Humbly with God."

Utility theory speaks of doing the most good, leaving the decision of whether or not the most good should be the most good for the most people or the "net most good." This is true regardless of whether or not only a few people benefit. Christians ought to be sensitive to at least two justice issues embedded in this situation. First, the concept of "net good" rests on the presupposition that good and bad are to be measured, and so long as the good outweighs the bad, the decisions fostering the "net good" are good ones. If people were not related and connected to the negative consequences that also accompany a "net good" decision, no further concern would be called for. But Christians should not ignore the hurt that so often accompanies otherwise good decisions. Neither is it altogether fair for institutions to march around making economic decisions that leave the negative residue to be cared for by other groups in the social structure.

The second issue of justice embedded in the distinction between the most good for the most people and the "net most good" is even tougher to grapple with than the first one. It is the tension between the individual and the community—the one and the many. Scripture clearly enunciates a concern for both, while not sacrificing one to the other. But it is difficult in a culture such as ours that so strongly champions individualism to effectively draw attention to the issues of justice related to the growing gap between the rich and the poor—the "haves" getting more and more while the proportion the "have-nots" receive continues to shrink. It is all too easy to applaud the innovative skills, education, and effort of those climbing the ladder of economic success while enumerating a standard list of reasons for the failure of the "have-nots" to keep pace.

Christians must ask if the economic/legal/political system is creating and protecting special opportunities for those already in positions of opportunity and restricting others unjustly. The question will generally generate some affirmative responses that frequently lead us to pockets of injustice that need to be highlighted and redressed. God's children cannot rest easy with the soothing ointment of the marketplace—so long as the most "net good" is being achieved, all is well. All is not well. Injustices exist and need to be addressed.

Loving mercy—The three considerations listed under the "Loving Mercy—Kindness" subheading in column (3) of figure 14.1 really begin to expose the distinctions between a secular world view and a biblical world view, where people are called on to act in ways that manifest (a) charity toward their neighbors, (b) concern for the rights of the powerless, and (c) a willingness to distribute economic wealth (under certain conditions) without regard for profits. These considerations are at the heart of being kind and loving mercy in the marketplace.

When economic justice in the marketplace can be brought alongside utility theory in such a comfortable manner, it is easy for people who are positively positioned in life to take advantage of the market's opportunities to stop short of making further inquiries into what biblically authenticated work ought to take into account. Mercy and humility are also biblical prerequisites along with righteousness, fairness, and efficiency. There are times, in fact, when in God's eyes showing mercy is more important than following the norms of utility theory where efficiency is paramount.

When Micah answered the question about "what the Lord requires of us," "to love kindness [mercy, goodness]" appeared as the second of the three enunciated ingredients. The etymological origin of the Hebrew word used in this context for "mercy"—*hesed*—expresses the idea of being devoted to people in spite of their unworthiness and lack of any right to be treated kindly. Mercy is not correlated with what is deserved. It is an attitude of the heart related to a commitment to help those who need help, even when the problem may be self-induced.

The ungodly are generally defensive about a call to be merciful if the act of mercy requires them to sacrifice something they personally own or desire. The first reason offered for refusing help is usually related to the fact that the helpless are undeserving. That may well be true! If they were deserving, the call would be for justice and righteousness. But God's children know that we have abundantly received God's mercy, so we will be merciful to the undeserving. We know from Scripture that the unmerciful have never truly received (acknowledged in the heart) God's mercy.

The second objection usually raised to being merciful in the corporate culture in the marketplace is that the wealth being administered belongs to the owners and using it for acts of mercy is inappropriate. That is true in an important sense, but all too frequently that response hides a hard heart. Administrators of corporations have no trouble asking stockholders for permission to establish stock option plans and severance pay protection plans that will benefit them. Why are these same people so unwilling to ask the owner(s) for permission to be merciful to the disadvantaged and helpless through the means of the business world?

Most opportunities to be merciful are stifled at the point where the need for mercy is first observed. The need for it is generally rationalized away. It is rarely defeated by an economic incapability. Furthermore, many acts of mercy require not money but an advocate in the corners of power. That is certainly implicit in the following declarations:

> The righteous is concerned for the rights of the poor,
> The wicked does not understand such concern. (Prov. 29:7)

> Open your mouth for the dumb,
> For the rights of all the unfortunate.
> Open your mouth, judge righteously,
> And defend the rights of the afflicted and needy. (Prov. 31:8-9)

> "They are fat, they are sleek,
> They also excel in deeds of wickedness;
> They do not plead the cause,
> The cause of the orphan, that they may prosper;
> And they do not defend the rights of the poor.
> 'Shall I not punish these people?' declares the LORD." (Jer. 5:28-29)

Biblically authenticated business conduct will always have room for mercy in its affairs. If it does not, the business leaders are acting idolatrously in their service of the corporation or are working for owners devoid of compassion.

Walking humbly with God—The opportunity to walk humbly with God is simply not available to those who have not been reconciled to God. Humility, an attitude devoid of false perceptions about oneself, is generated by the Holy Spirit's enlightening us regarding both our fallen nature (character and conduct) and the presence and perfection of our Savior. Humility is also grounded in our coming to a full and proper understanding of our true dependence on God. When we are enabled to rightly compare ourselves with God, we become humble.

Three aspects of what will be manifested when we walk humbly with God are noted at the bottom of column (3) of figure 14.1. First, people who walk humbly with God will walk humbly with their neighbors. Arrogance, haughtiness, and pride cease to infect the relationships of humble persons. The evidences of the fruit of the Spirit (see Gal. 5:22-23) will appear and grow in their attitudes and dealings with others. By their attitude and spirit, they will enhance the well-being of others rather than diminish or trade on their worth.

Second, those who walk humbly with God become more concerned about doing what is pleasing to God. The godly manager is no less aware of the need for profits than is the worldly manager, but the ideas about an optimum profit and how to achieve it may be very different. If you will, righteousness is worth more to the person of God than unjust economic profits. To the person whose identity is in the world, rather than God, forgoing the rewards of the world for the sake of holiness and righteousness does not make much sense. But the righteous prefer fellowship with God above all else (see Ps. 73:25-28). King David asked, "O LORD, who may abide in Thy tent?" The answer was, "He who walks with integrity, and works righteousness, and speaks truth in his heart. . . . He [who] swears to his own hurt, and does not change" (Ps. 15:1-2, 4).

Finally, those who walk humbly with God have come to the sure realization that God has commanded them to do justice, to love mercy, and to walk humbly with Him, and God also has given them the motivation, authority, right, and power to respond to His commands. This is one of the most fundamental truths of Scripture—God commands, we discover we need help to obey His commands, and God enables us to obey. I first became aware of this doctrinal truth (I had frequently experienced it) when studying the book of Deuteronomy. God commanded the people to love Him with all their heart, soul, and might (see 6:5); then God told the children of Israel He would circumcise their hearts, and the hearts of their descendants, so they would be able to love Him (see 30:6). This same truth is evident in John 15 where Christ describes Himself as the true vine and us as the branches: "As the branch cannot bear fruit of itself, unless it abides in the vine, so neither can you, unless you abide in Me. I am the vine, you are the branches . . . *apart from Me you can do nothing*" (vv. 4-5, emphasis added).

God's sought-after outcomes—God is not egocentric. He has never had any needs or experienced any shortcomings. He did not create us in His image because He needed someone corresponding to Himself to love and to be loved by. Eve was created to be a helper, corresponding to and complementing Adam, but God has eternally enjoyed love and fellowship in the Godhead—Father, Son, and Spirit. Then why did God create us? This question will be answered in two stages. The first part of it is outlined in column (4) of figure 14.1, and the final, most comprehensive, answer is capsuled in column (5).

The sentences opening the preceding paragraph are biblically defensible. Part of the content of this paragraph, however, cannot be backed by biblical proof texts. The part that cannot point to special revelation is defensible on the basis of logic, though. It is deduced from what we know of God's character, not directly from His revealed mind. God, absolutely perfect in His qualities of being, decided before times eternal to create a universe and an environment in which to place a created image bearer who would have the capacity to truly know Him and be righteous and holy. Why? If God did not need us, why did He create us and subject Himself to so much rejection, rebellion, and sin on the part of His creatures? God's intentions, thoughts, and actions in this matter manifest the character and nature of His love. He created us so we could have the incredible privilege and opportunity to truly know Him. There is no greater love than to be granted the eternal privilege of knowing God who is pure perfection and infinite in all His qualities.

We may also surmise that had there been no Fall, there still would have been the need for human intellectual growth and development. We can deduce this from two known facts. Adam and Eve were to exercise dominion in a world they had to discover, name, and rule. Everything associated with those ordained tasks would have added to their store of knowledge. We also know that Christ, who knew no sin in His being, was subjected in His humanity to the experience of intellectual growth when He became incarnate (see Luke 2:40, 52). He also learned obedience and was made perfect (completely mature) through His suffering (see Heb. 5:8-9). We may conclude that intellectual growth and developmental maturity were planned for mankind before times eternal. (Both 2 Tim. 1:9 and Titus 1:2 speak of God's activities "before times eternal.")

Adam and Eve were created without knowledge of good and evil, but with the inherent capacity to know it (see Gen. 2:17; 3:2-7, 22). The Fall, shattering and deforming the image of God in us, created the need for intellectual, moral, and behavioral renovation if we were to be restored to the likeness of God (see Rom. 12:2; Eph. 4:23-24; Col. 3:10). And even though God knew before He created anything or anybody that the Fall would occur, He had already planned before times eternal to reconcile and restore His Son's inheritance (us; see 1 Kings 8:51-52; Eph. 1:18), so that it would be renewed to the image of His Son (see Rom. 8:29).

We can reasonably conclude from this that God has an enormous interest in the development of our moral character and our intellectual capacities. In column (4) of figure 14.1, these things are referred to as moral capital and human capital. The third item in column (4) simply recognizes that God, having created us to tend, keep, and rule over the created order, wanted us to enjoy the fruits and benefits that could be derived from the basic elements He had made available to all of us. These three objectives—development of moral capital, development of human capital, and development of goods, services, and productive capital—are extremely significant and were eternally part of God's plan for us.

THE CHIEF END

"Do not fear, for I am with you;
I will bring your offspring from the east,
And gather you from the west.

I will say to the north, 'Give them up!'
And to the south, 'Do not hold them back.'
Bring My sons from afar,
And My daughters from the ends of the earth,
Everyone who is called by My name
And *whom I have created for My glory,*
Whom I have formed, even whom I have made."
    (Isa. 43:5-7, emphasis added)

God created us for His glory (see Isa. 43:7); He will not give His glory to another (see Isa. 48:11); He is to receive glory forever (see Rom. 11:36); and we are to do everything for His glory (see 1 Cor. 10:31). What does all of this really mean? We become so familiar with some things in life that we fail to contemplate their significance. For example, most Christians know they have been created in the image of God, but few have a clear understanding of what that really means. In the same way, many Christians have been taught the old catechism question (and answer), "What is the chief and highest end of man? Answer: Man's chief and highest end is to glorify God, and fully to enjoy Him for ever." And some especially well-trained Christians can even cite the proof texts for the catechism answers—those used in the opening sentence of this paragraph. But that fails to explain what it means to glorify God.

The root meaning embedded in the Hebrew word for *glory* is "heavy." In the Greek it is "reputation." Perhaps you have heard somebody exclaim upon learning something significant, "Man, that is really heavy." Behind these words—*glory, heavy, reputation*—is the notion of something being so awesome, profound, weighty, and majestic that it both manifests and elicits the ascription of worthiness. In the case of God, a true knowledge of Him elicits our acknowledgment of His worth, and true worship of Him will of necessity follow.

Another way to consider the whole matter of glory is to look at it from a parallel perspective. How does an orange tree glorify God? An orange tree glorifies God by growing oranges (whether or not anyone stops to ponder the awesome wonder of all that is involved in the development of an orange). God's glory is manifested in the awesome wonders of His acts of creation. King David was speaking of this truth when he said, "I will give thanks to Thee, for I am fearfully and wonderfully made; wonderful are Thy works, and my soul knows it very well" (Ps. 139:14).

We are now in a position to answer the original question: What does it mean for us to have been created for God's glory? We glorify God (point to or to a degree manifest His glory, not add to His glory) when we live in a manner that fulfills His intentions for us and when we worship Him in spirit and truth. Or putting it another way, when we think and behave as God wants us to, and when we truly comprehend God's awesomeness so as to praise and adore Him, we glorify our Redeemer.

The final objective for the CHRISTIANS IN THE MARKETPLACE Series was stated in the first Preface: "to encourage a *response* to God's revealed will regarding business, economics, and public policy, so that *justice* will be done in the marketplace" (page 9, volume 1). What we have done is to seek ways to stimulate and encourage one another in Christ so we will respond to His expressed purposes as they pertain to the marketplace and thereby glorify Him and more fully enjoy Him forever. To God be the glory!

NOTES

CHAPTER 1

1. Ed. Michael Cromartie, *Evangelicals and Foreign Policy: Four Perspectives* (Washington, D.C.: Ethics and Public Policy Center, 1989).
2. Paul Johnson, *Washington Times*, February 21, 1989, page 5.

EDITOR'S PERSPECTIVE

1. Other materials in the CHRISTIANS IN THE MARKETPLACE Series germane to the discussion on hermeneutics are found in (1) vol. 1, Preface, pages 8-9; (2) vol. 1, chapter 1, pages 11-17; (3) vol. 1, Section B, "Ethics of the Covenants: Does the New Covenant Supersede the Old?" pages 55-91 (esp. pages 89-91); vol. 1, chapter 14, pages 263-264; vol. 3, Part IV, "The Marketer in Biblical Perspective," see "Editor's Perspective," pages 87-89; vol. 3, chapter 13, pages 252, 254-256; vol. 3, Part XIII, "The Higher and Lower Laws," see "Editor's Perspective," pages 269-271.

CHAPTER 2

1. Lewis B. Smedes, *Mere Morality: What God Expects from Ordinary People* (Grand Rapids, Mich.: Eerdmans, 1983), page 240.
2. For an illuminating discussion of the tension between these principles, see Henry Stob, *Ethical Reflections: Essays on Moral Themes* (Grand Rapids, Mich.: Eerdmans, 1978), especially chapter 11, "The Dialectics of Love and Justice," pages 134-143.
3. Labor earnings account for close to three-quarters of net income generated by the economy. The remaining quarter is accounted for mainly by income from interest and dividends and rental income. Although the information on the distribution of income among persons and families includes

313

income from these sources and from government transfers, I do not discuss the determinants of the (relatively stable) labor earnings share.

4. For a general discussion of income distribution and the measurements used to describe it, see Martin Bronfenbrenner, *Income Distribution Theory* (Chicago: Aldine-Atherton, 1971).

5. Families with children include at least one member eighteen years old or younger. Single mothers include divorced, separated, widowed, and never-married women living with children.

6. Scaling incomes on the basis of equivalency at the estimated poverty level is only one way of making adjustments to take into account differences in needs. Measures of equivalency should not be viewed as indicating that families with similar equivalence measures are equally well-off in economic terms; economic needs of children also represent only one dimension of their effect on overall well-being.

7. Nicholas Eberstadt, "Economic and Material Poverty in Contemporary America" (Working paper, Seminar on Welfare and the American Family, American Enterprise Institute, Milwaukee, Wis., Marquette University, April 20, 1987), table 31, and "Is Illegitimacy a Public-Health Hazard?" *National Review*, December 30, 1988, page 38.

8. Michael Novak et al., eds., *The New Consensus on Family and Welfare* (American Enterprise Institute, Milwaukee, Wis.: Marquette University Press, 1987), page 5.

9. Jacob Mincer, *Schooling, Experience, and Earnings* (New York: National Bureau of Economic Research/Columbia University Press, 1974), page 134.

10. Other choices influencing material levels of living include careful management of spending choices or practices of thrift and frugality, and the choice between spending and saving, which influences future income. Of course, incomes are also affected by factors other than choice, such as lack of opportunity or involuntary unemployment. Since the depression of the 1930s, however, inability to obtain work has been important mainly for relatively short periods during recessions and in particular geographic areas affected by major layoffs or more general depressed business conditions.

11. Genesis 3:18-19.

12. Programs to redistribute income to the elderly—particularly social security—have been quite successful in part because, for people in retirement, the influence of transfer programs on work choices is much less important than for people of normal working age.

13. For a careful and thorough discussion of how these questions were dealt with in the Old Testament, see John D. Mason, "Biblical Teaching and Assisting the Poor," *Transformation*, vol. 4, no. 2 (April-June 1987), pages 1-14.

14. Leviticus 19:9-10.

15. The role of the market in the context of moral questions is perceptively discussed in Cecil B. De Boer, *The Ifs and Oughts of Ethics* (Grand Rapids, Mich.: Eerdmans, 1936), especially in the chapter "Economic Justice."

16. For a useful contemporary discussion of income distribution policy, see Edward M. Gramlich, "Economists' Views of the Welfare System," *American Economic Review*, vol. 79, no. 2 (May 1989), pages 191-196.

CHAPTER 3

1. E.g., Pope Leo XIII, *Rerum Novarum*, 1891; Archbishop William Temple, *Christianity and Social Order* (London: SCM Press, 1950); Dennis Munby, *Christianity and Economic Problems* (London: Macmillan, 1956).

2. Social Affairs Commission of the Canadian Conference of Catholic Bishops, *Ethical Reflections on the Economic Crisis* (1983); and the U.S. Bishops, *Pastoral Letter: Economic Justice for All: Catholic Social Teaching and the U.S. Economy* (1986).

3. This is a view that Waterman takes and that I have answered elsewhere. See A. M. C. Waterman, "The Catholic Bishops and Canadian Public Policy," *Canadian Public Policy*, vol. 9, no. 3 (1983), pages 374-382; and Bruce W. Wilkinson, "The Catholic Bishops and Canadian Public Policy: A Comment," *Canadian Public Policy*, vol. 10, no. 1 (1984), pages 88-91.

4. J. M. Keynes discussed it, however, in his *General Theory of Employment, Interest and Money* (London: Macmillan, 1936), chapter 21, "The Theory of Prices," pages 292-312.

5. Alan Blinder, "Economic Policy and Economic Science: The Case of Macroeconomics" (Prepared for the Economic Council of Canada "Visions of Canada in the Year 2000" project, September 1988), pages 12-25, 30-32.

6. Alan Blinder, "Economic Policy" and "Keynes, Lucas and Scientific Progress," *American Economic Review: Papers and Proceedings*, vol. 77, no. 3 (May 1987), pages 130-136; George A. Akerlof and Janet L. Yellen, "Rational Models of Irrational Behavior," *American Economic Review: Papers and Proceedings*, vol. 77, no. 3 (May 1987), pages 137-142; Paul A. Samuelson, "Evaluating Reaganomics," *Challenge*, Anniversary Issue 1987, pages 58-65; Lester Thurow, *Dangerous Currents: The State of Economics* (New York: Random House, 1983); Arthur M. Okun, *Prices and Quantities: A Macroeconomic Analysis* (Washington, D.C.: Brookings Institution, 1981), and "Rational-Expectations with Misperceptions as a Theory of the Business Cycle," *Journal of Money, Credit and Banking*, vol. 12, no. 4 (1980); and Thomas K. Rymes, *On Lasting or Natural Unemployment*, Zadak Christian Economists Group, no. 2 (1985).

7. In suggesting the "Keynesian-type" analysis is relevant in no way should

be interpreted as acceptance or endorsement of Keynes the man. The moral debasement of his personal life is well known and cannot be condoned by any biblical standard.

8. Blinder, "Economic Policy," pages 12-25, 30-32.

9. Carl Christ, "Unemployment and Macroeconomics," in *The Catholic Challenge to the American Economy: Reflections on the U.S. Bishops' Pastoral Letter on Catholic Social Teaching and the U.S. Economy*, ed. Thomas M. Gannon, S.J. (New York: Macmillan, 1987), pages 116-127.

10. *The Economist*, various issues.

11. Paul D. McNelis, S.J., "The Preferential Option for the Poor and the Evolution of Latin American Macroeconomic Orthodoxies," in *The Catholic Challenge to the American Economy*, ed. Gannon, pages 138-150.

12. C. B. Chisholm, "The Psychiatry of Enduring Peace and Social Progress," *Psychiatry*, vol. 9, no. 1 (1946), page 31, cited in David Hollenbach, S.J., "Unemployment and Jobs: A Theological and Ethical Perspective," *Catholic Social Teaching and the U.S. Economy: Working Papers for a Bishops' Pastoral*, eds. John W. Houch and Oliver F. Williams (Washington, D.C.: University Press of America, 1984), pages 110-138.

13. U.S. Bishops, *Pastoral Letter*, paragraphs 141-143.

14. Eric Kierans and Walter Stewart, *Wrong End of the Rainbow: The Collapse of Free Enterprise in Canada* (Toronto: Collins, 1988); on page 7, note that "nine families alone control 46 percent of the value of all the shares of the 300 most important companies listed on the Toronto Stock Exchange."

15. Kierans and Stewart, *Wrong End of the Rainbow*, pages 123-128, 158.

16. Hollenbach, "Unemployment and Jobs," pages 124-125.

17. Hollenbach, "Unemployment and Jobs," page 125.

18. Hollenbach, "Unemployment and Jobs," page 125.

19. Hollenbach, "Unemployment and Jobs," page 125.

20. Pope John Paul II discusses these matters in his *Encyclical Laborem Exercens: On Human Work* (1981).

21. Edward J. O'Boyle, "On Reconstructing the Foundations of Policy Toward the Unemployed," *Review of Social Economy* (1985), pages 325-344, notes that in the early 1940s in the United States an attempt was made to have unemployment defined taking "hardship" into account, but the approach was never adopted. He suggests that perhaps the time has come to do so.

22. See U.S. Bishops, *Pastoral Letter*, paragraphs 99-100, 123-124, as well as the extensive footnotes that document the long tradition of this principle in Catholic social teaching. Milton Friedman seems to think the Bishops are inconsistent in both endorsing the principle of subsidiarity and advocating national measures, on occasion, to reduce unemployment. See his "Good Ends, Bad Means," in *The Catholic Challenge to the American Economy*, ed. Gannon, page 105. However, a careful reading of their work suggests

that this is not so. The Bishops suggest that some things can be done locally and some are better done nationally.

23. E.g., see Gary North, *An Introduction to Christian Economics* (Nutley, N.J.: Craig Press, 1973); and *The Dominion Covenant* (Tyler, Tex.: Institute for Christian Economics, 1982).

24. Both the U.S. Bishops' *Pastoral Letter* and the earlier 1983 release by the Social Affairs Commission of the Canadian Conference of Catholic Bishops, *Ethical Reflections on the Economic Crisis*, largely neglect the matter of workers' responsibilities.

25. Mel Hurtig, "Presentation to the House of Commons Committee on External Affairs and International Trade," Government of Canada, November 17, 1987.

26. Albert O. Hirschman, *The Passions and the Interests: Political Arguments for Capitalism Before Its Triumph* (Princeton, N.J.: Princeton University Press, 1977).

27. J. M. Keynes said, "Avarice and usury (and precaution) must be our gods for a little longer still. For only they can lead us out of the tunnel of economic necessity into daylight" ("Economic Possibilities for Our Grandchildren," in *Essays in Persuasion* [New York: Harcourt, Brace, 1932], page 372). He subsequently added that once we were out of the so-called tunnel, "I see us free, therefore, to return to some of the most sure and certain principles of religion and traditional virtue—that avarice is a vice . . . and the love of money is detestable, that those walk most truly in the paths of virtue and sane wisdom who take least thought for the morrow. We shall once more value ends above means and prefer the good to the useful."

28. The issue of interest is complicated and easily deserves a chapter or book unto itself. However, the Islamic nations have developed forms of finance deemed consistent with their prohibition on charging interest. See Zubair Iqbal and Abbas Mirakhor, *Islamic Banking*, Occasional Paper No. 49 (Washington, D.C.: International Monetary Fund, 1987).

29. Chris Wright develops this theme in his unpublished paper "Individual and Family Freedom: An Old Testament Perspective."

30. Mennonite Central Committee, Employment Concerns, *Final Report: City of Edmonton/CJE/MCC Housing Renovation Project (1987-88) and Lot Regarding Project (1988)*, February 1989.

31. *Only Work Works: Train Canadians and Create Jobs Without Increasing the Deficit, Inflation or Tax Rates* (Ottawa: The Queen's Printer for Canada, 1987).

32. E.g., Carey Rosen and Karen M. Young, "When Workers Are Owners," *Dialogue*, vol. 75, no. 1 (1987), pages 33-35.

33. See Charles Sperry, "What Makes Mondragon Work," *Review of Social Economy* (1985), pages 345-356.

CHAPTER 4

1. Other programs offering assistance to poorer citizens might be considered popularly as welfare if their size were more substantial, such as school lunch programs and the Head Start program (educational assistance to poor preschool children). In addition most states have their own programs to assist the poor, typically known as General Assistance.

2. Citing all biblical references to this concern would be too cumbersome. Psalm 33:5 states it boldly: "The LORD loves righteousness and justice." Abraham and his children after him are "to keep the way of the LORD by doing what is right and just" (Gen. 18:19), Job (see Job 29:14), David (see 2 Sam. 8:15), and Solomon (see 1 Kings 3:11) served God by administering righteousness and justice. The "child [who] is born" and who will "reign on David's throne" will establish and uphold His Kingdom "with justice and righteousness" (Isa. 9:6-7).

3. The biblical concern is for those who are poor and needy through little fault of their own: those who have become poor through the arbitrary circumstances of a somewhat fickle natural world. When poverty is a result of laziness, the Bible commends work for the individuals (see Prov. 6:6-11; 2 Thess. 3:6-15).

4. The arguments noted briefly here have been developed in much greater detail in J. Mason, "Biblical Teaching and Assisting the Poor," *Transformation*, vol. 4, no. 2 (April-June 1987), pages 1-14.

5. In the case of the loan even more work than normal was expected, so as to repay the loan. The gleaners, on the other hand, would expend less overall work than hired laborers. In early Israel a third-year tithe was to be used to assist the Levites, widows, orphans, and aliens (see Deut. 14:28-29; 26:12), and it seems plausible that this provision, in the form of a handout, would have assisted those who could not be expected to do work.

6. When one member of an extended family became poor, the other members of the family were to be the first line of relief (the book of Ruth, the fundamental social framework of the Old Testament, and 1 Tim. 5:1-16 all exhibit this), and only when that source proved insufficient would nonfamily members be obligated to assist.

7. To gain greater insight into ghetto realities, see W. J. Wilson, ed., *The Truly Disadvantaged: The Inner City, the Underclass, and Public Policy* (Chicago: University of Chicago Press, 1987); and "The Ghetto Underclass: Social Science Perspectives," *The Annals of the American Academy of Political and Social Science*, vol. 510 (January 1989).

8. In the widely heralded TV special on urban Newark ("The Vanishing Family," presented by Bill Moyers in 1986), Shahid Jackson was a police

officer assigned to work with young men to help them (primarily through sporting activities) escape the long-term dangers of "the streets."

9. His answer is that single parents should be expected to work half-time (once the youngest child is of a suitable age), thus balancing the obligations for financial support of the family with proper nurturance of the children. See D. Ellwood, *Poor Support: Poverty in the American Family* (New York: Basic Books, 1988).

CHAPTER 6

1. U.S. Bishops, *Pastoral Letter on Catholic Social Teaching and the U. S. Economy*, first draft (Washington, D.C.), November 11, 1984.
2. John R. W. Stott, "Developing a Christian Mind" (Lecture given in Ann Arbor, Mich., November 16, 1988). Also see Stott's *Involvement: Being a Responsible Christian in a Non-Christian Society* (Old Tappan, N.J.: Revell, 1984, 1985).
3. Stephen Charles Mott, "How Should Christian Economists Use the Bible? A Study in Hermeneutics" (Paper presented at Consultation on the Mixed Market Economy, Wheaton, Ill., September 18-20, 1987), page 36.
4. John R. W. Stott, *The Christian Counter Culture* (Downers Grove, Ill.: InterVarsity Press, 1978), presents an excellent framework for contemporary application of the principles embodied in the Sermon on the Mount.
5. Richard A. and Peggy B. Musgrave, *Public Finance in Theory and Practice*, 5th ed. (New York: McGraw-Hill, 1989), pages 6-14.
6. Historical information in this section is from F. F. Bruce, *The Hard Sayings of Jesus* (Downers Grove, Ill.: InterVarsity Press, 1983), pages 214-217.
7. Bruce, *The Hard Sayings of Jesus*, page 216.
8. Bruce, *The Hard Sayings of Jesus*, page 216. Also see R. V. G. Tasker's commentary, *The Gospel According to St. Matthew* (Grand Rapids, Michigan: Eerdmans, 1961), page 210.
9. The likeness and the inscription on the denarius were violations of Jewish law. The fact that the Pharisees were able to produce the coin so quickly in response to Jesus' request could have been a public embarrassment for them. Although they gave the impression of being serious about keeping the law, they were not serious enough to observe the prohibition against images. Thanks are due Bruce Robinson for suggesting this point.
10. Extrabiblical views of society agree on the importance of justice as well. Aristotle said that justice is the greatest of virtues, and "neither evening nor morning star" is so wonderful.
11. Ronald Pasquariello, *Tax Justice: Social and Moral Aspects of American Tax Policy* (Lanham, Md.: University Press of America, 1985).
12. James Gwartney has advocated this view stating, "If God were supportive

of schemes which take disproportionately from the rich in order to assist the poor, surely he would have used this techniques [sic] to finance his work. But he did not. The tithe treats the rich and poor alike. Both are required to contribute the same proportion of their income to the Lord's work. Thus, God's method of raising funds fails to provide support for progressive taxes and other redistributive policies" (from Gwartney's "Human Freedom and the Bible" [Paper presented at Consultation on the Mixed Market Economy, Wheaton, Ill., September 18-20, 1987]).

13. Mott, "How Should Christian Economists Use the Bible?" page 39.

14. Arnold F. McKee, *Economics and the Christian Mind* (New York: Vantage Press, 1987), page 76.

15. McKee, *Economics and the Christian Mind*, page 77.

16. The services furnished by the governments with the tax revenues provide benefits that increase utility. Thus the net benefits are the relevant concept to consider.

17. John F. Witte, *The Politics and Development of the Federal Income Tax* (Madison: University of Wisconsin Press, 1985), pages 32-36.

18. For a Christian criticism of modern welfare theory, see George Monsma, "A Christian Critique of Neoclassical Welfare Economics" (Paper presented at the Institute for Christian Studies, Seminar on the Relevance of Christian Studies, Toronto, August 3-11, 1978).

19. On this general point see Richard John Neuhaus, ed., *The Preferential Option for the Poor* (Grand Rapids, Mich.: Eerdmans, 1988). In particular, Max Stackhouse notes in his chapter "Protestantism and Poverty" in that volume: "While we are all equally sinners (the poor being as sinful as the rich), the sins of the rich are more threatening than the sins of the poor because of the greater power that wealth brings. This equality of sin and inequality of guilt demands that Christians side with the weak to constrain the more terrible evils of the powerful" (pages 29-30).

20. Christopher Wright notes that God's active concern for the weak and the poor must be stated carefully: "In championing the cause of the oppressed in this way, [the prophets] exonerate God from the suspicion of being actually on the side of the wealthy and powerful, who could point to their wealth and power as apparent evidence of God's blessing on them and their activities" (*An Eye for an Eye: The Place of Old Testament Ethics Today* [Downers Grove, Ill.: InterVarsity Press, 1983], page 147).

21. Selected Scripture references making this point include: Deuteronomy 27:19; Psalm 35:10; 41:1-2; 82:1-4; 103:6; 146:5-9; Proverbs 14:21, 31; 22:22-23; Isaiah 32:1-8; Jeremiah 22:1-5; Amos 4:1-3; 8:4-6; Matthew 25:31-46; Luke 4:16-19; 6:20; 14:12-14; James 2:1-7; 1 John 3:17.

22. John Mason, "Biblical Teaching and Assisting the Poor," *Transformation*,

vol. 4, no. 2 (April-June 1987), pages 1-14. Mason is cited and this point is reinforced by Michael Wiseman in "Poverty and Empirical Christianity" (Paper presented at Consultation on the Mixed Market Economy, Wheaton, Ill., September 18-20, 1987).

23. Robert H. Haveman, "Equity-Efficiency Trade-Offs and the Welfare State" (C. Woody Thompson Lecture, Midwest Economics Association meetings, Cincinnati, March 30, 1989).

24. Thomas F. Pogue and Larry G. Sgontz, "Taxing to Control Social Costs: The Case of Alcohol," *The American Economic Review*, vol. 79 (March 1989), pages 235-243.

25. See Daniel Suits, "Gambling as a Source of Revenue," in *Michigan's Fiscal and Economic Structure*, eds. Harvey E. Brazer and Deborah S. Laren (Ann Arbor: University of Michigan Press, 1982).

26. Congressional Budget Office, *The Economic and Budget Outlook: Fiscal Years 1988-1992*, Report to the Senate and House Committees on the Budget, pt. 1 (CBO, 1987).

27. Joseph A. Pechman, *Federal Tax Policy*, 5th ed. (Washington, D.C.: Brookings Institution, 1987), page 356.

28. Pechman, *Federal Tax Policy*, page 359.

29. Witte, *Politics of the Federal Income Tax*, page 303.

30. Witte, *Politics of the Federal Income Tax*, page 306.

31. Henry J. Aaron and Harvey Galper, *Assessing Tax Reform* (Washington, D.C.: Brookings Institution, 1985).

32. See Daniel R. Feenberg and Harvey S. Rosen, "Promises, Promises: The States' Experience With Income Tax Indexing" (Seminar paper, Harvard University, January 1987).

33. Michigan Department of Treasury, Lansing, Michigan, 1986.

34. Mott, "How Should Christian Economists Use the Bible?" page 43.

35. On this point see John Howard Yoder, *The Christian Witness and the State* (Newton, Kans.: Institute of Mennonite Studies, 1964).

CHAPTER 7

1. The classic work exploring these criteria and the tradeoff between the two is Arthur M. Okun, *Equality and Efficiency: The Big Tradeoff* (Washington, D.C.: Brookings Institution, 1975).

2. There have been some attempts to give fairness a more positive foundation than is found in moral philosophy, but these attempts are also controversial. See William J. Baumol, "Applied Fairness Theory and Rationing Policy," *American Economic Review*, vol. 72, no. 4 (September 1982), pages 639-651; see also Randall G. Holcombe, "Applied Fairness Theory: Comment," *American Economic Review*, vol. 73, no. 5 (December 1983),

pages 1153-1156; and Geoffrey Philipotts, "Applied Fairness Theory: Comment," *American Economic Review*, vol. 73, no. 5 (December 1983), pages 1157-1160, as well as Baumol's "Reply" in the same issue of the *Review*, pages 1161-1162.

3. An early expression of this argument is found in Joseph A. Schumpeter, *Capitalism, Socialism and Democracy* (New York: Harper, 1942).

4. I am indebted to Bruce W. Wilkinson and Douglas Vickers for helpful comments on the issues involved in this section of the chapter.

5. An annual Gallup Poll asks about levels of confidence in specified institutions. In 1989, only 25 percent of those polled said they had "a great deal" or "quite a lot" of trust in the institution described as big business. Other percentages were: organized labor, 26; Congress, 35; banks, 49; and the Supreme Court, 56. The military was ranked at 58 percent, just one point behind the most-trusted institution at 59 percent, religion.

6. For a discussion of the competing theories, see George J. Stigler, "The Theory of Economic Regulation," *The Bell Journal of Economics and Management Science*, vol. 2, no. 1 (Spring 1971), pages 3-21.

7. See James M. Buchanan, Robert D. Tollison, and Gordon Tullock, *Toward a Theory of the Rent-seeking Society* (College Station: Texas A&M University Press, 1981).

8. James D. Gwartney, "Human Freedom and the Bible" (Paper presented at Consultation on the Mixed Market Economy, Wheaton, Ill., September 18-20, 1987; reprinted in *Christian Perspectives on Business & Government*, vol. 1, no. 3 [Winter 1987], pages 6-12).

9. The next footnote of the NIV on 5:22 indicates that some manuscripts read "brother *without cause*" (emphasis added).

10. For a discussion from a Christian perspective, see Jim Halteman, *Market Capitalism and Christianity* (Grand Rapids, Mich.: Baker Book House, 1988), chapters 1-2.

11. Arthur D. Austin, "Negative Effects of Treble Damage Actions: Reflections on the New Antitrust Strategy," *Duke Law Journal* (January 1978), pages 1353-1374.

12. Kenneth G. Elzinga and William C. Wood, "The Costs of the Legal System in Private Antitrust Enforcement," in *Private Antitrust Litigation: New Evidence, New Learning*, ed. Lawrence J. White (Cambridge, Mass.: MIT Press, 1988), esp. pages 131-134.

13. Executive Order 12291 by President Reagan (February 1981) required cost-benefit analysis of regulatory proposals from agencies in the executive branch. For a discussion, see Douglas F. Greer, *Business, Government, and Society*, 2d ed. (New York: Macmillan, 1987), pages 413, 457-458.

14. See the NIV text note on Matthew 16:26.

CHAPTER 8

1. See especially Lynn White, Jr., "The Historical Roots of Our Ecological Crisis," *Science*, March 10, 1967, pages 1203-1207.
2. For a compilation of different ethical statements on the environment, see Donald Scherer and Thomas Attig, *Ethics and the Environment* (Englewood Cliffs, N.J.: Prentice-Hall, 1983). For a thoughtful critique of New Age environmentalism, see Loren Wilkinson, "New Age, New Consciousness, and the New Creation," in *Tending the Garden: Essays of the Gospel and the Earth*, ed. Wesley Granberg-Michaelson (Grand Rapids, Mich.: Eerdmans, 1987), pages 6-29.
3. See Ezekiel 34 for an example of God's stern rebuke to those who do not exercise their responsibility carefully and wisely.
4. See, for instance, Isaiah 53 and Philippians 2 for explication of Christ's servanthood.
5. Since the concept of accountability is so basic to the Christian message, it would hardly seem necessary to list supporting passages. A few are Genesis 9:5 and several of Christ's parables, especially those in Luke 16:1-12 and Matthew 25:14-30. Some have argued that our accountability to God is the unique feature distinguishing humans from the rest of God's creation. See Loren Wilkinson, ed., *EarthKeeping: Christian Stewardship of Natural Resources* (Grand Rapids, Mich.: Eerdmans, 1980), pages 224-238.
6. The argument that an adequate information and incentive structure is necessary for good choices to result does not imply that only external incentives and information are all that matter in acting responsibly. As discussed earlier, the value structure of the individual is also crucial, and it is difficult to imagine a well-functioning property rights system without an adequate moral base.
7. In some cases, moral constraints are so strong that they override the badly structured incentives of common property. This usually occurs when the group is small and there is a deep level of commitment to one another and to a shared ideology. For instance, families, local churches, and certain clubs have elements of common property and yet are quite stable over long periods of time. Thus not all common property arrangements are doomed to failure.
8. See, for instance, Michael Maloney and Bruce Yandle, "Bubbles and Efficiency: Cleaner Air at Lower Cost," *Regulation* (May-June 1980); and Michael Levin, "Statutes and Stopping Points; Building a Better Bubble at EPA," *Regulation* (March-April 1985).
9. John Baden, "Destroying the Environment: Government Mismanagement of Our Natural Resources," NCPA Policy Report No. 124 (Dallas: National Center for Policy Analysis, 1986), page 9.

10. Peter M. Emerson, Anthony T. Stout, and Deanne Kloepfer, "Wasting the National Forests: Selling Federal Timber Below Cost" (Unpublished manuscript, the Wilderness Society, 1984).

11. Baden, "Destroying the Environment," page 14.

12. Baden, "Destroying the Environment," page 14.

13. See, for instance, John Baden and Richard L. Stroup, eds., *Bureaucracy vs. Environment: The Environmental Costs of Bureaucratic Governance* (Ann Arbor: University of Michigan Press, 1981); and Eric Zuesse, "Love Canal: The Truth Seeps Out," *Reason*, February 1981, pages 17-33. For a theoretical explanation of bureaucratic incentive structures, see William A. Niskanen, *Bureaucracy and Representative Government* (Chicago: Aldine-Atherton, 1971).

14. For a defense of private property beyond social pragmatism, see Carl F. H. Henry, "Christian Perspective on Private Property," in *Property in a Humane Economy*, ed. Samuel Blumenfield (LaSalle, Ill.: Open Court, 1974). Henry presents biblically based arguments for private property.

15. For a more complete history of Rosalie Edge and the Hawk Mountain Sanctuary, see R. J. Smith, "Special Report: The Public Benefits of Private Conservation," chapter 9 in *Annual Report, Council of Environmental Quality* (1985).

16. Smith, "Public Benefits of Private Conservation," page 390.

CHAPTER 9

1. An excellent review of the role of agriculture in Old Testament and New Testament times can be found in Madeleine S. and J. Lane Miller, *Harper's Encyclopedia of Bible Life* (San Francisco: Harper and Row, 1978).

2. Willard Cochrane, *The Development of American Agriculture* (Minneapolis: University of Minnesota Press, 1979), provides an in-depth historical analysis of the evolution of U.S. agriculture and agricultural policy.

3. The data for the tables and figures in this chapter were obtained from various issues of the U.S. Department of Agriculture's *Economic Indicators of the Farm Sector* publications. The best and most recent compilation of policy-related data is by Milton C. Hallberg, *The U.S. Agricultural and Food System: A Postwar Historical Perspective*, no. 55 (The Northeast Regional Center for Rural Development, Pennsylvania State University, 1988).

4. Writings of numerous authors reflect the force of agrarian fundamentalism. Many take a strict conservationist position while others argue for a sustainable agriculture on family-operated and -owned farms. Several examples are Aldo Leopold, *A Sand Country Almanac* (New York: Oxford University Press, 1966); Wendell Berry, *The Unsettling of America: Culture and*

Agriculture (San Francisco: Sierra Club Books, 1977); and West Jackson, *Altars of Unhewn Stone* (San Francisco: North Point Press, 1987).

5. This land ethic has been clearly outlined by Leopold and later by M. Douglas Meeks in "God and Land," *Agriculture and Human Values*, vol. 2 (1985), pages 16-27.

6. Much of the rent-seeking literature is academic in nature. Several useful guides are W. A. Niskanen, *Bureaucracy and Representative Government* (Chicago: Aldine-Atherton, 1971); and Gordon Tullock's seminal work *The Politics of Bureaucracy* (Washington, D.C.: Public Affairs Press, 1965). The *Public Choice* journal is an excellent source of analysis of rent-seeking behavior.

7. Cochrane chronicles these developments up to the late 1970s. Chapters 10, 12, and 16 of *The Development of American Agriculture* are particularly relevant for the technologicalism position.

8. Marvin Duncan, "U.S. Agriculture: Hard Realities and New Opportunities," *Economic Review* (Federal Reserve Bank of Kansas City, Kansas City, Mo.), vol. 74 (1989), pages 3-20, provides an excellent description of future policy choices. His discussion of technologicalism and internationalism, as defined in his paper, is compatible with the evolving position of economists but not necessarily policy makers.

9. There are many good references on God's covenantal relationship with the Israelites and later, through Jesus Christ, with the whole world. Suggested references include Page Ramsey, *Basic Christian Ethics* (New York: Charles Scribner's Sons, 1950), pages 367-388; W. Eischrodt, *Theology of the Old Testament*, vol. 1, trans. J. A. Baker (Philadelphia: Westminster Press, 1961), pages 36-45; and H. W. Wolff, *Anthropology of the Old Testament*, vol. 1, trans. J. A. Baker (Philadelphia: Westminster Press, 1961), pages 35-45.

10. Please see J. Bright's excellent discussion of obedience in covenantal agreements in *The Kingdom of God* (Nashville: Abingdon Press, 1953), pages 98-126, 228-230.

11. A more preliminary but more technical exposition of covenant economics can be found in the author's "Covenant Economics: An Application to Agricultural Policy" (Working paper no. 41, Department of Agricultural Economics, Tucson, University of Arizona, 1986).

12. A strong argument for God's sovereignty over the land resource is given by Meeks, "God and Land."

13. This claim is made by R. de Vaux in *Ancient Israel, vol. 1: Social Institutions* (New York: McGraw-Hill, 1965), pages 164-177.

14. These types of insurance proposals are not original with the author. Similar plans have been proposed by the Economic Council of Canada, *Handling the Risks: A Report on the Prairie Grain Economy* (Ottawa: Canadian

Government Publishing Centre, 1988), and Bruce Gardner, *The Governing of Agriculture* (Lawrence, Kans.: University Press of Kansas, 1981), as well as other authors. The distinguishing characteristic in the present treatment is that the rationale is based on fostering charity, stewardship, and justice rather than solely economic efficiency.

15. A recent series of articles in *Choices*, vol. 4 (1989), highlights the dilemma of rural poverty. Particular attention should be given to K. L. Deavers's article "Lagging Growth and High Poverty: Do We Care," pages 4-7.

16. See Sandra Batie's insightful analysis in "Agriculture as the Problem: New Agendas and New Opportunities," *Southern Journal of Agricultural Economics*, vol. 20 (1988), pages 1-11.

EDITOR'S PERSPECTIVE

1. Reverend Archer Torrey, Director of Jesus Abbey in Taebaek, Korea, wrote me after reading Dr. James Skillen's report on the fourth Chavanne Scholars' Colloquium in the September 1989 issue of the *Public Justice Report* (Center for Public Justice, Washington, D.C.). Included in that correspondence was a thirty-one page booklet entitled *The Land and Biblical Economics* by Mr. Torrey, 2nd ed. (New York: Henry George Institute, 1985). Although I cannot endorse all the ordering of the biblical data and conclusions drawn in Mr. Torrey's booklet, it has been nevertheless extremely helpful to me in that it led me to realize that the principle of land redemption was practiced in biblical times.

CHAPTER 10

1. For an introduction to a Christian idea of public justice and the nature of government's responsibility, see my article "What Does Biblical Obedience Entail for American Political Thought?" in *The Bible, Politics, and Democracy*, ed. Richard John Neuhaus, Encounter Series No. 5 (Grand Rapids, Mich.: Eerdmans, 1987), pages 55-80.

2. See Charles L. Glenn, Jr., *The Myth of the Common School* (Amherst: University of Massachusetts Press, 1988), pages 15-85; H. I. Marrou, *A History of Education in Antiquity*, trans. George Lamb (New York: Mentor Books, 1956), pages 41-42, 77-78, 147-153, 325-341, 400-418; and Fustelde Coulanges, *The Ancient City: A Study on the Religion, Laws and Institutions of Greece and Rome* (Garden City, N.Y.: Doubleday, 1956).

3. See Glenn, *The Myth of the Common School*, pages 179-235. My argument here is developed in more detail in "Changing Assumptions in the Public Governance of Education: What Has Changed and What Ought to Change,"

in *Democracy and the Renewal of Public Education*, ed. Richard John Neuhaus, Encounter Series No. 4 (Grand Rapids, Mich.: Eerdmans, 1987), pages 86-115.

4. See Glenn, *The Myth of the Common School*, pages 86-145, 236-261.

5. For more detail, see Rockne McCarthy, James Skillen, and William Harper, *Disestablishment a Second Time: Genuine Pluralism for American Schools* (Grand Rapids, Mich.: Eerdmans and the Christian University Press, 1982), pages 52-72; Skillen, "Changing Assumptions in the Public Governance of Education," in *Democracy and the Renewal of Public Education*, ed. Neuhaus; and Glenn, *The Myth of the Common School*, pages 249-261.

6. A more elaborate discussion of U.S. Supreme Court philosophy and reasoning can be found in McCarthy, Skillen, Harper, *Disestablishment a Second Time*, pages 73-106.

7. The argument here and in the following pages builds on the works cited above as well as on Rockne McCarthy et al., *Society, State, and Schools: A Case for Structural and Confessional Pluralism* (Grand Rapids, Mich.: Eerdmans, 1981). For recent popular expositions of some of these themes, see the articles by McCarthy, Richard A. Baer, Jr., and Charles L. Glenn, Jr., in *The Blackboard Fumble: Finding a Place for Values in Public Education*, ed. Ken Sidey (Wheaton, Ill.: Victor Books, 1989).

8. Many arguments for choice in education are now pouring forth. Not all "choice" proposals call into question governmental principalship, however. See Daniel C. Levy, ed., *Private Education: Studies in Choice and Public Policy* (New York: Oxford University Press, 1986); John E. Chubb and Terry M. Moe, "Politics, Markets, and the Organization of Schools," in *American Political Science Review*, vol. 82, no. 4 (December 1988), pages 1065-1087; Sy Fliegel, "Parental Choice in East Harlem Schools," in *Public Schools by Choice*, ed. Joe Nathan (New York: Institute for Learning and Teaching, 1989); John E. Chubb et al., "The Right to Choose: Public School Choice and the Future of American Education," Education Policy Paper No. 2 (New York: Center for Educational Innovation of the Manhattan Institute for Policy Research, 1989); and Edward Marciniak, "Educational Choice: A Catalyst for School Reform" (Report of the Task Force on Education of the City Club of Chicago, 1989).

9. For more on "secular," "religious," and the idea of "religious neutrality," see Richard A. Baer, Jr., "American Public Education and the Myth of Value Neutrality," in *Democracy and the Renewal of Public Education*, ed. Neuhaus, pages 1-24; and Baer, "The Myth of Neutrality," in *The Blackboard Fumble*, ed. Sidey, pages 49-64.

10. These points are elaborated in my essay "Changing Assumptions in the Public Governance of Education," in *Democracy and the Renewal of Public Education*, ed. Neuhaus, pages 86-115.

EDITOR'S PERSPECTIVE

1. Samuel L. Dunn, "Christianity's Future: The First-World Church Takes a Back Seat," *The Futurist* (March-April 1989), pages 34-37.

CHAPTER 11

1. *Demographic Yearbook: 1986*, 38th issue (New York: United Nations, 1988).
2. Victor Fuchs, "Economics, Health, and Postindustrial Society," in *The Health Economy* (Cambridge, Mass.: Harvard University Press, 1986), page 274.
3. President's Commission for the Study of Ethical Problems in Medicine and Biomedical Research, *Securing Access to Health Care: A Report on the Ethical Implications of Differences in the Availability of Health Services*, vol. 1 (Washington, D.C.: U.S. Government Printing Office, March 1983), page 20.
4. Victor Fuchs, "The Growing Demand for Medical Care," *New England Journal of Medicine*, July 25, 1968, pages 190-195.
5. Daniel Callahan, *Setting Limits* (New York: Simon and Schuster, 1987), page 130.
6. See also Luke 6:36; Philippians 2:5.
7. Mark V. Pauly, "A Primer on Competition in Medical Markets," in *Health Care in America: The Political Economy of Hospitals and Health Insurance*, ed. H. E. Frech III (San Francisco: Pacific Research Institute for Public Policy, 1988).
8. Callahan, *Setting Limits*, page 83.
9. A federal commission has estimated that from 22 to 25 million Americans lack health insurance during the entire year and that 34 million are uninsured for at least part of the year. These figures represent about 8.6 percent and 16.1 percent of the population, respectively (*Securing Access to Health Care*).

EDITOR'S PERSPECTIVE

1. *New Bible Dictionary*, 2d ed. (Wheaton, Ill.: Tyndale, 1987), page 386.

CHAPTER 12

1. One aspect of foreign trade policy that in principle could be covered in the present chapter—but is not in order to keep the topic manageable—is the choice of national policy for easing hardship of those harmed by

international competition or adjustments in national trade policy. This topic includes issues of unemployment insurance and trade adjustment assistance to workers and firms. A reference discussing many adjustment assistance issues is Robert Z. Lawrence and Robert E. Litan, *Saving Free Trade: A Pragmatic Approach* (Washington, D.C.: Brookings Institution, 1986).

2. Representative references include James A. Brander and Barbara Spencer, "Tariffs and the Extraction of Monopoly Rents Under Potential Entry," *Canadian Journal of Economics*, vol. 14, no. 3 (August 1981), pages 371-389; Brander and Spencer, "Export Subsidies and International Market Share Rivalry," *Journal of International Economics*, vol. 18-19 (February 1985), pages 83-100; Jonathan Eaton and Gene M. Grossman, "Optimal Trade Policy Under Oligopoly," *The Quarterly Journal of Economics* (May 1986), pages 383-406; Jagdish N. Bhagwati, "Is Free Trade Really Passe?" *Weltvirtschaftliches Archiv* (forthcoming); and Bhagwati, *Protectionism* (Cambridge, Mass.: MIT Press, 1988).

3. It could be asserted that there is a proper application of most of the principles embodied in the Sermon on the Mount to *national* dealings. Indeed, I think it would be more dangerous to argue that there are *different* rules of conduct for nations and individuals than to argue that there are the same rules of conduct, appropriately interpreted. Such an argument about the Sermon on the Mount is not needed in the present case, however, because the particular injunction to do unto others as you would have them do unto you is a principle found throughout Scriptures, in both Old and New Testaments.

4. Nationalist intervention here is taken to include managing trade in concert with other nations for the national advantage. Such arrangements have been proposed, for example, with respect to the international airframe market where U.S. industry and Airbus Industry governments would make arrangement governing "effects" of European subsidies to Airbus Industry that in practice would mean pricing agreements. Other nonmarket arrangements such as the Multi-Fiber Agreement would be put in this category since they are managed at the expense of nonmember trading countries.

CHAPTER 13

1. These are the views of the author in his private capacity and do not represent the official views of any organization with which he is affiliated.
2. Martin Buber, *Good and Evil* (New York: Macmillan, 1980), page 45.
3. Hans Kohn, *Nationalism* (New York: Krieger, 1982), page 47. See also Boyd Shafer, *Facing Nationalism: New Realities and Old Myths* (New York: Harcourt Brace Jovanovich, 1972).

4. Kohn, *Nationalism*, page 51.
5. Harold Laski, *Liberty in the Modern State* (London: Kelly, 1922), page 17.
6. Eric Fromm, *The Sane Society* (New York: Fawcett, 1977), page 29.
7. Carl von Clausewitz, *On War* (Harmondsworth, Eng.: Penguin, 1968), page 119.
8. David W. Ziegler, *War, Peace and International Politics* (Boston: Little, Brown, 1977), pages 215-230.
9. Martin Rein, *Social Science and Public Policy* (London: M. E. Sharpe, 1981), pages 75-93.
10. Joan Robinson, *What Are the Questions: and Other Essays* (London: M. E. Sharpe, 1981), page 24.
11. Barbara Ward, *Five Ideas that Changed the World* (New York: Norton, 1959), page 42.
12. Harry Blaimers, *The Christian Mind* (London: Crossway, 1970), page 23.
13. George F. Kennan, *American Diplomacy* (Chicago: University of Chicago Press, 1979), page 146. See also his *Nuclear Delusion* (New York: Pantheon Books, 1982) and *Soviet Foreign Policy* (Westport, Conn.: Greenwood Press, 1978) where his views are revised.
14. Zbigniew Brzezinski, *In Quest of National Security Policy* (New York: Farrar, Straus, and Giroux, 1988), page 101.
15. C. S. Lewis, *The Four Loves* (London: Geoffrey Bles, 1960), page 38.
16. As quoted by Lewis, *The Four Loves*, page 33.
17. "Just Defense and Nuclear Weapons" (Washington, D.C.: An Association for Public Justice Position Paper, 1983).
18. See James Skillen, *International Politics and the Demand for Global Justice* (Sioux Center, Iowa: Dordt College Press, 1981).
19. A. J. P. Taylor, *A Personal History* (London: Atheneum, 1983), page 95.